CRITICAL ACCLAIM FOR
TRAVELERS' TALES JAPAN

"Attack toilettes, sumo wrestlers, electric baths, and the inside scoop on Tokyo *rezubian* (lesbian) culture are just a few of the 46 good reasons to sit back and enjoy the odd and exotic stories in this anthology. Disturbing, enlightening, humorous, and sometimes sentimental, all provide insights into an often baffling, endlessly intriguing land."
—*San Francisco Examiner*

"If you are a first-time traveler to Japan, this book will help pique your interest in the country, its people and culture. The book is a good one-volume reader that will help increase the reader's insights. For those who have traveled to Japan before, this book will no doubt remind them of the unique people and events encountered on their journeys."
—*International Travel News*

"This anthology is the latest in a series of alternative guidebooks in which the practicalities of travel take a back seat to less tangible delights. The contributors are as diverse as the topics they cover. Readers of this entertaining anthology will be better equipped to plot a rewarding course through the marvelously bewildering, bewitching cultural land-scape of Japan."
—*TIME*

"The latest offering from the unique series from Travelers' Tales is about Japan, and it lives up to the reputation established by its predecessors."
—*Japan Airlines Newsletter*

"This collection of tales from a variety of authors will delight you, warn you, make you laugh, and even shock you."
—*Des Moines Register*

TRAVELERS' TALES

JAPAN

TRUE STORIES

TRAVELERS' TALES

JAPAN

TRUE STORIES

* ✶ *

Edited by

DONALD W. GEORGE AND
AMY GREIMANN CARLSON

Series Editors
JAMES O'REILLY AND LARRY HABEGGER

TRAVELERS' TALES
AN IMPRINT OF SOLAS HOUSE, INC.
PALO ALTO

Art Direction: Stefan Gutermuth
Cover Photograph: © *Donna Ikkanda/Getty Images. Woman by the Window.*
Map: Keith Granger
Interior design: Judy Anderson, Susan Bailey, and Kathryn Heflin
Page Layout by Cynthia Lamb, using the fonts Bembo and Boulevard

Frontispiece by Basho excerpted from *The Essential Haiku: Versions of Basho, Buson, and Issa*, edited by Robert Haas.

Library-of-Congress Cataloguing-in-Publication Data
Available upon request

10 9 8 7 6 5 4 3

Misty rain,
can't see Fuji
—interesting!

—BASHO (1644–94)

Table of Contents

Part Two
SOME THINGS TO DO

Japan: An Introduction

What is it about Japan that so enchants foreigners?

Partly it is the beauty of the country, from the palm-lined beaches and turquoise waters of Okinawa to the wide-open plains of Hokkaido, the hot spring-cradling Japanese Alps to the evergreen-cloaked mountains and glistening rice paddies of Kyushu and Shikoku.

Partly it is the ancient, intricate arts and crafts, from flower arranging and tea ceremony to pottery and *sumi-e* painting, the music of the *shamisen*, the movement of the Buyo dancer and the Noh and Kabuki player, the poetry of the *haiku* master and the woodprint maker.

Partly it is the bottomless depths of Zen Buddhism, and the disciplines and rites of martial arts such as *karate* and *kendo*.

Partly it is the entrepreneurial energy and manufacturing expertise of Tokyo and Osaka, and partly it is the spare tranquillity and aesthetic refinement of Kyoto and Nara.

Partly it is the cuisine—from the freshest *sashimi* to the miniature masterpieces of *kaiseki ryori*, lighter-than-air *tempura* to seaweed-wrapped rice balls, noontime bowls of handmade *udon* to midnight bowls of street-stall *oden*, all washed down with a steaming thimbleful of *sake* or a frothy glass of ice-cold beer.

And partly—and perhaps most persuasively of all—it is the kindness and sensitivity of the Japanese people, who will go to astonishing lengths to procure a special gift, direct visitors to their desired destinations, return a forgotten wallet, or see a friend off.

The truth, of course, is that all of these attributes interact in amazingly complex and compelling ways, creating the whole of

Japanese culture and countryside—a whole that is as enchanting as it is enigmatic.

This is not to suggest that everything in and of Japan is unblemished. On the contrary, as anyone who has lived in Japan knows, the culture is fraught with frustrations for the non-native: a powerful collective code of belief and behavior that seems to exclude all non-Japanese; a complicated inferiority-superiority mechanism that deflects visitors from ever probing into the real heart of the culture; racism directed against non-white visitors and residents; a long-hours work ethic and a sexual role-stereotyping that seem to run exactly counter to contemporary Western attitudes of family nurturing and gender equality.

These too are all interlocking pieces of the grand Japanese puzzle.

But frustrating and infuriating as Japan can sometimes be for foreigners, in its entirety it is a place that rewards persistence and open-mindedness with enthralling enlightenments, lessons that can change one's life—from the riches of artistic spareness to the splendors of recreated nature to the self-completing gifts of group harmony.

Both of the editors of this collection have lived in Japan, and both of us have found Japan mysteriously and ineluctably woven into our lives.

When you love Japan as we have come to love Japan, editing an anthology like this is especially daunting: there were so many good literary works that had taught us so much that it was almost paralyzing to have to choose among them. And as we undertook more reading and research, there was a powerful temptation to simply keep reading—and so postpone the choosing forever in a state of blissful, perpetual preparation. But at last, hard choices were made.

Now that our task is finished, one inevitable sadness is that not all the authors and works worthy of inclusion could be contained in this comparatively slim volume.

The other great sadness is that we can't simply sit down with all of the chosen writers—and with all of you reading them—and order some *sushi*, open some *sake*, and just enjoy all these tales together, as they should be enjoyed.

But let's do it in mind, anyway. We'll set the blanket under the cherry boughs here, and wait for the first faint breeze to stir the branches. See, there they fall, the first tremulous harbingers of summer, and fall, and winter—and, yes, spring. Now let's sing and dance and drink and, by all means, read—and celebrate all these stirring word-blossoms around us.

—Donald W. George and Amy Greimann Carlson

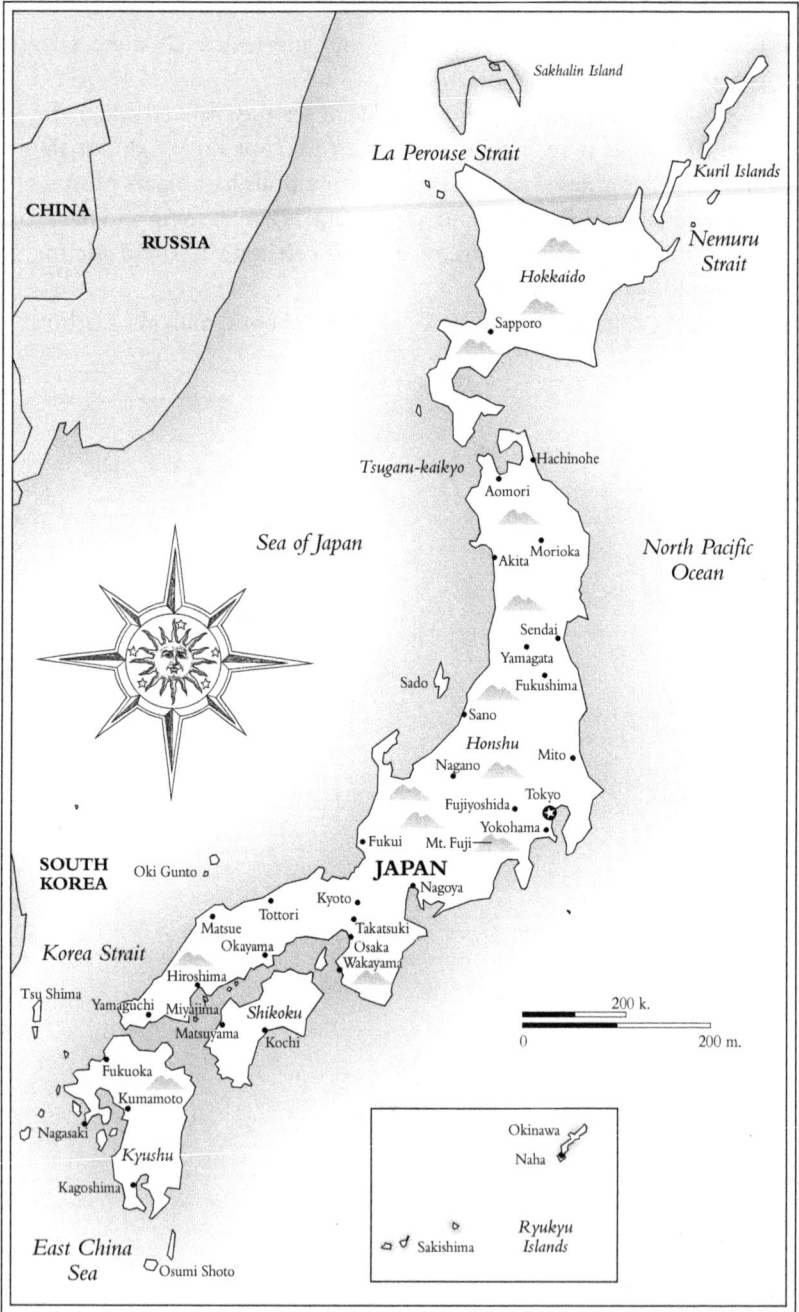

CHINA

RUSSIA

Sakhalin Island

La Perouse Strait

Kuril Islands

Ňemuru
Strait

Hokkaido

Sapporo

Tsugaru-kaikyo

Hachinohe

Aomori

Sea of Japan

Akita

Morioka

North Pacific
Ocean

Sendai

Yamagata

Sado

Fukushima

Sano

Honshu

Mito

Nagano

Fujiyoshida

Tokyo

Yokohama

Fukui

Mt. Fuji

SOUTH
KOREA

Oki Gunto

JAPAN

Nagoya

Kyoto

Korea Strait

Tottori

Matsue

Takatsuki

Okayama

Osaka

Wakayama

Tsu Shima

Hiroshima

Yamaguchi

Miyajima

Shikoku

Matsuyama

Kochi

Fukuoka

Kumamoto

Nagasaki

Kyushu

Kagoshima

East China
Sea

Osumi Shoto

200 k.

0

200 m.

Okinawa

Naha

Sakishima

Ryukyu
Islands

PART ONE

ESSENCE OF JAPAN

心

(Spirit)

ALAN BOOTH

✦ ✦ ✦

Taiko Drumming

A chance happening strikes
a different rhythm.

IN A LULL I REACHED THE TOWN OF HANAWA. IT WAS A LITTLE
after midday. I ate lunch in a restaurant where the walls were covered with posters announcing a festival, and the restaurant owner
stamped about, cursing the rain and worrying that the festival
would be canceled.

"You mean it's today?"

"Today and tomorrow."

"Here?"

"Over towards the station." The owner squinted at me from
behind the counter. "You mean to say that's not what you've
come for?"

"I'd no idea."

The owner scoffed. "There's no other damn reason to come
here. You might at least stay for that."

I needed no persuading. The weather was foul to walk in and
the prospect of a festival—however threatened—was the perfect
excuse for a dry afternoon. I took a room in a *ryokan* near the station, hung my dripping clothes over an oil stove, and spent a couple of hours sprawled on *tatami* mats, sipping green tea and listening to the thunder ripple across the valley.

By early evening the rain had stopped and I strolled out of the *ryokan* to find the road in front of the station transformed into an open-air bazaar. It was lined with dozens of pink-draped stalls, all hung with red-and-white paper lanterns, selling fireworks, gold-fish, stag beetles, terrapins, candyfloss, robot masks, octopus, and ginger. There were rifle ranges and hoopla stands, and in a shelter between the pumps of a petrol station sat six or seven policemen with megaphones, sipping tea and trying not to look enthused. Beyond the stalls, on the main street of the town, was a collection of large wooden platforms on wheels, and on each of the platforms stood a huge *taiko* drum. Hordes of young children in bright sum-mer *yukatas* were clambering over the platforms and beating the drums with curved wooden sticks. Out of the shops and houses flocked the fathers—firemen, bank clerks, postmen, farmers—dressed either in *yukatas* or in white shorts and the belted blue tunics called *happi*. There was mayhem as the fathers tried to wrest the drumsticks from their wriggling sons, and the noise of the drums and the screams and the laughter had reached a climax when the downpour began again.

It fell without thunder but it fell as solidly as it had fallen for most of the day, and the cries of the children when their mothers scuttled forward to drag them off the streets mingled with the curses of their fathers as they swarmed onto the platforms and struggled to haul tarpaulins over the drums. The tarpaulins were sodden and heavy with a day's rain and the drums were twice the height of a man.

I fled into the first dry space I could see—a canvas tent that turned out to be the festival organizers' headquarters. The orga-nizers sat behind a row of trestle tables, scowling at the rain, com-plaining to their wives, and drinking large quantities of beer. We gaped at each other for a few seconds, till I was invited to sit down at one of the tables and submit to beer and questions.

"What do you think of festivals?"

"I like them when it doesn't rain."

For a long moment my presence was ignored.

"That is to say, I like them anyway. Especially festivals in small towns."

An organizer topped up my glass.

"I like festivals where tourists are not important, festivals where they'd just as soon tourists didn't come. The festivals I've seen in large cities like Kyoto and Kanazawa seemed mainly for the benefit of the tourist trade, whereas a festival in a small town like this one is an event for working people and their families. That," I continued, growing radical, "is what a festival ought to be, not an annual bonus for some travel agent."

> *T*okyo Disneyland has become a mecca; a shrine; a temple to which millions pilgrimage each year,. On New Year's Eve, a time when traditionally families travel to shrines to ring in the New Year, Disneyland will host thousands and stay open for 36 hours straight.
>
> ♦
>
> —DWG & AGC

This heady speech earned me a plate of salami and a bottle of beer I was allowed to pour myself.

"And what do you think of Akita *bijin?*"

Akita is famous for its beautiful women (*bijin*), a fact that I had noted long ago and tended to dismiss as a partisan myth until, wandering about the streets of Hanawa in the rain, I found that my mouth kept dropping open and that I was devoting about a quarter of one eye to the *taiko* drums.

"My daughter is a *bijin*," an elderly festival organizer chuckled. "She's twenty-four."

"How very nice…"

"It's a pity she's married. You could have married her."

His wife, I supposed, was the woman choking in the corner. His daughter stayed wisely out of sight. And before I could ask about nieces and distant cousins, the rain stopped as suddenly as it had started, and the organizers packed me off to the station

square where "the real festival," they said, was about to
commence.

In the station square stood eighteen of the wooden platforms in
a semicircle facing the gathering crowd. Nine of the platforms
supported *taiko* drums, and on the other nine stood rectangular
paper lanterns, all taller by half than the massive *taiko*, and lit from
inside by candles so that the red-and-gold hand-painted pictures
on them glowed and flickered with life. Some were of heroes from
the Kabuki theater with masses of black hair, white-and-blue faces,
and bright scarlet eyes. Others were of feudal warriors, grimacing
under fierce horned helmets. On some, the warriors were locked
in combat, a tangle of long white-bladed swords and black, glint-
ing halberds. On others, a single warrior rode in arrogant splendor,
his horse's jaws a mass of foam, his armor bristling with arrows.

The nine drums thundered in unison, pounded by the fathers
now, not the sons. Each drum required two men to beat it, and
they hammered out a single rhythm that had already reached a
powerful crescendo and was still mounting as the noise and excitement of the crowd mounted with it. Sweat poured off the faces
of the drummers and the trails of it glistened in the light of the
candles. So violently did they hurl themselves at the drums, and so
powerfully did each stroke take its toll on the whole body, that a
man could not play for more than three or four minutes before
stumbling away, as another took his place, and collapsing on a
bench to tip cold sake down his throat and bury his face in a towel.

The *taiko* is an instrument that demands more than technique.
It is an obstinate instrument. It will resist and resist the drift of the
music until the sheer energy of the man who plays it at last excites
the god in the drum, and the rhythms then flow naturally from
him till his arms grow weak with exhaustion. The wise player cir-
cumvents the drum's resistance by taking so much sake into his
body that the god in the drum has no alternative but to assume
command at the outset.

I have to suppose that the god in the drum can also read minds,
for as I moved in and out of the crowd, past the lanterns and the
benches and the crates of bottles, a young man wearing a white

plastic raincoat came up and thrust a paper cup of sake into my hand and asked me if I would like to play. I said that I would, but that I would require more sake. More sake came. The crowd around us began to bubble. Three drummers offered me the use of their sticks, and after I had drained a third paper cup I took my place by the side of a drum and waited for the right-hand drummer to tire. Then, when my turn came, I stepped up to the drum, saluted it with the sticks, and whacked it.

The crowd went silly. "Look at this! Look at this! A *gaijin*! A *gaijin* playing the *taiko*!" Flash guns went off, crates were upended, parents pushed their children forward and craned their necks and stamped and clapped, and I felt the sake curl in my stomach and grinned at the drummer on the left of the drum, a middle-aged man who said "Yah!" and grinned back, and the god in the drum was kind to us both.

I have no idea how long I played. Twice the left-hand drummer changed and twice the drumsticks slipped out of my hands. When I came away I was drenched in sweat, and I sat on a bench with a towel round my head, guzzling sake and laughing like an idiot.

They had seen me from the *ryokan* windows, and when I got back, they danced about the entrance hall while I beat the floor with a pair of slippers. Then they ushered me into the front parlor where a college professor in a suit and spectacles presented me with his namecard and commenced to give us all a lecture.

"You see, the festival is a Tanabata festival and so it has its origins in eighth-century China where it commemorated the annual union of the two stars Altair and Vega. Up to the nineteenth century…"

Someone had poured me a cup of sake.

"Up to the nineteenth century the festival was celebrated on the seventh night of the seventh month, but when Japan adopted the Gregorian calendar Tanabata was incorporated into the general celebrations of August. The Nebuta lanterns of Aomori…"

"Excuse me, professor…," I said attempting a northern dialect to hisses of delight, "have you ever played the *taiko* after drinking three cups of sake?"

The professor admitted that he never had.

"The professor knows an awful lot about festivals," said the mistress of the *ryokan*, beside herself with joy.

In the streets the fathers were lighting fireworks for their sons. I felt happy for the firework sellers, who were the only stallkeepers that had not been doing a brisk trade. In the bath, when I let my ears sink under the water, the water throbbed to the rhythm of the drums, and when I got out of the bath and stood drying on the mat, my hands were still tapping out the rhythm on the windowsill. It was a long time before I could get to sleep, but I didn't mind. That night I knew an awful lot about festivals.

As a student from Birmingham University in England, Alan Booth traveled to Japan in 1970 to study the Noh Theater—and never returned home. He wrote extensively through the ensuing years, but is best remembered for his two epic accounts of his walks through rural Japan, The Roads To Sata: A 2000-Mile Walk Through Japan *and* Looking for the Lost: Journeys Through a Vanishing Japan. *He died of cancer in 1993.*

                                        ✳

We return home from the temple, just in time to see the end of the annual New Year's Eve competition between Japan's top male and female singers. This show, broadcast live from the Japan National Broadcasting Corporation auditorium in Tokyo, is a phenomenon: estimates state that up to 90 percent of the television-owning homes in Japan tune into the broadcast. The figure is staggering, but somehow right—it is emblematic of Japan, this picture of a nation transfixed in front of its collective television, watching the stars perform in all humility and humor and good-natured enthusiasm, eating tangerines and drinking sake and celebrating their unity as much as the new year.

This show ends shortly before midnight: the screen then switches to live broadcasts with correspondents stationed at famous shrines throughout Japan. We see Hokkaido blanketed in snow, Okinawa with palms and tropical bonfires blazing, and Tokyo's Meiji Shrine an immobile mass of humanity. This juxtaposition creates an intense intimacy, a sense that *the entire nation* is celebrating as one.

—Donald W. George, "Oshogatsu in Shikoku," *San Francisco Examiner*

DONALD RICHIE

* * *

The Magic of Miyajima

*A visit to a shrine blossoms
into a sensory paradise.*

As I was refolding the letter and putting it back into my pocket, I heard voices behind me. "You see," said one of the voices. "He has just received a letter and has come up here to read it. It is probably from a loved one and he wanted to get away so that he could read it in private."

"I see," said the other voice.

I turned around and there, directly behind me, stood a small, old lady in a kimono, and a boy, a middle-school student, black in his uniform and a cap too large for him.

"Good morning," said the lady, bowing.

I bowed in turn and she remarked on the weather and the view and what a nice place Miyajima was. "Oh, look at that bird," she suddenly said, indicating with a finger. "That was a sparrow."

"I see," said the boy.

"Sparrows are nice birds," she added. Then: "Oh, look, you can see the cable car from here. See, it is just now beginning to go up the mountain."

"I see," said the boy, looking in the other direction.

"This boy here is my grandson," said the old lady, smiling at me.

"I have brought him to Miyajima to show him the sights. He is old enough to be impressed now and remember."

She stood, small, bent, her hair silver in the sunlight, pulled back tightly into a bun, each strand like wire, her hands in front of her holding a large black bag. She smiled again and her face crinkled like paper. Then she sat down on a rock and patted one side of it to indicate that I was to join her.

One sometimes finds this directness in old people. One also finds it in the Noh drama, where the first character comes onto the stage and directly tells you who he is, where he is going, and why. Old people have gone through all the polite shufflings and mute longings of youth, all of the inarticulate and confused reasonings of middle age, all of the false politeness, the hanging back, that shyness creates and manners sanctify. Old women in Japan can do anything they please. They can be rude in bus or train, can pry into any matter, no matter how private, can be outspoken and impolite if they like, can wear the brightest colors without fear of censure, and can be so bawdy as to make their children blush. This was just such an old lady, and she was out showing her grandchild the sights.

She chatted on, pausing in her recitation of their adventures from time to time to point out a distant boat, a crow, a tree that had caught her fancy. It had not apparently occurred to her that I might not be able to speak Japanese—few foreigners do, despite the fact that it is among the easiest of languages to speak, if not to read. But then I remembered that once I had met an old man who had much pleased me by beginning at once in his native tongue, taking quite for granted that

> Due to the phonetic nature of the Japanese language, it is not as difficult as it appears to speak or read. The difficulty comes in the subtle nuances needed in varying contexts...and the writing of the Chinese characters takes years to learn.
>
> ◆
>
> —DWG & AGC

naturally, being here, I spoke. I was grateful to be spared the usual hesitancy, so often prolonged to the point where one begins to believe that they are seriously considering whether you can even think, much less speak. This I confided to the old man's youngster—old people in Japan always travel with children—and was told that it was not so much that he knew I could speak Japanese as it was that he was certain there was no other language on earth.

"And you," she was saying, "you must have come from far, far away. Where is it you come from, now?"

I told her I came from the distant and snow-covered province of Ohio.

"There, you see?" she told the schoolboy. "Just think of that. He came from some snow country far, far away. Consider that, now." Then, to me: "Why?"

"Why what?"

"Why did you come?"

No one had ever asked me that before. How did I come, that I sometimes heard; or, since I had come, how did I like it, that I always heard: but why, why had I come?—I didn't know what to answer.

"There, he doesn't know," she said, turning to the boy and nodding to emphasize her words. "He came all this distance, and he doesn't know why. Isn't that just like people though? You see, everyone is alike, really."

"I see," said the boy and looked at me with guarded black eyes.

"Perhaps he did something bad," she said, looking directly at me, her eyes smiling, her silver hair shining in the sunlight.

I opened my mouth, but no words came.

"Oh, if you did, you should be able to tell me. I'm no chatterbox. I'm able to keep a secret, I am. There, you see," this to the boy, "he did something bad and so he came here to the shrine."

"I don't think I did anything bad," I began.

"Oh, we all do bad things. Here." She reached into her black bag and produced a rice ball covered with seaweed. "Eat this."

"I've had breakfast—" I began.

"Eat it, eat it. One can't eat too much. Do you like rice balls?"

"Yes."

"Then eat it up." She put it into my hand. It was very heavy.

"Once when I was a girl," she said, "I liked a boy who did something bad. Can you guess what it was? You can't? Well, when I was a girl I lived in a fishing village over near Ise—you know where that is? Good. Well, this boy, his name was Ichiro, and he used to go out fishing like all the other boys did. And then one day he did a terrible thing." She went on with several sentences of explanation.

But I could not understand what the terrible thing was, though the boy did and nodded soberly. I tried to think of all the terrible things that a boy could do to a girl—getting with child, deserting, raping. I tried them out.

"No, no, no," said the old lady, shaking her head. "You men always think of things like that. Eat your rice ball." She rephrased the description, and this time I understood that Ichiro had cut something he wasn't supposed to.

"Is the rice ball good?"

"Very good," I said, my mouth full. I had reached the middle, where the sweetly sour pickled-plum lay.

She tried various words to tell me what she meant. Finally, the boy supplied one.

"Oh," I said, "he cut the nets."

After leaving an offering of food or money, people pray to the *kami-sama* for good weather, a safe firing, a prosperous year, good health, a son. At the large shrine in Kagoshima City one can buy gilt cloth and paper amulets for everything from health and marital harmony to success on exams and traffic safety. The traffic safety amulets come wrapped in plastic, with a suction cup for easy mounting on your windshield. I once rode in a car so laden with these that one could hardly see out.

◆

—Leila Philip,
The Road Through Miyama

"That's it. He cut the fishing nets. It was a terrible thing to do. They were all we had to get our food by."

"But why did he do it?"

"Well, it was terrible. They had a ceremony and then turned him out of the village. He had to go away and no one in the whole peninsula was supposed to ever help him or talk to him or speak about him again."

"Where did he go?"

She shook her head, smiled, her face creasing.

"But why did he do a thing like that?"

She smiled again and shook her head.

"Did he do it for you somehow?" I ventured.

She laughed, a dry little laugh, like husks shaken. "Oh, no. Not for me. This was for something in himself, deep down in himself. His name was Ichiro," she added. Then: "Shall we be going?"

Going down the rocky path in her kimono and slipper-like *zori*, she managed much more surely than either I or her grandson. She turned, offered the boy her hand, and said: "They didn't use to allow women here at all. I remember when I couldn't come here. And, oh, how I wanted to see it mainly because I couldn't, I suppose.... Why not? I don't know. Women were supposed to be unclean—not dirty, you understand, just somehow unclean. Men were supposed to be somehow clean."

"Even now you can't die here," suddenly offered the boy.

"That's right, I just told him that and it impressed him. If you feel that you're going to die, then you have to leave the island. I don't know what would happen if you didn't. Probably you'd just cause a lot of bother. You're not supposed to be born here either. Even now. I've never understood. I can understand about dying and disturbing people, but being born is such a happy occasion. Everyone likes to be born."

How old was she? I wondered. It is always difficult to tell, but with her it was almost impossible. She looked seventy but was descending the difficult path as though she were half that. Emulating her directness, I asked her.

"Me? Well, I was born in Meiji, I'm one of the last people from my year of the Meiji era." That is, she was born sometime between 1868 and 1912. In any case, she must be near seventy, I decided.

"Do you want another rice ball?" she asked as though this vertical, slippery path were the most logical place to eat it.

"No, thank you. It was very good, though."

"Very good indeed. Oh, see that bird? That was another sparrow."

"I see," said the boy.

Off the mountain, walking along the pier, she suddenly stopped. "Well, this has been very nice. It isn't often you meet a person you can talk to. We'll see you this evening. It's time for his nap now."

"No, it isn't," said the boy, whining, as is the way of Japanese boys forced to do something they don't want to do.

"Well, it's time for mine," she said. "It's past noon." Then she looked up at me. "This is our hotel. Please come about six and have something to eat with us." She bowed.

"Is this your first time here?" I asked.

She looked at me, her head to one side. "Now, how did he know that?" she asked her grandchild.

"I see," said the boy.

I too took a nap, in part recovered from the night before, and awoke to the late-afternoon sun covering me. It was warm in Miyajima. I listened and that familiar whirring sound began in the distance—the cicadas. It was summer again. It was as though, like Taro of Urashima, I had slept away a part of my life—the fall, the long winter, the spring—and here it was summer once more.

But it was deeper, mellower. The sky was a deep blue, as deep as the sea, and the air was thicker, it caressed the skin. It was not really summer, it was that miraculous counterfeit, Indian summer. I lay back on the pallet, the sun covering me like a blanket, and realized how happy I was. Then I got up and went to the shrine office.

She and her grandson were sitting at the table in their small hotel room facing the mountains and she greeted me with: "Who was that letter from?"

"It was from a boy in Takamatsu."

"What did he say?"

"He said he was well, and hoped I was."

"It was written in a foreign language," she said, looking up at me.

"No, it was written in *romaji.*"

"Well, that is almost a foreign language. We Japanese can't say very much in *romaji.*"

"He didn't really say very much, just that he was well and hoped I was."

"That's about all it's good for. Have some tea. Do you like *yokan*?"

I picked up a piece of the sticky bean-paste cake on a toothpick and ate it. It was

----)----

*R*omaji is the Japanese language written with our alphabet.

♦

—DWG & AGC

sweet, cloyingly sweet, sweet beyond the dreamings of all the children in the world.

"Good, isn't it?" she asked. "Nothing like *yokan.* Have another."

We talked on and on. There was no problem talking: we spoke of the habits of certain fish, of the magical properties of monkeys, of the grandchild's ability to draw (which resulted in a demonstration that produced a large cat with seven whiskers), of Momotaro, of the correct way to play the *shamisen,* of the Yomiuri baseball team, of what my mother was doing at this very minute, of life on other planets. When she asked after my wife, I said she was dead. During this we ate soup, more rice balls, of which she had brought a number and they would spoil if they weren't eaten, and spaghetti, the last being for some reason a specialty of the inn. We finished off with a tangerine and talk about the rabbit in the moon.

"But you don't see a rabbit, do you?" she asked, remembering.

"No, we see a man's face."

"Now, however do you see that? I heard that once, that you see

a man in the moon, and I went out in the garden and spent about an hour looking up at it, and I still saw the same old rabbit. Oh, look, that was a shooting star."

"Yes," said the boy.

I looked at my watch and suggested a visit to the shrine.

"But it's gotten dark," she objected. "We wouldn't be able to see anything."

"Let's go anyway," I said.

Her grandchild was also taken with the idea. "Let's go, Grandmother, let's go," he said.

She shook her head, two children being too much for her. "Very well, but I think it's stupid to go and leave this nice room and all this tea."

We walked along the dark sea wall, past the lighted hotel fronts and onto the small path that led around the tiny bay. She was no longer spry. She could not see. She held out her hands from time to time and complained. Then either her grandson or I would take her hand and guide her as she shuffled along in her *zori*, muttering, remembering the bright room, the undrunk tea.

"I hate the dark," she said. "I've hated it since I was a little girl." Then: "Oh, look…"

Because we had rounded the bend and there lay the floating shrine, illuminated, hundreds of candles in their hanging cages casting their reflections against the lacquer.

Two acolytes bowed as we entered and then, this duty done, went back to the others. One of the priests waved a handful of fluttering paper over us then took off his black-lacquered hat and went back to the television we could dimly hear in the distance.

Our shoeless, *zori*-less feet slid softly over the lacquered floor as we entered the labyrinth and then paused to look. It was extraordinary, all of these open corridors lit by the wavering light of candles, which flickered in the light sea breeze. It was like being in a forest at night, and the lacquered rails were cool to the hand as we slowly shuffled from one corridor to the next, moving farther and farther out over the pale sand that caught the flames and sparkled in the light.

None of us said anything as we wandered through the corridors, our shadows falling first before us, then behind us as we walked. We stopped at the farthest veranda and turned to look at the floating shrine, black and silver, touched with orange and vermilion where the candles showed the lacquer. Looking in the other direction, the sea was black, with just a sprinkling of lights. Hiroshima perhaps, perhaps some nearer port. The great *torii* was invisible, standing there but hidden in the night.

I looked at my watch in the flickering candlelight. It was time. And then, just as the priest had said, as though by magic, I heard the murmur and the lapping. I looked down and through the spaces in the lacquered flooring of the veranda I saw the first silver line racing through. The tide was coming in.

> he wooden shrines you see everywhere with the red *torii* gateways are Shinto places of worship. These *torii* are the easy way of telling a Shinto shrine from a Buddhist temple, which doesn't have them. *Torii* actually means "bird-perch," which is easy to remember because lots of birds do. If you can toss up a stone and make it rest on top of the *torii*, it is very good luck, but not for the birds.
>
> ♦
>
> —Robert Ainsley,
> *Bluff Your Way in Japan*

We sat, our faces dark, our backs illuminated by the candles, as line after line of waves, all silver, all rushing, pushed themselves up the shallow beach and disappeared under us. Soon we were afloat, as though we were sailing on some enormous and illuminated pleasure barge. Thicker, deeper, with crests, the waves rolled under us. Their sound was now a roar as they dashed among the pilings and raced beneath us. One expected the shrine to rock, to begin its long voyage out under the invisible *torii*, out onto the open sea.

Then—and this the priest had not told me would happen, though he must have known, he who knew the ways of the seas and the planets—then one of the crests of the mountains lightened, and the great orb of the autumn moon appeared and at once the sea was a silver plain in front of it, with the great *torii*, standing deep in the water, casting its shadow toward us over the waters.

We were all silvered, our hands, our faces, and in this cold light the illuminated shrine turned warm, an ornamental cavern with red and orange lights. Beneath us the silver sheet now flowed endlessly, like a river. The tide was fully in and the moon was sailing higher and higher, growing smaller and smaller, some mighty balloon, some great eye, receding farther and farther.

The spectacle was over. We turned again to the shrine, now as familiar as one's own room after the celestial visions of sky and sea. Already the few tourists whom the lights had attracted were leaving, already the acolytes were at work extinguishing the candles one by one.

Returning over the rocky path the old lady turned and—the first words she had spoken for an hour or so—said: "And how much did that cost you?"

"Not very much," I said, which was so. It had cost about ten dollars. Anyone could have the shrine illuminated; all you had to do was ask the priest in charge of the shrine office. The tide and moon were free.

"Well, it was very nice. I will never forget it," she said and, for

I am excited about two strange [glass balls] I find next to one another at Miniura Beach, a magnificent inlet with a rocky coast. This is where I finally hear the shiosai, the sound of the waves. When I read about it in a Mishima novel, I couldn't imagine the sound. But here it is. Not the sound of waves breaking. For the Japanese, the sound of the sea comes with the wave's aftermath, the crackling sound of water retreating through beach rocks.

◆

—Cathy N. Davidson,
*36 Views of Mount Fuji:
On Finding Myself in Japan*

once, did not draw her grandson's attention to any educational values the experience might have had. "There, see that shop there? I will now get us all some shaved ice."

While we were eating the ice, sweetened with synthetic strawberry syrup, our palates cold and our sinuses aching, she put down her spoon and said: "You like old stories, folklore, don't you? Very well, then, I will tell you the nicest I know."

She put down the spoon, pulled her kimono closer at the throat. Her grandson and I stopped eating and sat straighter. Then, as though ours was a picnic or a tea party, a pleasant, somewhat formal but unconstrained occasion, she cleared her throat, smiled at both of us in turn, and began:

"Once upon a time, after the last survivors of the Genji and Heike wars had fled, there was a beautiful young girl who lived in Shikoku. Every day she would draw water from the well and do the housework. One day, however, she forgot to draw the water and so it was night before she went to the well. It was a fine night, like tonight, and the moon was just as full as it is now.

"She bent over the surface of the water and there, far below, she saw a face looking up at her. At first she was frightened, for this was certainly a ghost. But as she looked she forgot her fear because the face was so handsome, and it looked at her with such longing. This, she told herself, is the ghost of a Heike warrior, long dead, and she gazed at him all night long.

"She had fallen in love with the ghost. Whenever the moon was full she went from her bed out into the courtyard and spent the night at the rim of the well, gazing through the depths at her handsome lover, who stared up at her.

"This went on for some time and she became thinner and thinner and finally had to take to her bed. She was pining away. Then one day she died and her ashes were buried in the temple graveyard. People forgot all about her and her strange story.

"Then, many years later, something was the matter with the well and they had to clean it. They took out all of the water and went down to fix it. And what do you think they found at the bottom? Skeletons, armor, a sword? No, not at all. They found down at the bottom, where someone had dropped it long, long before, a large, old-fashioned mirror."

She stopped. Then she smiled. It was to me—not to a foreigner, not to an American—that she had been speaking.

Of all the things I saw, of all the people I met, on my journey, it is this I remember most clearly: this beautiful old woman sitting back, smiling after her story, her grandson slumped against her asleep, the strawberry-colored ice melting in the dishes in front of us, the light bulb overhead and, over that, the millions of stars in a fall night. If I close my eyes now, the scene returns, all of us sitting there on our shadows, the ghost of that ravishing story slowly disappearing, the boy breathing through his open mouth, the old woman pleased, happy. And yet I don't remember her face. I've often tried to remember what she looked like, and I've failed.

Donald Richie is the author of numerous books on Japanese film and culture, as well as the travel classic, The Inland Sea. *He lives in Tokyo.*

※

There are no such sunsets in Japan as in the tropics: the light is gentle as a light of dreams; there are no furies of color; there are no chromatic violences in nature in this Orient. All in sea or sky is tint rather than color, and tint vapor-toned. I think that the exquisite taste of the race in the matter of colors and of tints, as exemplified in the dyes of their wonderful textures, is largely attributable to the sober and delicate beauty of nature's tones in this all-temperate world where nothing is garish.

Before me the fair vast lake sleeps, softly luminous, far-ringed with chains of blue volcanic hills shaped like a sierra. On my right, at its eastern end, the most ancient quarter of the city spreads its roofs of blue-gray tile; the houses crowd thickly down to the shore, to dip their wooden feet into the flood. With a glass I can see my own windows and the far-spreading of the roofs beyond, and above all else the green citadel with its grim castle, grotesquely peaked. The sun begins to set, and exquisite astonishments of tinting appear in water and sky.

Dead rich purples cloud broadly behind and above the indigo blackness of the serrated hills—mist purples, fading upwards, smokily into faint vermilions and dim gold, which again melt up through ghostliest greens into the blue. The deeper waters of the lake, far away, take a tender violet indescribable, and the silhouette of the pine-shadowed island seems to float in that sea of soft sweet color. But the shallower and nearer is cut from the deeper water by the current as sharply as by a line drawn, and all the surface on this side of that line is a shimmering bronze—old rich ruddy gold-bronze.

All the fainter colors change every five minutes—wondrously change and shift like tones and shades of fine-shot silks.

—Lafcadio Hearn, *Writings from Japan*

* * *

I Feel Coke

What does it mean? Does it matter?
Catch the feeling, not the meaning.

THOUGH I HAD BEEN FOUR MONTHS IN JAPAN NOW, IT STILL
seemed, often, as if I had landed, with an unseemly bump, on some
unworldly star. Whenever I walked down the street to my local
convenience store, the Familiar, I felt as if I were walking into a
surrealist's collage. On the wall of my lane, a sign informed me,
pleasantly:

> This is my STYLE
> The city is a 24-hour stage where we act out a life that
> is lively, free, and convenient. Be it day or night, we go
> out at any time to wherever we like, looking for some-
> thing new. This scooter is just right for a life-style.
>
> —City Motorbike

Around me were fresh-faced, bespectacled boys in warm-up
jackets that said "Neo-Blood," shy teenage girls whose coats said
"Dental Democracy."

Inside the store itself, where a Japanese Springsteen was delivering a Muzak version of the Boss's "Brilliant Disguise," I bought
some Chips Company potato chips, their box announcing, dis-
armingly, "We are the nicest friends in all the world." As a happy-

voiced announcer on the PA system advised us all to enjoy our stay in the store, I went over to buy a Clean Life Please dustcloth. "FACILE for your clean life," this helpful rag declared. "You grow to be beautiful in a pleasant and unforgettable mood." Nearby, goods were clamoring to reassure me: My Green Life utensils, Enjoy and Laundry cloths, hand soaps for "creating your dreamy life." Sometimes the objects here seemed almost more animated than the people.

As I headed home, newly befriended and more beautiful, in a pleasant and unforgettable mood, past the machine that offered Drink Paradise and Your Joyful Drink, I glimpsed a pink cushion embroidered with renditions of a cartoon cat. On it, entitled Fleçon Chat, was an atmospheric scene:

> There's a tranquil mood all over Montparnasse
> in the afternoon. The only sound is the gay chattering
> of Lyceenne and her mates. A Persian cat
> with a beautifully silky hair hunches down gracefully
> near the window. She looks a little like a lady
> putting on airs. Her fascinating blue eyes! What a
> brilliant, happy afternoon, as if we're in the world
> of Baudelaire's poetry.

These sunny, baffling sentiments were everywhere in Japan—on t-shirts, carrier bags, and photo albums—rhyming, in their way, with the relentlessly chirpy voices that serenaded one on elevators, buses, and trains; it did not take a Roland Barthes to identify Japan as an Empire of Signs. These snippets of nonsense poetry were also, of course, the first and easiest target of most foreigners in Japan, since they were often almost the only signs in English, and absurd; creamers called Creep, Noise snacks that came in different colors, pet cases known as Effem (whether in honor of the fairer sex or high-frequency radio, it was hard to tell). Every newly-arrived foreigner could become an instant sociologist when faced with this cascade of automatic writing, not stopping to think, perhaps, how often we may spray paint our t-shirts with elegant-looking Japanese characters that mean nothing to us, or something worse.

Nonetheless, it was hard not to notice how often certain words recurred in these slogans and contrived to create a certain atmosphere. Multimillion-dollar ad campaigns were no more random here than in America, and it was clearly no coincidence that they chose again and again to return to "dreams" and "feelings," to metaphors of community and gentleness, to imported notions of freedom and society. ("Coke is it," the slogan nearly everywhere else in the world, became, in Japan, the moodier, and more involving, "I feel Coke.") So too, it was hard to overlook how many of the t-shirts spoke of "clubs" and "tribes" and "circles," and how often kiosks or clubs or signs invoked the first person plural (Let's Archery or the Let's grocery store). Even packs of cigarettes announced themselves as "An Encounter with Tenderness," and Toyota and Honda gave their domestically sold models unusually soft and feminine names. Sometimes, in fact, the Dada fragments seemed almost to be inventories of cherished values, as in the Roget's exuberance of the ad for Nescafé's Excellent Coffee:

> It's happiness people loving casual time caring
> friendly tasty everyday relaxing cosiness fun intimate
> heart open likeable and togetherness. It's
> warmth heart embracing pure gentle comradeship
> you us family sharing sociable aroma liveliness
> tenderness smiling easy and yours.

Occasionally, too, they let out the other side of Japan: a group of S & M kiddies on motorbikes, fierce-eyed and demented, with hostile scowls, under the legend: "Though They're Hot-Blooded, Hard-Nosed and Crazy, Really They Act According to Their Principles. It's a Purple Story at Midnight." Rebellion made user-friendly; just another fashion statement.

Most often, though, the Japanese brought their poetic touch to English and created out of the imported sounds a haunting kind of synesthetic beauty, with an air of lulling, melancholy mystery; often, the buzzwords came together to create a kind of Pop Art haiku, rainswept and misty as a video.

SMOKE ON THE PURPLE TOWN
When time is softly
Veiled in a flower of black
tea, what dreams are your dreams?

ran an ad under a picture of a Picasso-like fellow enshrouded in fog on a Dantean New York street, under the warning: "All worldly things are transitory."

In the same magazine, another set of images again turned rough surfaces into poems:

BEYOND THE MEMORY OF MAN
my sepia memory
blurred with tears. I long
for it so much now.

These dreamy flights of inspired lyricism could work on one strangely, composed as they were not of words but associations: syllables used as moods, as ideograms. I came in time to find my imagination expanded by my Clean Mail writing paper, subtitled "Sound of Waves," or the monochrome photo album entitled Les Étoiles Brillantes (its subtitle sketching a Japanese ideal: "The wind whispers softly, the sun shines brightly all around, the flowers radiate joyfulness. Here the animals live cheerfully in peaceful cooperation"). Even the paper on my individually wrapped Fine Raisin Cookies declared, "Beautiful things are beyond time. Woman's history never ceases to yearn for beauty."

This poppy poetry was, in spite of itself, Japanese, I thought: in some sense, it meant nothing, and yet—in the Japanese way—it substituted atmosphere for meaning and so caught the aroma of a feeling. Meaning or its absence hardly mattered; there was no more point in belaboring a meaning here than in trying to pin one down in a photo or a *tanka*. Instead of analysis, one should simply surrender; surrender to the lovely, strange *trompe l'oeil*:

City streets at dawn
A soft mist
Fire on the mountainside.

Pico Iyer is one of the most popular travel writers of our time. He's journeyed the world covering distant places for publications like Time, Harper's, The New York Times, *and* The New Yorker. *His books include* The Global Soul, Sun After Dark, Cuba and the Night, Falling Off the Map, The Lady and the Monk, *and* Video Night in Kathmandu.

One night I had a Japanese lesson. My teacher is a very sharp 26-year-old woman. The reason I say she is sharp is because she understands me when I speak Japanese. Most people, understandably, can't make a grain of sense out of what I'm trying to say when I speak Japanese. And I can't make a microgram of sense out of their English, so I'm kind of committed to going to these classes.

The subject came around to food and I said: "My teeth hurt so I am on a liquid diet and eat mostly milkshakes and yogurt."

"No, no." My teacher swiftly corrected my Japanese. "You mean you're on a liquid diet but there are times when you also eat milkshakes and yogurt."

I repeated myself again. She looked blank. Suddenly, the only person who ever understands me wasn't understanding me. Then it occurred to me to ask a very silly question: "Is yogurt considered liquid food?"

"Did you use a straw or a spoon?" she asked.

"A spoon."

"Then it's not liquid food," she said.

"Is ice cream considered liquid food?"

"No."

"Is a milkshake?"

"Yes."

I explained that in the U.S., if someone says they are on a liquid diet, it usually means they are eating food that doesn't have to be chewed. My teacher seemed confused. "Such as milk, ice cream, etc.," I added. She was still confused. "Anything that isn't chewed," I repeated. No response.

Then it occurred to me to ask another silly question: "Do you chew milk?" I asked.

"I chew everything," she said, "even milk. We are taught in elementary school to chew milk."

—Amy Chavez, "Brace Yourself for a Diet with Guaranteed Results,"
The Japan Times

JOHN DAVID MORLEY

* * *

When the Heart
Becomes Quiet

*A Westerner tries his hand at the ancient art form
of shodo and finds only shuji.*

BOON HAD ORIGINALLY SOUGHT OUT A CALLIGRAPHY TEACHER IN
order to discipline his erratic, crab-like hand, but he soon found
that the strokes, points and spatial composition of the characters
he laboriously began to copy exerted a fascination entirely for
their own sake. They were not mere letters, the flat, inert tran-
scriptions of sounds; they were living things. Sprawled across
hoardings, rampant in the snarled vertical folds of cloth signs flag-
ging the narrow streets, they reminded Boon of dragons and he
regarded them with awe. His teacher, Suzuki Kazuko, was accordingly the dragon-slayer, and his first visit to her house in Nakano
a foray into dragon country.

The appearance of the large *tatami* room, bare of all ornament
and furnished with no more than a low black lacquered table, was
certainly austere but by no means forbidding. Here, every Saturday
afternoon, Suzuki Kazuko taught Boon and other small children
the abstruse art of calligraphy for a fee of two thousand yen per
month, to be paid in advance. Sometimes the children would arrive as Boon left, sometimes they did their exercises together, and
on these occasions their teacher showed herself capable of dealing
with two or three embryonic dragons all at the same time. With a

27

careless ease that Boon envied, seven-year-old children produced dragons of great natural splendour, but none of them satisfied the dragon-slayer and they were consigned ignominiously to the waste-paper basket.

On Boon's first visit he was received by Suzuki Kazuko alone. Dressed completely in black, with jet-black hair, she knelt at the glossy lacquered table in the centre of the eight-mat room, her hands in her lap and eyes fixed on the floor, withheld in a dark pre-scriptural trance, an attitude of concentrated repose, from which Boon's entry into the room abruptly released her. Somehow he felt the need for an apology.

"I hope I haven't come too early..."

"Oh no!"

Suzuki-san smiled brightly and ran her fingers over the polished table. "How are you? And Nakamura-san? Is he well too?"

Nakamura was the friend who had arranged their introduction. Suzuki-san invited Boon to sit down opposite her, and after they had chatted for a couple of minutes she produced a black plastic case and pushed it over to him.

"I bought this case for you. It contains everything you will need to begin with. And—well, I thought we'd start by going through the names of the things we shall be using." She opened the case and took out a large brush.

"All brushes used for calligraphy are called *fude*. There are all kinds and all sizes, but for the time being we shall be using only two: a small one, the *kofude*, and a large one, the *ofude*."

Suzuki-san spoke the word and held up the object she was naming in front of her eyes. Inserting her forefinger into the loop attached to the base of the bamboo shaft, she dangled the *ofude* between them, bushy tip down, and invited Boon to touch it.

"The tip of the brush is surprisingly hard, isn't it," she said.

"Shouldn't it be?"

"Later, you see, when you dip the brush into the *sumi* and knead the tip until it is moist it will gradually become soft. A good brush, depending upon the skill with which it is used, possesses both hardness and softness. In this way you can achieve contrasts, balance..."

Suzuki-san laid the brush down and asked Boon to repeat what she had said. In the cold air of the room a perfume, or the natural scent of her body, began to warm and unwrinkle, like melting frost.

Then she showed him the *sumi*-stick, coal-black and three inches long, looking like a chunk of sealing wax or solidified resin; and the smooth slate-like inkstone with a trough at one end into which she poured a dash of water. Moistening one end of the resin stick she began to rub it against the inkstone with steady, unhurried movements, lubricating the stone with a sprinkle of water whenever the stick jarred. After a short while the surface of the inkstone began to dissolve under the abrasion of the stick; coagulating with the fine dark grain of the inkstone, the water gradually thickened, pricked with tiny glistening bubbles, into the dense black fluid called *sumi*, blacker than any substance Boon had ever seen.

"What I am doing is called *sumi o suru*," said the young woman softly.

"When will the consistency be right?"

"It is right."

"But you still go on. How long should one go on?"

"Until the heart becomes quiet."

After a minute or two she laid down the *sumi*-stick, took out a piece of felt, a sheet of paper and a bronze paperweight. She placed the felt on the table, arranged the paper square in the middle and weighted it at the tip. Boon was startled by the sudden whiteness of the paper. The case, the felt, the resin stick, inkstone and *sumi*, Suzuki-san's hair, even her sleeves resting on the table—everything else was black. Greyish, jet-black, grained matt, glossy: a conspiracy of shades of black.

It was very still in the room, from the street outside only a faint murmur.

Arm outstretched, she held the brush poised over the paper for a second and then plunged it down like a sword. Moist, fat, black, lustrous in the instant but still spreading perceptibly, even after her hand had passed on, as the ink soaked into the fibre of the paper, suddenly all kinds of forms started up out of the whiteness in front of her: the woken dragons snarled. She wrote like a woman in her sleep, her hand moving with magical certainty, as if it had merely to trace the shapes that were already latent in the paper in order to make them apparent on its surface. Lines as straight and clear as pure sound, the slabby joints and hinges of the characters where the brush turned in its own damp track and swung down into the vertical; snarls, loops, and sometimes a breathless emptiness, the brush skimming the paper as a stone leaps water, leaving no trace. All these forms to Boon were sounds, and it did not occur to him that they also had meaning. Nevertheless Suzuki-san asked him if he were able to read what she had written.

"I'm afraid not."

"It's an old saying…"

Placing the sheet on the floor beside her, she took out a fresh piece of paper.

"You know the *kana*, don't you?"

"Yes," said Boon.

"Well, we shall only be using *hiragana* here. Once you have mastered the *hiragana* we can go on to the characters. Then it becomes a question of composition. But the basic technique, brush-stroke and so on, which you will acquire as you learn *hiragana*, applies

> *P*aper, I understand, was invented by the Chinese; but Western paper is to us no more than something to be used, while the texture of Chinese paper and Japanese paper gives us a certain feeling of warmth, of calm and repose. Even the same white could as well be one color for Western paper and another for our own. Western paper turns away the light, while our paper seems to take it in, to envelop it gently, like the soft surface of a first snowfall. It gives off no sound when it is crumpled or folded, it is quiet and pliant to the touch as the leaf of a tree.
>
> ◆
>
> —Jun'ichiro Tanizaki,
> *In Praise of Shadows*

equally to the writing of *kanji*. So one ought not to hurry at the beginning. The *hiragana* are the foundation of *shodo*."

Besides the more common Chinese characters, or *kanji*, as they were called, Boon had also been required to learn the two *kana* syllabaries, *hiragana* and *katakana*, consisting of forty-seven letters apiece. *Kana* were the contracted forms of characters that had gradually been systematised and developed into a phonetic syllabary much like any other alphabet. *Katakana* were used less frequently than *kanji* and *hiragana*, but all three scripts were indispensable for even elementary Japanese writing.

"And do you know the order in which they come?"

"Vaguely. It begins *i ro ha…*"

"Then we shall take those three first today. Just those three."

In her teacher's red ink Suzuki-san swiftly executed the three forms and spread them out on the table for him to copy. It looked quite easy. Meanwhile Boon plied the *sumi*-stick vigorously back and forth, watching the dark *sumi* well up out of the inkstone and waiting for his heart to become quiet.

But his heart refused to become quiet. For whatever reason, it knocked around terribly inside him, shying and rearing like a startled animal. He spent an hour spoiling good paper and returned home chastened.

The sheaf of rice-paper he had bought in Shinbashi would not be nearly enough to practise the three symbols. In the kitchen he unearthed a pile of newspapers as high as his knee, quality newspaper on coarse material whose texture was similar to the cheaper brands of paper used for *shodo*. Settling down on the *tatami* he immersed himself in newspapers and ink for two hours that evening and every evening throughout the following week.

Once or twice in an hour he could produce a form with a tolerable resemblance to the model which Suzuki-san had turned out in thirty seconds, but he never knew beforehand when this would happen. It was a fluke. Once or twice was not enough, not even eight times out of ten was competence, and real skill lay far, far beyond that. At even a basic level *shodo* demanded nothing less than

unbreached consistency. Neither more nor less gifted with a brush
than the average person, Boon would probably require at least a
year of regular daily practice in order to approach such consistency.
In fact for as long as he remained in Japan Boon never really em-
barked on the superior Way of Writing (*shodo*) but kept company
with its poor relation *shuji*, meaning simply the Practice of Letters.

And that was exactly what it was. Boon practised not in order
to become a master but to be able to claim familiarity, to acquire
a taste for and therewith some understanding of a form of art
which lay completely outside the terms of reference of European
culture. The word "calligraphy" was merely a convenience of
translation for the controlled explosions on paper which occurred
in true *shodo*. All decorative function, ideas of the smooth, pleasing
composition that does not jerk the eye, were alien to the aesthetics of *shodo*.

As a foreigner, new to the line and curve of the Japanese script,
Boon lacked the essential precondition for *shodo*: sleepwalking, unconscious familiarity with the letters he was shaping. This lack of
familiarity with the forms of letters could be compared to the differences between Japanese and European music. Boon had been
trained as a singer when he was a boy, and he did not have much
difficulty whistling or humming correctly any tune he heard. The
harmonics of traditional Japanese music, however, were quite unfamiliar to him; it surprised him to find how hard it was to learn
folk songs accurately or reproduce even quite simple melodies. He
discovered that his ear was as prejudiced as his eye, hand or any
other sense organ.

That apart, nightly practice of *shuji* on the *tatami* floor ac-
quainted him with two basic principles: pressure of the brush, and
rhythm of the hand between those moments when the brush was
actually touching the paper. One might even say that the "bloom"
of *shodo* emerged not from the apparent shapes but from the white
spaces they left on the paper. In *shodo* as in all Japanese art this
shaping of the negative form, the suggesting of enclosures and
continuous lines by ostensibly unrelated parts, was characteristic

and important. It could likewise be detected in everyday attitudes and the use of language, as Boon had already discovered.

Boon's first letter, the *i* which he had begun to practise, was a good example of the two principles. The symbol consisted of two separate, approximately parallel diagonal strokes. The tip of the brush had to strike the paper softly but full-on, broadside as it were, allowing the whole body of the brush to rest momentarily on the surface of the paper and creating an initial line at an angle of forty-five degrees to the top of the paper. Almost simultaneously with the impact the brush was gradually retracted as it was drawn downwards, until towards the base of the stroke only the tip of the brush was feathering the paper. At this point the line would be roughly half its width at the top, curving gently at first and then sharply down to the right. Again the body of the brush was brought to bear fully on the paper and swept vigorously up towards the right, relaxing the pressure so as to finish on a sharp point. Here the brush left the paper, having drawn a shape roughly similar to a capital L whose base is not horizontal but diagonal, at an angle of about forty-five degrees to the vertical.

The suspended brush continued to draw an invisible upward diagonal in the direction of the top right-hand corner of the page, until its tip again just pricked the surface of the paper and pulled firmly down, the full brush splayed. The brush was finally retracted from the page by doubling the tip back upwards into the line it had already drawn. When the *sumi* had dried, this overlap, the down-up of the brush, was naturally darker than the rest of the stroke in which it was contained and could be seen clearly. The finished stroke resembled an inverted comma, slim at the tip and broad at the base.

Attenuation of line, variation between the flat body of the brush and its tip, were the stock-in-trade of the *shodo* artist's technique. Accomplished calligraphists performed with the arm fully extended, but Boon's hand was not steady enough to do that; unless his forearm were supported by his left hand it began to waver. This posture was more typical of a rather delicate task, such as the

painting of miniatures or ceramics. It was a cautious posture, and
Boon felt that this already disqualified him, for caution had no
part in *shodo*. Beyond the discipline and concentration one would
naturally have expected, *shodo* also called upon resources or qual-
ities that were less obvious. The moment the calligraphist set his
brush to the page he was committing himself to something haz-
ardous. However good he might be he was always taking a risk.
He had to be bold, he must have moral courage. Boon accepted
the truth of this partly because it coincided with his own experience and, more importantly, because it was only within such terms
of reference that the profound respect, even awe, extended to the
shodo artist, and the ethical claims made on behalf of *shodo* could
be properly appreciated.

At this time Boon still had no inkling of the breadth and resonance of *shodo*. For him it was largely the sensual friction of contrasts, black and white, wet-dry, hard-soft. The dark illicit sexuality
with which *shodo* was flush, the rampant brush spilling onto the
page, all this had excited him from the very start, and by chance it
clashed with a discovery he made at about the same time he took
up *shodo*. After three or four inert months he had awoken to the
attractiveness of Japanese women.

There was nothing complementary in the nature of this attraction. It came to him as an awareness of unmistakable sexual antagonism; the male sought his opposite in the female, the female in
the male, opposite not in type but gender. Language, custom, education, superstition, everything in Japanese society bred artificially
what may or may not have been natural to woman but was at any
rate believed to be so: woman as repository, the pliant, concave element, a hollow acquiescence receiving the brunt of the extended
male as space receives body or dry earth soaks up rain. What man
imposed woman bore. In Chinese philosophy he had been repre-
sented by the *yang* principle; heaven, daytime, the positive charge.
Boon knew nothing of this. He saw only that Japanese women
showed themselves beautiful where they were also most vulnera-
ble: the nape of the neck.

Boon's sensual friction of contrasts, the vertical brush on the supine page, dark stain on porous whiteness, was a paradigm of this antagonism between male and female. The aggressive sexuality that lodged in *shodo* might not have been so clear to him had his teacher Suzuki-san not been a woman. She was an attractive woman; and she wore her hair fastened at the crown of her head, uncovering a fragile indentation at the base of her neck. In the cold room of the apartment where Boon knelt on the *tatami* practising his letters with numb hands this image generated a kind of ardour, not in Boon and not for any person, but in the feelings that materialised outside him on the page. For when he had done as best he could with *i* alone he coupled it with *ro*, a consort of syllables vertically arranged: *iro*. And by chance these first two symbols in the Japanese syllabary constituted a word meaning shade, colour, love, libido.

At first he botched it. *Iro* staggered miserable through an entire month of newspapers, the November issues of the *Asahi Shinbun*, superimposed on the faces of ministers, cancelling summits and mocking crises with a few brush-strokes, just as it pleased. In early December, as he became more sure of its form and found the dense print of political backgrounds rather distracting, Boon transferred *iro* to the advertising pages. On the whole they were emptier. Beside suits, aeroplanes and automobiles *iro* had more room to develop, and as it acquired maturity of form the need for successors became apparent. For basic technique it was enough to practise letters individually, but for flow and composition they would have to be rehearsed in combination. Accordingly he scanned his character dictionary for compound words with which *iro* could be eked out. It was an amazingly fertile word and not in the least fastidious, compatible with any partner, it seemed. Thus it could be drawn out into love affairs, dyed leather, crayons, coquetry and unbridled lust. All these words were the progeny of *iro*.

Boon did not show these exercises to his teacher, but when he returned the following week the marked improvement in his draughting of the first letters of the Japanese syllabary made it clear that he must have been courting *iro* with single-minded dedication. Suzuki-san was mildly surprised, calling her mother in from the kitchen to watch Boon wreak black mischief with his dripping lance.

"Ara!" crowed the old lady, guarding her lap with folded hands. Unfolded, knees parted, her daughter quivered.

What Boon had undertaken facetiously and as little more than a pastime became a serious occupation during the following year. His darting forays into dragon country led to wary encampment there; reconnaisance patrols developed into nightly skirmishes. His confidence grew, and finally he was stalking dragons in broad daylight.

He never spoke to Suzuki-san, even obliquely, of the admiration he felt for her or of the subtle fascination that flowed like a tide to him out of her darkness. There was no need. Everything that passed between them was already explicit, there, on the slab of paper that lay in front of them. The carnal Boon at her side she did not even see perhaps; but the dusky incubus who descended from the tip of his brush and dragged his spoor across the page she could admit into herself, to that she acquiesced; and more, she guided him to his mark. Side by side at the lacquered table she would sometimes get up and kneel behind him, reassuring his blind hand with two fingers pressing lightly just above his wrist. Week by week he knelt in the hush of her room, barely exchanging a word with her, the blunt winter light seeping through the paper screens, aware of a very slight cadence in the contours of her breasts beside him, rising faintly and falling.

Occasionally she broached herself to him.

"I am told my writing is masculine."

"Why?"

"It is strong, vigorous."

And she took out a long slim copybook with concertina leaves. Subdued marks and very fine lines, apparently fragmentary and to Boon utterly meaningless, like the descent of a spider with inky pads. He was disappointed.

"Is this you?"

"Oh no!"

She sounded horrified.

"This is *sensei*..."

Suzuki-san allowed him no more than a glimpse of her own work. It was not secret but sacred, her final intimacy. She would sooner have taken off her clothes and shown herself naked.

In this intimacy of her own calligraphy the *shodo* teacher was inaccessible. Some time, no doubt, she would marry, but Boon could not imagine her giving herself to any man. She talked, laughed, drank tea and shared biscuits with him, grinding the crumbs between her fingertips, but she was not really there. Her face was somehow shuttered, like a window netted with muslin. She was of impenetrable chastity, for in secret she had already taken her vows and become the bride of *shodo*. Not for any man.

John David Morley was born in Singapore and educated at Oxford University in England. He has worked in Mexico, Germany and Japan— where he studied at Waseda University. He is the author of Pictures from the Water Trade: Adventures of a Westerner in Japan, *and* Journey to the End of the Whole.

Moreover, as the seminar progressed, it became clear that these movements were not merely ornamental, but expressed a philosophy. For instance, I encountered the rhythm *jo, ha, kyu, zanshin*; basically this is quite simple, amounting to "slow, faster, fast, stop." When wiping the tea scoop with the *fukusa* in the tearoom, we were taught to start slowly (*jo*), speed up a bit at the center of the scoop (*ha*) and finish off at the end quickly (*kyu*). At the instant one draws the *fukusa* off the tip of the scoop, there is the closing *zanshin*, which means "leaving behind the heart." Then one returns to zero, in preparation for the next rhythm of *jo, ha, kyu*.

At first I thought this rhythm was a peculiarity of tea, but I soon found that it applies in exactly the same way to the foot movements and raising of the fan in Noh drama. In martial arts and calligraphy as well, this rhythm governs all movements. Over the course of the seminar I realized that *jo, ha, kyu* underlies every single one of Japan's traditional arts. The teachers went on to explain that *jo, ha, kyu, zanshin* is the fundamental rhythm of nature—it defines the destinies of men, the course of eras, even the growth of galaxies and the very ebb and flow of the universe.

—Alex Kerr, *Lost Japan*

✳ ✳ ✳

Smo

Hurry up and wait.

GENERAL ADMISSION WAS THIRTEEN DOLLARS, BUT I MANAGED TO
find a standing room ticket for just over two dollars—a prudent
move, as Kukugikan Sumo Hall had plenty of empty seats. I picked
one midway in the upper deck, settled in, and began scouting the
crowd through my binoculars. There were only three other *gaijin*,
all seated in the very front row. A yellow-haired young woman
with a long-lensed camera was scooting around the wrestling platform lining up shots, occasionally returning to sit between two
men. I counted 47 rows between my seat and hers.

I had arrived with the usual *gaijin* impression of sumo—fat men
with thick jockstraps butting bellies—and the evening's several
hours of matches did little to change that impression. By Western
standards the sport is painfully long on ceremony and short on action—the chorister's view of church. As I arrived, two groups of
sumos were impassively—no preening, no flexing—parading their
formidable stuff around the arena.

By any standard sumo wrestlers are fat, their fleshy arms carried
at 45-degree angles to their bodies, propped there by the sort of
medicine-ball bellies that horrify a tailor. This shape is neither accidental nor hereditary, a sumo's full-time job being the acquisition

and maintenance of bulk. He adds height by growing his hair long and wearing it in a knob atop his head; after meals he visits a masseur who manipulates his intestines, packing the food in, freeing up room for more consumption. In Japan, the citadel of sameness, this unorthodox lifestyle and appearance are widely respected. The best sumos earn enviable sums. Retirement must come reluctantly, since wisdom dictates massive weight loss, and custom demands a standard haircut and return to anonymity.

The parade's end was marked by a flurry of bowing—all the sumos hinging toward each other, toward the five black-robed judges seated at ringside, and toward the *gyoji*, a slight but all-powerful black-robed wizard who refereed from ring center. The *gyoji* had a ceremonial fan tucked into his belt in the same spot where his ancient counterparts (sumo dates from 200 A.D.) carried daggers, prepared to self-disembowel should they err in judgment.

Bowing completed, the teams squatted on opposite sides of the wrestling platform like twin rows of inflated lifeboats stood on end for storage. The blond woman, slim and nearly as pretty as my wife, must have used half a roll of film on this shot. She had plenty of time, as the *gyoji* filled the next half hour with a droning list of announcements, during which the people around me slept, drank beer, read, and munched snacks. Waiters in kimonos and slippers shuffled back and forth to the concession stands, like ballpark hot-dog vendors, only quiet.

Finally, after the announcements and the introduction of each wrestler, the first match began. Two wrestlers approached the platform, climbed the steps to their own corners, and shed silk kimonos to reveal the simplest of outfits—a wide sash fed through the crotch and anchored at either end to a thick leather belt girdling the waist.

Properly undressed, each of the bulbous giants began a slow limbering-up routine: stamping their feet to scare off demons; squatting to test knee joints and jockstraps; shaking the kinks from each leg; sipping water from a ceremonial dipper and then spitting it out. Each performed this ritual with sly attention on his opponent, so as to get neither too far ahead nor too far behind. At last each grabbed a handful of salt from a container at ringside and turned to face the other. Carelessly, almost disdainfully, they tossed the salt into the ring, ritually purifying it, and stepped in. With the speed of upright turtles, both waddled to the center of the circle, toed their respective lines, and went into a slow squat, a yard apart, face to glowering face, preparing to spring when the time was right.

But in sumo the time is almost never right. First one wrestler backed off, easing away, not breaking eye contact, and the other was obliged to do the same. They retreated to their salt bowls and their ceremonial dippers, slapping their thighs, each trying to convey the impression that *he'd* been ready, but the *other* guy flinched. More stretching, more salt, another mouth rinse, and they tottered back into the ring, deliberately toed their lines, and lowered back down.

> ——— ♪ ———
>
> *S*he quoted an aphorism that describes how well-bred women act. *"Tateba shakuyaku, suwareba botan, aruku sugata wa yuri no hana."* ("Standing and sitting she is as lovely as a peony; walking, she moves like a lily on a long stem").
>
> "Have you ever tried to move like a lily on a long stem?" she asked.
>
> "No," I answered.
>
> "When everyone wore kimonos it was easier. In modern clothes it's impossible."
>
> ◆
>
> —Linda Butler, *Rural Japan: Radiance of the Ordinary*

Amid small groans from the crowd, they repeated this backing-away process four times. Finally, on their fifth squat, the sumos lunged for each other; chests collided, fannies shook, feet clawed the clay floor; one of the men bullied the other backward to the edge of the ring and threw him across the line. Two frenzied seconds. The match was over.

There was no wild victory celebration. The loser picked himself up and moved to his corner; at a signal from the *gyoji* he waded off through the crowd, followed a moment later by the winner. The only person who paid them any attention was the *gaijin* woman snapping pictures. The spectators, sipping beer, browsing right-to-left newspapers, might have been at home watching TV in their living rooms.

The thirty-some matches that followed were much like the first one—long, slow buildups, instant endings. Only once did the sumos lunge for each other on the first face-off, and rarely did the actual wrestling last more than ten seconds. It didn't take long to see that the point of these contests was to match one's opponent ceremony for ceremony, politeness for politeness, pretense for pretense, and then—with all formalities evenly settled—throw his wobbly ass out of the ring. "If you understand sumo," the girl at the Tourist Information Center had told me, "you understand Japan."

Toward the end of the evening I felt a wave of the odd, lovely loneliness that haunts and soothes the solo traveler. Maybe it was better that my wife was at home. Were she with me, she'd have been jealous of my note taking, would long ago have suggested, and then *demanded*, that we leave, and would have spent too many yen on snacks. *She'd not tolerate three hours of sumo*, I told my notebook.

While jotting, I felt a soft tugging at my shoulder, and turned around. It wasn't my wife as I suddenly feared, or the *gaijin* photographer as I stupidly hoped, but a Japanese man from the row behind. He had a drink can in one hand, and was using his other to brush away a few clear beads of beer that he'd spilled on my down vest.

"*Bzz bzz bzzai,*" he murmured, rocking forward, smiling.

"It's okay," I said, waving him off. "It's okay."

He apologized some more, bowing, buzzing; excessive remorse, I thought, for something so small.

"It's okay. Okay." I turned back to the ring, hoping that was the end of that.

Below, the most exciting match of the evening was beginning. Two of the largest wrestlers were stomping through their warm-up rituals and actually showing anger!—slapping thighs, growling,

snapping their heads back and forth at each other. Instead of carelessly lofting their salt into the ring, they hurled it; the crowd
ooohed and aaahed as though some taboo were being broken. The
sumos squatted in front of each other and then broke away repeatedly, fourteen times I counted, glaring for long moments,
smacking thighs and chests furiously, and stomping back to their
corners through swirling clouds of salt and bluster.

When finally they did leap at each other, I was surprised by
their agility. They careened around the ring like runaway trucks—
tiny feet pummeling the floor in staccato bursts unexpected from
figures so sloppy. Suddenly the *gyoji* signaled them to stop in their
tracks: One of the men was losing his diaper! While they clenched
each other's shoulders—reminding me of an amorous bull I once
saw mounting a cow in an Illinois pasture—the *gyoji* matter-of-
factly arranged a new knot.

Three minutes into the match, there was a surprise ending. At
the same instant, both men flew from the ring in separate directions and appeared, to my untrained eye, to thud to the platform
simultaneously. With his fan the *gyoji* waved them to their corners.
The judges gathered at center ring; a long conference ensued.

Through my binoculars I was watching the judges and the *gyoji*
and the photographer, who had crept to within six feet of their
huddle (was that a ring on her finger, or part of her camera?), when
my vision was abruptly extinguished. I lowered the binoculars.
Floating in front of my face was a can of Kirin beer, dangled there
by the man behind me. He had slopped drink on a *gaijin*: amends
were called for. Here was liquid apology.

I looked back at him and smiled. He smiled. Indeed, the whole
row behind me was smiling, all teeth and crinkled cheeks.

"*Arigato*," I said, taking the can and popping the top. *Thank you.*

He lifted his can. "Sumo," he toasted. (He pronounced it
"Smo.")

I hoisted my can—"Smo"—and sipped. Everyone in the row
behind was tipped forward in their seats to watch me, one face
staggered behind another like a poker hand. I grinned and ducked
my head—setting off a chain reaction—and then turned away.

The three empty seats in the first row told me that the photographer had gotten what she wanted, and the judges scattering from the ring indicated that a verdict had been reached. The two wrestlers were silent, still squatting in their corners, and now they accepted the *gyoji's* announcement stoically—no exhibitionism, no self-congratulation, no dancing in the ring, arms raised. But the noisy ovation that accompanied their departure, and the crowd members reaching out to thump the winner's back, said that a good fight stirs the Japanese the same way it stirs the rest of us.

It was dark outside and drizzling when the last match ended. Police had closed off the street in front of the auditorium, allowing the crowd to march unimpeded to the subway. I was surprised to find myself walking next to one of the sumos. He was several inches shorter than I, and outside the ring he didn't look so fierce. In fact—wearing slippers and a flowered blue kimono, and squinting through thick glasses—he looked docile, bewildered, maybe even lost. He was peering back over one shoulder as though hoping to meet someone.

That, I thought, is how I look.

*Brad Newsham is a San Francisco cab driver and author of two round-the-world travel memoirs—*Take Me With You *and* All the Right Places, *from which this story was excerpted. On September 11, 2002, he founded Backpack Nation, an organization whose aim is to dispatch globe-roaming ambassadors to act as agents of peace in the world. For more information or to contact Brad, go to www.backpacknation.org or www.bradnewsham.com.*

*

Intermission over, I drained my Coke can and sat back down on my *zabuton*, sandwiched between two strangers and directly behind a wall of flesh; a wrestler awaiting his turn. To my delight, across the ring I spied Chuonofuji, nicknamed "Wolf Eyes," a fierce champion from the new school of "lean, but mean" sumo. Preparing to fight next, he sat meditating on his *zabuton*, arms crossed on his chest in a regal pose. His soon-to-be-opponent, sitting on the opposite side of the circle, occasionally cast fleeting glances at the champion and shivered. Wolf Eyes rose and confidently strode up the steps to the ring and began the ritual. Handsome and lean, his muscles shone in the bright lights overhead. Flexing, squatting, throwing, spitting, the two wrestlers took their positions in the center of the ring and bent over, trying to out-stare each other waiting for the referee. With a deep, dark, piercing gaze, Wolf Eyes once again rang true to his nickname.

The paddle lifted and, SLAP, flesh met flesh. With face turning red, his opponent strained to get a better grip, trying to maintain his balance. With seemingly little effort, Chuonofuji grabbed the loin-cloth belt of the other, subtly shifted his weight, and tossed the wrestler not only out of the ring, but off the mud platform, straight for my pillow. Lunging off my *zabuton*, I flew into the lap of a neighbor as the wrestler landed in a sweaty heap right where I had been sitting. Unaware of the drama unfolding beneath him, the champion stood glistening in the lights of the center ring. His eyes glowed triumphantly as the crowd roared.

I collected myself, apologizing profusely to those whose laps I splayed upon, and crawled back to my pillow.

—Amy Greimann Carlson, "Wolf Eyes"

DAVE BARRY

Somebody Stab Him Again

A sacrilegious account of a night
out at the theater.

AFTER STOPPING FOR DINNER, WE WENT TO OUR FIRST NIGHTLIFE cultural stop, the famous Kabukiza Theater, where we watched a Kabuki play. Or part of a Kabuki play. I have here a guidebook clearly stating that Kabuki is the "height of artistic perfection" and an "unforgettable experience," so I have to conclude that the problem, on this particular evening, was me.

I should note first that I've never been a big fan of any kind of classical performing art form. I am severely bored by opera, for example. The only ballet I ever enjoyed was one I saw on an outdoor stage, where instead of a curtain they had a large hedge that the dancers could duck behind. In the climactic scene, the lead ballerina got picked up by one of the male dancers, who was apparently supposed to waft her effortlessly offstage, but he had trouble keeping her aloft, plus her tutu blocked his vision, so he lunged forward, building up a head of steam, and rammed her headfirst smack into the hedge. Then he backed up, changed course slightly and ran her into the hedge *again*, before he finally managed to stagger offstage, with shrubbery clinging to both of their costumes. I was moved to *tears*.

So when it comes to the classical arts, I'm basically an

45

unsophisticated low-rent Neanderthal philistine kind of guy, which is why I'm probably just revealing my own intellectual limitations and cultural myopia when I tell you that Kabuki is the silliest thing I have ever seen onstage, and I have seen a man juggle two rubber chickens *and* a birthday cake.

For one thing, all the actors were wearing costumes that made them look like John Belushi on *Saturday Night Live* playing the part of the *samurai* delicatessen clerk, only with funnier haircuts. For another thing, since all Kabuki actors are male, a man was playing the role of the heroine. According to the program notes, he was a famous Kabuki actor who was extremely skilled at portraying the feminine character by using subtle gestures and vocal nuances perfected over generations. What he looked like, to the untutored Western eye, was a man with a four-year supply of white makeup, mincing around the stage and whining. It was Belushi playing the *samurai* whining transvestite.

In fact, everybody seemed to whine a lot. It was all that happened for minutes on end. Kabuki has the same dramatic pacing as

---

> oon was introduced to an entirely new dimension of aesthetic experience and sensual pleasure, best symbolised by the *geisha's* daring décolleté, which allowed the neckline of her kimono to drop revealingly not at the front but the back.
>
> Ms. Shimizu was dressed in Western-style clothes. Her luxuriant black hair was brushed upwards and fixed with a wide-toothed comb at the crown of her head; the exposed nape of her neck, naturally white and subtly powdered to make it appear even more so, somehow seemed very vulnerable. The sight of this exposed neck aroused in Boon a deep animal instinct, and he wondered if it was the draw of this instinct that made the sight so irresistible.
>
> ◆
>
> —John David Morley, *Pictures from the Water Trade: Adventures of a Westerner in Japan*

bridge construction. It's not at all unusual for a play to last *ten hours*. And bear in mind that one hour of watching Kabuki is the equivalent of seventeen hours spent in a more enjoyable activity, such as eye surgery.

From time to time, a member of the audience would yell something. This is also part of the Kabuki tradition; at key moments, audience members, sometimes paid by the performers, yell out a performer's family name, or words of appreciation. Our guide, Mr. Sato, had cautioned us that this yelling had to be done in a certain traditional way, and that we should not attempt it. It was a good warning—although I'm not sure what I would have yelled anyway. Maybe something like: "NICE HAIRCUT!" Or: "WAY TO MINCE!"

But the silliest part was the plot. We were able to follow it by means of earphones attached to little rented radio sets, tuned to a broadcast interpretation of what the actors were whining about. We watched for an hour, and here, according to my notes, is:

The Plot

Everybody is upset and whining. One reason is that they lost the sacred incense burner. Another reason is that some little boy is blind. And the heroine is extremely upset because she has to sell herself to the brothel so that she can afford to purchase the ointment her boyfriend needs for his hip ailment.

Meanwhile some assassins are lurking around.

So at this point, as you might expect, everybody stops for a few minutes to remember the way birds sing when they're alone.

Now the boy appears onstage. "He is blind," the interpreter informs us, "and earns money as a masseur."

The boy, played by a boy who was apparently selected for his ability to whine for extended lengths of time in an extraordinary high pitch, asks—why not?—whether his clogs are anywhere around. Everybody whines about this for three solid minutes (or fifty-one minutes in E.S.T., eye surgery time).

At this point the heroine goes off to sell herself to the brothel, which apparently has a big demand for women who look like John Belushi. Then the assassins reappear and the characters stage the World's Least Realistic Sword Fight.

Then the assassins go away and the heroine comes back and everybody squats around to whine for a while. A man who has been doing most of the whining—I think he might be the one who lost the sacred incense burner—announces suddenly (by which I mean, in only about five minutes) that he is going to commit suicide. He stabs himself in the gut, thereby causing a stirring of hope to ripple through the audience as it appears that the play might possibly be coming to an end.

But no. If you think this man could whine *before*, you should see him when he has stabbed himself. He kneels at center stage, holding his gut, and squalls at the audience for fifteen minutes. Meanwhile, other people appear and comment at length on how tragic the situation is. It is. And nobody *does* anything about it, such as call the *samurai* paramedic unit. They just whine about it, with the victim himself making more noise than anybody.

"SOMEBODY STAB HIM AGAIN!" is what I would have yelled, if I knew how in Japanese.

Finally he dies, possibly from overacting, and another guy announces that he's going to go off and find the sacred incense burner, and everybody is happy, especially us culturally myopic tourists, sprinting from the theater into the safety of the Tokyo night.

Dave Barry has written quite a few books, including Dave Barry's Guide to Guys, Dave Barry Slept Here, Dave Barry's Greatest Hits, Dave Barry Turns Forty, *and* Dave Barry's Guide to Marriage and/or Sex. *Notice a title theme here?*

✳

Kabuki, like all theater, is a world of illusion. With its extreme elaboration of costumes, make-up and the *kata* (prescribed "forms" of movement), it may be the most illusionistic of all: when the elegant court lady removes her make-up, one is left facing an Osaka businessman. Once, I was translating for Tamasaburo when an Englishman asked him, "Why did you want to become an actor?" Tamasaburo answered, "Because I longed for a world of beauty beyond my reach." I, too, was bewitched by this elusive world of illusion.

In the play *Iriya*, there is a scene where the woman Michitose is about to meet her lover after a long separation. Her *samurai* is being hunted by the police but has crept through the snow to see her. He waits in front of some *fusuma* sliding doors. Hearing of his arrival, she bursts into the room and the lovers are reunited. When Tamasaburo was once playing the part of Michitose, we were sitting together backstage, next to the *fusuma* doors and more or less on the stage itself, just prior to Michitose's dramatic entrance. Tamasaburo was chatting casually and was not the least bit feminine—very much an average man, although he was in full costume. When the time came for his entrance, he stood up, laughed, said, "OK, here I go!" and walked over to the *fusuma*. He adjusted his robe, flung open the *fusuma*, and in that instant was transformed into a beauty straight out of an Ukiyoe print. In a silvery voice fit to melt the audience's heart, he cried out, "*Aitakatta, aitakatta, aitakatta wai na!*—I've missed you, I've missed you, I've missed you so much!" A world of illusion had sprung up from one side of a *fusuma* to the other.

—Alex Kerr, *Lost Japan*

DONALD RICHIE

* * *

The Essence of Japan

An exploration of the mysteries of the natural
as shaped by Japanese hands.

JAPAN IS ENTERED; THE EVENT IS MARKED, AS WHEN ONE ENTERS A
Shinto shrine by passing beneath the *torii* gateway. There is an outside; then, there is an inside. And once inside—inside the shrine,
inside Japan—the experience begins with a new awareness, a way
of looking, a way of seeing. You must truly observe. Go to the garden and look at the rock, the tree. Ah, nature, you say and turn—
then stop. You have just observed that rock and tree have been
placed there, placed by the hand of man, the Japanese hand. A new
thought occurs: nature does not happen; it is wrought. A new rule
offers itself: nothing is natural until it has been so created. This
comes as a surprise to us of a different culture. The Japanese view
is anthropomorphic, unashamedly, triumphantly so. The gods here
are human, and their mysteries are on display. If we occasionally
find the Japanese scene mysterious, it is only because we find such
simplicity mysterious—in the West, cause and effect this clear tend
to be invisible. Look again at the *torii*—the support, the supported,
and that is all.

Observation, appreciation, and through these, understanding.
Not only in Japan, of course, but everywhere, naturally. But in Japan
the invitation to observe is strongest because the apparent is so

plain. Look at the architecture. The floor defines the space; from it the pillars hold the beams; on them the roof contains the whole. Nothing is hidden. Traditionally there is no facade. Take the shrines at Ise. Cut wood, sedge, air—that is all they are made of. The spatial simplicity extends temporally as well. The shrines have been destroyed and identically rebuilt every twenty years since antiquity. This cycle is an alternative to the Pyramids—a simpler answer to the claims of immortality. Rebuild precisely, and time is obliterated. Ise embodies the recipe for infinity: 100 cubits and two decades. That is all. Such simplicity, such economy suggests the metaphysical: the ostensible is the actual, the apparent is the real. We see what is there, and behind it, we glimpse a principle.

Universal principles make up nature, but nature does not reveal these principles, in Japan, until one has observed nature by shaping it oneself. The garden is not natural until everything in it has been shifted. And flowers are not natural either until so arranged to be. God, man, earth—these are the traditional strata in the flower arrangement, but it is man that is operative, acting as the medium through which earth and heaven meet. And the arrangement is not only in the branches, the leaves,

Surely we have something to learn from the people in whose mind the simple chant of a cricket can awaken whole fairy-swarms of tender and delicate fancies. We may boast of being their masters in the mechanical, their teachers of the artificial in all its varieties of ugliness; but in the knowledge of the natural, in the feeling of the joy and beauty of earth, they exceed us like the Greeks of old. Yet perhaps it will be only when our blind aggressive industrialism has wasted and sterilized their paradise—substituting everywhere for beauty the utilitarian, the conventional, the vulgar, the utterly hideous—that we shall begin with remorseful amazement to comprehend the charm of that which we destroyed.

◆

—Lafcadio Hearn,
Writings from Japan

the flowers. It is also in the spaces in between. Negative space is calculated, too—in the architecture, in the gardens, in the etiquette, in the language itself. The Japanese observes the spaces in between the branches, the pillars; he knows too when to leave out pronouns and when to be silent. Negative space has its own weight, and it is through knowing both negative and positive (*yin* and *yang*), the specific gravity of each, that one may understand the completed whole, that seamless garment that is life. There are, one sees, no opposites. The ancient Greek Heraclitus knew this, but we, in the Western world, forgot and are only now remembering. Asia never forgot; Japan always remembered.

If there are no true opposites, then man and nature are properly a part of one another. Seen from the garden, the house is another section of the landscape. The traditional roof is sedge, the stuff that flourishes in the fields. The house itself is wood, and the mats are reed—the outside brought inside. The garden is an extension of the house. The grove outside is an extension of the flower arrangement in the alcove. Even now, when land prices make private gardens rare, the impulse continues. The pocket of earth outside the door contains a hand-reared tree, a flowering bush. Or, if that too is impossible, then the alcove in the single matted room contains a tiny tree, a flowering branch, a solitary bloom. Even now that sedge and reed are rarely used, the shapes they took continue—the Japanese reticulation of space insists on inside, outside, man-made nature made a part of nature, a continuing symbiosis. Even now, the ideal is that the opposites are one.

A garden is not a wilderness. It is only the romantics who find wildness beautiful, and the Japanese are too pragmatic to be romantic. At the same time, a garden is not a geometrical abstraction. It is only the classicists who would find that attractive, and the Japanese are too much creatures of their feelings to be so cerebrally classic. Rather, then, a garden is created to reveal nature. Raw nature is simply never there. Paradigm: In Japan, you get up, go to take your morning bath, and you are invisible—no one greets you. Only when you are dressed, combed, ready—only then comes the morning greeting. Unkempt nature, unkempt you, both are equally nonexistent. The garden prepared is acknowledged as natural. What was invisible is now revealed, and everything in it is in "natural" alignment.

Thus, too, the materials of nature, once invisible, are now truly seen. Formerly mute, they are now "heard." The rock, the stone, are placed in view; textures—bark, leaf, flower—are suddenly there. From this worked-over nature emerge the natural elements. Wood is carved with the grain so that the natural shape can assert itself. In the way the master sculptor Michelangelo said he worked, the Japanese carpenter *finds* the shape within the tree. Or, within the rock, for stone too has grain, and this the mason finds, chipping away to reveal the form beneath. Made in Japan is a slogan we know, and one we now see has extensions—like silicon chips and carburetors. Not the same as carved wood or stone, but created by a similar impulse. And with

———☽———

*T*he only way I can speak of Japan is to express what disappears. "Gardens that a traveler cannot see are private gardens," Suzuki Hiroyuki writes. "And precisely because they are private, they have such a strong allure."

I came to Japan hoping to force my way into its private gardens; that is the way to destroy. Gardens are what they are only so long as they remain unseen. This is the art of seeing through the mirror, and I am just beginning to master it. As Suzuki writes:

> Private gardens lie hidden away in the recesses of homes on Kyoto's busiest, most bustling streets. The existence of these invisible gardens lends the city a stillness, an indescribable depth. Visitors from afar walk the city's streets aware of these countless unseen gardens, and their invisible presence lends the city a rare charm.

◆

—J.D. Brown, *The Sudden Disappearance of Japan: Journeys Through a Hidden Land*

such an unformulated national philosophy—nature is for use—it is
not surprising. Everything is raw material, inanimate and animate
as well.

Not only is nature so shaped, but human nature, too, is molded.
We of the West may approve of the hand-dwarfed trees, the
arranged flowers and the massaged beef, but we disapprove when
people are given the same attention. Our tradition is against such
control. Japan's, however, is not. It welcomes it. Society is supposed
to form. Such is its function. We are (they would say) all of one
family, all more or less alike. So we have our duties, our obligations.
If we are to live contentedly, if society (our own construct) is to
serve, then we must subject ourselves to its guiding pressures. As
the single finger bends the branch, so the social hand inclines the
individual. If the unkempt tree is not considered natural, then the
unkempt life is equally out of bounds. So, the Japanese do not
struggle against the inevitable. And, as they say, alas, things cannot
be helped, even when they can be. This simplified life allows them
to follow their pursuits. They may be flower arranging, or Zen, or
Kendo fencing. Or, on the other hand, working at Sony, Toyota,
Honda. Or *is* it the other hand?

The support, the supported. The structure of Japanese society is
visible, little is hidden. The unit is among those things most apparent. The module—*tatami* mats are all of a size, as are *fusuma* sliding
doors and *shoji* paper panes. Mine fits your house, yours fits mine.
Socially, the module unit is the group. It is called the *nakama*. Each
individual has many: family, school, club, company. Those inside
(*naka*) form the group. This basic unit, the *nakama*, in its myriad
forms, makes all of society. The wilderness, nature unformed and
hence invisible, is outside the *nakama* of Japan, and that wilderness
includes all nonmembers, among them, of course, us, the *gaijin* (foreigners). The West also has its family, its school, its company, but
how flaccid, how lax. They lack the Japanese cohesion, the struc-
tural denseness, and at the same time the utter simplicity of design.

Land of the robot? Home of the bee and the ant? Given this
functional and pragmatic structure, given this lack of dialectic (no
active dichotomies—no good, no bad, no Platonic ideals at all),

one might think so. But, no—it is something else. Let the Westerner sincerely try to live by Japanese custom, says Kurt Singer, Japan's most perspicacious observer, "and he will instantly feel what a cell endowed with rudiments of human sensibility must be supposed to feel in a well-coordinated body." Does this not sound familiar? It is something we once all knew, we in the West as well. It is something like a balance between the individual and his society—one lives within social limitations to be sure. But if you do not have limitations, how do you define freedom? In Japan, the result is individual conformity: each city, each house and each person is different from all the others yet essentially the same. The hand may shape the flower, but it is still a flower.

If one answer to the ambitions of immortality is to tear down and reconstruct exactly the Ise shrines, then one answer to the external problem of the one and the many (a Western dichotomy), to reconciling the demands of the individual and those of society, is the Japanese self in which the two selves become one. They are not, Japan proves, incompatible. The individual, and that individual playing his social role, are the same. As the house and the garden are the same. The *nakama* dissolves fast enough when desired—and freezes just as fast when not. To see Japan then is to see an alternate way of thinking, to entertain thoughts once deemed contradictory. Having defined nature to his satisfaction, the Japanese may now lead what is for him a natural life.

This natural life consists of forming nature, of making reality. Intensely anthropomorphic, the Japanese is, consequently, intensely human. This also means curious, acquisitive, superstitious, conscious of self. There is an old garden concept (still to be seen at Kyoto's Ensu-ji temple) that is called *shakkei*. We translate it as "borrowed scenery." The garden stops at a hedge. Beyond that hedge, space. Then in the distance—the mountain, Mount Hiei. It does not belong to the temple, but it is a part of its garden. The hand of the Japanese reaches out and enhances (appropriates) that which is most distant. Anything out there can become nature. The world is one, a seamless whole, for those who can see it; for those who can learn to observe, to regard, to understand.

*Donald Richie also contributed "The Magic of Miyajima" earlier in
Part One.*

★

As I walked, past houses lit up by a brilliant moon, I thought how much
the Japanese were a people of the moon, the central image of the first
Japanese story I had ever heard. And though they traced their lineage to
the Goddess of the Sun, the sun was mostly used now to describe the
modern or the public world—the Sun Plaza American-style convenience
store, the Sunflower Hotel, and rows of Sunny cars were all five minutes
from my home. The moon, by contrast, was the part they kept jealously
to themselves. In their hearts, I thought, the Japanese were still a people
of the Rising Moon. And just as I was dwelling on this, and recalling how
Kyoto itself had once been known as "Moon Capital," I turned on the
tape again and—out of nowhere—heard Van der Post talking about how
the moon in Japan was always three times larger than in any other place
and how the Japanese had a deep affinity with the moon, renewing themselves, after earthquakes or wars, as cyclically as the moon.

—Pico Iyer, *The Lady and the Monk: Four Seasons in Kyoto*

DONALD W. GEORGE

✳
✳ ✳

When the Cherries Bloom

*How a glorious annual sight became
a treasured national rite.*

THE SINGULAR SIGNIFICANCE OF CHERRY BLOSSOMS IN JAPANESE
culture is a phenomenon even the casual student of Japan is likely
to be familiar with. It was one of the few things I knew about
Japan when I went to live there on a two-year teaching fellowship
twenty years ago.

Of course, this knowledge was limited to what books could
teach: that cherry blossoms so suited the Japanese sensibility that
they had long ago become an unofficial symbol of the country
(the official symbol is the chrysanthemum), and the word for
flower, *hana*, had become synonymous with the cherry blossom itself; that cherry-blossom-viewing parties, or *ohanami*, had been ini-
tiated by the aristocracy in the 8th and 9th centuries and had
evolved through succeeding centuries into extravagant ritualized
excursions; that these parties had been whole-heartedly adopted
and popularized by commoners in the 16th century, and were still
so important that the country virtually shut down for the precious
few weeks in April when the blossoms bloom; and that the flowers are celebrated both for their beauty and for their brevity, which
have come to symbolize, for the Japanese, the haunting and glorious impermanence of life.

This knowledge blossomed into resonant reality my first spring in Japan. I had been living in Tokyo for about half a year when, in early March, anticipations of and predictions about the opening of the buds began. By the end of the month these had built to a crescendo, and it seemed that virtually every conversation somehow ended in speculation about the flowers.

When the first buds bloomed in the south, the media's cherry blossom bonanza began. Television newscasters and newspaper reporters tracked the pink- and-white trail as it slowly spread along the length of Kyushu and Shikoku, then moved through southern Honshu toward Kyoto and Tokyo.

At first, it was hard to understand what all the fuss was about. Then one morning, virtually the entire campus where I was living and teaching—a place famed in Tokyo for its cherry trees—had overnight exploded into a fragile, fleecy shower of impossibly delicate white-and-pink blossoms. It was magnificent, it was breathtaking—exquisitely ethereal and sensual at the same time.

And it was as if all of Tokyo had blossomed at the same moment: wherever I went, the incomparable flowers were, too— sometimes a single tree in solitary splendor by the bank of a river, sometimes a festive procession along a downtown street, and some-

> ───── ☽ ─────
>
> *T*he Japanese were famous, I knew, for their delight in *lacrimae rerum* and for finding beauty mostly in sadness; indeed, it was often noted that their word for "love" and their word for "grief" are homonyms—and almost synonyms too—in a culture that seems to love grief, of the wistful kind, and to grieve for love. So I was hardly surprised to learn that most of their stories were sad and that all of them ended in parting. Parting was the definition of sweet sorrow here.
>
> ◆
>
> —Pico Iyer, *The Lady and the Monk: Four Seasons in Kyoto*

times, on the grounds of a park, row upon row creating the effect of a fluffy pink cloud.

What first struck me about the blossoms was their elusively sexual character. At one point that youthful spring I even exulted into my journal: "On some of these bleached-blue days, when the cherry blossoms stand out so brave and submissive against the sky, I want to leap into the branches of the trees and never come down. Incomparably fluid and feminine, they somehow embody all that is sensitive and stoic, submissive and dominant, giving without ever being given, all that is lasting and eminently perishable in the Japanese woman."

This sexual nature still strikes me each spring, but there is much more to their allure than that. I was walking through Ueno Park, one of Tokyo's largest parks and famous throughout Japan for the beauty and breadth of its cherry blossoms. It was the first Sunday after the buds had opened, and raucous sounds of singing and laughter carried on the air. In the area with the most spectacular concentration of cherry trees, the lawns were blanketed with people sitting on reed mats and colorful quilts, their shoes neatly laid in rows beside them. Arrayed on their spreads were multilayered lacquer containers full of food—*sushi*, rice balls, pickled vegetables, boiled eggs wrapped in *tempura*-fried fish paste, salads, fried chicken—and big bottles of beer and sake. There were businessmen and blue-collar workers, house-wives and fashion models— all of Tokyo, it seemed—sitting side by side, feasting and drinking, breaking into song and dance, guffawing and shouting and swapping tales.

Such public celebrations, such freeing of pent-up emotions, are extraordinarily rare in Japan. This is one of the invaluable functions of the cherry blossoms as well: once a year, their opening makes it permissible for the Japanese people to bloom, too, to sing and dance and in general abandon themselves for a day under the benevolent, all-forgiving branches.

Even more amazing was the fact that one of the groups invited me to join them. I demurred, but they insisted, and I soon found

myself sitting cross-legged on a soft mat, surrounded by a Japanese
family who would probably never, under any other circumstances,
invite a foreigner into such intimate contact. They bade me feast
on *sushi* and sake, and as the liquid warmed through me and the
blossoms whispered in the breeze—a few frail petals already drifting around us like soft and softly scented snowflakes—I joined
their jokes and songs, even serenading the park with a warbly version of "Yesterday" before the afternoon was over.

In ensuing years I have seen this scene repeated throughout
Japan, on castle grounds and in city parks, along high mountain
trails and by the glittering sea. It is one of the glorious rituals that
unifies and enriches Japanese life, and no matter where you may
be in April, if the cherry blossoms bloom, you will see such rituals, too. It may be a grand reenactment of an early *ohanami*, with
aristocrats in gorgeous kimono proceeding in pomp and splendor;
or a company outing, where the president performs a snaky, sake-
inspired dance for his employees; or a simple family gathering
where children wheel and squeal and parents sup and sip and sigh
at the pink-petaled sky. Whatever version of the cherry-blossom-
viewing party you see, you will be witnessing one of the deepest
and best-loved rites of Japanese life.

It is a celebration whose sense and significance are at once social
and spiritual, a glorious affirmation of the present in the effusive,
efflorescent beauty—at once individual and collective—of the blossoms, and a transcendent renewal in the tangible demonstration that
the universe is proceeding as it should, and once again blessing the
world with these offerings of evanescence and eternity.

*Before becoming Lonely Planet's global travel editor, Don was travel editor at
the* San Francisco Examiner *for nine years and then founded Salon.com's
travel site, Wanderlust. He is the editor of* The Kindness of Strangers, A
House Somewhere, *and the author of Lonely Planet's* Travel Writing.

★

Weary as I was, the taxi ride proved my first cultural thrill. The seat covers were white lace—yes, lace! yes, white! And the driver flexed his fingers over the steering wheel inside a pair of spotless white gloves. In the

coming days, I was to ride in many taxis, each a bit differently appointed, but always the white lace and gloves. The back door panels in one were upholstered in lace covered with clear plastic; from the bottom of the dash in another hung a lacy skirt; and the headrests of many sported their own little crocheted slipcovers.

On each of my rides, I mused for a few moments on the immaculate state of these covers. I tried to envision the driver's morning. Did he (I never saw a woman driver) changed them with each day's dawn? Were they supplied by the taxi company—a routine of picking up a carefully folded fresh set in the morning and then stripping and tossing it into a laundry cart in the evening? Or did the driver's wife dutifully launder them? Or a crew of women rotate them in the manner of hotel maids changing beds? The worried-about-the-future-of-the-earth part of me mulled over how many gallons of bleach nationwide were washing into waterways as a requisite of the laundering? Of all my questions, I could only answer one: the source of desire for such presentation of a taxi. It embodied what I saw as the essence of things Japanese—cleanliness, beauty, order.

—Kathleen Meyer, "Toiletopia: Plunging into 'Things Japanese'"

JEFF GREENWALD

Into the *Denki Furo*

A dip into electrifying territory.

MY GOD, IT WAS HOT IN TOKYO. THE KIND OF HEAT AND HUMIDITY that makes the jaw go slack. Morning was to stagger toward the newsstand, shielding my eyes from the glare off scooters and vending machines. Afternoons were spent careening through Tokyo in search of information, or prone dumbly on the *tatami* beneath an oscillating fan, listening to Tony Bennett on the Far East Network:

> The little boy lost
> will find his way once more
> Just like before
> When lips were tender...

Our apartment, like most in Tokyo, had no shower. But when the cool evening finally arrived I climbed gratefully into my *yukata* (robe) and made for the *sento* (public bath).

How I loved our neighborhood *sento*! Big bright locker-room-cum-gym, spotlessly clean. Please Leave Shoes At Door. Never crowded. A handful of Japanese men—I was the only foreigner—attended themselves naked and unselfconscious, rubbing their bodies with rough towels.

The walls were lined with low mini-showers. One must squat. Also, Please Turn Faucet on Slowly; those little Japanese showers can knock you across the room.

The entire back portion of the *sento* was occupied with baths. First there was an Olympic-sized hot-tub/Jacuzzi. Next to that was a cold bath, then a green bath, and at the end a small mystery bath, perpetually empty, with an alarming lightning bolt emblazoned in red on the white tile wall above.

Glancing now and again at that placid final bath, the surface of which seemed supernaturally calm, I felt a nagging curiosity. For all I knew it might have been a device for sterilizing surgical tools, or hyper-cleaning jewelry. Why was I seized by a crazy intuition to climb recklessly in?

There are no beggars and few elderly people on Tokyo streets. The city seems to belong to a youthful post-bomb generation that moves at ease among high, clean buildings and throbbing electrical billboards. As if there had been nothing before this. As if Tokyo had elected to submerge its history under canyons of steel and glass and especially plastic, infinite quantities of plastic. Flowers wrapped in plastic. Plastic eel in the windows.

Another day ended. I sweated and staggered from subway to subway, swooning in the unspeakable heat. Home at last and all I wanted was a bath. Collecting my toiletries in a plastic bucket, I set off for the *sento*.

There were men in the mystery bath.

Two old men, covered from neck to waist with outrageous tattoos. Their faces wore expressions of the purest transcendence, like *samurai* warriors under torture. One of them motioned to me with his head—a mere twitch really—in what seemed to be a gesture of invitation.

Silence prevails in the *sento*, but foreigners are expected to breach every custom and who was I to disappoint the Japanese? Pointing to the fateful pool, I inquired of the young man on my right.

"*Denki furo,*" he explained. Electric bath.

There is a moment we have all experienced, on the edge of a diving board or at the threshold of a bedroom, when we know that to take another step is to commit ourselves irreversibly. I walked, naked, to the wall of the *denki furo*. The water within pulsed invisibly, and I felt the fascination and aversion one experiences when bending over to touch a completely still animal that may or may not be dead. But to touch the water hand-first would be, I imagined, shameful, as if I lacked the strength of my convictions.

Every eye in the room was upon me as I swung my leg into the bath. Electricity swarmed up my calf, buzzing and stinging. I uttered no cry. Bracing on rubber arms, I swung my other leg in. Face be damned; this was as far as I was going to go.

But wait—the bath was doing something, not unlike love, to my loins. They were turning to *soba* (noodle). Wearing the resigned grin of a fall guy in some '50s comedy, I began to sink gradually into the water.

There was no point trying to escape; my feet would not respond. The most important thing, I understood, was to remain unflinching as my testicles went under. Every situation in Japan is a test. I would not disgrace myself.

Contemplating the *wu* (essence) of the white tile wall I sank, expressionless, up to my neck. The men in the adjoining bath watched my eyes, staring with impassive,

> The next week we skied in Nagano, famous for its natural outdoor baths as well as its superb mountain slopes. These baths are much prized by the residents of the area, and not only the human ones. Snow monkeys indigenous to the area have discovered the joys of relaxing comfortably in the hot springs. The monkeys, among the very few species of their clan which do not inhabit the tropics, counter the cold by taking a nice warm bath. As the snow falls, entire families including monkey babes in arms take to the waters and soon the gray fur coats in the hot springs outnumber the nude bodies.
>
> ◆
>
> —Naomi W. Caldwell, "Japanese Bath"

cat-like gazes.

What did it feel like? Imagine the howling physical rush of a blow to the "funny bone," generalized over your entire body. Or think of yourself as a silver filling, and the *denki furo* as a mouth full of foil. Did it hurt? The exquisite intensity went far beyond pain. My only hope was that there would be no permanent physical damage; that, like the cartoon cat whose tail is thrust into a wall outlet, I would sizzle for a while then reappear, unscathed, in the next scene.

I do not recall how I left the *denki furo*. Perhaps the two old men lifted me, a recalcitrant tumor, from their buzzing province. Perhaps I mustered a supreme effort of will and climbed from the tub myself, like Batman in a fix. Or maybe I never left the bath at all. Perhaps I'm still in it, existing in a Borgesian dream-state of compressed time. It often seems that way.

I live in America now, where the burgers are charcoal broiled. People take baths at home. I have never met anyone else who has taken an electric bath. We have all seen movies or read newspaper stories of people getting electrocuted when their radio or blow-dryer decides to take a bath with them, and I would go so far as to say that electrified water, like darkness or sharks, is a deeply rooted fear.

The men in the Japan National Tourist Organization laughed when I asked them what I had encountered in Japan.

"*Denki furo*," they replied, unable to elaborate.

Still mystified, I called a *shiatsu* school specializing in oriental healing techniques.

"It obviously affects the polarity of your electrons profoundly," speculated the director. "It can probably alter your brain waves. After all, we're nothing but masses of electrons to begin with…"

Which explains some things. But sometimes, in Japan, there is no explanation save that single four-word mantra, uttered by the visitor in awe and italics:

They are the Japanese.

Oakland-based Jeff Greenwald is the author of five books, including Shopping for Buddhas *and* The Size of the World. *He is also the director of Ethical Traveler, an international alliance uniting travelers to help protect human rights and the global environment (www.ethicaltraveler.com). He launched his stage career in 2003, with a one-man show called "Strange Travel Suggestions."*

✳

There is a quality I've noticed in Japanese women, and I think it comes from generations of tending to men: they know the male anatomy and psyche very well and have no revulsion or embarrassment regarding them. In the larger bathhouses in Tokyo, the attendants in locker rooms were middle-aged, middle-class, respectable women, fully clothed, who moved about the naked men, picking up towels and tidying up with the benign neutrality of a librarian shelving books. Being around this was very comforting and easy; I have never felt this comfortable around women in the West. Their manner of serving men, which some call subservient, did not seem that way to me. They were playing a role, and it seemed they knew they were playing a role; this made for a small detachment from it, and in this space I could see the soul shining through.

—George Vincent Wright, "A World of Bathhouses"

BRUCE S. FEILER

* * *

P's and Q's and
Envelope Blues

It's all in the elaborate packaging.

ONCE, DURING MY EARLY MONTHS IN SANO, I WROTE A LETTER TO
some Japanese friends while I was at my office. When I had finished, I put the letter into an envelope, copied the address of my
friends on the front, and gave it to Arai-san, the affable "office
lady" who daily gathered the mail.

Several days later, Mr. C approached my desk with my letter in
hand. "Mr. Bruce," he said in a low voice, squatting beside my chair
as he did when he had important matters to discuss, "I'm afraid we
cannot mail this envelope."

"Why not?" I asked in a similar hushed tone. I assured him that
the letter contained important office business.

"It's not the letter," he said, "it's the envelope. You have not prepared it correctly."

"But the address is accurate on the front," I protested, "and I
wrote the return address of our office on the back. Can you not
read my writing?"

"Oh no, your writing is very beautiful—more lovely than
mine," he said in one of those fatuous compliments that usually
warned of something harsh to come. "But you have forgotten a
very important detail. You left out the character for *sama* [a more

67

formal, written version of the honorific *san*]. I'm sorry, but we cannot mail this letter without it."

Was this a joke, I wondered—a parody, perhaps, of the Japanese obsession with detail? Would the authorities in this office really not mail my letter without the Japanese equivalent of "Mr." or "Mrs." scripted on the front? Did they really check every letter that passed through the mail bag to make sure that all the names were anointed and all the *kanji* were crossed? The truth, I realized, was that this was no joke. The senior secretary of the Ansoku Education Office of the Tochigi Prefectural Board of Education had delivered my mislabeled letter to her section chief, who had conveyed it in turn to *my* section chief, who had passed it finally to my boss, who had dutifully come to inform me that the Japanese government refused to spend 60 yen to mail any envelope that did not contain the proper appellation of respect.

I thanked Mr. C for his advice, apologized for the inconvenience, and told him I would solve the problem. But instead of just adding the missing character, as any humble civil servant would have done, I vowed to prove that my officemates had grossly overreacted. I took the errant letter to the post office, purchased a stamp, and mailed the envelope myself—*sans sama*. Any friend of mine, I thought, would not be offended by this trivial lapse of etiquette.

The next time I visited these friends—a middle-aged couple in Osaka whom I had known for some time—I related this story to them, expecting us all to share a hearty laugh. But when I reached the end of my story, my friends didn't laugh. They didn't even titter.

"Mr. Bruce," they said with utter sincerity, "your boss was right. We always know when we get a letter from you, because you never address an envelope in the proper way. Form is very important, you know."

Envelopes, as I learned the hard way, are more than mere packaging in Japan. They are more than simple wrappers that protect a private letter and are later thrown away. As a school uniform defines a student or knickers a mountain hiker, an envelope actually becomes a part of the message itself. "In Japan, the package is a thought," wrote the philosopher Roland Barthes. Within minutes of reprimanding my poor form, my friends led me to a special drawer in their home which they reserved exclusively for new envelopes. Inside they kept containers for every occasion—from births to deaths, from New Year's gifts to mortgage payments. Some were wrapped in ribbons of red, while others were garnished with silk cherry blossoms. They even had a special envelope for the tooth fairy. The last, and most elaborate, package they drew from their drawer actually consisted of two wrappers in one. On the inside was a white sheet of paper, folded twice to conceal its secret contents, and on top of this slid a thicker slip of paper which was sheathed in red and white twine, knotted around the midsection, and adorned with springs of pine.

"This is the most precious kind of envelope in Japan," my friends said as they handed me this paper bouquet that seemed more suited for framing and hanging than licking and stamping. "We put a crisp yen note in the inner fold, tuck this into the outer sheet, wrap both sheets inside a silk handkerchief, and give it to a bride and groom on their wedding day. This is our Japanese custom."

In early June I got the chance to put my new envelope expertise to a test and spend a Sunday afternoon away from the tensions of Sano: I was invited to attend the wedding of my new friend Hara, the banking tycoon from Tokyo, and his bride, Emiko, from the "Up River" Real Estate Company. Cho and I drove together to Tokyo and arrived several minutes before noon at the canopy-covered entrance to the Mikado Hotel, across the tree-shrouded moat from the estate of the Japanese emperor. Upon arrival we were obliged to give a present—in cash. This courtesy contribution, currently running at 20,000 yen (or $150), defers some of the cost of the ceremony, but mostly pays for the gifts that the couple is obliged to give the guests. For my gift I got to witness the marriage ceremony, have my picture taken, savor a five-course meal, and—according to the complex calculus of gift-giving in Japan—receive *four* presents in return: a chocolate cake, a bag of rice, a pair of crystal goblets, and an economy-sized bag of dried fish shavings.

Later I also received a box of macadamia nut chocolates from the couple's honeymoon in Hawaii.

After registering at a table in the lobby and handing over our envelopes, we were hurried up a winding staircase and ushered into a cramped waiting room where the two families sat facing each other in resolute silence, like rival diplomatic delegations across a negotiating table. The groom's family sat to the right in three even rows of ten people each, and the bride's entourage sat directly across in a similar, formal phalanx. Like most modern couples, Hara and Emiko held two ceremonies: a private religious service for family members, followed by a large reception for friends, colleagues, and obligatory guests. Cho and I, the only friends invited to the private ceremony, were placed between the two families on a third side of the square, directly across from the bride and groom.

Hara, his face somber, wore a black silk kimono with embossed family crests, wrapped by a pure white sash, while his bride wore an ornate white kimono with winglike sleeves embroidered with peacocks and birds of paradise. Her usually beaming face had been powdered over with white cake make-up and quieted with a submissive smile drawn with red lipstick. On her head Emiko wore a crowning, boxlike white hat that rose ten inches from the top of her hair and hung out over her eyes like a Greek pediment. This elaborate headgear, known as a *tsunokakushi*, is designed to hide the "horns of jealousy" that all new wives are expected to sprout.

"Would both the mothers please stand," the hotel attendant announced from the front of the room, "give your name, and your place of birth. Would the grandparents please rise..." I felt as if I was on jury duty, watching witnesses being sworn in. Ten minutes later, with the formal introductions completed, we moved two doors down the hall to a more traditionally appointed Japanese room for the nuptial ceremony itself. Black wooden chairs lined three sides of the room, spaced evenly across the lustrous wood floors that shone like melted butter. Narrow screens with charcoal strokes of bamboo leaves leaned in from the ivory walls. The guests took their places along the outside of the chamber; the bride and groom stood on virgin *tatami* mats in the middle of the room before a miniature Shinto shrine. The freestanding mahogany shrine had all the poise and strength of an antique armoire, with a carved frontal piece, several shelves holding gems and fruit, and a mirror that reached up from behind the altar and was trimmed with garlands of green summer leaves.

A white-robed priest emerged from a door behind the shrine, made some opening remarks, and then removed a white sheet from atop a large straw keg of sake which was resting before the altar. Moving slowly, he blessed the couple with his hands, waved streams of white paper over their heads, and poured some clear sake into a cup at their feet. The bride knelt down, lifted the scarlet cup to her lips, then offered it to the groom. When he had finished, the priest refilled the cup. The groom drank first this time and tendered the cup to his bride. Finally, each of us in the wedding party retrieved a cup from under our chair and waited for the priest to fill it with rice wine. The priest returned to the altar and clapped twice to summon the gods; we all bowed as one, then drank from our cups. What wine has joined together, let no one put asunder.

Throughout the short ceremony, the priest gave no indication of having met the couple before. He read standard prayers from a photocopied sheet of paper, and at each stage of the ceremony he leaned over and whispered instructions into the groom's ear: "Put on the ring.... Bow! Start walking out.... Now." The Shinto element to Japanese weddings is relatively new, added only after Christian missionaries poured into Japan a century ago and introduced their religious ideals of marriage. Before that time, marriage was viewed as a secular union between two families. Nevertheless, the ceremony itself seemed devoid of any religious ambience. There was no music except for a few tape-recorded reedlike sounds piped in over scratchy speakers, and no prayers were uttered by the bride, the groom, or either of the families. The only other people who participated in the ceremony were an older couple who sat behind the wedding pair for no apparent reason.

"What were they doing in the middle of the room?" I asked

Mr. Up River after the ceremony had ended and we were having a group picture taken.

"They played the part of the *nakodo*," he said, "the formal go-between."

"But I thought Hara and Emiko met through friends," I said. "They didn't have an arranged marriage. They were a love match."

"That's right. But the hotel told us we had to have a *nakodo*, so we asked the neighbors to sit in."

After the modest ceremony, we moved back downstairs for the reception and joined 150 of the couple's assorted friends and co-workers in the grand ballroom of the hotel. Far from the refined elegance of the Shinto chapel, this room was about as understated as the palace at Versailles. Mauve velvet curtains swooped like condors from above and draped the sides of the gilded shutters that covered nothing but wall. Buxom chandeliers bobbed from the ceiling like frilly hoop skirts at an antebellum Southern ball. The round tables were heaped with twinkling topiaries; satin ribbons tied to the top dribbled over the edge of the linen tablecloths and dragged along the floor. Cho and I found our assigned seats, along with Hara's other college mates, and sat in front of silver platters brimming with cold meats, sliced fish, and pickled vegetables—all covered with plastic, so we could look but not touch.

The reception itself was so elaborate that it required a five-page printed program and a rented emcee to narrate the show. In the beginning was the word—speeches, to be precise. The happy couple, now changed from their ceremonial garb into a less regal but still formal pair of kimonos, marched down the center of the room and took their places on a raised platform for everyone to see. The acting matchmaker then assumed the microphone and proceeded to recapitulate the life story of the groom. "Hara-*kun* was born in a small wooden house on…As a boy, he obeyed his parents and worked long and hard at…He attended elementary school at…In junior high school he was a member of the… His favorite class in high school was…" The only thing omitted from this exhaustive résumé was a list of his former girlfriends. The matchmaker's wife then did the same for Emiko, followed by more character testimonials from the groom's boss, the bride's sister, several high school friends, and even Emiko's junior high school homeroom teacher. Cho, in his capacity as honored university elder, gave a short address about the virtues of traveling with long-time friends and the difficulty of traveling with Hara, who always came away with the girls. The audience applauded politely, like white-gloved guests at high tea.

After the last formal toast, "To the wedding of Toshiaki Hara and Emiko Kawakami," we were finally able to open the wine and remove the plastic wrapping from the food, which had been growing steadily more appealing on the table before us. With the start of the meal, tuxedoed waiters hurried to our sides, dishing out portions of French onion soup, Caesar salad, and lobster not-quite-Newburg made with processed cheese, since the Japanese don't care much for *fromage verité*. The real show, however, was on the stage. After a pause long enough to admire the meal but not long enough to eat it, the lights were dimmed and a movie screen descended magically. Through sips of soup and sweet German white wine we watched a slide montage of childhood pictures of both the bride and the groom, set to the rueful tune of "Time in a Bottle."

When this high-tech montage was finished, the emcee called for the lights to be blackened completely, and his band of loyal retainers rolled out a small computerized machine about the size and shape of a grocery cart. As the speakers whined with Lionel Richie singing "Endless Love," tiny beams of red, white, and green light burst from the box with a shower of brilliance and began to dance in the dark. "It's the Mikado Hotel's Laser Light Extravaganza," the emcee wailed as the light beams outlined frolicking butterflies and dancing hearts on the wall in the back of the room. "TOSHIAKI AND EMIKO—TOGETHER HAPPY ECSTASY," the laser scripted in classic Japanese-English. "LOVE IS 4-EVER." The crowd shrieked its approval. "Isn't it spectacular!" said a woman at a nearby table. "It's better than the Magical Light Parade at Tokyo Disneyland." I thought for a moment I had found the ultimate trophy of Japanese technological ascendancy: a portable electronic box that painted multicolored sea gulls on hotel walls to the squealing delight of hundreds of guests.

But we were not through yet. Just as the laser show drew to a close, a spotlight reached out from the darkness like a shining sword and revealed the bride and groom, now dressed in chiffon wedding dress and tuxedo, being lowered into the room inside an eight-foot-tall white-picket gazebo suspended from the ceiling. As this Cinderella-like coach touched the ground, the crowd oohed and aahed and two dozen children wearing pinafores and sailor suits stepped forward to greet the newlyweds with pink carnations in hand. Emiko kissed the children on the cheek; Hara shook their hands; and my *go-con* companion Prince Charming, in his capacity as cameraman-at-large, rushed forward to capture the scene on his portable video camera. Moving back toward the front of the room, the happy couple mounted a small round stage alongside a three-tiered pink wedding cake, which was festooned with lacy icing, supported by plastic Ionic columns, and topped with a Caucasian wedding couple underneath a canopy. The lights dimmed. The crowd hushed. The master of ceremonies announced into his microphone, "This is the climax." The bride and groom brought down the knife together with all the ardor of an aspiring *samurai*, and suddenly the stage began to rotate, the cake began to shake, and pink smoke came billowing out from beneath the lowest tier. As the tape-recorded violins soared to the crescendo of "Love Is A Many-Splendored Thing," white spotlights drowned the stage and the entire platform began to rise on the shoulders of three hydraulic beams, like a UFO taking flight. I held my breath, thinking for a moment that the cake was going to lift into the air on a web of red and white laser beams. Yet the crowd could contain itself no longer. Roaring their approval, the guests jumped to their feet in riotous applause and swarmed the swiveling cake with an arsenal of flashbulbs and dessert forks.

So much for the myth that Japan is a land of understated elegance.

When I went with Hara on our failed *go-con* in January, he told me about a new era of love in Japan—or at least in Tokyo—in which sex comes first and then comes marriage. In this new romantic age, he said, boy meets girl, propositions girl, then takes her home to bed, "just like in America." The apogee of this modern love is the modern wedding. More than any other event I witnessed, this reception showed how material wealth is changing the lives of the "way out, but classic" generation. In the past, weddings were more sober affairs, befitting the *kejime* of moving from one stage of life to the next. Mr. C, for example, was married in the shrine I had visited on New Year's Eve. But weddings today have become showcases for wealth and gadgetry. The average Japanese couple spends $53,000 to get married—about half from the cash contributions and the rest from the parents of the bride and groom. The high cost of tying the knot includes not only the price of the wedding and reception but also $1,000 as a finder's fee to the real or stand-in *nakodo*, $2,000 for photographs, and an estimated $10,000 in dowry money exchanged between the two families. Since a wedding is a milestone for an entire community, many families are willing to splurge to enhance their position among their friends and neighbors.

As I witnessed the parade of these high-priced toys, from laser-light moonbeams to hydraulic-powered cakes, it occurred to me that some money-conscious Japanese may have fallen victim to their own brand of "conspicuous consumption"—spending enormous sums of money for extravagant tokens of wealth and status. If anything, money has allowed the Japanese to explore their wildest fantasies, especially of romantic love. Magazines like *Seventeen* and *Jump!*—modeled after prototypes in the United States—have saturated Japan with their dreamy tales of Western love. Comic books, soap operas, and

—————)—————

*N*obody likes a loner. Hiroaki Kono, director of the National Institute on Alcoholism, told the *Los Angeles Times* that to be branded *tsukiai ga warui*—"no good at socializing"—was "the most fearful thing that can be said about a person in Japan."

◆

—Clayton Naff,
About Face: How I Stumbled onto Japan's Social Revolution

bubble gum pop music all urge young people to spurn the for-
mulaic methods of courtship which their parents pursued and set
out to find the perfect match for themselves. Young people have
taken this foreign custom and carried it to extremes. The Japanese
imported Valentine's Day from the West, for example, and promptly
added a parallel holiday one month later called White Day. On
February 14 girls give boys gifts of chocolate, and on March 14
boys return the favor with batches of homemade cookies. Hikaru
Genji—a popular musical band of beatific roller-skating teenage
boys named after the gallivanting hero in *The Tale of Genji*—
received an astonishing eighty tons of chocolate one year from
weak-kneed junior high school girls all across Japan. Even though
marriage is still primarily an institution in which the wife is expected to show duty toward her husband, a glitzy wedding can
provide a temporary escape from this reality. On its wedding day,
at least, a couple is elevated from the bonds of obligation to the
realm of *romansu*.

Yet in the course of the entire reception, no speaker made any
reference to the future happiness of the bride and groom. No
person even mentioned their "love." Besides exchanging rings—
another Western adoption—the couple did not touch and, as far
as I could tell, did not even look at each other throughout the entire four-hour ceremony. Not until the end of the day, after we
had all filed out of the hotel with our shopping bags brimming
with chocolate cakes and crystal glasses, did the newlyweds
emerge, in their fourth change of clothes, to reward us all with
their official "first kiss." As I watched, I remembered Hara telling
me on the evening of our *go-con* that he would ask his wife to
quit her work as soon as they were married. He wanted modern
love, all right, but with a traditional wife. Despite all the bells and
whistles, the new age of love imported from the West has been
unable to bridge the age-old gap that separates men from
women, even those who are married to each other. The wedding
itself was simply an "event," with little spontaneity, little emotion,
and, despite the laser valentines and sentimental soundtrack, little
heart. After all the excitement was over, the wedding reminded

me of its own envelope—an elaborately crafted package stuffed with brand-new money.

Bruce Feiler is the author of several books, including Walking the Bible, Looking for Class, Abraham, Under the Big Top, *and* Learning to Bow, *from which this story was excerpted.*

＊

It turned out that the family had taken their daughter into Yamaguchi city that day for an *omiai*—the first meeting between a potential couple and their family representatives to test the waters for a possible marriage. The *omiai* normally occurs after an exchange of photographs, and it is arranged by a go-between, often an old friend of one of the families, who has unearthed what he considers an eligible prospect. The young people and their families meet, usually at a hotel restaurant or coffee lounge, and talk about nothing in particular, smiling with studied politeness while they furiously size each other up. Marriage will not be mentioned, although jobs and hobbies may be discussed, and afterwards the young people will decide separately whether they want to see each other again, and if they both do, dating can commence.

The daughter was busy serving us all sake with a twinkling smile on her face, and everyone else, including her mother and father and the go-between—Mr. Kobayashi, an elderly reporter for the local newspapers—sat staring glumly at the floor.

"How did it go?" I asked the daughter when I found out how they had spent the afternoon, and if looks could kill, the father's and mother's would have flushed me straight down to the Ninth Circle.

"Not a success," the daughter said brightly, and I then compounded my felony by pouring her a cup of sake with the remark that it would do her good after such a hard day.

Eventually they all cheered up, even Mr. Kobayashi—until I beat him in a game of *shogi* which was watched by a cluster of the *ryokan's* guests who kept congratulating each other on witnessing an international sporting event. Public defeat was the last straw for the poor go-between, and he ended his day of sorrows peddling home on a wobbly bicycle while the twinkling daughter got happily sloshed for what I suspect was the first time in her life.

—Alan Booth, *The Roads to Sata: A 2000-Mile Walk through Japan*

KEVIN O'CONNOR

* * *

Illiteracy and the Attacking Toilet

A lost battle with some baffling electronics.

PERHAPS THE GREATEST CHALLENGE FACING WESTERN TRAVELERS in Japan is illiteracy. Relying on a mixture of Chinese ideographs and two supplemental syllabary character sets, Japanese script is one of the most complex writing systems on earth. Given the demands on the modern business traveler, it is difficult to find the vast amounts of time necessary to master the language's arcane symbols. But, in hindsight, we should have, at least, learned some basics.

Unfortunately for Dennis and Scott and me, our pre-trip preparation contained all business and no language instruction. Therefore, upon arriving in the northern Japanese port city of Hachinohe, we—three highly-educated members of America's high-tech workforce—had the reading skills of dried squid, dangerously combined with the hubris of being corporate managers. This volatile mixture could only have one result—two violent, and losing, confrontations with a Japanese toilet.

This story starts, as many plumbing tales do, with the consumption of alcohol. One night, after a particularly high-pressured, twelve-hour day, Dennis, Scott and I decided to relax over a few beers in a small, side-street neighborhood bar adjacent to Hachinohe's commercial center. Being illiterate, we didn't know the establishment's name (it was the Night Inn), but the hostess was friendly enough and the suds were cheap (600 yen) by Japanese standards. We spent an amusing hour rehashing the day's business and exchanging pantomime with the jovial clientele. We fancied ourselves as unofficial ambassadors for the United States, and by the time 60 minutes and several beers had passed, we were doing well enough to expect an appointment with the U.S. Secretary of State himself.

Besides improving our diplomatic skills, the beer also filled our bladders. Soon, Dennis was heading for the men's room, where he encountered a commode from another dimension. The cutting edge of toilet tech, this porcelain device had a mysterious control panel, with a myriad of buttons, all labeled in Japanese. It also lacked an obvious flushing mechanism, so Dennis, based on 45 years of bathroom experience, decided that the wisest course of action was to press one of the hieroglyphically-labeled buttons.

Calmly, Dennis watched the results of his decision. A little robotic arm, resembling an evil, mutant silver pen, protruded into the bowl, and suddenly began spraying water around the three-meter-by-two meter bathroom. Jagged jets of water were fired from the toilet in all directions. Dennis danced and dove, pressing more random buttons—further enraging the porcelain Poseidon. This ensured that the streams were continual and abundant enough to flood the floor with two inches of liquid. Dennis emerged beaten and stunned, with all the aplomb of a man who had just walked through a car wash. He was followed by three rivulets of toilet water, all merging to form Great Commode Lake. Despite the graciousness of the bar lady, who had squelched the fountain and mopped up the puddles, we quickly paid the bill and slid out the door.

Over the next two days, Scott and I relentlessly kidded Dennis

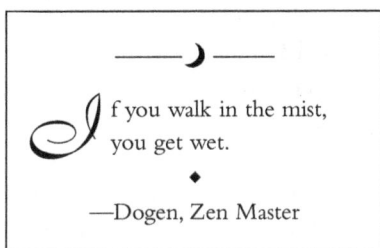

> *If you walk in the mist, you get wet.*
>
> —Dogen, Zen Master

about his inadequate toilet training, and retold the story to any English speaker who even feigned interest. Dennis's consistent rebuttal was that neither of us had even seen the toilet, so we were not worthy judges of his behavior. After hearing Dennis similarly respond the third time, Scott and I reached a momentous decision—we were going to return to the toilet bar, and see the toilet for ourselves.

That night, we went back. We entered humbly, as we were expecting to be remembered, but not necessarily forgiven. However, the bar lady's greeting was warm, and her smile even cracked into a slight giggle when Dennis said his hellos. Instantly, she passed us cold Kirins and a tray of dried plums and pinenuts, and involved us in an animated conversation of charades with two secondary school science teachers. When the talk and mime slowed, the mama-san was quick to pull out the karaoke mike, and the teachers eagerly burst into song.

After a few beers, I inconspicuously slipped away to the john. My bladder was empty of urine but my brain was full of curiosity, and this was my first chance to see the now-legendary crapper. Though cleaner and brighter than your average public toilet, it was immediately notable for what looked like a large Japanese calculator attached by several colored wires to the ceramic basin. Quite possibly, this device could solve several fluid dynamics equations, auto-pilot the space shuttle and send e-mail all at once. It seemed incongruous and excessive that such an advanced box should be strapped to such a lowly appliance.

Taking advantage of the camaraderie and exuberance of the teachers, and my own beer-bolstered confidence, I returned to the bar to enlist one of them as a toilet tour guide. Gently tugging on the sleeve of the man who claimed to teach physics, I motioned him towards the bathroom. In Baltimore, this would get you kissed or punched, depending on whom you asked, but in Hachinohe, it gained me an education.

Once in the water closet, I pointed to the control panel, and shrugged my shoulders—the international gesture for cluelessness. The physics teacher commenced to demonstrate. He pressed one button, causing a thick column of water to pour from the rim to the water line. He touched another key, causing the toilet to emit a puff of perfume, and filling the room with a fresh pine aroma. He then showed me where I could also produce a lemony scent, and how I could adjust the temperature of the water. Finally, he showed me a rather ordinary looking handle on the side of the tank. With that, just like in America but unnoticed by Dennis, he flushed the toilet.

Always a fan of participatory learning, I decided to make use of the presence of the teacher to push a button of my choice. I reasoned that, if I was about to do something dangerous, my Japanese friend would be there to stop me. So I slowly moved my pointed index finger towards the lower left-hand key. Not receiving any protestation from my *sensei*, I kept going until impact.

Immediately, what looked like a thick robotic radio antenna unfolded from under the rim. At once, the teacher bolted from the room. I, having heard Dennis' tale, also quickly realized what was happening and threw myself flat against the wall. Within seconds, a jet of water blasted across the ten-foot room, knocking a picture off the wall. Panicking, I slammed shut the toilet lid, but that didn't contain the water. It flowed out under the seat in all directions, like a parody of a 20th century water sculpture, soaking the floor.

Stunned, I could do nothing. Soon, the bar lady appeared, spewing streams of harsh-sounding Japanese words. She quickly silenced the fountain. I don't speak Japanese, but she was probably yelling, "I can't believe they did it again! I know lab rats that are smarter than Americans!"

Embarrassed, horrified, but laughing uncontrollably, I curled up in the only dry corner and wiped my face clean. About a minute passed, then the mama-san returned with towels, a note pad, and a pencil. As I began soaking up the bodies of water at my feet, she wrote a simple Japanese character on the paper.

"Stop," she said, pointing to the character.

"Stop," I repeated, a bit quizzically.

"Stop," she said again, this time pointing to the lower right-hand button on the toilet's control panel, labeled with the character she just drew. Then she smiled and said, in a voice touched with song, "Don't worry—you are my most funny customers." I would have been surprised at her attitude, had it not reflected the same friendly helpfulness I had encountered everywhere in the Land of the Rising Sun.

And so I learned my first Japanese character. I have since learned a few more, though I am still far from being what demographers would call "functionally literate." Dennis, on the other hand, was clearly more traumatized by the incident. Upon returning to the U.S., he immediately started taking Japanese courses. He has told me that he wants the Hachinohe Toilet Affair to be his last losing battle with a Japanese appliance.

In the meantime, we were not ostracized or summarily ejected from the bar, as might happen in Baltimore. Instead, I was treated to a dry towel and an explanation of the toilet—it was meant to save toilet paper by cleaning the user with water. By the end of the night, I was even tending bar, serving whiskeys and coffees to several customers with whom I could not communicate except to exchange smiles. And of all of my customers, my favorite was the magnanimous and tolerant bar lady, who chatted with Dennis and Scott amiably as I poured her glasses of beer—on the house.

Kevin O'Connor is a businessman from Elliott City, Maryland who sometimes travels for his company to places far away.

★

I never climbed Mt. Fuji because my students advised me not to.

"Why?" I asked.

"It smells," they replied, "for there are so many people and not enough toilets…in the summer heat."

Need I say more?

—Amy Greimann Carlson, "Sensory Notes from Japan"

LINDA BUTLER

* * *

Tea with an Old Friend

*An intimate invitation to understand
a heart over a cup of tea.*

MY SEVENTY-YEAR-OLD WIDOWED FRIEND, ITOGA SENSEI, LIVES
with her ailing mother-in-law. Until four years ago, she was an active career woman, but now she rarely leaves home. Since traditional Japanese families do not hire outsiders to nurse sick relatives,
she alone cares for her mother-in-law.

On my spring trip, a mutual friend accompanied me to her
home. When we arrived, we joined the ninety-three-old *obasan*
(grandmother) around a square lacquer table in the main room of
the house. Despite her age, the grandmother's color was good and
she was mentally alert. She bowed deeply when she saw us.

The day was warm and the sliding doors to the garden were
open. The air hummed with the voices of tiny frogs that breed in
the water of rice fields. Itoga Sensei asked us if we would enjoy
o-matcha (the tea ceremony). While we talked, she offered us bean-
cake sweets on small lacquer plates. The sweetness would create an
excellent balance for the bitterness of the tea.

I was curious about her life as a young woman and asked about
the postwar period. In response to my questions, Itoga Sensei
shared a memory from her younger days. In those days there was
never enough to eat even in rural areas, and she had a houseful of

83

children to feed. One evening a neighboring farmer brought over a tiny pig, the runt of a large litter. The baby pig was near death, and the farmer didn't have time to take care of it. If she was willing to feed it, he would give it to her. She still remembered covering it with a blanket and slipping a baby bottle into its mouth as if it were a child. Of course it was improper to keep a pig in the house, so she built a small pen for it and fed it with whatever she could find. In time it became bigger than its brothers and sisters; her children loved it. The pig let them ride on its back and slide off its rear end. She even built a wagon, and the pig took the children for rides.

None of her neighbors had cars, and she did her errands by either walking into town or taking a bus. It was inconvenient, and she envied her friends who had bicycles. When the farmer offered to sell her pig for her, she accepted. The money she would receive would allow her to purchase a bicycle. She remembered seeing her pig for the last time and feeling too ashamed to look into its eyes. More than forty years had passed and she still regretted her decision.

She poured some hot water into a pottery bowl that she would use in the tea ceremony. In addition to cleaning the bowl, the water would warm the bowl so the tea would stay hot. Emptying it, she then added two scoops of green tea powder and a precise amount of hot water. Using a bamboo whisk, she whipped the tea in a clockwise direction for a full minute and offered the first bowl to the grandmother. Itoga Sensei meticulously prepared my tea in the same manner and offered it to me with a bow. The soft green of the tea in the rust-colored bowl was exquisite. I drank it in three swallows, holding my left hand under the bowl and my right hand on the side.

"It is an exceptional bowl. What is its history?" I asked.

Someone had given it to her deceased husband twenty-five years ago. It was made by a famous potter in Shigaraki who never used glazes. She explained that the flecks of color on the bowl were caused by wood ashes falling on its surface while it was firing in a mountain kiln.

To get a better look, I lifted the bowl up to eye level, holding it in my left palm. In the meantime, Itoga Sensei whisked the tea in the final bowl for our mutual friend.

Just as we finished our tea, our conversation was interrupted by a sudden shrillness in the chirping of the frogs. "They are crying because it is about to rain," she said. As if by signal, a downpour began. Itoga Sensei rose from the table to see how hard the rain was falling. The blossoms on her three large cherry trees were almost open. In a few days she would be having an *o-hanami* (a flower-viewing party). If it rained too much, the blossoms, under the weight of the droplets, would drop to the ground, leaving nothing but fallen petals. Her guests would be disappointed.

When she came back to the table. Itoga Sensei excused herself for being un-Japanese, but she felt that she could speak openly to me since I was a foreigner and she was a modern woman. She explained that the bowl appreciation must be done within an inch of the table's surface, so that if my hands slipped, the bowl would not break. It was a mistake to hold a valuable bowl in the

———⟩———

"What precisely are the most important things that must be understood and kept in mind at a tea gathering?" A disciple of Sen Rikyu once asked him this question.

His answer was, "Make a delicious bowl of tea; lay the charcoal so that it heats the water; arrange the flowers as they are in the field; in summer suggest coolness, in winter, warmth; do everything ahead of time; prepare for rain; and give those with whom you find yourself every consideration."

The disciple, somewhat dissatisfied with this answer because he could not find anything in it of such great importance that it could be deemed a secret of the practice, said, "That much I already know..."

Rikyu answered, "Then if you can host a tea gathering without deviating from any of the rules I have just stated, I will become your disciple."

◆

—Soshitsu Sen XV,
Tea Life, Tea Mind

air because it made everyone nervous, thus destroying the feeling of calm that the tea ceremony was trying to create.

I thanked her for teaching me; she had saved me from making future mistakes. I appreciated her frankness; it was one of the reasons I cherished her friendship.

She asked if I knew the proverb *"Ichi go, ichi e"* ("One meeting, one chance"). "It is an old proverb," she explained. "It is said to have originated with a *samurai* who offered the tea ceremony to a friend about four hundred years ago. They were leaving for war and did not know if they would ever see each other again.

"Our lives seem predictable compared with the lives of the ancients, yet even we cannot be certain if we will meet again. The tea ceremony trains us to focus on the uniqueness of our moments together."

I asked if she would explain the meaning of *teisai buru* (doing something for appearances' sake), a Japanese concept that I didn't fully understand.

"We older Japanese always worry what other people think," she began. "For instance, at funerals it would be easiest to invite a country priest with a black robe to tap *poku, poku*, on a country drum and chant the last rites for one's deceased relative. But instead we invite five priests from city temples. They bring fancy altars and beautiful parasols and wear shiny purple and gold robes and bring cymbals. For the *kamisama* and the dead relative, a simple ceremony is adequate, and in fact, the chants are exactly the same. But for appearances' sake, the family must have the fancy ceremony to make a good impression on the guests." During this explanation, the grandmother had dozed off.

"When we bring gifts to someone's house, even if the gift is not from a famous department store, we carry it in the bag of a famous department store, and sometimes we even rewrap it in the box of a famous department store. The person who receives it feels more valued if it is from a place of high repute.

"At country weddings, the parents still give the bride a *tansu* (chest) full of kimonos. After the wedding ceremony, the neighbors come over to see the contents of the chest. Each drawer is pulled from the chest and each kimono is unwrapped so the neighbors can evaluate the quality. It is, of course, a foolish custom because young girls never wear kimonos anymore, so thousands of dollars go to waste. Sometimes the daughter begs her mother not to do this, but the parents must give a chest full of kimonos for appearances' sake."

As we excused ourselves, the grandmother woke up. We had intruded for a long time, and we knew both of them were tired. To say good-bye, the grandmother knelt in a prostrate bow, her head on the *tatami* floor and her arms extended. According to Japanese custom, I bowed as deeply as the grandmother to show respect. I stretched myself into a prostrate position and inched out of the room crawling backward.

As we walked home, I asked my friend how someone as bright and active as Itoga Sensei could bear staying at home constantly. My friend explained that Japanese women were expected to care for their in-laws. What was unusual was that Itoga Sensei loved the *obasan* as if she were her own mother. Of course the work was hard and stressful, but Itoga Sensei had much endurance. In giving her mother-in-law such good care, she had achieved an inner peace; she would be lonely when the grandmother was gone.

Linda Butler, born in Appleton, Wisconsin, attended Antioch College in Ohio and the University of Michigan, becoming a fine arts photographer. She has exhibited her work in many one-person shows and is in the collections of Boston's Museum of Fine Arts and other major museums across the country.

✳

"I've been studying tea for three years," the woman went on. "See, the thing about it is that it combines calligraphy, lacquer-work, scrolls, flower arranging, all the rules about bowing and manners. So everything's right there; tea's like a compilation of all the Japanese arts."

"But to a typically uninitiated viewer, it's a little hard to see the subtleties."

"Sure, but they're *incredible*. Believe me, they are amazing. Like, in pouring the tea, you've got to curl your finger into this exact shape?"—

she curved it prettily—"which is meant to be the exact shape of the moon two days after it's new. No way you can do the second-day moon, no way you can do the fourth. You've got to make it the third. And there's a different tea, not just for every season and every month, but for every week! So you have to have this amazing concentration—like *aikido* too."

"Do you enjoy it?"

"Yeah. But I kind of think it's time to quit. The truth is, the longer you do it, the more you see what you're supposed to be doing. You get more self-conscious, more uptight—more Japanese, I guess. I remember one day I had been doing tea for two hours, and then I was arranging a flower, while looking out a window. Nobody could see me. Nobody! But this lady came up to me and told me I was sitting wrong. I felt like saying to her, "Fuck it! Who cares how I'm sitting if nobody's here?" But you can't do that. So I had to sit the right way, and there's no way I can sit the wrong way again. I've got to be self-conscious even when I'm fucking sitting down! When I first came here, I was just like this kind of happy idiot, stumbling over everything: a real bull in a china shop. But the more sensitive I became to the Japanese, the more self-conscious I had to become. I think I'm burned out."

—Pico Iyer, *The Lady and the Monk: Four Seasons in Kyoto*

GREG DVORAK

Back to Izumo, Back to Springtime

A long overdue return home to family.

AN OLD WOMAN SMILES AS SHE WHISPERS STORIES TO HER LITTLE grandson, stroking her hand gently across his shaven head. Just outside her window, on her side of the train, the Sea of Japan rambles lazily past the slick tracks. The grey drizzle of early April is subsiding, and through the chalky spring mist beams of light ride each wave to the jagged beaches below.

On my side all is green. Before Japan, I didn't understand the color green, but now it is an old friend; no matter how long I live or travel in Japan, this infinitely vivid green never ceases to seep into my soul. Mountains and hills and valleys off in the distance almost seem to be upholstered with cedar trees. Emerald fields of rice interspersed with patches of fluffy purple flowers shimmer as they sway gently beyond where I sit. A white heron stretches its neck out at me. Every now and then a lone cherry tree in full bloom emerges in the landscape, blurred by the runny condensation on the glass.

Indeed, this is the *San'In*—the land that dwells in the shadow of mountains. I remember it so well, despite the two years we have been apart. And the sea is the same—studded with strange old rocks jutting out of the water; tiny, weathered *torii* built of wood sitting amid the craggy ridges. Grey, moody, muted—it is enchanted but welcoming all at once.

----)----

*E*ven schoolchildren know that life in the *tokai*, or big city, is different from their routine in the *inaka*, or countryside. Several junior high school girls in a nearby town approached my friend Jane one day while she was teaching at their school.

"Miss Jane," they asked, "have you ever kissed a boy?"

"Yes, I have," she replied. "Have you?"

The girls blushed and covered their mouths in shock.

"Of course not," one squealed.

"I don't even have a boyfriend," said another.

"I'm only going to kiss the boy that I decide to marry," a third girl insisted.

"But I'll tell you a secret," one of the girls whispered in a conspiratorial tone, drawing the others in tight. "In Tokyo, they start much earlier. Some even kiss at thirteen."

◆

—Bruce S. Feiler, *Learning to Bow: Inside the Heart of Japan*

And within the *San'In* lies the old country of Izumo. This is my Japan, the one I knew from the first time I came here. The Big City is far from here; it was there that I nearly lost faith that this Japan was still even here. But in these few minutes of riding the *San'In Hon Sen* I remember that this is the place I have been trying to return to. And yet when I am away from here, it is only a dream, just as America is now.

Memories of my Japanese family flash through my mind: Strangely, I only stayed a month with them, but with all the letters we had exchanged it seemed as if I'd grown up with them. I promised them all that I would come back, and that when I did I would speak Japanese fluently. Here I am, doing just that. I remember my brother, Hiroya, teaching me my first words of Japanese, how we talked so much the first night in a noodle shop that we missed a whole fireworks festival, or how we sat at dinner saying *"arigato"* and *"doitashimashite"* repeatedly until I finally got it right. I think of my *okachan*, my Japanese mother, giggling as she watched me fumble with my chopsticks, trying to understand my English— or *otochan*, my father, doing the tea ceremony and throwing pots while he had Hiroya translate his lengthy explanations of history. I went to the beach often with my younger brother Kosuke, and we talked about soccer and America while digging for *sazae* in the damp sand and skipping stones across the water. My little sister Wakako would hide shyly under the table, pulling my leg hairs and laughing hysterically. And there was *ojichan*, my grandfather, who stood up in front of everyone at our farewell party and sang an old good-bye song to me with tears in his eyes. That was the last time I would ever see him.

The sound of this slow train on the rails is soft, kind of muffled, like popcorn exploding in a very faraway place. *Chug-a-chug-chug, chug-a-chug-chug…chug-a-chug-chug-ka-chug….* Soon I'll be back in Izumo. The little boy has fallen deep asleep and crumpled up against his grandmother, his mouth hanging open. The four o'-clock sun is beginning to cast a huge shadow on the earth that races along next to us. I see the shadows of all the sleeping passengers in the grass and daffodils. I see my own shadow, too. At least in the world of shadows, I could easily pass for Japanese. And the *San'In* is indeed a world of shadows.

An hour later, I am walking towards the turnstile in Matsue station. I can see my Japanese parents already. They stand alone, eagerly beaming with happiness—they are not embarrassed to show their emotion, even though the other strangers in the crowd around them look so restrained and polite. I can feel my own smile bursting off my face. We ignore Japanese custom and engage in a group hug there in the middle of the station. I don't understand how I could have been away for so long.

We hop into the white Toyota and drive off into the town. There are several huge, new futuristic buildings near the station, but for the most part, Matsue looks the same. Soon we are winding our way through a maze of tiny roads into the familiar district of Edo-era houses, wood turned black with the ages. And there is the house, the same as before. No sooner can I get out of the car than seven-year-old Wakako comes racing through the front gate and leaps upon me. It is amazing how much she's grown, and maybe even more amazing how much she remembers me. The last time we met I couldn't even understand a word she said. I feel as if we both were five years old then. Last time she had given me a speechless tour all around the little old house and gardens, and we sat on a rock counting up to 100 in Japanese together. I look at her energetic, smily face and realize that now I understand all that she says to me; I understand everyone. Soon Hiroya joins us in the entryway, and Kosuke, and all the cats. It is such a dream to be back in this house. Everyone is obviously overjoyed to have me back, but they all seem to be trying to conceal it from me. I turn around to see Kosuke looking up at me. "How are you?" he says shyly in English, shaking my hand. Hiroya puts his arm around me and welcomes me back.

I am always amazed by this house, how despite its 300 years it still manages to feel so alive. Whenever I tell my friends, whether they are Japanese or not, they can never believe that houses like this still exist. *Otochan* says if at least some people don't hold onto the old Japan, it might just slip away. So he and *okachan* do their best to keep the house just as it always was. Everyone always sleeps on *futon* in the same

---

*I*n ancient China, the size of a building was defined by the number of pillars or "bays" lining the front and side of the structure. Japan inherited this arrangement, and standardized the width of one bay to be the same as the length of a *tatami* mat. It is from this system of bays and mats that Japan's modular architecture developed. Land is also measured in terms of *tatami* mats. The standard used even today, when all other measurements have gone metric, is the *tsubo*, defined as one square bay or two *tatami* mats (3.3 m^2). The land my house sits on measures one hundred and twenty *tsubo*.

◆

—Alex Kerr, *Lost Japan*

room together; they don't keep any furniture except the low tables for eating; and they still heat their bath water with a wood furnace. But of course, they have a TV, a computer, and a new washing machine, and Kosuke and Wakako are always playing video games.

The air smells familiar, of spicy plum incense, *tatami* flooring, and ancient cypress. We all walk through the shadows of the house, lit softly by the dusk outside. The six of us sit around in the main *tatami* room by the *tokonoma* alcove, where *okachan* has artfully displayed a white lily. Eating Shimane grapes and drinking tea, we all talk together about how things have and haven't changed. They ask me about my family back in America. For a second, I don't even know what or where America is, and everyone laughs at me as I stumble over my words.

"Tonight we're going to have a night picnic dinner under the cherry blossoms," says *okachan* with a grin of delight, "*yozakura*." My "siblings" help me to carry my two super heavy bags out onto the veranda. No matter how many times I travel in Japan, I still haven't learned to pack as well as my Japanese counterparts and never fail to bring much more than enough.

"Do you like koala bears?" Wakako asks me, as she shoves a few boxes of koala-shaped cookie snacks into a Snoopy-pattern drawstring bag. She packs some gummy candies and a packet of blueberry stick gum for me.

We all set out on foot through the garden, stepping carefully on the flat stones that rise up out of a thick carpet of moss. A bird cries out above me, and Kosuke whispers in his raspy voice, "That's an *uguisu*." I want to carry something and help out, but no one will let me. The path opens out to a narrow road lined with red-and-white-striped festival lanterns, and quite a few people seem to be headed in the same direction. Hiroya runs over to a small booth, buys a white, steaming package, and yells to me, "Hey, do you remember these?"—*takoyaki*, octopus dumplings. He and I had shared a package together back on that first night I came to Japan.

In what seems like no time at all we are walking up the cool, grassy slope of the hill where Matsue Castle stands. There are vendors on either side of the path selling sweet skewered *mochi* balls, barbecued corn-on-the-cob, more dumplings, masks of every Japanese cartoon hero imaginable, and soccer fan paraphernalia. Kosuke casts a longing look at the latter, but his mother subliminally disapproves.

In my bliss, I have somehow failed to notice the rows and rows of trees overspilling with blossoms. Against bark turned black by the day's drizzle, the *sakura* glisten pink and white in the light reflected from the festival booths. Each tree is so plump and ripe with fleeting beauty that for a moment I lose all sense of time and space.

Matsue Castle looms hauntingly above the crowd of festival-goers, a tremendous monument of tradition and the past illuminated all around by huge floodlights. It is like a huge rock or cliff standing straight out in a desert. Unlike most Japanese castles, it is mostly black, but in the strange light it all seems to glow against the blue-black Izumo sky. Tiny petals dance through the breeze, flying high and swirling like pink seraphim around the mossy tiles and black wooden rafters in the altitudes of the fortress. Blossoms brush across our faces in a silent blizzard.

Everyone else seems to be as amazed as I am, even though they must see this every year. Without words, my Japanese family and I lay out our lacquered-wooden boxes of food on a large plastic sheet. I am starving. All varieties of *sushi* are spread out before me, with *sashimi*, *yakisoba* and pickled vegetables.

Otochan cracks open four cans of portable sake that heat up as soon as they are activated. Kosuke and Wakako fill their cups with green tea.

"Let's *kanpai* to my second eldest son," announces Otochan. We all hold our drinks in the air.

"*Okaeri nasai,*" they shout. Welcome home!

"*Tadaima,*" I'm home, I say. I have been wanting to say that for so long, but I just wanted to make sure I wasn't dreaming. And even if this is a dream, it's the best one I've ever had in my entire life. Drunk by the sweet sake, the smell of spring, and the love and laughter of my Japanese family, I feel myself carried up tenderly on the evening breeze. When tomorrow comes, all the blossoms will have fallen, and the trees will be bare. But I know I will always have a home right here in Japan.

Greg Dvorak is a writer from Medford, New Jersey. This story won Grand Prize in a writing contest conducted by the Japan National Tourist Organization.

⁕

Johen sits among thickly forested hills and lush green fields in a rugged and virtually untouched region of Shikoku. Very few foreigners have ever visited there, and sometimes wandering its streets—seeing adults stop in their tracks to gape at me, and little children turn away in terror or, conversely, run up to touch this strange being's skin—I felt like a medieval European explorer. It is a quiet village of fishermen and farmers, a place of wooden houses arranged along roads that follow the contour of the land, of rice fields and vegetable plots and shops open to the street where housewives in kimonos gather every day for groceries and gossip.

In the days before our wedding, we visited Kuniko's friends and relatives in the area, bringing small gifts, and explored the country around the town. Certain memories stand out: a conversation over tangerines and green tea at one relative's house, about the "other foreigner" who married a girl from the town across the hill; random nods and smiles from grandmotherly shopkeepers; a thatched-roof farmhouse in the middle of distant rice paddies; fishing villages with their nets strung out to dry, and men and women in white sunbonnets sitting under tents surrounded by oysters and seaweed, beckoning to us and smiling great gap-toothed smiles, while they patiently planted pearls; the quiet streets and wooden houses after sundown, lit from within; a gathering of mothers and children in the late afternoon, flying long-tailed kites in a field; and a Chinese lion dance a group of elementary school students put on in a garage in our honor, the kids in shorts and crew cuts beating the drums with all their might and the lion thrashing about under the garage's single bulb.

It was in the accumulation and sharing of such experiences—of the meticulously tended gardens outside even the simplest houses, of mornings loud with wind and rain and bird-song, of the wooden steps at the local shrine grooved by centuries of soles—that I first began to understand the Japanese sense of richness in simplicity, of vitality in the unadorned.

—Donald W. George, "Unforgettable Journey," *San Francisco Examiner*

PART TWO

SOME THINGS TO DO

動

(Activity)

T.R. REID

* * *

The Great Tokyo Fish Market

*Frozen carcasses for auction turn
into* sushi *in no time flat.*

THE LONG, COLD TRIP TO TOKYO CAME TO AN END FOR TUNA
number 197 with a *thud*, a *bonk*, and one last cavernous *clunk* as the
huge fish toppled off the truck and skittered across the slippery
concrete floor. Two, maybe three days earlier, this torpedo-shaped
bluefin had been searching for its supper in the chilly waters off
Boston. Now—netted, gutted, flash-frozen to 76 degrees below
zero, and transported via cargo jet halfway around the world—197
was itself on the verge of becoming somebody's supper, served up
on the polished wooden counter of a *sushi* bar where diners would
pay dearly for this succulent delicacy.

The place that transformed 197 from just another fish in the sea
to one of the world's most expensive foodstuffs is a sprawling,
teeming, cacophonous corner of reclaimed land on the edge of
Tokyo Bay. Its formal name is the Tokyo Central Wholesale
Market, but in Tokyo everybody calls the place Tsukiji (pronounced skee-jee), for the neighborhood where the market stands.
Fairly substantial quantities of meat, mushrooms, maple syrup,
pickles, potatoes, peaches, and other foods move through this market every day. But the heart and soul of Tsukiji is fish.

Tsukiji is a fish market in the sense that the Grand Canyon is a

ditch or Caruso was a crooner. Among the wholesale fish markets
of the world, Tsukiji ranks at the top in every measurable category.
It handles more than 400 different types of seafood, from penny-
per-piece sardines to golden brown dried sea slug caviar, a bargain
at almost $500 a pound. It imports from 60 countries on 6 conti-
nents—indeed, the list of shipments reaching Tsukiji on any given
morning reads like a verse from John Masefield's poem "Cargoes":
eel from Taiwan, sea urchin from Oregon, octopus from Athens,
crab from Cartagena, salmon from Santiago, tuna from Tasmania,
and on and on for hundreds of entries. Tsukiji moves about 5 million pounds of seafood every day—7 times as much as Paris's
Rungis, the world's second largest wholesale market, and 11 times
the volume of New York City's Fulton Fish Market, the largest fish
market in North America. In dollar terms, that comes to nearly 30
million dollars' worth of fish. Per day.

Handling that incoming ocean of seafood is the work of some
60,000 people and a fleet of 32,000 vehicles that seem to operate
in a near-constant state of gridlock. At the midpoint of Tsukiji's
workday (6 a.m. or so) the crowded sheds and narrow passageways
are so clogged with trucks, vans, motorcycles, fork-lifts, handcarts,
and bicycles (with the rider balancing, say, 4 cases of live shrimp
on a shoulder) that you literally can't find walking space.

Not that it's safe just to stand still—if you do, there's always the
risk of being mowed down by a *ta-ray*, a three-wheel, gas powered
wagon that zips through the market carrying stacked cases of fish.

The first couple of times I went to Tsukiji, I was overwhelmed
by the vastness of the place, the frenzied activity, the constant roar
of voices and vehicles. I was struck both by the presence of so
many fish and by the mysterious absence of any fishy aroma (it's
actually no mystery at all, I learned later; the produce sold at
Tsukiji moves through the market so fast that it's long gone before
it starts to smell). I remember wondering—as I stepped over long
rows of tuna, walked past blue plastic trash cans filled with squirming eels, slipped between stacked wooden cases of flounder flapping their tails—how any city could eat this much fish in a month,
much less one day.

But going back more often, I gradually realized that to focus on the bigness was to miss a key point. The real secret here, the reason the place does its job so well, is that Tsukiji is a small town. It's a community where everybody knows everybody else, and everybody works together toward the common goal of moving fish as fast as possible from the sea to the *sushi* bar or the supermarket.

"Of course, we know that time is money," says white-haired Kikuo Takayanagi, president of the wholesale firm Daitoyo and a respected elder statesman of the marketplace. "Even so, you always take the 30 seconds to bow, to say hello. We are all neighbors here."

"To understand how Tsukiji works, just remember that Tsukiji is a *mura*," smiles Makoto Nozue, director of the Tsukiji Tuna Association, using the Japanese word for a traditional village. "We feel we work in a community called Tsukiji-mura. Yes, we are all competitors. But we spend a lot of our lives in this crowded village, and we need to get along."

Like every Japanese *mura*, the small town called Tsukiji has a clear hierarchy. At the top of the pecking order are the employees of the seven major first-tier wholesalers, who buy up fish around the world and get them to Tokyo. The big seven, in turn, auction off the daily catch to more than a thousand middle wholesalers, who cut, package, and deliver the goods, sometimes to yet another tier of distributors, sometimes directly to stores or *sushi* bars. There is a separate world of small businesses—knife sharpeners, boxmakers, bootsellers, and three dozen restaurants—on the site to serve the fishmongers.

And yet the privileges of status at Tsukiji tend to yield to the fundamental Japanese social principles of harmony, community, and the avoidance of confrontation. I saw that one morning when I witnessed a traffic accident in the market. A rampaging *ta-ray* cart slammed into a bicycle. The biker was wearing the uniform of one of the seven top-tier firms; the *ta-ray* driver, who worked for a small wholesale outfit, seemed to be in the wrong. But it quickly became clear that this incident would be resolved by the Japanese version of a no-fault settlement: both drivers got off their vehicles, took off their caps, bowed deeply to each other, apologized, and then worked together to straighten the bicycle's bent fender and to gather up the cases of fish sent flying in the crash.

Like every Japanese *mura*, Tsukiji has its own Shinto shrine, a handsome dark-wood structure with a black fluted roof and an imposing twelve-foot-tall *torii*, or gate, out front. It was built here 350 years ago, when the ruling *shogun* first reclaimed the land, to appease the gods; that explains its name, Namiyoke Inari Jinja, or "hold-back-the-waves shrine."

"People in the fish market come to pray more often than the average salaryman," the amiable chief priest. Hidemaro Suzuki, told me one day as he sat cross-legged on the *tatami* floor of his shrine. "They are buying and selling every day in auctions, and auctions are a function of fate. So people working here need more contact with the gods."

Sometimes the shrine is a place for carefree escape, such as the festival each June when hundreds of fish-market people pull on bright orange *happi* coats for a grand procession through the neighborhood. Sometimes the shrine is for contemplation; several times a year Suzuki-san leads prayers for the fish that die here. Gathering up his long black kimono, the priest led me over to a large rock in the temple garden, placed by the Association of Sushi Suppliers.

"We have pleased many humans with fine *sushi*," the inscription reads, "but we must also stop to console the souls of the fish."

Tsukiji puts heavy emphasis on education to pass along essential skills to the next generation—yet another resemblance between this place and Japan's small towns. On any given day there will be classes at the market on topics like auction protocol, knife handling, or time-tested techniques for making a spicy *kamaboko*, or fish sausage.

One day I happened upon a course that had literally life-or-death implications. Officials from Tsukiji's Fugu Harmonious Association were teaching the proper way to carve a fillet of *fugu*, the bulbous fish usually known in English as blowfish or puffer. For reasons I've never understood—the stuff always tastes like cardboard to me—*fugu* is an expensive and cherished delicacy in

Japan. Unfortunately, it can also be lethal. Enzymes in organs of the fish are fatal to humans; almost every year some unfortunate diner expires in Japan after feasting on fugu that was not properly prepared.

Accordingly, a national license is required for every fugu chef. The class I saw was preparing candidates for the rigid licensing exam. "I've only got a month to go before the test," 26-year-old Kazuya Yawatagaki told me nervously, hefting an 18-inch knife as he practiced cutting slivers of *fugu* so thin they were translucent. "There's a written exam that lasts two hours. The next day they hand you a *fugu*, a knife, and two pans. In 20 minutes you have to put every poisonous part of the fish in one pan and all the edible parts in the other."

Another reason the people of this teeming place see themselves as neighbors in a village is that everyone in the market is bound to an upside-down daily schedule known as Tsukiji time. The market's workday begins just before 3 a.m., when the truck convoys begin to arrive, hauling fresh and frozen fish from around Japan and around the world. By sunrise it is time

*A*n average of thirty Japanese people die each year from globefish poisoning. One of the most publicized cases occurred in January 1975 when the Kabuki actor Bando Mitsugoro who had been designated a Living National Treasure—died after eating globefish prepared by a licensed chef at a restaurant in Kyoto. The five or six companions with whom the actor had dined that night were rather less keen than him on the delicacy, so he gobbled all their portions too— despite which the chef was charged with professional negligence and received an eight-year suspended prison sentence.

Basho has a haiku poem on globefish:
Would you believe it—nothing's happened!
Yesterday's vanished, and so has the globefish soup.

♦

—Alan Booth,
The Roads to Sata: A 2000-Mile Walk Through Japan

for the lunch break. When the day's work is essentially done, the people of Tsukiji sit down for dinner and a cold beer-at around 8:30 in the morning. "Someone working here might live in a nice neighborhood like Shibuya or Funabashi, but how can you have any friends there?" says Masami Eguchi, a round-cheeked, crew-cut 41-year-old who has worked at Tsukiji for 20 years. "You get up at, what, 2:30 a.m. to go to work, and when you get home, you're already thinking about going to bed. So for us, our 'neighborhood' is really Tsukiji."

As a rising star in the ranks of Chuo Gyorui, the largest of the seven first-tier wholesale firms, Eguchi-san says he has no complaints about his inverted workday. "But my daughter is four now, and she's starting to complain," he adds with a half smile. "She says, Papa, you're a grown-up! Why do you go to bed before I do?"

Eguchi-san needs his sleep, because around five every morning he plays a leading role in Tsukiji's most lucrative daily drama: the tuna auction.

Longer than a man and weighing from 200 to 1,000 pounds each, hundreds of tuna arrive in Japan by cargo jet every day. So voracious is the Japanese appetite for fish that even the swordfish caught by a tourist off the coast of Florida is more likely these days to end up frozen in Tsukiji than stuffed on the fisherman's wall; Chuo Gyorui and other first-tier wholesalers contract with agents on the charter docks in Miami to buy those big prizes as soon as they reach shore.

From the airport, the tuna are trucked to Tsuikiji and bounced out onto the floor of the big tuna shed. They are lined up in long rows, like so many toppled bowling pins, while workers weigh them and label them with bright red characters. Number 197—a monster of a fish at 622 pounds—happened to be the 197th tuna delivered to the Chuo Gyorui auction area the day it arrived; the man with the writing brush quickly stroked the essential information on the tuna's belly: #197, Boston, 282 kg.

In the crowded market the frozen fish quickly begin defrosting, and a cold, eerie mist rises from the long lines of tuna. Around 4 a.m. an army of phantom figures starts moving through the mist.

These are the buyers from several hundred second-level tuna wholesalers, who cut a morsel of dark red meat from each tuna; they feel it, smell it, check its color and oil content, constantly making notes on their hands or scraps of paper.

Eventually, the auctioneers join the throng. Proudly putting on his brown-and-white Chuo Gyorui cap, Eguchi-san sets up shop on a small wooden pedestal, ringing his handbell to announce the start of the sale.

"There are dozens of auctioneers working for the big seven wholesalers," Eguchi-san explained to me one day. "And each one has his own chant, his own rhythm. You have to pick a style that works for you and for the buyers. And you have to work fast. You know, the tuna I sell go for 600,000 yen [$6,800 U.S.], even one million yen apiece, and I have to sell 200 of them in about half an hour each morning."

Eguchi-san's style of selling might be described as "total involvement." With his right arm high in the air and his chubby belly bouncing rhythmically along, he roars out his sing-song call. He constantly scans the arcane hand signals of the buyers circled around him, stepping up the pace, and his own rate of bounce, as the bidding goes higher. When one fish is sold, he swipes quickly at his sweat-soaked face with a sleeve or handkerchief and moves on to the next without missing a beat.

Implicit in this complex ritual of inspection and auction is a concept that might not be immediately obvious to Americans—one that I was educated about over an exquisite dinner of tuna *sashimi* when I asked Eguchisan's boss, Hiroyasu Itoh, senior managing director of the Tuna Department of Chuo Gyorui, if all tuna taste alike.

Itoh-san, who has put in some 40 years with his firm, bore my ignorant query with a gentle smile, and replied with a question of his own.

"Reido-san," he said, "why is it that Americans think any fish is just like every other fish? They're not made in a factory, you know. It seems perfectly obvious to us that a bluefin from the cold, rough seas around Tasmania will have different meat than a bluefin from tropical waters. I guess if you cook your tuna with lemon and seasonings, then it all starts to taste the same. But that's another thing I can't understand."

Itoh-san deftly scooped up a slim rectangle of deep red tuna meat with his chopsticks and held it out to me. "Why would you take fish this good, fish that cost 7,000 yen a kilo [about $36 a pound], and cook it? I mean, you kill the flavor! It seems so wasteful."

In fact, virtually all the tuna and more than half of all the seafood Tsukiji sells each day will be eaten raw—either sliced into small rectangles as *sashimi* or placed as the topping on a cube of *sushi* rice. And it will all be expensive.

Japan is famous for outrageous prices, of course, and the country's famously inefficient distribution system is a key reason. This is all part of Japan's basic social contract: to make sure that almost everybody has a job, extra layers of labor are added to virtually every economic activity. This is costly in terms of prices, but it also saves a good deal of money, pain, and disruption by ensuring a secure and peaceful population. As the central seafood distribution hub for a nation of fish lovers, Tsukiji vividly illustrates how this works.

Consider, for instance, tuna 197. It was caught by an American fishing boat. Sold to a Japanese trading company. Shipped via air and truck to a first-tier wholesaler at Tsukiji. Sold at auction there to a smaller Tsukiji wholesaler. Cut, packaged, and transferred to various distributors. Delivered to restaurants throughout central Japan. By the time the fish finally got to the end consumer, tuna 197 has passed through at least seven intermediary companies, each one taking a profit along the way. No wonder some salaryman in a *sushi* bar ended up paying five dollars or so for each half-ounce bite.

But if Tsukiji serves to prove the common Western view that Japan is expensive and inefficient, it tends to undermine another piece of conventional wisdom about Japan—that its markets are closed.

Almost every developed nation is running a trade deficit with Japan, and companies around the world still face problems getting many goods and services into this rich country. But when it comes to food, either from land or sea, Japan is the biggest net importer on earth. Tsukiji, of course, is the largest importer of seafood, and people working in the market seem proud that their daily labor helps offset Japan's big trade surplus.

"You know, your president ought to give me a medal," laughs Tetsuya Ishizaki of Chuo Gyorui, a man who greeted me wearing an orange plastic squid in place of a necktie. "I mean, he says he wants Japan to import more American products. Well, I get up at three every morning to buy American imports."

The import that Ishizaki-san brings in from California, Oregon, and Maine is *uni*, or sea urchin, a fist-size shellfish with a buttery soft meat of yellow red, or bright orange. Many Americans probably wouldn't know a *uni* from a unicorn, yet the U.S. has become the biggest exporter of *uni* on earth. And every last exported *uni* goes straight to Japan.

"I went to Portland, Oregon, to teach them how to get the *uni* out of the shell and into the wooden shipping box," Ishizaki-san says. "The California red sea urchin is one of the largest *uni* in the world, and it is delicious. But we had to explain to the Americans that if you handle the meat too much, it will go bad."

The reason that Tsukiji buyers had to develop a U.S. *uni* industry involves a familiar problem in the fishing business these days. The *uni*-picking grounds in Japan and Korea have been overfished, and it is necessary to give them time to replenish. Japan has sharply limited *uni* picking in its waters—they can be fished no more than two hours a day—and other countries (as well as California and Maine) are moving in the same direction.

The sea urchin is hardly the only marine species facing depletion, and many people at Tsukiji are coming to sense a tension between the desire to sell as much fish as possible today and the need to have more fish available to sell tomorrow. "We all think about this," says Itoh-san, the 40-year veteran of Chuo Gyorui. "My father was in this company, and I would like for my children and grandchildren to have a future in it. And that means we must have healthy fish stocks."

The need for healthy stocks around the world will continue, because the world's biggest fish market must continue to sell fish. Its appetite is huge, and its reach is broad. In almost any corner of the seven seas, buyers from Tsukiji are at work right now, on the lookout for tomorrow's number 197.

T. R. Reid spent many years in Tokyo as the bureau chief for The Washington Post. *He has written numerous articles on Japanese affairs for* National Geographic *and other major U.S. publications.*

✳

On the way, the old man, between yawns, gives me information.

We are between the islands of Samejima and Seijima, where the sea is so shallow that at low tide one may walk the considerable distance from one island to the other and the water will come no further than here—the breastbone of this short, gnarled, wrinkled, smiling old man whose black eyes, sunk deep into his face, sparkle like coal.

Also when he was a boy, back in the Meiji period, they used to have great sport out here with the octopus, which grows to great size in these shallow seas. They would catch a large one and bring it into the boat. Then they would put it on the back of one of the boys, like a knapsack, the large, snakelike tentacles wrapped around his chest, the monster first struggling, then holding like a python. With it on his back, the boy would dive into the sea.

Though the octopus was free to escape, it never did. It was too used to holding onto things; once onto something, it would never let go. Since it was back in the sea, however, it swam in its own fashion, shooting water out behind while firmly attached to the boy's back, and he could half-guide it, much as one directs a stubborn donkey. In this way the youngster could enjoy an exhilarating ride, held up by the half-submerged octopus, propelled at a great rate, diving, gradually turning around and being propelled back to the boat, where the other boys were waiting to take their turns.

But what about the beak, I wanted to know, that awful beak I had read about, right in the middle of the body where the eight legs meet, that parrot-beak which can break a thighbone as a sparrow breaks a twig.

Oh, they never use it, not unless they are really frightened. And then, it is so brittle that, though it can make a nasty cut, there is more danger of it itself breaking than of its breaking anything. The most that can happen is that the octopus gets so frightened that he releases his ink and then—and the old man laughed to remember—you come up black as a man from Africa, covered with the not-unpleasant but strong-smelling India-black ink of the octopus.

But, wasn't anyone afraid of the monster? Of course not.

And it is true. Japan, unlike the West, has no horror legend about the gentle octopus. In Japanese folklore the octopus is always playful, no matter how large. He often wears a towel around his head and a roguish look. He is also eaten in various ways and is delicious. Japan has no more need of horrid stories about the octopus than we do of frightful legends about the cow.

But when it came time to get out of the water, what then?

Well, alone it would have been hard to take him off, that's true. One would have had to wear him home. But friends always managed to tear off those great suction-cupped arms, though they left marks. Oh, after a day of play out in the boat they would all go back home all spotted up, as though they had smallpox.

And what would happen to the friendly octopus after they had tired of their playmate?

Oh, they would cut him up and eat him.

—Donald Richie, *The Inland Sea*

JIM LEFF

* * *

Department Store Panic

*A search for a bow tie turns
into an urgent escape.*

ON THE SURFACE, TOKYO SEEMS MUCH LIKE ANY OTHER BIG CITY.
It's easy for a Western visitor to fit comfortably into its familiar
urban facade, only rarely glimpsing the breathtaking exoticness
that lurks just beneath the surface.

Notice the mohawked, body-pierced Japanese youth coming
toward you on that Shinjuku sidewalk. You've seen punkers before;
he's hardly worth a second glance. But watch as he bows to an elderly stranger out of respect for her age.

You're not in Kansas anymore.

I was there to perform with a mostly black jazz band, and was
appalled when the promoter's welcoming party featured a table full
of cut-up watermelon. I was more horrified still—for different
reasons—when I learned that off-season watermelons in Japan run
a cool $100 per. So...it was more an ostentatious show of respect
than adherence to a stereotype. Or was it?

It's nearly impossible to say; East/West cultural correlations are
slippery, and sometimes the more you probe and analyze, the less
you understand.

In those moments when the apparently ordinary suddenly bares
its alien underpinnings, even avowed Asiaphiles—caught off

guard—may find themselves plunged into confusion. Or worse. All I wanted was a bow tie…

With dress rehearsal set at 1 p.m., I had time to dash out in search of emergency neck-wear. Afflicted with 12-hour jetlag, I'd risen at the unmusi-cianly hour of 5:30 a.m. and thus found myself first in line outside one of the big down-town department stores. Precisely on the hour, a uni-formed doorman—having completed a martial ceremony akin to London's changing of the palace guard—unlocked things and allowed in the sea of customers.

I had read that when Japanese department stores open, their staff lines up to bow to the incoming shop-pers, and therefore took the spectacle in stride. Amused by the incongruity of such surrealistic pageantry in a set-ting as familiar as, say, Macy's, I mirthfully strode down the aisle, each employee bending deeply at the waist as I passed by. To be polite, I returned a jerky, short nod every few feet. But peering front-wards—at columns of clerks

———❩———

*I*t was the fifth birthday party last year for my son Gregory, and he had invited all his Japanese friends over from the Tokyo kindergarten that he attended. My wife and I ex-plained the rules of musical chairs, and we started the music.

It was not so awful for the Japanese boys. They managed to fight for seats, albeit a bit lamely.

But the girls were at sea.

The first time I stopped the music, Gregory's 5-year-old girl-friend, Chitose-chan, was next to him, right in front of a chair. But she stood politely and waited for him to be seated first. So Gregory scrambled into her seat, and Chitose-chan beamed proudly at her own good man-ners. Then I walked over and told her that she had just lost the the game. She gazed up at me, her eyes full of shocked disbelief, looking like Bambi might after a discussion of venison burgers.

"You mean I lose because I'm polite?" Chitose-chan's eyes asked. "You mean the point of the game is to be rude?"

◆

—Nicholas D. Kristof, "Is Japan Too Civilized for the '90s?" *The New York Times* receding into the horizon (well...at least into Housewares), all awaiting our passage—I felt a stab of self-consciousness. I wasn't going to nod my way across the store; it seemed ridiculous.

So I decided to ignore them. Chin high and eyes straight ahead, I marched resolutely toward the faraway escalator. Very quickly, though, I began to feel unbearably regal, like the child-king in *The Last Emperor*. No, my "ignore the peasants" gambit was not working either.

I started to sweat. And to walk faster.

If I'd been the second or third to enter—anything but first—I could have stayed behind the front runners, looking to them as behavioral examples. What's more, since the crest of bowing seemed always to break over Esteemed Customer Number One, I'd have been relieved of much of the focus. But no; first I was, with all attention on me, and I couldn't bring myself to spin around and prod the guy behind me into the coronation position. Nor could I escape by veering into one of the departments: side aisles were blocked by my obsequious, bowing tormentors.

As icy panic built deep inside my roiling, jetlagged, digestive tract, a voice inside my head—one I'd heard from before in times of dire need—piped up with the following advice "Jim, just be YOURSELF." It was the kind of inane platitude that seldom helps but is manna for the desperate, so I grabbed the straw. I speak no Japanese, but figured that my cordial hand-waving, thumbs-up greetings of "Hey! How's it goin'! Howareyuh!" would meet with international recognition. But it wasn't getting over. Eye contact wasn't being returned, and I felt preposterous and gauche. What's more, legions of expectant employees still loomed in the distance, waving in my now-undulating visual field.

So I broke into a dead run for the escalator. Lungs heaving, heart palpitating, I reasoned that the Loss of Face was more than offset by my not having had to face the mortification of a blackout halfway through the brassiere department.

If I spoke Japanese, I'd have broken into the store's intercom booth and screamed "AS YOU WERE!" through the microphone, but this was not an option. Of course, I had forgotten all about my bowtie, hoping only to hightail it out of there and come back later, when the perfume sample girl had commenced her spritzing, the alterations guy his busy chalking up of trousers.

But the relief of my escalator sanctuary was short-lived. As my eye level escalated to the second story, I realized that I was entering virgin territory: untold clutches of clerks waiting shoulder-to-shoulder for the arrival of Esteemed Customers to their humble floor. And this time I was completely alone—bereft of the meager buttress provided by that rear brigade of fellow shoppers. *Gaijin* nightmare time.

I don't remember much—having blacked out the subsequent few minutes of vertiginous panic—but I did somehow manage to get out of the building. An hour later (after much tranquilizing noodle soup), I returned to find that I perhaps had made as much of an impression of the staff as they had on me. After accepting payment for my purchase, the saleswoman made a small bow of thanks, giggled, and watched slyly to see if I would attempt to bow back. Was she teasing me because of my earlier escapades? I'll never know. Some things are simply unfathomable.

Jim Leff is a New York–based jazz trombonist and food and travel writer. He is the author of The Eclectic Gourmet Guide to Greater New York City: The Undiscovered World of Hyperdelicious Offbeat Eating in All Five Boroughs *and is the Big Dog at www.chowhound.com, his website for those who live to eat. His tale of culinary frustration while on tour in Morocco appears in* Travelers Tales: Food.

✳

I caught myself bowing while talking on the phone the other day and realized just how much I've internalized the customs of this country I'm living in.

In Japan, bowing is the most basic form of social intercourse. Saying hello, saying goodbye, thanking, apologizing, are all accompanied by a bow. It is done dozens of times every day. The short-term visitor, surrounded by bows from store clerks and business associates, soon begins to bow back. For someone here a bit longer, bowing becomes second nature.

One day I was in the elevator with one of the higher-ups at my company whom I knew by sight but had never met. We made some small talk and introduced ourselves. Later the rumor floated down through the ranks that she had been impressed with how naturally I bowed when giving my name. For me, it had been completely unconscious.

It is a habit that wears well in Japan, where gentleness and respect in personal relations count for a lot. It's respect for their fellow man that marks Japanese behavior, and that respect is symbolized by the bow.

The Japanese start bowing early and do it often. Infants are always carried on mother's back and ride up and down along with mother's bows. The bow becomes so ingrained, so closely associated with the words that go with it, that it is common to see Japanese bow on the phone: office workers nodding their heads as they say goodbye, businessmen at public phones bowing from the waist to their unseen partner.

I had found this amusing. In fact, the Japanese find it amusing if it is pointed out. But I thought it something only a lifetime of practice would instill, nothing I would ever do. One Westerner described the moment he found himself bowing on the telephone as the moment he realized he had stayed too long. I've been here just a bit over a year; I caught myself bowing on the phone.

—Dennis Normile, "Taking a Bow"

CATHY N. DAVIDSON

* * *

Bilingual Laughter

*It's not just language
that needs translation.*

PERHAPS BECAUSE I WAS STRUGGLING SO HARD TO LEARN EVEN
the most rudimentary Japanese, I was eager to teach these students
English. My dislike of the traditional Japanese way of teaching
English also made me feel almost a missionary zeal upon entering
my Oral English course at KWU. I'd never taken any courses in
the field of TOESL, Teaching of English as a Second Language, but
I certainly knew from colleagues that the way English is taught in
the Japanese schools is exactly the wrong way to encourage people to really communicate in a new language.

I tried a different track, beginning with the conscious demotion
of *sensei*. Unlike many language teachers who refuse to speak anything but the language being taught, I delighted in speaking to the
students in my execrable Japanese. Partly this was selfish; I practiced
more Japanese in beginner's Oral English class than anywhere else.
But it was also pedagogical. I figured if they realized that *sensei*
wasn't ashamed to make mistakes, they certainly didn't have a right
to be—a way of using the Japanese proclivity for authoritarianism
and punctiliousness against itself. To show what I expected on the
first formal presentation, a requirement in all of the Oral English
sections, I initially prepared the same assignment—in Japanese. At

first I thought I'd intentionally throw in a few mistakes, but quickly realized my Japanese was quite bad enough on its own without my having to invent errors.

I came up with a whopper. It is the kind of mistake often made by native English-speakers, who have a hard time differentiating between repeated consonants. Mine, I found out later, was already a famous mistake; it happened when an American introduced the oldest and most revered woman in the Japanese parliament on national television. The American meant to say that this legislator was not only "very distinguished" but also "very feminine" (*onna-rashii*). She ended up saying the legislator was both distinguished and *onara shi* (which means, roughly, to cut a fart).

"That double *n* is hard for foreigners," I said when one of my students started to giggle. "We can't really hear the difference between *onna ra* and *onara*."

The students were now all laughing, but in polite Japanese-girl fashion, a hand covering the mouth.

"*Wait!*" I shouted in my sternest voice. "This is Oral English class!"

The laughter stopped. They looked ashamed.

"No, no. In this class, you must *laugh* in English. Think about it. You've all seen American movies. How do you laugh in English?"

I could see a gleam in Miss Shimura's eye, and I called on her: "Would an American woman ever put her hand over her mouth when she laughed, Miss Shimura?"

"No, *sensei*, I —mean, teacher."

"Show me. Laugh like an American movie star."

Miss Shimura kept her hands plastered at her side. She threw back her head. She opened her mouth as far as it would go. She made a deep, staccato sound at the back of her throat. *Hanh. Hanh. Hanh.*

We all laughed hysterically.

"Hands down!" I shouted again. "This is Oral English!"

They put their hands at their sides and imitated Miss Shimura's American head-back, open-mouth explosive laugh.

"What about the body?" I asked.

I parodied a Japanese laugh, pulling my arms in to my sides, bowing my head and shoulders forward, putting a hand coyly to my mouth.

Again they laughed. This time it was American-style.

"Oral English is about bodies too, not just words." I smiled. Miss Kato raised her hand.

"*Hai*?" (Yes?)

"Americans also laugh like this." She put her head back, opened her mouth, and rocked her upper body from side to side, her shoulders heaving and dodging, like Santa Claus.

There were gleeful shouts of "Yes! Yes!" and again a roomful of American-style laughter. It would start to die down, then someone would catch her friend doing the funny American laugh, and she'd break into hysterics again, the hand going to her mouth, me pointing, her correcting herself with the Santa Claus laughter. I continued to laugh Japanese-style, which made them laugh even louder, bouncier. We were off and running, laughing in each other's languages.

Cathy N. Davidson is currently Professor of English and Director of the John Hope Franklin Humanities Institute at Duke University. In 1980 she traveled to Japan to teach English and ended up writing a book about her experiences, 36 Views of Mt. Fuji: On Finding Myself in Japan. *She has written and edited over a dozen books since then and her work appears regularly in major U.S. magazines.*

✳

"Do anything you want," he once said with a grin, pantomiming the throwing of an enormous pot. Then he added seriously, "Anybody can get good on the wheel if they practice. Monday through Thursday, learn the Nagayoshi workshop forms, but Friday, make your *own* pots—cups, bowls, whatever." I was also not to address him by his official title of *sensei*, because in the workshop, he explained, he too was always learning. In an American art school these policies of independent study versus rote learning would be standard, but in Japan they turned the traditional concept of learning by repetition on its head. After the discipline of repeating the same forms all week, throwing without a model and a definite plan was unsettling. I was as lost as in the very first days of my apprenticeship, floundering to discover where to begin.

—Leila Philip, *The Road Through Miyama*

JONATHAN ALTER

* * *

The Indoor Slopes of Tokyo

The Japanese take mimicry to new heights.

IT WAS BROILING HOT ONE EVENING IN TOKYO, SO A FRIEND AND I decided to go skiing. Japan is like that—a bit upside down for the Westerner—and the indoor recreational experience at Ski Dome did not disappoint in the weirdness department. The skiing was decent, too.

That afternoon, T.R. Reid, a *Washington Post* reporter who wrote a book on Japanese skiing, had briefed us on the unusual genesis of Ski Dome. His account itself demanded that we check the place out. Apparently N.K.K. Steel, a huge Japanese manufacturer, was worried about a shipbuilding subsidiary that couldn't compete anymore. In typical Japanese fashion, the 800 employees had been guaranteed life employment, so the company tried to figure out how to apply their skills to something new. Because the workers were good at welding, the company first tried to go into the stretch-limo business. But it discovered that Toyota already made a good stretch limo.

Hmmm…The company had built some icebreakers, knew metal boxes, ice and snow. How about skiing? So they opened this place in 1993, the first of its type in the world. Ski Dome is the biggest, but Japan now boasts more than a half-dozen indoor ski areas (not to mention plenty of good regular skiing in the winter).

Our own run began shortly after 6 p.m. Wearing business suits, we joined the white-collar crowd commuting home to the suburbs on the JR Keiyo line. A mere half-hour from downtown Tokyo (a short commute by local standards) we emerged from the Minami-Funabashi station to see what looked like a 300-foot-high gray caterpillar against the night sky. Its spindly steel girders evoked George Lucas-like legs in some horror flick. The bug had lain down in the middle of Japanese mall-land, surrounded by charmless housing projects and a race track. Walking through tall, surprisingly untended grass, we found the place eerily deserted. Was it closed? We'd been told that on weekends the skiers were packed so closely together they could barely turn. We later learned that Ski Dome (full name: SSAWS Gelande) is most popular in winter, just as Wild Blue Yokohama, the indoor beach owned by the same company, gets most of its visitors during the summer.

Soon we entered a ticket-booth area and were greeted by the first of scores of earnest young Japanese ushers, all wearing bright yellow sweaters. *"Konnichiwa!"* ("Good evening"), they chirped. This night, we estimated, there were at least three times as many well-scrubbed employees on duty as skiers. We were the only foreigners on the premises, and the only skiers over age 25. All eyes were on us, and our eyes were on the strange interior. Imagine a Trumpish Tower transmogrified in the Japanese suburbs.

We were handed a computer card that would electronically tote up lift tickets, rentals, food and other expenses for payment on exit. For 2 hours of nighttime skiing, it was 4,300 yen, which is roughly $50, depending on the exchange rate, plus 400 yen for every additional 15 minutes. With another $20 each for ski clothes and rental equipment, the whole excursion would come to under $100 each. For an evening out in Tokyo, that's almost cheap.

We took an escalator past the boutiques selling $600 Bogner ski wear, a swimming pool, fashion videos. This could be just another high-end health club and shopping center but for these young people on the escalator carrying skis, and closed-circuit TV of what lay ahead. On the fourth floor we rented ski suits and warm gloves—extra large even though we're of ordinary size for Americans. We were outfitted with Nordica boots, Rossignol skis and generic Japanese poles. Weren't we missing something? Of course—no goggles, sunglasses, lip balm or sun block necessary.

The clientele tonight consists mostly of Japanese teenagers traveling in friendly, giggling packs. Two 20-something women walk toward the boot-rental desk in matching lime-green snow suits and high heels. We buy a cardboard camera to take pictures of our new friends in the men's locker room or no one will believe it; three ponytailed sumo wrestlers, dressed in their warm-up robes. Each had to bring his own king-size ski clothes, though some rental boots and skis were finally secured. Lots of smiles and bows and special hospitality for these minor-league celebrities in our midst.

Through more turnstiles, some glass doors and…hey, it's cold in here! A little colder and we'd need hats. But there's no wind-chill factor because there's no wind. The man-made snow is respectable packed powder, though it feels a little different, as if some chemicals have been added. When we start skiing it turns out to be slower than even man-made outdoor stuff, which is a good thing because one wrong traverse and the retaining wall beckons.

It is empty—no lines at the two bright yellow quadruple chair-lifts that bracket the two runs, each of which is about 1,600 feet long, or the escalator that serves the bunny slope. The shed-like structure is 328 feet wide at the bottom, but each run is only 115 feet wide at the top, a narrow trail even by Vermont standards. It feels a bit like skiing in the Javits Center, though the place is refreshingly undecorated; no cloud decals or faux alpine motifs.

The lift takes exactly two minutes, which is about how long it takes to get down if you don't pause to soak up the landscape. The view from what the brochure calls "the summit" consists mostly of steel rafters and lift operators sitting in high-tech booths that seem to belong in a nuclear power plant. We do glimpse the sumo wrestlers trying to ski, though the acoustics are so poor that we can't tell whether their exertions are accompanied by trademark grunts.

Soon we are racking up the runs. We made more than 15 the first hour before breaking for some Japanese fast food. This is Illinois or New Jersey skiing—262 feet vertical drop, which is enough for anywhere from 3 to 10 turns. The Red Course on the right has some steep moguls; the Yellow Course on the left doesn't, though the pitch is not so gentle. Several well-behaved young Japanese hotshots are practicing their expert bump skiing. Even they couldn't take the whole thing in a tuck. It is just too steep to handle without at least a few turns. And there's always that plate-glass window looming ahead.

Ski Dome closes at 10 p.m. and by then we have about had it anyway. The experience has been invigorating but not refreshing; after a while it is as if we had stuck our heads in a slightly stuffy freezer. Apres-ski has that grunge feel; too much recirculated air. But back in our street clothes and riding the perfectly safe subway downtown, we conclude that the experience certainly beat another evening of karaoke. When it comes to the art of imitation, better to try Steamboat Springs with a roof on it than Buffalo Springfield after too much sake.

Jonathan Alter's work has appeared in Newsweek *and* The New York Times.

✳

When I got home, I went up on the roof. I'd been meaning to do this since Okubo, the real-estate man, had shown us our apartment. As I stepped onto the gravelly surface, the skyline of Tokyo hit me on all sides—the shopping center of Ikenbukuro, with its thrust of skyscrapers, a little to the left; then to the right, Shinjuku, and beyond that Shibuya, the ring of centers along the Yamanote-sen line. All my travels through the city had been by train or subway. My sense of the city was from the ground, winding through small streets, looking for this shop or that class, or trying to choose a restaurant. I felt as if I'd just climbed up from a system of tunnels, was suddenly seeing sunlight and distance, with a new sense of space and vertical heights.

I could see dozens of apartment buildings within a block, and dozens of balconies with clotheslines. Tiny walkways ran between the buildings. No yards, though here and there a single pine or a large jade plant fronted a building. The balconies indicated that each apartment was about twelve feet wide, rabbit hutch after rabbit hutch. The scene had an Asian sense of space. Inside, the apartments were cluttered with goods, the people well fed, the refrigerators full.

Down below, I heard the *yaki-mo* man and his loud-speaker recorder blaring out his selling song. *Yaki-mo* were mountain potatoes roasted in charcoal (most apartment, like ours, did not have an oven). His song, a folk tune, seemed ear-splitting and obnoxious, rather than charming and quaint.

The skyline suddenly reminded me of the panoramas at the beginning of cop shows. Television gave no sense of Tokyo space. Either the small rooms looked large on the tiny sets, or the streets, seen one at a time, lacked the curves and dead ends, the layout which was designed in feudal times to ward off invaders and which gave the city its labyrinthian feel.

So, I thought, this is where I live. I've become one of them, an anthill dweller, a member of the hive.

—David Mura, *Turning Japanese: Memoirs of a Sansei*

SUSAN ORLEAN

* * *

Transcendence

Do we transcend before or after we purchase
the commemorative eel cakes?

THE SMALLEST MOUNT FUJI I SAW WHILE I WAS IN JAPAN WAS IN
the backyard of a Shinto shrine that sits next to a Tokyo fire station and across the street from a grocery store where you can buy
sake in a box and $18 cantaloupes. The shrine is called Ono-
Terusaki, and the little Mount Fuji in its backyard is called
Fujizuko, and they are located in Shitaya, an unfancy lowrise
neighborhood you would never visit unless you were looking for
miniature mountains. I went to see Fujizuko on a blazing hot July
Sunday when the sky was the color of cement and the air was so
thick it felt woolly. The real Mount Fuji is only 60 miles from
Tokyo, but the scrim of smog around the city cut off the view. No
one was on the streets of Shitaya that morning, and all the houses
were perfectly still except for a few damp kimonos flapping on
balcony clotheslines. I wandered around the neighborhood for half
an hour before I finally found the shrine, a homely 9th-century
building dedicated to a scholar of Chinese classics who died in
A.D. 852 and was said to have enjoyed landscapes. I walked around
to the back of the shrine, and there I came upon the mountain. It
was made of blackish lava chunks and was shaped like a piece of
pie propped up on its wide end, exactly like the real Mount Fuji,

only this Fuji was about 16 feet high, whereas the real one is 12,388. Someone who really liked Mount Fuji built the mountain in 1828. The mountain was flanked by a pair of stone monkey-faced dog-lions, and there was a sign that said, FUJIZUKO IS A MINIATURE MOUNTAIN THAT AN IMITATION MAN MADE IN THE IMAGE OF MOUNT FUJI. THIS PRECIOUS MOUND IS PRESERVED ON GOOD CONDITIONS.

I looked at the mountain for a while and rang a doorbell, and after a moment a student priest came out and gave me a look. He was dressed in a snow-white robe and slippers and had kissy lips and a grave handsome face. He didn't speak English and I don't speak Japanese, so we just smiled at each other until a middle-aged gentleman who was also visiting the shrine said he would attempt to translate for the priest. The gentleman said that the priest said that there was a time when Japan was not in order and people felt a pain about the abusement of the land, and there were problems, lots of problems, with the gods, or maybe it was problems with the crops, but anyway then a man went climbing Mount Fuji and by climbing he tried to make the world in order and he prayed many crops or gods would come in good condition and then the world of Japan became in order and through his feelings he built the mountain. As the gentleman was translating I felt a profound sense of mystery and confusion in my very own mind but I also sort of understood what he was trying to say. I then asked the gentleman to ask the priest if he had ever climbed the full-scale Mount Fuji. The priest giggled and shook his head, so I asked whether the priest planned to climb it anytime in the future. The two men chatted for a minute. At last the gentleman turned to me and shrugged his shoulders and said, "I believe he says, 'No way.'"

The reasons people don't climb Mount Fuji are various. Sometimes they just forget to do it. Sometimes the reasons people have for not climbing are more existential than forgetful. When I first got to Tokyo I went to visit Kunio Kaneko, an artist who makes woodblock prints of Mount Fuji. At his studio, every wall was hung with his pictures of the mountain—in indigo blue, in orangy-red, covered with gold leaf, outlined with silver ink. There were drawers full of Fuji prints and racks of note cards of Fujis and one wall with pictures of kimonos and *happi* coats and those traditional Japanese wooden platform sandals that make you walk like you're drunk. Kaneko is in his late forties and has longish hair and broad shoulders, and he was wearing beat-up khakis and green Converse sneakers. He spread his pictures out for me to see and told me that he divided his life into two: the years before 1964, when the air was still see-through and Fuji was always visible from his backyard in Tokyo, and the post-1964 years, when pollution got so bad that he almost never saw Fuji except on rare stainless winter days. Kaneko said that he thought about the mountain all the time. Since he seemed slightly outdoorsy and had devoted so much of his work to the mountain, I assumed that he had climbed it, maybe even several times. When I asked him about, it he looked bashful and replied, "No, I have never climbed it." He shuffled together some of his prints and slid them into a drawer. "I always stay at a distance at the bottom so I have a perfect view," he said. "I don't climb it because if I were on the mountain I couldn't see it."

There are lots of reasons the Japanese do climb Mount Fuji. They climb it because it's tall and pretty and has a grand view, because some of them think God lives inside it, because their grandparents climbed it, or because climbing Mount Fuji has been the customary Japanese thing to do for as long as anyone can remember. In a way, the enduring attraction of a Mount Fuji pilgrimage is a remarkable thing. The Japanese have always revered their landscape and scenery, but they seem perfectly at peace with fake nature, too—only in Japan can you surf at an indoor beach and ski on an indoor slope and stroll through exhaustively manipulated and modulated gardens of groomed pebbles and dwarfed trees and precisely arranged leaves. Sometimes it seems that the man-made Japan has eclipsed the country's original physical being. Still, the symbolism and reality of Mount Fuji remain. The mountain may have pay phones on the summit and its own brand of beer, but otherwise it persists as a wild and messy and uncontrollable place—big, old-fashioned, and extreme. That is, nothing like what I expected Japan to be. I wanted to go to Mount Fuji because I imagined it would be a trip to the un-Japan, a country I wasn't sure even existed anymore except in nostalgic dreams.

It was a terrible year to climb Fuji, really. The official climbing season opens July 1 with a ceremony at the base of the mountain in the Segen Jinja shrine, and usually thousands of climbers would attend the ceremony and ascend the mountain that day. Some would be dressed in traditional pilgrim costumes: white kimonos and pants, straw *waraji* sandals, a mushroom-shaped hat, a walking stick. Most of the rest would be in Gore-Tex and t-shirts saying MOUNT FUJI: THE MOST HIGHEST MOUNTAIN IN JAPAN and WELCOME TO MELLOW VILLAGE and JOYFUL MY SCENE MORNING BUNNY MOUNT FUJI. In Tokyo that same day, less ambitious climbers hold another ceremony at the Ono-Terusaki Shrine and scramble up all 16 feet of the miniature Fuji; similar observances would take place at each of the 40 or so other miniature Mount Fujis in greater Tokyo. But this was the summer of ghastly weather in Japan. In the weeks before opening day two typhoons passed through; the first one hit Tokyo and raked across Fuji, covering the climbing routes with snow and filling the access roads with mud and rocks, while the tail end of the second typhoon added to the mess on the mountain. The opening ceremony was held but was sparsely attended, and access to Fuji itself was postponed until July 10, then postponed again for another 24 hours. The day I arrived in Japan the tanker *Diamond Grace* had run aground and was bleeding crude oil into Tokyo Bay. In the south yet another storm struck, and on the island of Kyushu mud slides killed almost two dozen people. In Tokyo a heat wave jacked the temperature above 100 degrees, and everyone walked around looking broiled and stoic, dabbing their foreheads with washcloths and flapping lacquer fans. I was so hot that I had to hide from the sun every afternoon in my hotel room. I started wondering why exactly I wanted to climb Mount Fuji, but I did, and even after an earthquake bounced me around my hotel room I was still good to go.

Mount Fuji is the highest mountain in Japan. Its peak is nearly two and a half miles above sea level, and its base has a circumference of 78 miles and spans both Yamanashi Prefecture and

Shizuoka Prefecture. The mountain is a 10,000-year-old volcanic cone that last erupted in 1707. Scientists believe it is dormant rather than extinct. A nearby mountain named Yatsugatake used to be higher than Fuji, but then the jealous and bellicose Fuji goddess Konohanasakuya-hime decided to knock over Yatsugatake so Fuji could be supreme. The first documented ascent of the mountain was made by a Shintoist pilgrim named En no Ozunu in the 8th century; the first Westerner to climb was Sir Rutherford Alcock, the British consul, who ascended in 1860 with his Scottie dog Toby. The world's oldest mountain-climbing picture, painted in the 15th century, depicts monks climbing Mount Fuji. Only religious pilgrims were allowed to climb until the 19th century; women were not allowed at all until 1871.

Fuji's six climbing routes are divided into stations; the route I planned to take has ten. The Fuji Subaru highway to the Fifth Station was opened in 1965, and with it came millions of visitors by

---

*I*t is said that the ancestral god, Mioya-no-kami, was making calls on a number of gods all over the country and happened to arrive at a place near Mt. Fuji at dark, so he asked the god of Mt. Fuji to accommodate him for the night. Just at that time the god of Mt. Fuji was so busy in the preparations of the local Good Crop celebration he could not manage to put the ancestral god up for the night. The latter became so annoyed that he denounced the god of Mt. Fuji for being so lacking in filial piety and declared that cold snow would cover its top throughout the ages, so that few people would climb up to offer food. That is why Mt. Fuji has always had snow on its top from that time on. The Mioya-no-kami then went to stay with the god of Mt. Tsukuba for the night and there he was treated most kindly and lavishly, and for that reason Mt. Tsukuba has many people climbing the whole year round.

◆

—Chiang Yee, *The Silent Traveller in Japan*

tour bus and subsequently tons of trash and erosion problems that continue to threaten the mountain. Mount Fuji is so pretty and so weirdly symmetrical that people have always believed it was supernatural and sanctified. The most fervent Fuji worshipers are the members of the Shintoist sect Fuji-ko, whose founder, the 16th-century monk Fujiwara no Kakugyo, supposedly climbed Fuji 128 times and lived to be 106 years old. Fuji-ko pilgrims stay in special shrine lodges at the base of the mountain, wash themselves in the purifying water of the five lakes nearby, get blessed by a priest, and then time their ascent so that they arrive at the summit at sunrise. During the 17th and 18th centuries as many as 10,000 Fuji-ko would climb each year, but these days they are far outnumbered by ordinary Japanese and tourists.

Before I left for Japan I obtained an introduction to a man in Tokyo named Fumiaki Watanabe, who was going to have me over for dinner as part of an official international friendliness program. All I knew about him was that he was recently retired from his position as an internal auditor at an Exxon subsidiary. The minute he heard from our intermediary that I was planning to climb Fuji he proposed skipping the dinner and instead going with me on the climb. This to me was a huge surprise. I kept being told that every year half a million people drive to the Fifth Station of Fuji and 20,000 climb to the summit, but so far I hadn't managed to find a single person who had done either. I was starting to wonder how much of the Japanese devotion to climbing Mount Fuji is abstract and conceptual and how much of it involves the material experience of putting on shoes and walking. It turned out that Mr. Watanabe was a materially experienced climber. He had climbed Fuji more than ten times, had skied into its crater and down its side, and was 70 percent of the way to his goal of climbing the hundred highest peaks in Japan.

It was decided that Mr. Watanabe and I would climb together but that our dinner would go ahead as planned, and one evening I rode the subway to the southern edge of Tokyo, where he and his wife and son live. He met me at the station and almost without a word gestured toward the exit. He walked quickly, pushing his bicycle, which like every Japanese bicycle I saw was low-built and sturdy, like a Fifties Schwinn, and had a plastic bag wrapped around its seat. Mr. Watanabe was low-built and sturdy himself, with a baldish head and bright eyes and a small, solid body. In the very best possible way he looked a little like Jiminy Cricket. That night we spoke about the beautiful dinner Mrs. Watanabe had made for us, about the differences between Americans and Japanese, about how tradition in both countries is melting away. Mrs. Watanabe was wearing Western-style casual clothes, but she decided to show me the formal kimono that she said she hardly ever wears any-more. Once she brought it out she decided to dress me in it. The kimono was cool and silky and as heavy as water. It required special underwear with multiple belts and bows, and had a wide sash tied over a pillow that sits in the small of your back. It took about 15 minutes to get the whole thing on. Then, as I sat there trussed up like a fancy turkey, Mr. Watanabe began laying out his plans for our climb.

We left two days later on a bus that threaded through the steep hills and rice fields between Tokyo and Fujiyoshida, the town at the base of the mountain where we were going to spend our first night. The bus was full of vacationers carrying take-out *bento*-box lunches and overnight bags. Mr. Watanabe brought a big rucksack and was dressed in a long-sleeved shirt, a gray pinstriped vest, wool knickers, and hiking boots with bright red laces. The boots looked well-worn. He said that he managed to go climbing about ten times a year. I wondered whether he was going more often now that he had retired. "Yes, I have had the opportunity," he said. He shifted in his seat. Everything he said sounded measured and ele-gant. "My plan is to now climb the highest peak on each conti-nent. I would begin with Kilimanjaro, then Aconcagua, and then, of course, McKinley."

Entering Fujiyoshida, you pass a McDonald's and a *pachinko* gambling parlor and then a Mount Fuji made of flowers—a mound of red salvia and impatiens in pink and white. Just beyond it was the famous Fuji Sengen Jinja shrine. The long pathway to the shrine was dim and unearthly and lined with stone lanterns and tall red trees. Mr. Watanabe said the trees were called *fujitaro-sugi*, which translates as "boy cedar tree to Fuji." There are thousands of cedars encircling the mountain, forming what people call the Sea of Trees or the Forest of No Return. This forest is one of the most popular places in Japan to commit suicide—every year several dozen bodies are recovered in it—and it is one of the most popular places to headquarter a religion. There are almost 2,000 officially registered religious organizations located around the base of the mountain, including a number of Nichiren Buddhist sects, the faith-healing Ho no Hana Sanpogyo group, and the ancestor-revering Fumyokai Kyodan religion. Until it was evicted recently, the subway-gassing Aum Shinri Kyo cult had its headquarters here, too.

We stopped at the Fuji Sengen Jinja shrine and walked under the boy cedar trees to the main structure, an ornate building made of reddish wood that had been slicked to a dull shine by the drizzle. The place was deserted except for a little boy who was studying his reflection in a puddle and a priest who was padding around in his white *tabi* socks, closing up for the day. The priest was in a hurry to leave but he agreed to give us a condensed version of the traditional Shinto preclimb blessing. He motioned for us to stand in front of the shrine. As he chanted and banged on a small brass drum, the rain began to patter and a gust flicked the water in the trees onto the ground.

We finally arrived at our hotel, a Western-style high-rise building that had its own amusement park, called Fujikyu Highland, whose attractions included a Ferris wheel and the highest roller coaster in Japan. On the hotel grounds there is a perfect 1:200 scale model of Mount Fuji and the five lakes to the north; guests can climb the small mountain and also visit the Mount Fuji museum located inside the artificial peak. The enormous picture windows in the hotel lobby would have offered a staggering view of the real Fuji if the weather had been clear, but it wasn't, so that night after dinner we sat in the lobby and gazed in the direction of the rain-shrouded Fuji, over the top of the scale-model Fuji, to an outline of Fuji made of neon glowing in the spokes of the Ferris wheel.

You can walk up Mount Fuji, or you can run up (the Mount Fuji Climbing Race has been held every year since 1948), or you can roll up in a wheelchair (first done in 1978), or you can wait to go up until you're really old (as old as Ichijiro "Super Grandpa" Araya, who climbed it when he was 100, or Hulda "Grandma Whitney" Crooks, who did it at 91). Or you can ride a horse to the Seventh Station, the rental horse drop-off point, and then walk the rest of the way. The next morning, as Mr. Watanabe and I were sitting in a cold mist at the Fifth Station getting ready for the climb, a horse rental guy walked over and introduced me to his pony, Nice Child. The guy was wearing a Budweiser hat and rubber boots that had articulated toes. Nice Child looked like a four-legged easy chair, and I was really tempted to take the man up on his suggestion that I ride rather than walk. It was a lousy day to climb a mountain. Many of the pilgrims at the trailhead were wearing garbage bags, and the only scenery we could see was the Fifth Station gift shop and a cigarette vending machine that had the phrase TODAY I SMOKE printed on it at least a hundred times. "I believe only crazies will be climbing today," Mr. Watanabe said, looking at a group of climbers who were eating rice balls and hot dogs and shouting at one another.

After Mr. Watanabe talked me out of renting Nice Child, I put on my pack and tightened my laces and went into the gift shop and bought a traditional pilgrim's walking stick—plain and squared-off, with jingle bells hanging from the top to ward off evil spirits and plenty of room for *yakiin*, the brands you can get burned into your stick at each station along the way to the top. I also wanted to buy the Fuji-shaped cookies or cheesecakes or bean-paste patties or jellies, or the Milk Pie biscuits in a box that said, FUJISAN: NATURE IS A GREAT EXISTENCE. IF YOU BECOME ANGRY OR NERVOUS HOLD COMMUNION WITH NATURE. The trouble was

> ──── ☽ ────
>
> *T*o climb Fuji once is wise, to climb it twice is to proclaim oneself a fool.
>
> ◆
>
> —Japanese saying

I'd already picked up some eel jerky and some octopus jerky at a 7-Eleven near the hotel.

We planned to climb to the Eighth Station by sunset, spend the evening in a mountain hut, and wake up at 2 a.m. to finish the climb so we would reach the summit by sunrise. We had reserved space at a hut called Fujisan Hotel. From the sound of the name I thought maybe it was a luxury hut, but Mr. Watanabe rolled his eyes and assured me that all the accommodations on the mountain were more hut than hotel. "Do you know how silkworms live?" he asked. "They live on wooden shelves. That is what the huts are like—silkworm shelves."

I was taken aback. "You mean the huts are infested?"

"No," Mr. Watanabe replied, "the huts have shelves, and we are the worms."

I walked a few feet behind him, stepping on and around nubbly black lava rocks and loose pebbles of red pumice. The terrain was sheer and treeless. On a sunny day it would have been beastly. Rock larks flitted around, and green weeds grew under some of the overhangs, but otherwise the mountainside was blank. After about an hour I started wondering where one would relieve oneself in such a lunar landscape. "We will be at the Sixth Station in just a few more minutes," Mr. Watanabe said. He hesitated for a moment, pressed his finger to his lips and then said, "There you will find a cozy adjacent hut." In a few minutes we did in fact reach the station, a big wooden lean-to hut with a cozy adjacent unisex hut beside it, both clinging to the mountainside like barnacles. Inside the big hut you could get your walking stick branded and buy crackers and souvenirs and any one of a dozen brands of beer, as well as a $12 canister of Mount Fuji Congratulations Do It Now Oxygen. About 40 climbers were milling around, dripping and sweating and gobbling snacks. One delicate-looking older woman dressed in what looked like pajamas was taking gulps from a canister of oxygen, and the man with her alternated gulps of oxygen with swigs of beer. Four U.S. Navy enlisted men came into the hut. They seemed quite excited. "Hey!" one of them hollered. "Anyone got any sake?" I went outside on the deck, where a bunch of Chinese students were eating dried fish and cookies and taking snapshots of one another. Two of them were speaking to each other on their cellular phones and were shrieking ecstatically. One of the Chinese girls came over to me and gasped, "We are wanting to speak *Japanese!* We are wanting to speak *English!* But our heads are filled with *Japanese!*"

Mr. Watanabe wanted to push ahead, so we soon left and plodded up the jagged trail for another hour. By then the clouds had broken up, and below them we could see a big green patch that Mr. Watanabe said was a Japanese Self-Defense Forces training ground and some of the 117 golf courses that lie at the base of the mountain. I wanted to look at the view for a while, but the trail was getting clogged with other climbers, so we turned and continued. We beat the Chinese students to the Seventh Station and went in to get my walking stock branded. The stationmaster was a young man with bristly black hair and bright-red cheeks. He motioned me over to a fire that was burning in the center of the hut and then pulled out a branding iron that had been heating in it. After I paid $2, he branded my stick with his symbol—some Japanese characters and a drawing of Fuji. Then he told me he'd been working at the hut for 20 years and that he was the sixth generation of his family to run it. In the winter he works at a gas station. During the two-month-long climbing season he leaves his wife and children in the flatlands and comes to the Seventh Station with his mother, and they don't go back down until after the Yoshida Fire Festival, which marks the season's close. On a busy day he brands the sticks of 600 climbers. On a slow day, he said, he gets lonely.

Mr. Watanabe and I reached the Eighth Station two hours later. That is, we got to the first of the seven Eighth Stations. The seven Eighth Stations are strung out along about an hour's worth of trail. All of the stations on Fuji are family businesses that have had the same owners for a hundred years or more, and they enjoy the spirited competition of the free-market system. The first Eighth Station calls itself The Authentic Eighth Station; the second one calls itself Originator of the Eighth Station; the third is The Real

Eighth Station. As it happened, our Eighth Station, the nonluxurious Fuji-san Hotel, was the seventh of the Eighth Stations. By the time we wended our way past the preceding six stations it was dusky, and I was eager for dinner and the use of a cozy adjacent hut. The Fuji-san stationmaster was a jolly guy with a mustache and tobacco-stained fingers. When we arrived he and a few friends were sitting inside the hut watching the Yankees game in which Japanese pitcher Hideki Irabu made his debut. The television and a fire were the hut's sole amenities. Otherwise it was outfitted with a couple of wooden benches in the main room and, in another, two levels of wooden platforms that formed a communal bunk bed—the silkworm shelves. Mr. Watanabe grinned when he saw me surveying the quarters.

"On the mountain for women it is very...*harsh*," he said. "I believe the goddess of Fuji was said to be very jealous and did not favor women climbers."

Because of the lousy weather, the mountain was unusually quiet that night. Typically there would have been about a hundred people at the hotel, but instead there were only two young Sony employees from Nagasaki and three of the stationmaster's friends. The Sony men went to sleep almost immediately. The rest of us ate a dinner of rice and then tried to warm up by the fire next to the television set. I stepped outside to see what I could see from 11,000 feet up. It was a cold, black night, and the cloud cover was still cracked open; below I could see the little lights of Fujiyoshida and the carnival neon of the Fujikyu Highland Ferris wheel.

After I went back inside, Mr. Watanabe offered everyone refreshments: banana chips and cocktails of Johnnie Walker Black and Takara Multi-Vitamin Water. "Very healthy," he said to me, holding up a can of Takara Water and a plastic cup. "It has many important minerals. Please, allow me to give you some." The stationmaster's friends introduced themselves as Boss-o Guide-o, Guide-o Carpenter-o, and Mr. Shinto Priest. Boss-o explained that he was in charge of all the guides working on Mount Fuji. After his second scotch and Multi-Vitamin Water he offered to make me an assistant guide next summer. Guide-o Carpenter-o was an

assistant mountain guide in the summer and a carpenter in
Fujiyoshida during the winter. He was the brother of Mr. Shinto
Priest, who was a Shinto priest and also a part-time carpenter. Mr.
Priest was a wild-eyed semibald-headed man who chain-smoked
Virginia Slims Menthols and was wearing a padded coat, a terry
cloth towel around his neck, a wool beanie, and knee-high rubber
boots, which had the combined effect of making him look like a
cross-dressing Tibetan heavyweight boxer. He kept lighting his
cigarettes with one of the station branding irons and then whipping off the beanie and rubbing his remaining hair while growling
something crusty-sounding in Japanese. "That's a joke!" Guide-o
Carpenter-o yelled to me, pointing at Mr. Priest. "That's a Japanese
joke!" Even Mr. Watanabe, who may be the most gracious and
proper human on earth, was roaring at the priest. "To tell you the
truth, I believe he's quite crazy," he whispered to me. By then we
had all had lots and lots of multivitamins. Mr. Priest was getting
sort of sentimental, and when he was done with his hair routine
he wanted me to sit on his lap or next to him and look at snap-
shots. I had my doubts, but they turned out to be pictures he'd
taken of the shadow thrown by Mount Fuji at sunrise—a perfect
sheer-gray triangle cast across an ocean of clouds, as amazing a
sight as I've ever seen.

At that point there was no real point in going to sleep, since we
were going to wake up in an hour to finish the climb. I lay down
on my shelf and listened to the Sony men snoring and the rain as
it started to dribble, then pour, then slam down on the tin roof of
the Fuji-san hotel. At about two in the morning, I heard the
rustling of ponchos. Some two dozen climbers had arrived at the
hotel, rain running off them in rivers, and outside on the trail I
could see a dotted line of lights zigzagging up the mountainside.
Most of the climbers wore their lights on their heads, so for a moment the scene looked like a subterranean mining expedition
rather than the final stretch of a mountain climb. We dressed in a
rush, and then Mr. Watanabe warned me about the end of the
climb. "What we have left is the heart-attacking final 800 meters,"
he said, looking at me solemnly. "You must inform me before you

become completely ex-
hausted." Climbers were ma-
terializing all around us in
the dark mist, each with a
Cyclops head lamp shining in
the middle of his forehead.
We took our places on the
trail and began trudging up
the final steep stretch.

The line of climbers' lights
now reached up to the summit and down to the seventh
Eighth Station, where it vanished into the fog. The rain
was falling in gobs, coming
down harder and harder, and
the fog was building up into
a solid white wall; I would
never have known we'd
reached the summit except
that Mr. Watanabe said we'd
reached the summit and
should stop under a shelter
and have something to eat.
The crater was there but I
couldn't see it, and the whole
of Japan was spread out underneath us but you'd never
know it, and there were
scores of people all around us
but I couldn't make them out
even though they were probably just a few feet away. I
didn't really care. I was completely thrilled just to be on
the summit. I was the highest

———) ———

ometimes I would stop
to rest at a small shop or
to ask how many kilometers it
was to the next village. And
sometimes, especially when the
shopkeeper was getting on in
years, she would tell me she had
no idea how many kilometers it
was, but that it was perhaps a *ri*
or a *ri* an half. The *ri*, the old
Japanese measure of distance, has
disappeared entirely from road
signs and maps, and within ten
years it will have vanished from
the language. One *ri*, say the
conversion tables, equals 3.927
kilometers, but that is nearly
irrelevant. One *ri*—as I came to
know in practice—was the distance that a man with a burden
would aim to cover in an hour
on mountain roads. The kilometer was invented for the convenience of machinery. The *ri* was
an entirely human measure,
which is why it had no chance
of surviving. We tell the time in
digits and bleeps, and distance is
not distance if you can't divide
it by ten.

◆

—Alan Booth,
*The Roads to Sata: A 2000-Mile
Walk Through Japan*

thing in Japan! I wanted to run around the crater, but the wind had picked up to about 60 miles an hour, which would have meant running sideways if at all.

It is traditional for climbers to mail a letter at the Mount Fuji post office on the summit and to hike around the crater to each of the two shrines on the rim before descending. Mr. Watanabe suggested we should skip the post office and the shrines and simply head down right away. I wanted to stay. We held a vote and it was a tie, but then the wind punched me so hard that I changed my mind. I got the official summit brand burned into my walking stick and then started down into the fog, sliding hell-first into the loose pumice, the sheets of rain in my face.

For a while, everyone who saw Mount Fuji wanted to write a poem about it or tell a story about it or make pictures of it. It was described by a writer in the 8th century as "a lovely form capped with the purest white snow...reminding one of a well-dressed woman in a luxuriously dyed garment with her pure white undergarment showing around the edge of her collar"—in other words, like a lady with her bra straps showing. Unquestionably the consummate Fuji artist was the 19th century printmaker Katsushika Hokusai, who made pictures of the peak for 70 years. Hokusai often called himself a crazed art addict and sometimes used the name Hokusai the Madman. *Thirty-Six Views of Mount Fuji*, a collection of his prints, was published around 1823 and was a huge hit in Japan. Hokusai depicted Fuji covered with snow, half-covered with snow, bare, hidden by mist, capped by an umbrella cloud, in nice weather, with pilgrims climbing, with storks bathing in front of it, as seen from the bow of a boat, and viewed from a bridge in Tokyo. In some of the pictures the mountain fills up most of the space, whereas in others it is just a pucker on the horizon while the foreground is dominated by *geisha* girls loafing around or a guy building a barrel or someone trying to talk his horse into walking over a bridge. A few years later, when Hokusai was 74 and worried about his career, he recharged it by publishing a new collection, *One Hundred Views of Mount Fuji*. It was another huge hit. Hokusai was an inconstant man who moved 93 times, but for the 70 years he made pictures of Fuji, his image of the mountain never changed; it was always steep-sided, narrow-peaked, wide-bottomed, solitary, and simply the loveliest mountain you could ever hope to see.

When we got to the bottom of the mountain, Mr. Watanabe apologized for the weather and said he very much wanted me to come back so I could see Mount Fuji on a good day—that is, so I could see Mount Fuji at all. I told him that I wasn't the least bit disappointed and that anyway this seemed like the Japanese way of seeing the mountain, less with my eyes than with my mind's eye. I was a material climber but I had been won over to the conceptual side.

If we wanted a view, I told him, we could always go back to the Ferris wheel at Fujikyu Highland. "I suppose," Mr. Watanabe said. "However, I do not believe we will have the time or opportunity to ride such a vehicle." He was right, so we just blotted our soaked clothes and kicked the pebbles out of our boots and caught the next bus back to Tokyo, and before I left Japan I bought myself a copy of Hokusai's *Thirty-Six Views of Mount Fuji*.

Susan Orlean is a staff writer for The New Yorker *and the author of* The Orchid Thief, The Bullfighter Checks Her Makeup, *and* My Kind of Place: Travel Stories from a Woman Who's Been Everywhere.

✳

"Every morning make up your mind how to die."

So advises an eighteenth-century handbook for *samurai*. I couldn't agree more.

"Every evening freshen your mind in the thought of death," it continues. "And do this without ceasing. Thus your mind will be prepared. When your mind is set always on death, your way through life will always be straight and simple..."

This is the precise course I have set to reach Mt. Takachiho in Kirishima National Park, an hour north of Mt. Sakurajima by train. I go alone in the morning, food packed, timetable and map in hand. I go as if this is my final journey in Japan. And no place could be more final. This is the beginning of Japan, at least in myth.

Takachiho-no-Mine is the volcanic peak where Niniji-no-Mikoto, grandson of the Sun Goddess, Amaterasu Omikami, first touched earth on a mission to rule the world. He descended to the peak bearing three symbols of the Sun Goddess: sword, mirror, and jewel. The sword of heaven he cast down to earth like a blot of lightning, implanting it deep in the crater rim. His feet on the ground, Niniji immediately went shopping for a wife and found one, Konohanasakuya-hime, whose name means tree-flower princess. At the same time, he was offered her ugly sister as a consort, but Niniji rejected her. Shamed, the father set a curse upon the offspring of Niniji, that their lives would be as brief as flowers upon a tree. Thus was the race of mortals born on the slopes of Mt. Takachiho.

—J.D. Brown, *The Sudden Disappearance of Japan: Journeys Through a Hidden Land*

JAMES D. HOUSTON

Sandbath Resurrection

*Two dislocated souls search for home and
find it in the black sands of Kyushu.*

KAGOSHIMA IS THE SOUTHERNMOST CITY IN JAPAN, AND WE HAD
not planned to go beyond it. But somewhere in our travels another
American had told us we should look at Ibusuki, down at the
lower end of the last peninsula on the island of Kyushu. The town
was small, this woman said, and cheap, and close to the water, and
warm most of the year, which is something to think about as fall
turns to winter. It was the kind of thing that happens when you
are on your way from Point A to Point B and you meet someone
on a subway platform who has just come back from Point X, a
place you've never heard of or thought of visiting, but a few days
later there you are, wandering into an unknown town for reasons
that are still not entirely clear.

House hunting, we told ourselves, as we walked out of the
depot, hailed a cab, and taxied over to a low-budget inn we'd
found in the pamphlet that comes with the Rail Pass. House hunting, we said again the next morning—though each day now it was
harder to fight down the growing sense of dislocation. By that time
we had moved in and out of too many inns and hotels and cabs
and train stations. The bags were getting heavier, and after two
weeks on this gypsy path, the quest, the adventure, the challenge

141

of Japan was wearing thin. This country was too strange, and perhaps more trouble than it was worth.

As I woke the next morning I was having the second thoughts,
or third thoughts, that can grip you in the early days of a long trip,
when you begin to fear the whole expedition may be a terrible
mistake. Remembering all the loose ends and unfinished business
I'd left behind, I woke in the predawn of Ibusuki thinking, "What's
going on? A week ago we had never *heard* of this place. And what
am I really *doing* over here seven time zones away from my phone
and my desk and my work and my stuff, all my carefully assembled
time and stuff?"

Well, as they often say, when you are ready for the answer, the
question will appear. And the answer was about to present itself,
there in the strangest of all the strange places we had seen.

In this land of the unexpected, Ibusuki is the farthest from
what we had expected to find. It does not resemble any of the
Japans you see promoted or publicized. There are no world-class
shrines or gardens. You don't find Kabuki there or sumo wrestling
or cherry trees in bloom. There is no fast-track urban life, no sidewalk multitude streaming toward the underground trains. It was
October. The streets were almost empty—a few honeymooning
couples, a few elderly retirees, a few off-season site-seers from
China and Korea. In the yards around the houses we saw a lot of
cactus, and bushes of red hibiscus. Palm trees lined the boulevards,
royal palms, date palms, palms with the spiky leaves Hawaiians use
to make *lauhala* matting. The latitude is more southerly than San
Diego, in line with northern Baja. Later a fellow from Tokyo who
has been to the U.S. would tell us, with a condescending city
smile, "That part of Kyushu is what you might call the Alabama
of Japan."

At the southern end of the island, two long peninsulas, like two
facing crab claws, form Kagoshima Bay. Ibusuki lies inside this bay,
on the protected inner edge of the peninsula called Satsuma, with
a view across still waters toward the worn-down cliffs of former
craters, now green and razor edged, much like the cliffs that line
the north shore of the island of Kaua'i. Maybe this in itself has

prepared me to surrender, something about the Polynesian look of the volcanic landscape that shaped the glassy bay, the steeply eroded peaks, the palms, the blue water lapping porous lava rocks.

After a morning of halfhearted apartment pricing, we do what Japanese heat seekers travel hundreds of miles to do and stroll over to the bath house, where steam from subterranean springs comes percolating right up through the sand. For three hundred yen you get a locker and a clean *yukata*, a long robe, blue on white. You can't wear anything underneath, says the woman who takes the money. "All off. No underpants. Nothing."

Inside the locker room you strip and don the robe and feel the crisp, freshly ironed cotton on your skin. (Half an hour later it will be dark with sweat and with the fine black sand you carry back to the bath house where you'll drop it in a soggy heap with all the other spent *yukata*, then shower off the sand and soap down and shower again and slide into *furo*—the tile lined tub filled with mineral water piped from the springs—for the finishing work, the final polish.)

Outside the bath house door rubber thongs, *zori*, are piled in a heap, several dozen, of varying sizes. We each grab a couple of these and clop along the concrete walkway, looking out across the dark sand turned black by wetness. Steam curls from the low-tide flats, much as it rises from the vents and fissures in the floor of Kilauea Caldera on the Big Island of Hawai'i. An important difference is that here the bonneted women await you, shovels in hand, standing by their rows of shallow graves.

We stretch out in the sand, attended by these shovel-bearing women, and one leans in so close to me, her eyes gazing into mine with an intimacy so tender, so disarming, I have to relax. I have to surrender. She wraps the white towel around my head and gently pulls it snug beneath my chin. She does not speak. She steps back and throws the first shovelful across my shoulder, black and hot and wet enough that it does not spread. Each grain seems to lie where it lands, making weight against the skin. The next shovelful lands on my belly, the next on my hips. Soon she has me buried to my neck, the dark sand pressing along my body, and steam rising through the sand beneath me, from the hot springs. Only my head shows, one head in a row of towel-wrapped heads lined along the black sand beach.

She looks to be about sixty. She wears the clothes of a country woman dressed for field work, baggy blue trousers, white apron, blue bonnet. She laughed when she saw me coming, laughed at my height. She spoke to the other women, all dressed alike, all carrying long-handled shovels, and they all laughed as she trenched an extra foot of sand so I could stretch at full length and join the others staring at the sky.

Now she leans on her shovel, and I am breathing slowly under the weight of all the sand, while the heat cooks my neck, my legs, my back. The women move away to meet some new arrivals who have walked down from the bath house. I close my eyes. For the first time in two weeks I feel at ease, at rest. Why? Is it just the sand and the beach air and the heat of this outdoor Asian sauna? Something I'd been barely aware of is being steamed away, some deep anxiety is dissolving, floating upward with the whispers of the moisture and the heat. For the first time since we landed in Japan, I feel connected. But how? And why here?

I doze.

The lap-lap of tiny waves revives me. My nose revives me. Both together. Splashing surf and itching nose. I cannot scratch. My arms and hands are buried. My eyes begin to itch. My chin. My neck. Suddenly each second is a little test of the will. I can force my arms upward through the sand to scratch away at my face and eyes, but that would break the crust, break open the cocoon of heat, break the spell.

> *W*hen Margaret finally throws off the hot blanket of sands, she spreads her arms as wide as the wings of a crane. "Not one more minute," she declares. "I feel like one of Edgar Allan Poe's catatonic damsels in a heated crypt."
>
> ◆
>
> —J.D. Brown, *The Sudden Disappearance of Japan: Journeys Through a Hidden Land*

I concentrate on voices. Whose are they? From Jeanne, from other towel-surrounded heads along the beach I hear nothing but the occasional intake—Ssssssss—a stoic hissing through the teeth, a long exhale. The voices come from the women with the shovels. Softly they chatter, in words I can't comprehend, as they move the sand around, smoothing, preparing it. I listen while the minutes pass. I can't say how many minutes. Two. Or ten. I listen until my itching subsides, and the nearby scratch of a shovel digging—chk...chk...chk...—is a gentle drumbeat calling me back to life.

It is the same woman, in her blue cotton trousers, white apron to her knees. She is working right next to me, clearing another space. She glances my way. Again our eyes meet, just a glimpse, an instant, and here at last I find the touchpoint—after two weeks of dislocated gypsy roaming—a first point of entry into this unknown and foreign land.

It is not the town of Ibusuki that touches me. We'll be out of here and on our way tomorrow afternoon. The touchpoint is located somewhere else. It is in the dark sand. It is inside the earth and the steam. It is in the eyes of this unnamed woman gazing out from under the brim of her white, farm-country bonnet. Sweat is pouring off my face, into the towel. I am cooking in my sweat, inside the wet cotton skin of my *yukata*. My back is stinging with the slow burn of steady heat you know is going to be good for you. And what comes rising through me, along with the heat, is a liberating form of knowledge, or perhaps memory—that the land is not foreign. It is familiar. This is the sand and the steam and the subsoil and the hot spring and the mountain peninsula of the globe we all inhabit. And the look in the eyes of this woman is familiar too. You would recognize it anywhere. She is the tender-eyed lover, and the mother tucking you in at night, and the one who has come to bury you so that you can be born again.

James D. Houston is the author of numerous works of fiction and non-fiction—including the novels Love Life, Gig, Continental Drift, The Last Paradise, *and* Snow Mountain Passages. *He has won a number of presti-*

*gious awards, including the Wallace Stegner Fellowship, the Humanitas
Prize, and a Rockefeller Foundation residency.*

*

The year 12 of the Tembun era, a great boat moored in the cove of
Nishimura. Impossible to know where it was from. A hundred men were
aboard. Their faces were different from ours and they did not know our
language. All those who saw them found them strange…(I see one of
those sparkling sand coves that you find in the south of the country, a blue
sky full of an immense wonderment, and the people of this fishing village
scattered along the beach, unsure what to make of this junk with its high
quarterdeck decorated with demons painted in flashy colors.)

Among the men, there was a young Chinese by the name of Gobo.
(Probably the reason he is mentioned is that he is the only one who
knows how to write.) The mayor of Nishimura, who is literate, talks to
him by tracing Chinese characters in the sand with his cane.

"The men on this ship are unusual-looking. What country are
they from?"

"They are merchants who belong to the race of the Barbarians of the
South. In general, they know justice and the rules governing relations between lords and subjects, but they are completely ignorant of the laws of
etiquette. They drink without cups (probably they drink from the bottle),
they eat without chopsticks, and they pick up food with their hands.

They only know what they like and only do what pleases them. They
do not read characters and they do not understand their meaning…

They are merchants. They are not dangerous."

—Nicolas Bouvier, *The Japanese Chronicles,*
translated by Anne Dickerson

STEVE BAILEY

* * *

Of *Gomi* and *Gaijin*

The hunting is good in the garbage!

ABOUT ONCE A MONTH THE CITY OF OSAKA DISPATCHED EXTRA garbage trucks to each neighborhood to haul away oversized household junk. On such days great heaps of furniture, appliances and assorted cast-offs would sprout on residential street corners. My *gaijin* colleagues liked to brag about their latest finds in these *gomi* heaps. "Boy, I really scored in the *gomi* last night," was not an unusual comment to hear in the teachers' room. We *gaijin* competed among ourselves to see who could out trash-pick the other. We concealed the locations of particularly lucrative *gomi* piles—the ones that offered CD players and bilingual color TVs—in the same way that anglers guard the streams and ponds where they catch their biggest fish. An element of luck made the contest exciting. The contents of a *gomi* pile could never be predicted, and in my entire time in Japan, I never once met a *gaijin* who could decipher the neighborhood *gomi* schedules. The heaps simply appeared without warning, as unpredictable as the weather.

The contents of the unfurnished apartment that my wife and I rented in the Yata district came almost exclusively from the *gomi*—refrigerator, gas rings, stand-up mirror, color television, VCR, chairs, bookshelf, corner couch, and a beautiful cherrywood

147

table—as did the contents of many *gaijin* apartments. Not every item came in perfect shape, of course. Our VCR cast movies in lurid tones of blue and pink; my neighbor, a Canadian named Graper, once yelled frantically for help when his *gomi* microwave nuked itself into flames of molten plastic. But our refrigerator worked perfectly, and our furniture looked as good as any we'd ever owned anywhere else.

When Japanese consumers buy a new model—which they do quite often—the old model goes out with the trash. They simply haven't got the space in their tiny homes to hoard useless items, and passing on hand-me-downs is simply not done. I asked my students if it would be acceptable, once I had a new TV, to offer the old unit to a friend who didn't have one. My students looked mortified and tried to warn me away from such a horrendous breach of etiquette. They remained too polite to tell me not to forage in the *gomi*, and when the topic came up they simply laughed. The *gaijin* preoccupation with *gomi* struck them, no doubt, as the most inexplicable and undignified of eccentricities.

Some lower-class Japanese compete with *gaijin* for *gomi* pile pickings. Not far from our apartment lay a massive heap of appliances, bicycles, and metal furniture collected from various *gomi* piles by a scrap company. To the ire of the junkmen, *gaijin* periodically raided the unfenced lot in the middle of the night. Moving through the dark, narrow streets, gas heaters and electric fans hoisted on their shoulders, they looked like rioters out for a night of looting.

I once ran afoul of a junkman while wobbling home late at night on a stolen pink ladies' bicycle with flared handlebars, not quite flat tires, and a jingling warning bell. I wore a suitjacket and tie; the junkman wore a plaid porkpie hat and drove a Honda van stuffed with all manner of *gomi*. We followed the road beneath the elevated trainline, and in the thick summer darkness it was like exploring a giant *gomi* warehouse. Each intersection offered a neat jumble of discarded refrigerators, rice cookers, bicycle tires, toys, scrap lumber, stereo components, books, and a thousand other items.

The junkman waved me away with angry sweeps of his arms as he scouted each pile. My presense annoyed him; he did not want to trash-pick with a *gaijin*. Those things of value he hadn't room to take he shattered on the pavement with great violence. He muttered angrily as he did so, and I guessed him to be saying: "If I can't have it, then neither can that goddamn *gaijin* on the pink bicycle."

The junkman couldn't get to every *gomi* pile first, however, and when I'd reach a virgin heap of discarded consumer goods I'd smash a few items in return. I gleefully stomped a few unidentifiable appliances, but I could never bring myself to wreck anything truly valuable. Since I could not haul such items away on my bicycle, the junkman won out in the end. I watched him cram a giant stuffed panda into the bowels of his van, and then I pedaled home through the darkened, *gomi*-filled streets.

My wife and I gave away the contents of our apartment when we left Japan to resume our travels. Virtually everything we owned had come from the *gomi* anyway, but we had some particularly hard to find items—chairs and the cherrywood table, a toaster oven, an ironing board and iron—that our *gaijin* friends could really use. We gave everything away, or returned it to the *gomi*, and it felt liberating to distill our belongings down to what we could fit into two backpacks. Our traditional-style apartment had always been rather untraditionally clogged up with the accoutrements of modern life, but on that last night our tiny apartment took on the character of an idealized Japanese home—a spartan *tatami* mat cubicle furnished with nothing more than a futon—whose clean, simple austerity calmed us both for the next morning's departure on the ferry to Shanghai.

Steve Bailey is a writer from Fairbanks, Alaska.

✳

Not everything I learned in the Tokyo office had to do with economics. The only employees were Mrs. Chida and myself, and the floor space was barely seventeen *tsubo*. Even so, visitors would often comment, "How spacious, It has that nice foreign look." Mrs. Chida and I racked our brains to figure out what it was that gave us that "foreign look," and we could only think of one possible reason: the lack of clutter. For some reason, Japanese businesses cannot get the hang of managing office space. Even when the building and office are brand new, heaps of documents cover the desks and boxes jam the corridors. Our office looked different because we kept only what we were using on view; everything else was filed in the appropriate spot.

A pure *tatami* room, empty but for a single flower in a vase, is an almost archetypal image of Japan. Such spaces do exist, but only in tearooms, temples or formal meeting rooms—locations where people do not live or work. Anyone who has spent time in a Japanese home or office knows that they are usually flooded with objects. From the old farmhouses of Iya to the apartments of modern Tokyo, living in a pile of unorganized things is a typical pattern of Japanese life. In my view, this is what led to the creation of the teahouse. In the Muromachi period, tea masters grew weary of a life crowded with junk. and created the tearoom: one pure space with absolutely nothing in it. It was where they escaped from the clutter. The culture of the Japanese is bracketed by the two extremes of "clutter" and "emptiness." But when it comes to the middle ground of "organized space," that is, space with objects organized for daily use, their tradition fails them.

—Alex Kerr, *Lost Japan*

ALEX KERR

* * *

Osaka: Bumpers and Runners

A city one would never think of putting in a
"must see" itinerary until....

WELCOME TO OSAKA. FEW MAJOR CITIES OF THE DEVELOPED
world could match Osaka for the overall unattractiveness of its
cityscape, which consists mostly of a jumble of cube-like buildings
and a web of expressways and cement-walled canals. There are few
skyscrapers, even fewer museums and, other than Osaka Castle, almost no historical sites. Yet Osaka is my favorite city in Japan.
Osaka is where the fun is: it has the best entertainment districts in
Japan, the most lively youth neighborhood, the most charismatic
geisha madams and the most colorful gangsters. It also has a mo-
nopoly on humor, to the extent that in order to succeed as a popular comedian it is almost obligatory to study in Osaka and speak
the Osaka dialect.

A few blocks away from [the neighborhood of] Shinsekai is
Tobita, Japan's last *kuruwa*. In Edo days, prostitution was strictly reg-
ulated, and the courtesans lived in small walled towns within the
cities, which had gates and closing times. These cities-within-the-
city were known as *kuruwa* (enclosures). In Kyoto, the old gate to the
kuruwa of Shimabara still stands, although Shimabara itself is defunct.
The largest *kuruwa* was Yoshiwara, near Uguisudani Station in
Tokyo. Within the walls of Yoshiwara, there was a lattice of streets

lined with pleasure houses, a scene familiar in the Kabuki theater, where such streets form the backdrop of many love plays. The entrance to each pleasure house featured a banner with the name of the house on it; inside, women wearing gorgeous kimonos were on display. Today, Yoshiwara is still in business, but the boundaries, the street grid, the houses and the banners have been replaced by a jumble of streets sprinkled with love hotels and saunas, with the result that it looks not much different from most of the other places in Tokyo. If you can't read the signs, you might not realize the nature of the neighborhood. Tobita, however, survives almost completely intact. There are no walls, but there is a precise gridwork of streets lined with low tile-roofed houses. In front of each house is a banner, and inside the entrance a young woman and the madam sit side by side next to a brazier. This is as close to Kabuki in the modern age as you can get.

A word of caution: it is best not to stroll around Shinsekai or Tobita without a Japanese friend if you are a foreigner, as you might be accosted by a gangster or an unfriendly drunk. I usually go there in the company of an Osaka friend, Satoshi; he looks so tough that once, when he was on his way to a wedding dressed in a black suit and sunglasses, the police

---

Oh, yes—that's right: They have gangsters in Japan. The gangs are called yakuza, *and their role in the System is to operate the extortion, loan sharking, and prostitution industries. As long as they don't carry guns, sell drugs, or harm innocent civilians, the police pretty much leave them alone. The* yakuza *are about as clandestine as the National Football League. Everybody knows who they are. Many of them get large tattoos and chop off finger joints to demonstrate loyalty or some other important gangster quality. Also they're the only people in Japan who wear double-breasted suits, white ties, and sunglasses. "Hi!" their outfits shout. "We're gangsters!"*

◆

—Dave Barry,
Dave Barry Does Japan

picked him up on suspicion of being a gangster. Many Japanese are afraid to enter the downtown neighborhoods of Osaka. There is one area in particular that taxi drivers will not go into at all because of the *atariya* ("bumpers"), who make a living from bumping into your car and then screaming that you have run over them. The whole neighborhood rushes out to support the *atariya*, threatening to act as witnesses in a lawsuit against you until you pay up. Even so, this pales in comparison to what can happen in New York and many of Europe's large cities. The gangsters of Osaka and Kobe, known as Japan's most vicious, keep largely out of sight, and in general, violent crime is rare. One of Japan's greatest achievements is its relative lack of crime, and this is one of the invisible factors which makes life here very comfortable. The low crime rate is the result of those smoothly running social systems, and is the envy of many a nation—this is the good side of having trained the populations to be bland and obedient. The difference in Osaka is only one of degree; the streets are still basically safe. What you see in Shinsekai is more a form of "misbehavior," rather than serious crime. People do not act decorously: they shout, cry, scream and jostle one another; in well-behaved modern Japan, this is shocking.

Osaka does not merely preserve old styles of entertainment, it constantly dreams up new ones. For example, Osaka premiered the "no panties coffee shops" with panty-less waitresses that later swept Japan. In other places, the boom remained limited to coffee shops, but in Osaka they now have "no panties *okonomiyaki*" (do-it-yourself pizza) and "no panties *gyudon*" (beef-and-rice bowls). The latest, I hear, is "breast-rub coffee," where a topless waitress, on delivering coffee to the table, rubs her customer's face in the way the name would suggest.

The entertainment is by no means limited to the sex business. Osaka pioneered a new type of drive-in-public bath at Goshikiyu, near the Toyonaka interchange on the expressway. In general, public baths are slowly dying out in Japan, as the number of homes with their own bath and shower increases. However, an Osaka bathhouse proprietor with an entrepreneurial bent promoted the idea that an evening out at the public bath was the perfect family entertainment. He built a multi-storied bathhouse with a large parking lot to service Japan's new car-centered lifestyle. Inside, he installed restaurants, saunas and several floors of baths with every type of tub: hot, cold or tepid; with jacuzzi, shower or waterfall. On a Saturday night you can hardly get into Goshikiyu's parking lot; the place is jammed with families with small children.

Fashion in Osaka is not like fashion elsewhere. Tokyo is the home of trends: all the businessmen wear the same blue suit, housewives wear the same Armani, artists wear the same pastel shirts with high collars, and the young people hanging out at Yoyogi wear whatever the latest craze happens to be. Kyoto people are afraid to do anything that might make them stand out, so they dress rather drably—like Tokyo on a bad day. But Osaka is a riot of ill-matched color, tasteless footwear and startling hairdos. Satoshi puts it this way: "In Tokyo, people want to wear what everyone else is wearing. In Osaka, people want to shock."

Japan's national problem is homegeneity. The school system teaches everybody to say and think the same thing, and the bureaucracies restrict the development of new media, such as cable TV, the information highway and even movie theaters. As a result, no matter where you go, from Hokkaido to Kyushu, all the houses look the same, the clothes look the same, and people's lives center around the same humdrum activities. With everyone so well behaved and satisfied with their mediocre lives, Japan specializes in low-level pleasures. *Pachinko* is the perfect example. Why has *pachinko* swept Japan? It can hardly be the excitement of gambling, since the risks and rewards are so small. During the hours spent in front of a *pachinko* machine, there is an almost total lack of stimulation other than the occasional rush of ball bearings. There is no thought, no movement; you have no control over the flow of balls, apart from holding a little lever which shoots them up to the top of the machine; you sit there enveloped in a cloud of heavy cigarette smoke, semi-dazed by the racket of millions of ball bearings falling through machines around you. *Pachinko* verges on sensory deprivation. It is the ultimate mental numbing, the final victory of the education system.

In a department store in Tokyo recently, I saw a girl at the Shiseido cosmetics counter who summed this up. She was seated demurely at the counter, while the attendant did something with her make-up kit. The girl's head was tipped forward, and her long black hair hung around her on all sides, completely obscuring her from view. Her hands were folded with eternal patience in her lap; her down-turned head faced the table. The passivity, the way in which her hair shut out the outside world—it was a distinctive posture which I have seen in Japan so many times. Sensory deprivation? Passive silence? Fear of the world? I wish I could find the right words for it, but Japan is becoming a nation of people like this.

Donald Richie, dean of the Japanologists in Tokyo, once made this observation to me: "The people of Iya were not the only ones who escaped regimentation during the military period. There was one other group: people living in the downtowns of big cities like Edo and Osaka.

> ——⟩——
>
> *achinko* is a sort of vertical pinball machine ("invented after the war by a ball-bearing manufacturer who had a surplus load of balls," you can say truthfully). *Pachinko* halls are huge arcades lined with machines stretching as far as the eye can see. No one knows how big they are because they fill with cigarette smoke before they can be measured. They resound with the infernal clatter of a million balls plinking around the game consoles. They're not difficult to spot; every main street has one.
>
> ◆
>
> —Robert Ainsley,
> *Bluff Your Way in Japan*

The merchants in these cities were a different breed from the farmers, with their need to cooperate in rice growing, and the *samurai*, with their code of loyalty and propriety. The *samurai* despised the merchants as belonging at the bottom of the social totem pole, but at the same time, the merchants had the freedom to enjoy themselves. The brilliant realm of the "floating world"— Kabuki, the pleasure quarters, colorful kimonos, woodblock prints, novels, dance—belonged to the old downtowns. Even today, people from these neighborhoods are different from ordinary Japanese." This is especially true of Osaka. The downtown neighborhoods of Tokyo, while they still exist, have largely lost their identity, but Osaka maintains a spirit of fierce independence which goes back a long way. Originally, Osaka was a fishing village on the Inland Sea called Naniwa. The writer Shiba Ryotaro maintains that the colorful language and brutal honesty of Osaka people can be traced to Naniwa's seaport past.

Osaka dialect is certainly colorful. Standard Japanese, to the sorrow of Edan and Trevor, has an almost complete lack of dirty words. The very meanest thing you can shout at somebody is *kisama*, which means literally, "honorable you." But Osaka people say such vividly imaginative things that you want to sit back and take notes. Most are unprintable, but here is one classic Osaka epithet: "I'm going to slash your skull in half, stir up your brains and drink them out with a straw!" The fishwife invective and the desire to shock produced the playful language that is the hallmark of Osaka dialect. When Satoshi describes a visit to the bank, it's funnier than the routines of most professional comics. It begins with the bank, and ends with the dice tattooed on his aunt's left shoulder. Free association of the sort he employs is called *manzai* in the blood. That's why comedians have to come here to study.

During the early Nara period, Naniwa was Japan's window to the world, serving as the main port of call for embassies from China and Korea. Osaka was so important as the seat of diplomacy that the capital was based there several times in the 7th century before finally being moved to Nara. In the process, numerous families from China and Korea emigrated to the Naniwa region, and Heian-period censuses show that its population was heavily of continental origin. In the late 16th century, Osaka's harbor shifted from Naniwa to Sakai, a few kilometers south. As Chinese silk and Southeast Asian ceramics flooded into Japan, the Osaka merchants grew rich; among them was Sen no Rikyu, founder of tea ceremony. For several decades Osaka was again Japan's window to the world, and outshone Kyoto as the source of new cultural developments. During the Edo period, the Shogunate closed the ports and three hundred years of isolation set in. But Osaka continued to thrive, its merchants establishing themselves as wholesale rice brokers and moneylenders. Certain unique occupations grew up, such as "runners," who still exist even today; their job is to visit one wholesaling street and jot down prices, then dash over to the next street to report them to competitors—and then do the same thing in reverse.

The mercantile ethos in Osaka resulted in many of Japan's largest businesses being based there, such as Sumitomo and the trading house C Itoh, which did more volume of business in 1995 than any other company in the world. Osaka's good fortune lay in the fact that the government left the city almost totally free of control. In Tokyo there was the Shogun; in Kyoto there was the Emperor; but in Osaka there was nobody on top, except a skeleton staff of the Shogun's officials holed up in Osaka Castle, pitifully unprepared to join in a battle of wits with wily Osaka merchants. The ratio of *samurai* to population was so low that people could go their whole lives without meeting one. In Edo, the Shogunate built bridges; in Osaka, private businessmen built them. In other words, in Osaka, the people ran their own lives.

In recent years, the fact that certain areas like Shinsekai have become slums has acted as a protection, scaring away the developers and investors who raised land prices and transformed the face of Tokyo. Osaka preserved its identity, which goes right back to the old seaport of Naniwa. So when friends ask me to show them the "true Japan of ancient tradition," I don't take them to Kyoto: I take them to Osaka.

---

*T*he Edo Period (1603-1867) A time of stability through hierarchy, when Shogun Tokugawa Ieyasu unified the country via military rule and established a feudal system: under the Shogun, the *daimyo*; under the *daimyo,* the *samurai*; and so on down to the peasants.

◆

—DWG & AGC

*Alex Kerr first experienced Japan at age twelve as the son of a naval officer.
He returned to the States and earned a degree in Japanese Studies from
Yale, then went to Oxford University for a degree in Chinese Studies. In
1977 he returned to Japan and began collecting art, writing, and lecturing.
This story was excerpted from his book,* Lost Japan.

※

I started a conversation with a middle-aged, cheerful, freshly shaved, stout
Japanese who sat next to me. He looked like a well-fed reveler who had
spent his night sitting on soft pillows drinking tepid sake and watching
the *geishas* of Kobe dancing. He would have escaped from the monotony
of his home life to enjoy a free evening. "The sweetest woman," says a
Japanese proverb, "is first the wife of your friend; then, the *geisha*; then,
your maid; and finally, your wife."

I was wrong. He spoke a little English. He was a businessman. He lived
in a villa in a suburb of Kobe and commuted to his office in Osaka. He
spoke to me about his huge city with its two and a half million people
and his face shone with pride.

"It is the Manchester, or, better, the Chicago of the Far East. Look at
its chimneys, a forest. We send our cotton fabrics all over the world. We
have 6,700 factories. We are the economic capital of Japan."

As he talked, his eyes sparkled. You felt that his thick, smooth body was
inhabited by indomitable energy. In my life, I have often encountered fat
people, full of energy and soul. You think their spirits are nourished by
spreading their tentacles in the thick, abundant flesh.

The Japanese lit a big cigar and continued: "We work. All day.
Telephones, telegrams, statistics, invoices, exchanges. But in the evening,
we enjoy ourselves. No other city in Japan has so many nightclubs, so
many secret gay restaurants, so many beautiful *geishas*. We have six thousand *geishas* in Osaka."

I enjoyed listening to that fat man talk. I looked admiringly at his
short, plump hands, that knew so expertly how to earn money and caress
the *geishas*.

"Are you a Buddhist?" I asked, just to tease him.

He laughed and looked at me slyly.

"Of course," he said. "Sometimes, when my business goes well, I go to
a temple and put a few flowers at Buddha's feet. I have nothing to lose!"

"The world is an illusion of the five senses. Open your eyes, wake up,
free yourself from the net of need."

"Yes, I know it," replied the reveling businessman, laughing. "That's what Buddha said and it certainly was right in his times, when his people lived in tropical forests. But if Buddha lived today and had his home in Osaka, I am sure he would be like me!"

I turned and looked at him as if I had seen him for the first time. Once, I had seen a wooden statue of Buddha, with a protruding huge belly, with laughter bursting out which spread from his mouth to his whole fleshy face; it extended through his neck, his three-fold belly and his naked legs to his swollen soles...Yes, surely when this covetous businessman, who looked at me slyly, took his bath in the morning and, after it, sat naked, steaming, with crossed legs on the cool straw mat while his silent wife brought him green tea, he was exactly like gentle Buddha and looked at the futile world as at a soap bubble—tea, woman, business—which in a little while will burst and vanish in the air...

May this fat businessman of Osaka be well and his business go well because, thanks to him, for a moment I saw and felt all the contrasts of the mysterious oriental soul.

—Nikos Kazantzakis, *Japan China,* translated by George Pappageotes

DONALD W. GEORGE

* * *

Ryoanji Reflections

A simple plot of ground that makes you stop—
before you can really see.

WHEN I THINK OF THE SACRED PLACES I HAVE ENCOUNTERED IN
my own travels, I recall the Temple of Poseidon on the cliff of
Cape Sounion in Greece, where I spent a wild night huddled in
my sleeping bag among the moonlit columns, surrounded by tear-
ing wind, the crashing of waves and ghostly, godly dreams.

I think too of Bali, of the lush, lovingly sculpted land and the
gentle people, more profoundly imbued with a sense of sanctity—
of life as a holy gift to be celebrated—than any other I have met.

But most vividly of all I think of a simple plot of sand and rocks
and moss in Kyoto—the rock garden at Ryoanji Temple.

The guidebooks will tell you that the rock garden was built in
the 15th century, probably by a renowned, Zen-influenced artist
named Soami, and that it is considered a masterpiece of the *kare-
sansui* ("dry landscape") garden style. It consists of fifteen irregu-
larly shaped rocks of varying sizes, some surrounded by moss,
arranged in a bed of white sand that is raked every day. A low
earthen wall surrounds the garden on three sides, over-hung by a
narrow, beamed wooden roof; on the fourth side, wooden steps
lead to a wide wooden platform and the main building of the temple itself. Beyond the wall are cedar, pine and cherry trees.

Such a description gives a sense of the history and look of the place, but to understand its power, its pure *presence*, you have to go there. The first time I visited Ryoanji I was overwhelmed—first by the spareness of the site and second by loudspeakers that every fifteen minutes squawked out a recorded message about the history and spirit of the garden to the busloads of obedient schoolchildren and tourists who filed through.

But something held me there. Morning passed to afternoon, and still I sat on the well-worn platform, staring. Kids in black caps, tiny book-filled backpacks and black-and-white school uniforms passed by, studying me while I studied the garden, and adults in shiny cameras and kimonos clicked and clucked and walked on.

Clouds came and went, and the branches beyond the garden bent, straightened, bent again. I saw how the pebbly sand had been meticulously raked in circles around the rocks, and in straight lines in the open areas; and how those lines stopped without a misplaced pebble when they touched the circular patterns, and then resumed unchanged beyond them. I saw how pockets of moss had filled the pocks in the stones, and how the sand echoed the sky, the moss echoed the trees, the wall and roof balanced the platform, and the rocks seemed to emanate a web of intricate, tranquil tension within the whole.

It was an exquisite enigma, telling me something I couldn't put words to, and so it has remained. I have seen

> *A*nother fact of prime importance to remember is that, in order to comprehend the beauty of a Japanese garden, it is necessary to understand—or at least to learn to understand—the beauty of stones. Not of stones quarried by the hand of man, but of stones shaped by nature only. Until you can feel, and keenly feel, that stones have character, that stones have tones and values, the whole artistic meaning of a Japanese garden cannot be revealed to you.
>
> ◆
>
> —Lafcadio Hearn,
> *Writings from Japan*

Ryoanji in spring, when the cherry trees bloomed, and in fall, when their branches were bare; in winter, when snow covered the moss, and in summer, when the cicadas buzzed beyond the wall. I have been there among giggling teenagers and gaping farmers, bemused Westerners and beatific monks. By now it has become a part of me—and still it eludes me.

I love the place partly because it is so emphatically not a ten-minute tourist stop. Its dimensions defy the camera—I have never seen a true picture of the place—and its subtle simplicity defies quick assimilation. It makes you sit and study, slow down and stare until you really see it—in its particularity and in its whole, simultaneously.

And yet—and here the enigma expands—you cannot see all of Ryoanji at one time: the rocks are so arranged that you can see only twelve of the fifteen stones wherever you stand. You have to visualize, imagine, the other three.

How wonderful! It is in this sense that Ryoanji is, for me, the essential sacred place: it is complete in itself, but for you to completely perceive it, you have to transcend the boundary between inner and outer—to travel inward as well as outward, to find and finish it in your mind.

And the gigglers, the camera-clickers, and the squawking loudspeakers are all, in their exasperating reality, part of this completion. Beyond a great irony of modern Japan—loudspeakers instructing you to appreciate the silence—they embody a much larger meaning: you must embrace them all—the monks and the moss and the trees, the schoolkids and the stones—to really be there, to be whole.

Donald W. George also contributed "When the Cherries Bloom" to Part One.

*

Every time I am shown to an old, dimly lit, and, I would add, impeccably clean toilet in a Nara or Kyoto temple, I am impressed with the singular virtues of Japanese architecture. The parlor may have its charms, but the

Japanese toilet truly is a place of spiritual repose. It always stands apart from the main building, at the end of a corridor, in a grove fragrant with leaves and moss. No words can describe that sensation as one sits in the dim light, basking in the faint glow reflected from the *shoji*, lost in meditation or gazing out at the garden. The novelist Natsume Soseki counted his morning trips to the toilet a great pleasure, "a physiological delight" he called it. And surely there could be no better place to savor this pleasure than a Japanese toilet where, surrounded by tranquil walls and finely grained wood, one looks out upon blue skies and green leaves.

—Jun'ichiro Tanizaki, *In Praise of Shadows*

KATHERINE ASHENBURG

* * *

The Arithmetic of Beauty

A class in flower arranging is an introduction
to the exacting esthetics of Japan.

IN FUJI BANK'S FALL AD CAMPAIGN, A SURPASSINGLY ELEGANT young man considers the relationship between a sunflower and a vase.

On the Tokyo subway (but not during rush hour), passengers, mostly women, can be seen tenderly carrying long, quiver-like containers.

In Japan's ubiquitous flower shops, blossoming boughs up to six feet long jostle for space with smaller blooms, shelves of flat and cylindrical containers, and the metal holders we call frogs.

The explanation of these minor Japanese mysteries is *ikebana*, the art of flower arrangement. *Ikebana* is studied up and down the country, at an impressive number of levels. Just how seriously the Japanese take *ikebana* can be glimpsed at Sogetsu Kaikan, a huge glass-and-steel rectangle designed by Kenzo Tange across from the Crown Prince's Palace in downtown Tokyo. Except for the company art gallery on the top floor, the entire six-story building is occupied by flower-arranging classes and their administration. And, as an unusual bonus for foreigners, a two-hour "international class" is taught in English every Monday and Friday morning.

On the way to my first class, in the two-story lobby designed by Isamu Noguchi as a showcase for gargantuan *ikebana*, I summon up half-remembered notions of flat containers, gnarled branches and off-center, contorted arrangements. Of the Sogetsu school itself, I know only that its director, Hiroshi Teshigahara, is a former film director best known for *Woman in the Dunes*. I am in for a very steep, very Japanese learning curve.

Our classroom has low tables, low stools, and a sunny view of Tokyo's sprawl below. There are perhaps half a dozen people, including one young man, choosing flowers and containers and working more or less independently. Appropriately enough the first name of the *sensei*, or teacher, Seishu Kawasaki, means "blue autumn flower." She gestures to the wall lined with containers, from classic cylinders to spiky metal creations, and to the buckets filled with branches and flowers: "Please, select." I choose my materials, as they are called here: deep blue gentians, curly dragon willow, a triangular black container. Then she motions me to sit for an introduction.

Ikebana began simply in the 4th century, she tells me, as floral offerings to Buddha, and gained prominence as an accessory to the tea ceremony around the 15th century. As with the tea ceremony itself, at first *ikebana* was an aristocratic masculine accomplishment. By the beginning of this century it had evolved into an essential part of a young lady's education.

Today there are three main branches of *ikebana*: the very traditional Kyoto-based Ikenobo school, the Ohara school and the Sogetsu school. Ohara began at the turn of the century, in response to the importation of Western flowers such as dahlias, tulips, and anemones. Sogetsu, the most free of the main schools, was founded in 1927 by Sofu Teshigahara, the father of the present director, in protest against the rigidity of the Ikenobo and Ohara systems. He insisted on using anything—plastic, wire, styrofoam—as long as each arrangement had some fresh plant life. "Sogetsu is modern art using fresh materials," *sensei* concludes.

Then she starts me on my first arrangement ("Would you please stand up when you arrange"), explaining how to calculate the three main stems, called *shin, soe,* and *hikae*, traditionally symbolic of heaven, earth, and man. She measures the diameter of my vase, doubles it, and adds its height. That makes the height of my main stem, *shin*, *soe* is three-quarters the height of *shin*, and *hikae* is half as tall as *soe*. Using the willow for the first and second stems, *sensei* slants the first branch about 15 degrees from the center to the right, the second about 45 degrees; the third branch, a gentian, she tilts 75 degrees to the left.

The arithmetic, the low tables and stools, the frequent use of the word "materials," and *sensei's* smiling encouragement make me feel I'm in a Montessori school for grown-ups. Now she detaches her arrangement from its *kenzan*, or frog, and tells me it's my turn. As firm with her esthetic pronouncements as she is with the unruly willow tendrils, she leaves me with a few maxims: "Make a triangle." "Keep space between the main stems." In a breathtakingly condensed demonstration of a major Japanese concept, she moves the frog from its off-center position to the center of the container: *"Not interesting."* It's only 10:30 a.m. and I've absorbed important Japanese attitudes to beauty: the importance of structure, restraint, and asymmetry.

> At home again, I slide open once more my little paper window, and look out upon the night. I see the paper lanterns flitting over the bridge, like a long shimmering of fireflies. I see the spectres of a hundred lights trembling upon the black flood. I see the broad *shōji* of dwellings beyond the river suffused with the soft yellow radiance of invisible lamps; and upon those lighted spaces I can discern slender moving shadows, silhouettes of graceful women. Devoutly do I pray that glass may never become universally adopted in Japan—there would be no more delicious shadows.
>
> ◆
>
> —Lafcadio Hearn,
> *Writings from Japan*

Left to myself, I measure happily, choose "materials" from my bucket, fill in *jushi*, or secondary branches, behind the main stems for depth. Confident that if I follow the basic rules I'll have room to express myself "freely," as *sensei* promised, I quite like my finished arrangement.

Sensei doesn't. When she returns, without speaking she pares, prunes, and deconstructs my rather unkempt Western arrangement into something more…Japanese. Now she smiles. "Simple one is most difficult. Don't use so many materials."

At 11 a.m., she mounts the platform at one end of the classroom and demonstrates two more advanced styles for the whole group. Eyeballing flowers ("Keep the best blossom to hide the frog"), cutting delicate grasses in a vinegar-and-water solution to lengthen their life, chanting "*shin, soe, hikai*" like a mantra whenever she considers her triangle, she seems to have a sixth sense of how the smallest grass will contribute to the general effect.

The second demonstration involves a long, modernist pottery trough on legs, a very heavy berry branch, and some pod-bearing millet stalks. While the class watches in absolute silence, *sensei* cuts a section from a stick and fixes it as a brace inside the trough, near one end. That supports the berry branch, which droops artfully over the container, accompanied by the millet. *Sensei* snips, twists grasses, assays her creation constantly and smiles in relief at the end. When the class claps, she murmurs, as a modest diversionary tactic, "It's very important to fix heavy material."

Now *sensei* returns to me, teaching a tricky method of supporting material in a tall vase by means of two branches split at the tops and interlocked. Again, she's unimpressed by my efforts but in an objective way that leaves my pride unhurt: her loyalty is to beauty, and she assumes mine is too. Remaking my stiff arrangement, supporting the Turkish bellflowers and grasses high but obliquely on her little holder, she admonishes, "You must slant in tall vase." Holding the flowers straight, she says: "This is *not* beautiful." And then she tilts them and says: "This is."

As the class winds down, we drink cold tea from a thermos and cruise the room, admiring the others' arrangements. *Sensei* commends the young man's avant-garde arrangement of anthurium and gloriosa: "This is free-style. Please. Look."

My own two arrangements are best passed over in silence, but the class has been more than rewarding. As well as the pleasure of spending a morning with flowers, I've experienced something of Japanese education and esthetics up close. When *sensei* deflects my parting compliment by demurring, "I've been studying *ikebana* more than twenty-five years," she embodies one of the central Japanese virtues—*gaman*, or persistence. Resolving to persist, I take my *Sogestsu Text Book* (Grade One), bow to everyone, and start to leave. The whole room bursts into delighted laughter at my *faux pas*. It's the morning's last lesson in things Japanese: everyone picks up after oneself. I dutifully return scissors, tray, water bowl, vases, and all those fragrant materials to their proper places.

Katherine Ashenburg lives in Canada where she writes and edits. Having received an Asia-Pacific Fellowship, she spent an autumn in Japan.

✳

The philosophies of China and Japan are to be found in different places. Beginning with Confucius and Mencius, the first of a long stream of eminent philosophers and theorists, the Chinese skillfully put their thoughts in writing, thus leaving them behind for later generations. One can scour the history of Japan, however, without finding much in the way of articulated philosophy; to put it strongly, Japan is not a country of thinkers. As a result, before coming to Oomoto, both David and I had felt far greater respect for China than for Japan. But at the seminar I discovered that Japan does have its own philosophy, every bit as complex and profound as China's. Rather than being expressed in words, it flows within the traditional arts—although Japan had no Confucius, Mencius or Chu Hsi, it did have the poet Teika, Zeami, the creator of Noh drama, and the founder of tea, Sen no Rikyu. They were Japan's philosophers.

—Alex Kerr, *Lost Japan*

* * *

Rain Droppings

A journey into the art of meditation
and the terror of the bamboo stick.

TANI HOUSE, THE INN WHERE I STAYED IN KYOTO, WAS A DARK,
older two-story box with winged Japanese roof and a palisade of
fifteen-foot bamboo trees surrounding it. Women guests slept on
futons in a large room on the lower floor, men on an upper floor
that also had three or four smaller rooms for couples or groups.
Some nights more than forty people were shoehorned into the
house, including latecomers that the owner, Mrs. Tani, let sleep on
the second-floor porches. Her accommodating disposition (for
fifty cents she'd do your laundry) was one reason for the inn's pop-
ularity. Other factors were price ($6 a night) and location, a quiet
district half an hour by bus from the hooting rush of downtown.

The sprawling parklike grounds of Daitoku-ji Temple surrounded Tani House; from the inn's back porch I saw temple
buildings and acres of gardens, and orange-robed monks pacing
manicured, rock-lined paths. A graveyard of marble shrines and
markers butted up to the back fence, and in the mornings the
sound of chanting carried from the temples, floated over the head-
stones, and bothered Tani House's late sleepers.

But not everyone slept late. Many people were there for the
novice Zen meditation classes offered next door. Six-thirty each

morning brought a quiet rustling of fabrics as the meditators whispered each other awake, dressed, clomped down the wooden stairs and out the front door. They would return in a rowdy mood a couple hours later, just when the heathen were beginning to stir.

> "*I* remember this one Zen teacher told me, soon after I arrived, that the appeal of Zen to many foreigners was like a mountain wrapped in mist. Much of what the Westerners saw was just the beautiful mist; but as soon as they began really doing Zen, they found that its essence was the mountain: hard rock."
>
> ◆
>
> —Pico Iyer, *The Lady and the Monk: Four Seasons in Kyoto*

As the cast of lodgers changed every day, so did the cast of meditators. During my first few days I noticed one older man serving as head meditator. The registration book identified him as Daniel Davidson, a 47-year-old from Chicago who listed his occupation as "teacher." Indeed, he looked professorial—black-rimmed glasses, full beard gone gray, and hair headed the same direction. In conversations that were always lively but never broke down into argument, he discussed Zen with many of the other travelers. He had a good backlog of Zen lore and parables, talked engagingly about the different levels and stages of study, and described how Zen masters think and how they differ from the rest of us.

I had been meditating off and on for a few years, sitting quietly for twenty minutes once or twice a day, trying to observe the constant parade of thoughts through my consciousness without becoming seduced by them. Sometimes I've reached a mildly euphoric state of seeming transparency, relaxed and happy, with a rather pleasant "nothing" going on in my consciousness.

"That's probably the state of *reverie*," Daniel said, "something common to all novices, the same state one might experience in a cathedral under the influence of organ music. But a Zen master has attained the ability to go into a state far beyond reverie, beyond tranquillity, a state where he is completely conscious and aware of everything—the chirping of a bird, the closing of a distant door, the thoughts of the person next to him—without being attached to or affected by any of it. It's ungraspable to others, but accessible to a Zen master under all circumstances, not just the special conditions of church or temple."

It was raining the next morning as Daniel and I and two other novice meditators shuffled beneath umbrellas toward the temple.

"The monk might hit you with his stick," Daniel said.

"What?"

"The monk might hit you with his stick. But don't worry. He knows how to do it so you'll feel it, but it won't injure you. You might even *ask* him to hit you—just for the experience. If he comes and stands in front of you with his stick, just bow your head and he'll whack you on the back of your shoulders. He canes someone every day."

The other two initiates were Steve, a freshman from Yale, and Rhonda, a married lady from New Zealand whose husband was still sleeping. "He's into volleyball," she said. "He stays out late in the gyms, I'm up early in the temples." Both Steve and Rhonda had been to the temple before, and both had been caned.

"It smarts at first," said Rhonda, "but it helps get my attention off my knees. After about twenty minutes of that half-lotus position, I feel like screaming."

The session's format was to be this: one forty-five-minute meditation, then a five-minute break for walking in a silent circle, another forty-five minute meditation, then ten minutes of chanting. Everything had an exact prescribed form. "But don't worry," said Daniel. "If you're doing something wrong, the monk will tell you."

Puddles were forming on the walkways, gray pebbles washed clean by the bouncing rain. Daniel led the way through a maze of bushes, buildings, and trees, through wooden archways and around corners. At one point he slid aside a bamboo gate and held it until the four of us were through. Finally we came to a series of flat stones placed a couple of feet apart on a green lawn; the path they formed brought us to a small gazebo-like prayer building with steeply pitched roof.

"Take your shoes off," Daniel said, whispering now. We left shoes and umbrellas under an awning in front of the sanctuary, and stepped into the ever-present slippers. At the doorway Daniel stopped, pressed palms together breast high, and bowed deeply. On a table in the center of the room was a shrine of bells and a small Buddha. Along the right and left walls were two raised platforms where we would sit and meditate; two other Westerners were already there squatting on cushions, looking into space.

"Get lots of cushions," Rhonda whispered to me.

I grabbed four of them from a stack near the door and arranged them under my buttocks so that when I began crossing my legs I was a foot off the floor, easing the strain on my knees.

It was a building of windows. The roof was anchored in each corner by thick posts, but the walls were merely bamboo screens that slid back to allow a free flow of air through the room. I was the only one looking around; the others were sitting cross-legged, hands clasped in laps, staring at the floor with barely opened eyes. Across from me was an attractive woman my own age with the word WIND-SURFING arched across the front of her sweatshirt.

We sat for several moments, listening to the tick of rain on the roof, until there was a motion at the doorway. Out of the corner of my eye I saw "the Monk" changing from outdoor slippers to indoor ones. He straightened

---

inally, it began to rain, pittering and pattering on all the flimsy roofs and walls.

"*Shito-shito,*" said Joe softly. "And *goro-goro* for thunder. *Za-za* for heavy rain. *Pica-pica* for starlight. You don't have words for these things. Just sounds, man, perfect sounds."

And I thought how well you could always hear rain here, on wooden walls and roofs, in every Japanese poem and home.

◆

—Pico Iyer, *The Lady and the Monk: Four Seasons in Kyoto*

at the door, bowed to the Buddha, and strode effortlessly across the room without looking at any of us. His head was bald—shaved and gleaming. He wore a gray robe made of expensive material. His motions and gestures had obviously been practiced at great length, each one flawlessly smooth and connecting naturally with the next.

The others in the room adjusted noiselessly into the half-lotus—one foot twisted up onto the opposite thigh, the other pretzeled beneath them—a painful contortion, which I imitated. On a mat at the far end of the room the Monk assumed the full-lotus position. He tapped on a high-pitched bell, three times, precisely spaced.

Pingggg!

Pingggg!

Pingggg!

The first few moments passed unnoticed. I studied the rounded contours of "Windsurfing" several times and entered a mammareal reverie, comparing the docile, small-bosomed Japanese women with the busty, briefcase-toting ones back home. I thought about how long it had been since I'd hugged anyone, and I considered proposing marriage, or at least adultery. I watched my breathing for a while. In, out, in, out, in, out. And then I noticed my legs. How long before my ankles snapped? Was I doing this wrong? Was there something deficient about me? Hadn't there always been? Was I supposed to focus my eyes on a spot on the floor, or was I supposed to let them drift? Was there something particularly holy about this pagoda that I should try to pick up on? Was today the day that I would finally "get it"? Had some critical nugget of divine inspiration crept out of the Himalayas and into China several centuries ago, wound its way down the Yangtze, leaped the Japan sea, and lodged at Daitoku-ji Temple, where today it would be gloriously revealed?

Would the Monk be insulted if I moved around a bit? Would he come over and beat me with his stick? Was there some suggested reading I should have done? Shouldn't I have asked all these questions before coming? What sort of thoughts were the others having? How long had it been? Ten minutes? Fifteen? Or only two? Oooh, my ankles...

I tried to will the blood to circulate in my legs, tried mentally to heat my feet, but it did no good. My ankles and knees screamed to be moved. Around the room there was stillness and complete silence. I wiggled my toes, flexed an ankle, started to remind myself about being in the right place and all, but my body congress jeered and threatened impeachment. *I will never be Japanese*, it occurred to me. *Never be Buddhist. I've come to see the country, not convert.* Japan had granted me temporary asylum; that was all I could ask. Any understanding would be strictly a bonus.

Just as I was preparing to ease my foot off my thigh, the Monk rose to his feet. Without turning my head, I saw the rod in his hand. *He's read my thoughts. He's coming to cane me!*

Instead, he paced slowly in front of the three people across from me—Daniel, Windsurfing, and a Western man I didn't know. His back to me, the Monk stopped in front of Daniel and presented the cane. I raised my head to watch. Daniel leaned slowly forward. Using precise, choreographed motions, the Monk placed his stick flat against Daniel's left shoulder blade. Without hesitation, he lifted it high and slapped it down sharply. Four times.

Crack! Crack! Crack! Crack! The noise sounded and resounded through the room, the temple complex, the quivering universe. I thought: Rhonda was right. My blood-starved legs were long forgotten.

The Monk shifted slightly and placed his cane on Daniel's other shoulder blade. He showed no doubt, no indecision, and he did not look to see how Daniel was receiving his correction.

Crack! Crack! Crack! Crack!

Daniel straightened. The Monk bowed. Daniel bowed. The Monk moved away. I looked back at the floor, pretending not to have seen anything, pretending to be above it all, pretending to have been lifted to some other, loftier plane of being. But my legs were jeering again. It was hopeless; when the Monk came to me, I would ask for a rain check, beg permission to leave, promise to come back tomorrow. He was pacing my side of the room now;

he stopped in front of Rhonda and Steve and punished both of them with the cane. Again the universe shook.

And then my time came. The Monk stopped in front of me, gray robe obscuring my field of vision. I kept my eyes lowered, pretending to meditate, and waited for something to happen. It was a very short wait.

I heard a gasp, and looked up. The Monk's eyeballs had inflated and the individual black hairs of his eyebrows were frozen into concerned arches. He was staring at my aching feet.

"Zzox!" he hissed in a whisper. Was he expecting me to speak Japanese? "No zzox!" He reached out and touched my socks.

"Oh."

"Teek zzox uff." He pointed toward the open doorway.

A miracle! A reprieve from the governor! I unkinked my legs and my pulsing ankles, slid down off the platform and into my slippers, and walked to the door, trying to imitate the Monk's graceful motions. Blood poured into my legs; my toes tingled. I took my time at the door, pulling off my zzox and tucking them into my zzhoes. I debated making a run for Tani House, but decided against it. With restored legs, I climbed back onto the meditating platform, but scaled my half-lotus down to about one-quarter.

The Monk had gone back to his mat, and for the rest of the session stayed there. "Teek zzox uff," turned out to be his only words of instruction.

When it was all finished, we novices stood quietly under the awning, pulling on footwear, claiming umbrellas. The Monk joined us, a blank expression on his smooth face. No one spoke. He stood there a moment watching us, then studied the leaking sky. He stretched a hand out from under the awning and caught several wet splats.

"Rain droppings." He stared at his palm.

"Yes," said Daniel, liaison for all of us. "Rain."

The Monk looked up, chuckling, his face now a network of wrinkles. "Not animal droppings." He smiled at his own play on words. Soon we were all smiling.

"Rain droppings," he said again, whimsically. "Not animal

droppings." And then, still chuckling, the Monk shook open his umbrella and padded away, into the rain.

Droppings.

Brad Newsham also contributed "Smo" in Part One.

★

There were many things he found offensive but which he learned to accept because they were necessary, and equally a number of things that were unacceptable because they were offensive without being necessary. The worst of these was noise. Hour by hour and day after day columns of vans and cars, loudspeakers blaring, circled the estate laying a cordon of noise from which there was no escape. Occasionally there were political announcements, but on the whole they dealt with the price of fish and vegetables or some forthcoming attraction in a local hall, always couched in the most effusive courtesy language; a futile palliative, for the damage had already been done. Most Japanese had become resigned to this violating of their peace and assured Boon that he would soon get used to it, but he didn't. In fact it became steadily worse. The first jarring notes of the tinny melodies that were always churned out before these announcements were enough to drive him to fury.

—John David Morley, *Pictures from the Water Trade:*
Adventures of a Westerner in Japan

PICO IYER

* * *

An Alchemy of Absences

The depth and elegance of sparseness
is discovered in an ancient inn.

EVERYTHING INTERESTING, CELINE ONCE SAID, HAPPENS IN THE
shadows. The great elegiac Japanese novelist Junichiro Tanizaki actually wrote a whole treatise called *In Praise of Shadows*, a virtual
handbook of Japanese aesthetics, suggesting, as it does, how everything essential takes place in the corners, the silences, the inter-
stices. In life as much as in art, Japan proceeds by indirections, to
find directions out.

The Tawaraya, the oldest and most famous traditional inn in the
ancient capital of Kyoto, is a masterpiece in the poetry of absences,
a sonnet on the wealth of having nothing. There is no lobby there,
no restaurant, no menu, no room-key. Each of the eighteen rooms,
individual as haiku, contains, on the surface, little more than a single flower, a small bowl for incense and a scroll against the wall. If
you wish to see how ceremony and quietness and precision alone
can make an empty room full, go to Tawaraya.

The particulars of the place often known as the world's best
hotel (it is surely its most secret one) are almost legend now: 300
years ago, a textile merchant from the southwestern area of Tawara
asked his son to find a hostlery in Kyoto for business-trips. Soon,
the unprepossessing building on a forgotten back-street was

attracting other guests, and serving as a *ryokan*, or traditional inn. By now, it has housed everyone from Prince Ito, the first Prime Minister of Japan, to Tom Cruise. And, with its unique system of two staff to every room, built up a deserved reputation for exclusiveness: the first time I rang for a reservation, I was told that the only rooms available on a weekday night several weeks from now would go for $900 or more. The guest-book of the small inn is, not surprisingly, a roll-call of the great names of the century, from Robert Oppenheimer to Liza Minnelli and Gerald Ford to Jean-Paul Sartre. Elliott Richardson sketched his garden in the book, Leonard Bernstein scribbled off fragments of a score, and Marlon Brando invited the proprietors to stay on his island forever. Alfred Hitchcock wanted to have the Tawaraya's bathroom reproduced at home. And on his official visit to the city, King Carl Gustav XVI of Sweden got so carried away by the beauty of his garden that he almost missed his tour.

Yet none of that catches the essence of Tawaraya, which is, in a sense, an education in a whole way of refinement, a crash course in the music of inflections. The inn itself is hidden away in the center of Kyoto, on a tiny, elegant lane tucked among pink love-hotels and *pachinko*-flashy shopping-malls. When first I arrived, on a chill November evening, when the last leaves were red and golden in the temples, and the city was eccentrically celebrating its 1200th birthday (I arrived too late for the Great Tea Ceremony, but just in time for the Housewives' Volleyball Tournament and the International Dioxin Conference), I stepped out of a taxi, and under a little gate, and into a wonderland of lanterns and secrets. A man was waiting to take my shoes at the entrance. A kimonoed lady-in-waiting was ready to take me to my room. And, almost immediately, I was in a different kind of consciousness, catching the way the maple leaves were scattered across the garden, the reflection of a candle off the polished wood, the whisper of stockinged feet on bamboo mats.

The room in which I found myself was simplicity itself: a paper lantern, a low lacquer table, the faint gold tracery of butterflies on the closet-walls. An adjoining waiting-room, a heated toilet, and an exquisite space with a cedarwood bath, its water perfumed by the sap. The Tawaraya acknowledges the need for a few modern conveniences—there is a rotary phone, a small TV, and a fire sensor or two—but all these encumbrances are covered in cloth so as not to disturb the harmony of the space.

As the silence and the space around me deepened, I felt my mind expand, and grow attentive to the details: the single perfect maple leaf under a bowl of pineapples; the Noh texts around the lantern-like brazier on which I was invited to cook beef; the postcards in the rice paper stationery kit that changed each day. Every morning, my personal maid came to wake me up with a glass of chilled tangerine juice, preparatory to a fifteen-course breakfast; the ashtray she removed from my table turned out to be a 200-year-old antique.

And slowly, I found, the place began to seep into me, to put me into a different state of being, until I felt I could spend all day in my room, just watching the sun make stripes across the *tatami*, and the light wind touch the bamboo screens outside. Slowly, I felt myself sinking into a different kind of rhythm, and simply staying where I was, watching the sky darken and the shadows deepen; listening to the crickets in the courtyard; raising my screens to see silver lanterns against an indigo sky. The Tawaraya is the only hotel I know that enters the guest as much as the guest enters it.

It is also, of course, an alchemy of absences, a celebration of what isn't said, what isn't seen, and what isn't known. "Very few of the staff speak English," Mrs. Toshi Okazaki Satow, the 11th generation owner of the inn told me in her fluent (and, of course, self-deprecating) English. "But I tell them it isn't necessary to speak good English if you have a heart." (And it's true: the staff here are famous for sensing one's needs before one even knows one has them.) One of the inn's great illusions is that every guest feels he's got the whole place to himself. And few visitors realize that to sustain the air of calm, workers have to scrub the floor daily by hand, change the flower-arrangements every morning, pick stray leaves out of the garden. "Even by Japanese standards, it's understated and bare," says Diane Durston, author of *Old Kyoto*, and the leading foreign expert on the city. "The Tawaraya preserves a *wabi* (cultivated simplicity) style, a tea-ceremony aesthetic," comparable to the reticence of the nearby imperial villas.

Its sovereign blessing, though, is simply service. "Here in Japan we talk of *okyaku-sama* (customers), and give them the same honorific as an emperor or a god," says Yuko Yuasa, a cultured Japanese scholar, "and we mean it often in a warm, and slightly cynical, way. But in somewhere like the Tawaraya, a guest really is treated like a king." When I went out for a walk my first day in the inn, dawdling for twenty minutes in the library en route, I came out to find my shoes laid out on a clean-washed stone; my maid was there to see me off; the shoe-keeper handed me an umbrella in case it rained; and as I walked away, my maid stood at the entrance, bowing and bowing until I was out of her sight.

Once upon a generation ago, such delicacy and decorum were part of our stereotypes of a quaint, gossamer Japan of cherry-blossoms and *geisha*. Yet as Japan and the U.S. have traded places, eco-

---

> *W*hen we bow *"Oyasuminasai!"* to one another, the rough equivalent to "pleasant dreams," Kazue-san starts to giggle. She says my house makes her feel joy. Here, she's a child again. She tells me it's been years since she's slept in a *tatami* room, on the floor, snuggled between *futon*.
>
> "What about at a *ryokan*?" I ask. Surely she's slept on *tatami* at a traditional Japanese inn.
>
> "Yes," she nods thoughtfully. "But a *ryokan* is a kind of make-believe. That's the point. We visit temples or famous tea houses on vacations. We stay in a *ryokan* and it makes us feel good about our serene and beautiful Japanese life. But how many people really live like that anymore? We live in apartments, cement boxes, in cities that are noisy and huge."
>
> ◆
>
> —Cathy N. Davidson,
> *36 Views of Mt. Fuji: On Finding
> Myself in Japan*

nomically, it has grown increasingly hard, even for the Japanese, to discern their traditional values of spareness and elegance. The Japanese sun has risen again thanks largely to its masculine powers. Thus the grace of a place like Tawaraya, as of the city around it, is that it serves as a monument to the feminine, the private, the imaginative Japan. Where modern Japan is full of energy, it instills a sense of calm. Where contemporary Tokyo is all speed, it teaches one slowness. And where modern Japan produces objects as impersonal and practical as the Honda Civic and the Walkman, it is particular and personal.

Such virtues are especially precious in the old capital of Kyoto, the soul and source of Japanese tradition, and long a kind of shrine to the religion that is Japan. Now, though, it seems that the same men who are celebrating the city's 1200th birthday are trying to demolish it. The number of cars in Kyoto's narrow lanes has risen from 5,000 after the war to 450,000 today; in the past decade alone, 40,000 *machiya*, or traditional wooden houses, have been razed to the ground. Only last year, over the vehement protests of monks, a new fourteen-story hotel was built downtown, disfiguring a skyline that had remained unchanged since the time of Genji. Now, many fear that the city will be turned into a kind of theme-park replica of itself, served up for the 40 million tourists who visit every year.

In that context, Tawaraya, with its light-dimming switches catching reflections off the paper screens, is a model of how to move with the times in order to stay where you are. Like Issey Miyake or Isamu Noguchi, in fact, the inn has preserved a highly distinctive and traditional Japanese style in part by incorporating elements from the modern and the foreign world (Mrs. Satow includes items from Indonesia, China, and Egypt). "The spirit of Tawaraya has not changed in 300 years," she says, "but the style has to change to keep that spirit alive." Thus Tawaraya is not just an antique on the country's mantelpiece; it is more like the *rakkon*, or elegant red stamp, inscribed in the right-hand corner of the country's self-portrait, to show its maker. Or, indeed, like the only other visitor I saw in my days in the Tawaraya: a famously rebellious apprentice *geisha*, now launching the first lawsuit in history against the *geisha*-world, who came shuffling out of the darkness early one evening, in six-inch wooden sandals and silk kimono, and slipped into the inn, a huge black boom-box in her hands.

Pico Iyer also contributed "I Feel Coke" in Part One.

We do not dislike everything that shines, but we do prefer a pensive luster to a shallow brilliance, a murky light that, whether in a stone or an artifact, bespeaks a sheen of antiquity.

Of course this "sheen of antiquity" of which we hear so much is in fact the *glow of grime*. In both Chinese and Japanese the words denoting this glow describe a polish that comes of being touched over and over again, a sheen produced by the oils that naturally permeate an object over long years of handling—which is to say grime. If indeed "elegance is frigid," it can as well be described as filthy. There is no denying, at any rate, that among the elements of the elegance in which we take such delight is a measure of the unclean, the unsanitary. I suppose I shall sound terribly defensive if I say that Westerners attempt to expose every speck of grime and eradicate it, while we Orientals carefully preserve and even idealize it. Yet for better or for worse we do love things that bear the marks of grime, soot, and weather, and we love the colors and the sheen that call to mind the past that made them. Living in these old houses among these old objects is in some mysterious way a source of peace and repose.

—Jun'ichiro Tanizaki, *In Praise of Shadows*

MARY ROACH

* * *

Monster in a *Ryokan*

*Crushing rules and furniture like Godzilla, an ungainly
American sent the locals running for cover
in a traditional Japanese inn.*

A MONSTER IS A RELATIVE THING. IN GODZILLA'S HOMETOWN, everyone was fifty feet tall and scaly. The sidewalks were wide enough that no one had to trample parked cars and knock over buildings. Only in Tokyo did Godzilla become a monster.

Likewise myself. In my own country, I am not thought of as brutish and rude—or anyway, no more so than the next slob. But in Japan, I am suddenly huge and clueless. I sprout extra limbs and make loud, unintelligible noises. In Japan, I am a monster.

I came to this conclusion following a recent stay at a *ryokan*, a traditional Japanese inn. It was raining the night I flew in to Tokyo, and the cab had dropped me at the wrong place. Having walked the remaining distance, stopping every few blocks to perform the quaint flailing pantomime of the lost foreigner, I was drenched and disheveled by the time I arrived at the right place.

I lumbered down the foot-path, crashing into bicycles and trampling tiny ornamental trees. As I opened the door, several of the staff could be seen fleeing from the room. Others crouched behind traditional Japanese furnishings, which, though pleasing to the eye, offer little in the way of protective cover.

183

"HRRARGGHH ARGGHH HAARGH RARRRRHSCHRVRANN."
(Hello, I have a reservation.)

I lurched forward and stepped up to the reception window. The woman's face crumbled in distress. A large portion of this appeared to be directed at my feet. She pointed to a shelf of shoes and then she pointed to mine. The shoes on the shelf were dainty and immaculate. The shoes on my feet were wet and battered and huge.

I apologized for the size and condition of my footwear. This was not the problem. The problem was that I was wearing them *inside the ryokan.*

As an American, I was raised to believe that the simple act of passing one's soles across a nubbly plastic mat sporting a cute saying will somehow magically dislodge an accumulated eight hours of filth, muck, and germs. The Japanese do not share our faith in doormats. The Japanese remove their shoes at the door.

As a *ryokan* guest, you are expected to do the same. Inside the front door is a bench for you to sit on and take off your shoes. This is normally located directly across from the reception window, enabling the staff to tell at a glance that your socks a) don't match, b) need washing, and c) have little threadbare patches at the heels. You are then provided with a pair of Japanese slippers, which are open in the back so that the staff, over the course of your visit, can see that, indeed, all of your socks have threadbare heels.

The slippers, you soon learn, are special hallway slippers, not to be worn inside the rooms. In the rooms you wear only socks. That is, unless you are in the toilet room, in which case you exchange your special hallway slippers for special toilet slippers, which are never, under penalty of shame and humiliation, to be worn anywhere but the toilet.

I do not mean to imply that Japanese people are needlessly fastidious. I mean to imply that Americans are needlessly squalid—especially in hotels. In American hotels, the whole idea is to create as much of a mess as possible, as someone else will be cleaning it up. Do unto others as you figure they'd do unto you if you had a job cleaning hotel rooms.

Properly shod, I was shown to my room. It was approximately

nine feet square and contained three or four pieces of traditional ankle-high furniture. To someone accustomed to the vast prairies and vistas of the American hotel room, this takes getting used to. In America, a single-occupancy room must contain a bed—heck, make it two!—large enough to accommodate lumberjacks and NBA centers lying spread-eagle in any direction. Though guests will be leaving their belongings strewn about the bed and floor, there must be a dresser, a desk, and a closet the size of Maine. There must be six bars of soap and a telephone in the bathroom. A *ryokan* room, on the other hand, serves the simple purpose for which it was designed: that is, to provide a neat, comfortable place to sleep for a few nights.

Though I appreciated the rational scale and modest aesthetics of my accommodations, I was nonetheless hopelessly disoriented. I kept running into walls and stumbling over traditional ankle-high furniture. Someone had spread bedding out all over the floor, which caused me to trip and smash headlong into a low-hanging lantern. Tea cups were capsized. Miniature dressers toppled and rolled. Soon the Japanese national guard would arrive with rifles and tranquilizer darts.

I tried to get a grip on myself. Thrashing violently in a small Japanese room is a dangerous proposition, as the walls are fashioned not from plaster, but from delicate sheets of waxy rice paper. It's like living inside a Dixie Cup. One false step and you come crashing through to the adjoining room, which in this case happened to be a carp pond, and god only knows what sort of slippers are required for that.

I decided to go soak in the tub. Like other large reptiles, I am plodding and ungainly on land, but surprisingly graceful underwater. I asked the staff for a robe and entered the steamy, tiled sanctum. To my great relief, the bath was already drawn and everything seemed self-explanatory.

Later, back in my room, I noticed a small booklet on the table. It was called *Information on How to Enjoy a Ryokan*—a "guide book" to "living, eating, and sleeping as the Japanese do." According to a section titled "Tips for Taking a Bath," I had committed no less than three ablutionary offenses. For starters, the bathtub is not for bathing, but for relaxing. To soap and rinse yourself inside the tub is an unthinkable act, akin to peeing in the pool or drinking milk straight from the carton. The cute plastic baskets are not floating soap dishes; they are for storing your clothes. The traditional Japanese robe closes left side over right, not right over left, and is called a *yukata*, not—as I had called it—a *yakuza*. (*Yakuza* are Japanese mafiosi, the guys who chop off their pinkies for dishonorable behavior, such as cowardice or soaping oneself in the tub.)

While I contemplated my sins, there was a knock (rustle? thwap?) on the wax paper. It was the proprietress, bearing a tray of tea. She seemed displeased. "I'm sorry about the soap," I blurted. "I didn't see the instruction book."

She smiled—the sort of bemused, resigned smile Fay Wray used to give King Kong after he tipped over the garage or stepped on the house pets. Without a word, she set down the tray and left.

Shortly thereafter, I noticed the toilet slippers on my feet. It was almost a relief. Every wrong thing that could be done had been done. I could only go uphill from here. I rested my huge wet head on my little prehensile arms and went to sleep.

Mary Roach has traveled to all seven continents, yet to this day she cannot remember to order special meals. She has written about her travels for Salon, Islands, Condé Nast Traveler, Health, Vogue *and* American Way. *She lives in San Francisco with her husband Ed and their three pieces of luggage.*

⁜

Ah, the *furo*. I had been looking forward to meditating in the hot tub ever since I first learned about it in my Japanese class at the local community college. And here I was, at last in Japan, the home of the hot-tub soak.

We arrived in Kobe after the lengthy flight from New York, which included another plane from Narita airport to Osaka and then a bus ride to our destination. Not possessing the ability to sleep while in transit I was exhausted and looking forward to embracing a bed. However, I discovered my longed-for tub in the hotel room that had been assigned to me.

Sleep could go begging, I thought, here was my *furo*. I prepared for immersion while the tub filled with hot water. Over the high side wall I climbed and sat down in the small square tub. I soaked and sighed great sighs of contentment. Fatigue finally won out and I ached for sleep. I attempted to leave this paradise. But it was not to be, I am a tall woman and while I could bend my knees to fit into the tub, I couldn't unbend them to emerge. I looked for a handle or anything to grab onto to rise from the water. There was nothing. In my exhaustion all I could think of was my epitaph—"She died, trapped in a *furo*." Finally, rocking my entire body, my hands were able to catch onto the edge of the connecting sink and I pulled myself out of my temporary prison.

—Marge Wyngaarden, *"Nippon No Tabi"*

PART THREE

GOING YOUR OWN WAY

探

(Quest)

JAMES D. HOUSTON

* * *

Unforgettable

You're going to do what to that shrimp?!

I FEEL COMPELLED TO INCLUDE THIS DINNER PARTY WE WERE
invited to a while back, where I had the chance to talk with a fellow who sounds a lot like one of our neighbors in the States. He
watches the concentration of money in the hands of a few very
powerful families and consortiums, and he doesn't like the effects
of this. Property values go up and up. He works long hours with
fewer rewards awaiting him in the future.

"Nobody in Japan can buy a house now," he says. "My parents
have this house. But the younger people…everyone works long
hours, and we save our money. We are all very good about saving
money, as you know. I don't remember the percentages. Better than
in the U.S., I think. But what difference does it make? We are supposed to be one of the richest nations in the world. This is what
you hear today. But what is 'rich'? What does it mean to be rich
when you can work for your entire life and not be able to earn
enough money to buy a house?"

I will call him Reijiro. We are sitting on *tatami* mats on the floor
of his family's dining room, around a low wooden table inlaid with
mother-of-pearl. He is a slender fellow, as are most young Japanese
men. Except among the wrestlers, you seldom see obesity here,

191

male or female, seldom see anyone you would call "heavy." Reijiro has a narrow waist, wide shoulders, slightly curly hair (perhaps some family gene from Okinawa).

His eyes are full of questions. He doesn't speak much English, but his sister does. She studied it for years, and for a while she dated an American man from Texas. She translates what her brother can't say. The sister, Kimiko, is 28. Reijiro is 30. He works in a camera shop. She does clerical work and moonlights nights at a karaoke bar. Neither of them has married yet. Neither owns a car. They use subways and buses. They both still live at home because it's cheaper. The father isn't here much. He spends most of his time in Tokyo. A businessman, they say. Sometimes they don't see him for six or seven months. It was an arranged marriage, so the mother and the father have never been close. "No love," Kimiko will tell us later on.

Information trickles out during an hour or so of sipping sake. They are friends of some friends, and they have invited us for a dinner toward the end of the season the Japanese call "Forget the Year." It corresponds roughly to our Christmas season and occupies most of December. They are intrigued with the idea of getting to know some Americans, who are not as visible here as in Tokyo and Kyoto. Maybe the cultural mixture appeals to them too. Jeanne has brought a conversation pocket dictionary, which she holds in her lap for ready reference. So we are laughing and sipping and groping along in a kind of broken bilingual chatter, which grows easier after the sake cups have been refilled a few times.

No one in the family has been to America, but they have seen the films and a lot of TV coverage and they have listened to the songs. They want to know how many cars we have. They want to know what we think about Japan. They want to know about our families. They tell us about theirs. In the room where we sit, half of one wall is occupied by the family altar. Two folding doors stand open to reveal shelving decorated with gold leaf, a golden Buddha, columns of fresh chrysanthemums. Above a low table with candles and with incense sticks in a bowl, there are small framed photos of grandparents and great-grandparents. On another wall, directly above our heads, hang larger portraits of the grandparents wearing traditional dress, kimono and *yukata*. Beside these, a framed panel shows their names in thick black calligraphy, and over each name a grandparent has left a red handprint, thread lines of white across the palms. They preside over the afternoon and evening and all the food and drink we are about to consume—the ancestral portraits and the bright red prints of the hands of the grandparents who have been dead for many years.

After an hour of sipping, the food begins to appear, one dish at a time, delivered from the kitchen by the gracious and self-effacing mother, who bows and mutters an apology each time she sets something fabulous before us. It is odd to watch this. Kimiko the daughter is outspoken, bold, vivacious. She usually wears jeans, leather jacket, scarlet lipstick. Today it's a smart blouse and miniskirt. She pours our sake with a *geisha* bow that is also a parody of a *geisha* bow, having some fun with the tradition of the sub-servient female.

"Jim-san, Jeanne-san," says Kimiko with a playful smirk and a glance at our empty cups, "we are honored that our Fukuoka sake pleases you so much."

> ───)───
>
> At noon the Fujitas' grandmother asked me to take a break from my photography to join her family for lunch. She was planning to serve a rural delicacy that is now rarely eaten by the Japanese. In the kitchen, she placed a two-inch cube of tofu (bean curd) and several small, live eels at the center of lacquer bowls. Just before the soup was served, she poured soup stock into each bowl. To escape the heat, the eels plunged into the cool tofu and smothered.
>
> ◆
>
> —Linda Butler, *Rural Japan: Radiance of the Ordinary*

She is in a way imitating her mother, yet not mocking her. They both enjoy the daughter's little game. The mother dresses in a plainer, older style of western clothing, slacks, a simple sweater. Not dowdy, but more sedate. There are probably kimonos hanging in a

closet somewhere, but this is not a kimono day. You seldom see
them now, unless it's a formal occasion, like the photos the grandparents posed for, or New Year's at the local shrine, when everyone in the neighborhood is out buying good-luck charms, burning last year's charms, and promenading in the courtyard. Later we
learn that the mother, Nobu-san, grew up on a farm in this region,
where her people have lived and farmed for a thousand years. Her
parents negotiated with a well-to-do city family, so she had married "up," as they say, the first from her family to leave the countryside and move into town.

We start with *tsukemono*, homemade by Nobu-san, bits of pickled carrot, turnip, cucumber. Then comes roe of halibut, clusters of
golden fish eggs. We have salty/sweet black beans the size of
peanuts and cooked to be eaten like peanuts, one at a time. We
have strips of salmon, an inch or so wide and rolled into bite-size
morsels, and daikon that has been cooked in a broth of beef and
beef gristle, and tiny shrimp, their bodies the size of the end of
your finger, fried spicy and eaten whole, and beef seared on the
outside, still raw at the center, and another kind of fish egg, very
small and red, smaller than pin-heads and presented with thin-
sliced squid. And there are glistening silver shrimp about eight
inches long, served alive, so that their feelers are still waving around
as the platter is set upon the table. On their undersides the tentacles are flailing. The idea is to select one, break off the head, peel
the skin immediately, and eat the raw, living flesh.

Jeanne and I are not squeamish about exotic dishes, but we can't
go this far. I identify with the shrimp, squirming as if they know
their minutes are numbered. But Nobu-san, the self-effacing
mother who has prepared most of this food back in the kitchen
with the help of her microwave, has now joined us at the table. She
has emptied her first cup of sake, poured by Kimiko. She gestures
for another, then reaches with both hands and breaks off a shrimp's
head, dips the flesh into her side dish of soy sauce and horseradish,
and announces in her soft, motherly voice that this is indeed
"*Oishi*." Delicious.

It is about this time that a second platoon of visitors shows up, friends of the family, a man named Kato, with his wife and their 15-year-old son. Kato looks about 45, a muscular fellow with a rascal glint in his eye. He is a marble cutter who was once a fisherman. He had brought along some *sashimi*, a specialty from the small offshore island where he grew up. His wife carries a platter of what smells like Kentucky Fried Chicken.

Kato's older son is a sumo wrestler who did well in the recent tournament. This is like having a son playing in the NFL. He is the proudest of fathers, was probably something of an athlete himself in his day. We pass around some photos of the husky, bulging son, while Kato and his wife begin to catch up with the party by downing two fast shots each from a quart of Johnny Walker Red Label that has appeared from somewhere. He wants to know if I speak any Japanese.

"*Sumi-ma-sen,*" I say. "*Nihongo-ga wakari-ma-sen.*" ("Please forgive me, I don't know any Japanese.")

He gazes across the table for a moment, as if deciding how to handle this. At last he says, "*¿Como está?*"

"*Muy bien,*" I say.

"*¿Habla Español?*"

"*Un poco,*" I say.

"*Si, muy poco,*" he says with a laugh, pointing a finger at himself, at the tip of his nose.

He bites off some sashimi and takes a long pull of the Johnny Walker and says, "*Parlez-vous Français?*"

"*Un petit peu,*" I say.

"*Voulez vous de cognac?*" he says, lifting the bottle.

"*Merci, non,*" I say, pointing to the sake.

"Ah, sake," says Kato, framing his face with widespread fingers. I look at Kimiko to translate.

"Makes your eyes bright," she says.

As a young man Kato lived for four years in the Canary Islands, he explains, via Kimiko, so he has met fishermen from all around the Mediterranean. "*Molto bono,*" he says, pointing to his platter of Kentucky Fried.

While the chicken and the *sashimi* are making the rounds, one of the long silver shrimp leaps into the air, startling everyone. It has been lying there for half an hour as if dead. Suddenly it springs to life, makes a twitching arc across the table, and lands on another platter a foot and a half away. Kato-san takes it as a sign that this shrimp's moment has finally come. He grabs it and breaks the head off and peels the shell from the body. He dips the quivering flesh into his little cup of sauce and gives it a gleeful chomp.

"*Oishi-des*," says the mother. ("It's tasty, eh.")

"*Muchas gracias*," says Kato with his rascal smile. Many graces. Much thanks. To the shrimp. To the whiskey. To the hostess-cook.

Reijiro decides it is music time. He rises from the table, slides back a *shoji* screen decorated with a garden scene, bonsai trees, a rippling brook. In the next room he has what looks like a thousand-dollar sound system. He wants to know if we recognize the voice on his newest CD. He comes back in and stands watching us, awaiting our reactions, as we listen.

It's a new reissue of Bobby Vinton singing "Blue Velvet." When I tell him Jeanne and I grew up with Bobby and that there will always be a place in our hearts for this song, a huge grin fills his face.

Again he slips past the *shoji* screen. "Blue Velvet" fades away. The next thing we hear is Natalie Cole singing "The Very Thought of You." I tell Reijiro we grew up with this song too, but we love it even more.

"*Arigato go-zai-mas*," I say with a low bow to the table. ("Thank you very much.")

At this he bows deeply from the waist, grateful that I have allowed him to please us with this choice of song. Kimiko tells us it is his CD of the season, his "most favorite."

"*Domo*," he says. "*Domo arigato go-zai-mashita!*" ("My gratitude runneth over.")

This is of course the hit collection *Unforgettable*, featuring all of Nat King Cole's great tunes from the 1940s and '50s as re-sung by his daughter. What astounds us is that everyone at the table knows the words to all these songs—Kato the marble cutter who once lived in the Canary Islands, and Kato's wife and their 15-year-old son who, until this song, has not opened his mouth, and Kimiko, age 28, the daughter who once dated a man from Texas, and Reijiro, age 30, who claims to know very little English, and Nobu-san, the 55-year-old mother who knows no English at all. When "Mona Lisa" comes on, Nobu's lips begin to move, as she sings quietly to herself. Pretty soon everyone's lips are moving, humming.

I don't think what happens next could have happened much earlier. Without a few drinks to loosen everyone up, they would not be willing to sing aloud in front of their American visitors and risk humiliation for mispronouncing words. But now some time has passed. Some trust has accumulated. To the kinship that comes with food and drink, we are ready to add the kinship of song. One by one we start singing along with the recording, led by Kato-san and by Reijiro, who can hardly contain his passion for these lyrics.

"Mona Risa, Mona Risa, men have name you. You so rike a raydee wis a mystic smire…"

By the time the album's title song comes through the speakers, some kind of dreamy-eyed, head-wagging nostalgia has taken over the room. They mouth these tunes and hum along with an amazing mix of familiarity and affection. We are all swaying with the melody of "Unforgettable," as if the double-track voices of the famous father and the devoted daughter singing this early '50s classic has transported them all back to the same high school dances Jeanne and I carry around in our personal data banks of pop song memories. Not to that exact place in the memory bank. But maybe somewhere similar.

That's how it looks and feels, at any rate. You never know for sure what's running through another person's mind. You can only guess. Are they just acting dreamy-eyed to make us feel at home? According to the legend, the Japanese are supposed to be inscrutable, mysterious, and governed by rules we Westerners will never understand, the kind of people who will sooner or later sneak up on you when you least expect it. But I have a hunch that just the opposite may be true, given the way the world is going.

Maybe they are starting to remind us of someone we know too well. They love to eat. They love to sing and party. They love to drink. They drink more than is good for them. They get

sentimental. They are shameless consumers. They wear jeans and
running shoes and ball caps. They line up at McDonald's. They are
sports nuts and media nuts. They love high-tech equipment. They
covet brand names. Meanwhile, their political leaders move in and
out of the corporate power structure, in and out of favor, in and
out of scandal and disgrace. Maybe the Japanese are a little too familiar now, like a brother you grew up with who learned whatever
he knows from the same place you learned it, and when he annoys
you it is because he reminds you of yourself.

When the song ends, and our voices subside, Kato-san bows
with a silly grin and says, "*Muchas gracias. Très bien.*"

We all break into loud applause. For Nat. For Natalie. For
Reijiro's CD. For the black beans and the *sashimi* and the Kentucky
Fried Chicken and the strips of salmon and the salty, savory fin-
gertip shrimp, for the Fukuoka sake and the Johnny Walker and
the spectacle of the long silver cylinders of shrimp still wiggling on
their platter. We applaud the mother who has prepared this feast,
whose family has farmed the same farm for a thousand years, and
the grandparents too, who have watched and listened from the
gold-leafed altar and from the wall overhead, their bold red hand-
prints shining as if the ink were wet and fresh.

James D. Houston also contributed "Sandbath Resurrection" in Part Two.

⋇

"Now I will teach you the proper way to eat Japanese food," Denver
said with characteristic enthusiasm as he returned to his seat. "First, take
a little rice and put it in your mouth. Then take some meat, and finally
some salad."

I followed his instructions as he spoke.

"Now chew them all together at once. Rice. Meat. Salad. These are
the three sides of the triangle."

Soon all of the students at our table of desks were demonstrating the
proper technique. "One, two, three, chew. One, two, three, mix."

"You see, rice has no taste," he explained. "So it is best to take other
food and mix it with the rice. This is why we don't use plates at home.
Each person holds a small bowl of rice while we place several serving

plates of food in the center of the table. We pick up the food with our chopsticks, bounce it on our rice, and then put it in our mouths. This way the food tastes more delicious, and it's better for your health."

"How can putting all of that food into your mouth at one time be good for your health?" I asked.

Some of the students giggled at the question.

"It's not *how* you eat," he said. "It's *what* you eat."

By now most of the students had finished their meal and were straining to hear our conversation.

"In Japan, we have certain eating habits," he continued. "When we are young—like these students—we eat a lot of meat. It's good for us while we're growing up. But when we get a little older—like I am—we begin to eat more and more traditional Japanese food, such as mountain vegetables and *miso* soup [a plain broth made from soybean paste]. By the time we get older—like the principal—we eat *only* Japanese style food."

—Bruce S. Feiler, *Learning to Bow: Inside the Heart of Japan*

* * *

Land of Wonder,
Land of Kindness

Biking at night brings delight, anxiety, and a welcome encounter.

YAKUSHIMA IS A VOLCANIC MOLAR OF LUSHLY VEGETATED ROCK that rises out of the Pacific between Kyushu (the southernmost of the four main Japanese islands) and Okinawa. It is, in my own words, a Japanese Galapagos—home to rare and unique ecosystems, harboring plants and animals found nowhere else in the world—and the short honeymoon week I spent there with my wife showed us not only how beautiful rural Japan is, but also just how kind its island-folk can be.

My wife, Nozomi, is Japanese. I met her while teaching English in a small city on mainland Kyushu, and it was she who initially told me about this amazing island. Yakushima is one of few places in the world where one can go from tropical coral reefs to alpine tundra—on the peak of the highest mountain in all of Kyushu. On random beaches between the scatter of dark, jagged coastline, sea-turtles come ashore in the spring to lay their eggs. The forests are made of Yaku cedar trees, some of them living for 3000 years, others more than 130 feet in diameter. It also harbors its own unique species of several Japanese flowers, as well as Yaku monkeys, and the shy Yaku deer.

To save the ferry charge (ours was a low-budget honeymoon), we'd decided not to take our car, but rather to bicycle from the ferry to our camp, a challenging but certainly do-able 58 kilometers. What we hadn't counted on was the heat—110 degrees in the shade, and what we'd thought would take an afternoon had taken two full days. While the week spent camping and sightseeing was wonderful, the return trip hung heavy in the backs of our minds, and eventually we decided to bike back to the ferry at night to avoid the unbearable heat.

"And that way," my wife said optimistically, "we can sleep on the ferry and save the cost of a night in a hotel!"

Night-time biking turned out to be a wonderful way to travel—and as we coasted silently down the shallow hills, I was surprised to find myself enjoying an entirely different side to the island: its smells. Undistracted by sight, I found myself marking the journey not by the island's vistas and brilliant azure waters but rather by what my nose could identify—a farmer's field, freshly fertilized; cool moisture on a bridge above a rushing stream; horses; forest; monkey dung; heady tropical flowers; and, occasionally, the smell of salt from the shores we were leaving behind.

About an hour into the trip, my flashlight became loose, and, while trying to attach it more securely to my handlebars, I dropped it soundly on the unforgiving pavement.

I'd broken it, and then we had only one light between us! Even though driving while under any influence (even traces) of alcohol is not permitted, neither Nozomi nor I were comfortable with the idea of continuing the trip without each of us having a bright light to alert unwary drivers. Unfortunately, we had no choice. Our ferry left early the next morning, and we estimated the ride might take as long as ten hours. Light or no light, we had to keep going.

By ten o'clock p.m., we'd climbed much of the "hilliest" part, and were looking forward to a long series of smooth downhills, when Nozomi screeched to a halt just past a store that appeared to be open.

"Maybe we can get batteries, and even a bulb to fix the light."

"Great," I said. "Go in and ask."

"No," she said. "You go."

She wouldn't go in and ask because one of my wife's peculiarities is a phobia of talking to people she doesn't know. Thus it was I, speaking only a small amount of Japanese, who went inside to discuss flashlights, while she, the native and fluent one, stayed outside and sipped a cola, bathed in the florescent glow of the vending machines.

There were three women at the counter when I walked in, and my blond hair and 5'9" height instantly stopped their conversation. In the silence I walked up, then down, the tiny, cluttered aisles, looking for batteries.

Because they see so few foreigners, the Japanese often make assumptions about visitors' ability to speak Japanese, and it's a great benefit, once one has become partially fluent—to overhear what might otherwise have been spoken in a much lower voice. Thus, when the conversation resumed, I feigned absorption in the ingredients of a *sukiyaki* sauce and listened.

"So handsome," whispered one of the older women to the young one. "Look at his blond hair."

"What's he doing?"

"I don't know…"

Again, the older to the younger, "Are you going to marry a foreigner someday?"

Knowing Nozomi was tapping her foot outside, I interrupted in fluent but accent-laden Japanese: "Excuse me ladies, but, do you have any batteries for a flashlight by any chance?"

"Oh," tittered the older lady, "he speaks Japanese!"

I gathered by this time that she was the owner of the store, and the attractive girl at the counter was her daughter. The third, middle-aged woman, was a friend who had stopped in for some evening gossip perhaps.

"You speak Japanese very well," said the friend, smiling.

"Oh, not-so-well I'm afraid. I make many mistakes." This was in keeping, I hoped, with the Japanese custom of being modest.

"No, it's very good!" exclaimed the owner, beaming, delighted to have a new direction for the conversation.

"Where are you from?" asked the friend.

"Kagoshima," I said, enigmatically. I knew they wanted to know which country I was from, but as I had married a Japanese woman and considered Kagoshima not only my destination but to a large degree my home, I left it at that.

"What country are you from?" asked the owner, smiling broadly.

"Oh," I answered, "America."

"America," the two ladies said in unison. "Oooh!"

And then, as I was preparing to get to the matter at hand, as often happened in many a Kagoshima conversation, the friend said that she had a relative who had mar-

———)———

I met a man on an overnight boat going from Osaka to Matsuyama. We enjoyed each others company and he invited me to stay a night with his wife and two young boys. I did, and we had a wonderful time together. I wrote them a letter when I returned to the U.S. but never heard back. My bicultural friend Hiroshi said that they would not write back for fear of displaying their less than perfect English.

♦

—George Vincent Wright, "A World of Bathhouses"

ried an American. Every time I heard about an intercultural marriage there I was touched because Kagoshima's people—despite being bombed severely by the Americans during World War II— always seemed happy and even proud to talk about their contact with foreigners.

"He was a very nice man," she said. "She lives in San Francisco now."

"Are you married?" asked the owner, eyeing my ring.

"Yes, my wife's outside."

"Oh, too bad!" she laughed, elbowing her daughter who tittered shyly, a hand politely covering her mouth.

"What are you two doing though, at this time of night?" asked the friend.

"Biking to Miyanoura City."

"WHAT?!!" all three gasped, even the girl.

"You're making your wife bike eight hours?"

"Well," I began, "it really isn't that bad. We both like biking…" but the damage was done. I could see from their shocked expressions that I had, once again, impressed on those three how odd Americans are, and I knew that weeks would pass before they stopped talking about us. I decided to cut my losses and run.

"Do you have any flashlight batteries?" I asked.

"Oh, of course we do!" said the girl, brightly, reaching down under the counter and pulling out a packaged set of C cells. "Will these do?"

"Perfect! And do you have replacement bulbs?"

"Certainly." She bent down again and popped up with one.

"Oh open it!" said the owner. "Here in the store where there's good light! No point in fiddling around out in the dark. Are you sure your wife doesn't want to come in?"

"No, I'm—"

"Ask her!"

So I opened the door (the ladies peering out behind me) and called to Nozomi to come inside.

"I'm fine!" she called.

"Oh! She's Japanese!" said the friend, beaming, proud. "Japanese make very good wives, you know."

"Well, she's not quite 'typical' Japanese…" I began, but was interrupted by the owner putting her hand in mock sadness on her daughter's shoulder.

"You missed your chance!"

"But why are you making her bike all that way in the dark?"

Fixing my light quickly, I thanked the three of them and left, waving goodbye as Nozomi and I peddled our red-blinking rears and white flashlighted steeds off into the darkness. We were through the little town in a flash, and soon slicing through the dark, quiet, countryside absorbed, again, by the sea of smells.

I had just finished recounting the events in the store when a dog came bursting out of the darkness, barking madly, chasing us for a few feet before finishing with a few final barks.

Oddly, that one dog triggered a case of the night bogeys in both of us—soon we were peering into the darkness trying to discern lurking dogs, pulling our bikes off to the side to let cars pass by, our hearts pounding as we pedaled.

We really got worried, however, when a white mini-van passed us, turned around ahead just within sight, came back past us again, then turned around behind us.

Japan is magnitudes safer than the United States, and yet, oddly, in that post-dog darkness, the night closed in and I found myself, as the van slowed down and began following us up a short hill, readying myself for the worst. My knees started aching from the excess of adrenalin, yet I resolved to keep cool.

Then the car stopped, and, to our great relief, a woman's voice called out: "Do you need a ride?"

Nozomi pulled over, and I followed. The van pulled closer, and then the stranger shot out a burst of Japanese that I didn't understand. Nozomi turned to me:

"Do you know this woman? She says she met you somewhere."

I squinted to see through the reflection on the windshield who was inside. When she hopped out I broke into a smile—it was the "friend" who I'd been talking with inside the store.

"I have to pick up my husband in Anbou," she said. "I saw you two biking along, and since I've got this mini-van..."

"No, we really couldn't impose," said Nozomi, but I could tell from her expression that the idea of a free trip as far as Anbou was attractive.

"No," I added, "we really can't...two bikes, they wouldn't fit...."

"No," the woman beamed, "I can take down the seat. I even brought plastic wrap to protect the cushions!"

"Well..." said Nozomi cautiously.

"If it's really not a problem..." I added. I had the advantage because, being a foreigner, I could be "rude" here and there and people would let it slide. If Nozomi, being Japanese, was rude, it would be far more offensive.

"No, it's no problem at all!" she said, smiling ear-to-ear. "In fact, it was getting lonely driving all by myself, and I'd love the company!"

So, ten minutes later, we were rumbling along at 60 kph towards Anbou, Sasahara-san chatting merrily away with Nozomi, me looking out the window at the no-longer-frightening darkness, amazed at the charity we had stumbled upon. In the warm car, I realized what a luxury it is to live in a country that is actually safe—where one doesn't have to worry about psychopaths or murderers and where hitchhiking is actually a valid mode of transportation. A fellow teacher of mine never even rode his bike to his various schools—but rather spent three years doing all his commuting via the thumb, and he was never short of tales, yet never once had to worry if his life would be in danger. I felt guilty—after the ride (Sasahara-san took us almost the entire way, driving two hours past her destination before pulling over and saying goodbye), pedaling the remaining hour with the lights of Miyanoura in sight—thinking about what similar treatment a trusting Japanese in the States might get.

Of course, Sasahara-san's kindness created a new dilemma—as we had planned on biking through the night, we had no hotel reservations, and many of the smaller, less-expensive hotels and *ryokans* had already closed for the night.

"Of course," grinned Nozomi, "the four star *Shiisaido* Hotel Yakushima is still open…and still has vacancies…"

Later, lying down on the immaculate bed, having handed our sweaty backpacks to the smiling *Shiisaido* porter, I couldn't help but think that my time in Yakushima had been similar to what I'd found all over Japan: very beautiful landscapes and friendly, kind-hearted people. The unexpected ride had been a perfect ending for a wonderful honeymoon.

My only regret, is, of course, that like so many debts to so many people, we can never return the favor to Sasahara-san. We sent a postcard, but were unsure of the address, and never heard a

reply...so if you happen to visit Yakushima, please stop by a grocery store in Onoma and say hi for my wife and me.

Ray Bartlett is the author of In the Sunlight of Sakurajima, *from which
this story was excerpted. He lives in Massachusetts.*

✳

Jeanne and the wife of Shimazawa-san begin to talk, half in Japanese, half
in English, which she once studied at the university. With Jeanne here, the
wife suggests, perhaps she can practice her English on a regular basis.
When Jeanne tells her she already speaks very well, the left hand flies up
to her face, waving back and forth as if insects have attacked her.
    "No no no no no, my Engrish very bad."
    Whether the English is good or bad is not the point, of course. We will
see this gesture repeatedly, everywhere we go, the head inclining, the hand
brushing past the face, the frantic wave of denial, waving away every kind
of compliment.
    "No no no no no, my English no good."
    "No no no no no, the food too cold."
    "No no no no no, my son should try harder in school."
                —James D. Houston, *In the Ring of Fire: A Pacific Journey*

MICHAEL FESSLER

* * *

The Tangerine Buddha

You never know what's at the end of the tunnel.

I CAME TO TOKYO AT THE AGE OF FORTY-ONE. I WAS A TEACHER, mainly. I had had an interesting life up to that point, seen a lot of interesting places, met interesting people, but in the process I had ruined myself financially. My net worth was zero; actuarially speaking I was not on the screen. I owned nothing, I was a non-statistic. So what did I have to lose by going East? Exactly: nothing. My projected schedule was a year in Japan. After that, we would see. I felt I would not be a whole person—of this planet anyway—until I had experienced Asia.

My first days in Tokyo were spent at a small *ryokan*, or Japanese inn. Though this little place was tucked behind a gas station, it was very Japanesey, the manager humble and inscrutable, *shamisen* music was always plucking, water dripping, and bamboo plonking down on stone. Unfortunately, as inexpensive as it was, it was too expensive for me. If I were going to spend a year in Tokyo, I would have to get something dirt-cheap. And that was how I found Edo House.

One afternoon of my first week I was hanging around Shinjuku and somebody told me about *gaijin* houses. *Gaijin* are westerners— me. Maybe you. *Gaijin* houses were cheap places, communal, shared bathing facilities, etc. They were cheap because you, the westerners, would speak English and the Japanese who lived there would learn from you. The guy who informed me about all this gave me the addresses of several, and since Edo House had some historical resonance (Edo is the old name for Tokyo), I chose that. One morning I walked to it, talked to the manager, and was in. I returned to my *ryokan*, thanked the inscrutable director (who seemed not to stand but to hang in mid-air), and then went back to Edo house where I claimed my place in the men's section.

Edo House was a three-story building. The men's section was in the basement and contained eight bunk beds. There was a series of double rooms on the second and third floors, and a few much-coveted single rooms here and there. There was a big kitchen and rec-room on the second floor, plus two showers. On the roof was a washing machine and lines for drying clothes. Such a layout doesn't seem too bad. Now reduce your mental image of Edo House to one-third of what it was. Throw in lots of junk and dirt. Now throw in lots of people, both Japanese and *gaijin*. Got it? Everybody on top of everybody. Absolutely no privacy. What no money will buy you anywhere.

I went to my bunk, put my suitcase under it, and sat there, surveying my surroundings. The men's section was warmed by a kerosene heater which was about three yards from my bed. There were some lockers. A used band-aid was stuck to one of them. The bunks had curtains, some of which were drawn. I could hear heavy breathing behind them. Late sleepers. It was 11:00 a.m. As I was sitting there, studying the scatter of hair-balls, waxed-on ear swabs, nail clippings, bunched tissues, and other personal detritus, the door opened and a guy wearing a sweat suit came in. About thirty-five. Barefoot. He sat down on a swivel chair and we struck up a conversation. He was kind of a nervous guy and he kept swinging his leg as he talked. The big toe on his right foot looked like a Chinese almond cookie—the nail was pinched and narrow.

"Not much room, is there?" I said.

He gave me a kind of quizzical look, as if I were saying something he didn't want to hear. He wiggled his foot and the Chinese

almond cookie went round and round. It was hypnotic—maybe he
had a magic foot and were going to put me in a trance.

"Isn't it?" I said.

"Isn't what?"

"It crowded in here."

"You can overcome it," he said. And then, "Catch you later."

He jumped up and left the room.

Little by little the curtains were drawn back, people from outside came back to their bunks, and I got to see the mates with
whom I would be living. Two Ghanaians, two Brits, one Yank, and
one Japanese. One bunk open. The Ghanaians were, well, I never
found out. They were nice guys though, the one quiet and softly
observant; the other chipper and bouncy. Of the two Brits, the first
was a resourceful type, a trekker who had been all over Asia and
was replete with the tools of traveling: Swiss Army knife, sewing
kit, compass, and so on. He was always saying that things were dear
(expensive). The other Brit was from London, platinum-headed,
frenetic, always in a sweat and trembling for a cigarette. The Yank
was not actually a Yank—he was more properly speaking, a Rebel.
A South'n boy. He didn't know anything that his Ol'Daddy had-
n't told him. The Japanese was a pleasant kid who had lived in the
States and was getting re-started in Japan. He was mild and a little
wishy-washy in the opinion area. He could fall asleep on a dime,
or a one-yen piece.

I introduced myself and then basically listened in, feeling I had
more to learn than teach. A lot of the talk was house-gossip. There
was a young lady that several of them were sleeping with and they
all had her cold. Several joked about conversation classes they were
teaching. Paid off small debts that they owed one another. The
phone rang and the Rebel answered it.

"No, this is Cameron," he said and cupped his hand over the receiver. "They're looking for a pair of hands."

I wondered what he was talking about. One of the Ghanaians—
the chipper one—volunteered.

"White hands, fella," Cameron said.

The Ghanaian looked disappointed.

Cameron got back to the caller and said, "Sorry, no hands."

"What was that about?" I asked.

"TV commercial. They need a pair of *gaijin* hands to open a jar of something."

I turned my palms over. Maybe the next time. Cameron explained that modeling was an easy way to pick up money. He himself did only face and chest, or full body.

"Mah Daddah always tol' me that the whole is greater than the parts," he drawled, dressing slowly and deliberately.

I went topside. The TV was blaring and people were sitting around. Some watching it, some reading the newspaper, some playing the Japanese board game Go. I was hungry. A couple residents were cooking food that they kept in one of the two communal refrigerators, but since I had none in there, I went out to reconnoitre the neighborhood and find a cheap stand-up restaurant. Instead, I bought some tangerines and rice crackers and ate them as I walked. The neighborhood, I soon found out, was different from anything I had previously encountered. The streets were narrow and winding. Many of the homes had yards whose walls abutted the street, so you felt you were walking in a maze. I found myself getting disoriented, since I was used to grid-patterned U.S. and European cities. I noted the trees and plants: lots of bamboo, palms, and a number of bushes with red or white flowers, which I later learned were camellias. I kept saying to myself, "I'm in Asia. I'm in Asia." In fact, though, it was a little disappointing: it was bleak and gray and muddy. Many paths off the side streets were stones laid down in dirt. There were no large and easy to read street signs. On and on I walked, stopping only now and then to sit on steps or lean against walls and eat my tangerines and rice-crackers.

I spent most of the afternoon that way, and finally tired out, I looked forward to getting back to Edo House for some company and then a good night's sleep. When I returned, I went to my bunk and read for a while (Basho's, "Oku No Hosomichi"). The place was relatively quiet, since as I found out, most of the *gaijin* taught at *eikaiwa* [English conversation] schools in the evening and didn't get back until nine or ten. I spoke to a few of the ladies in the lounge. One had very black teeth and seemed to dislike foreign men. The saliva frizzed in her mouth when she spoke. There was a Middle Easterner who may have been part-dog. He barked rather than spoke, and it was hard not to wince at his rough delivery. (His Japanese was good though.) I went up on the roof to check out the view. The high-rises of Tokyo stood out in illuminated clusters. Overhead, Orion was visible, and the Pleiades, though just. Same basic sky. That was comforting. I came back down, went below, read some more by the kerosene heater, and then decided to turn in. I undressed, got into bed, pulled the curtain closed. For a while I dreamed, assessed my prospects, decided I would try to get some kind of work, and maybe I could make it for a year in Tokyo. I was vaguely aware as I mused on my plans that it was hard getting to sleep. Then I realized why: the TV, the barking man, the woman with black teeth, and every pot, pan, and refrigerator slam in the lounge were almost as loud as if I were up on the first floor. The walls of Edo House were paper thin! I was tired but couldn't drop off to sleep with all the noise. As the night progressed, it got louder and louder. The teachers returned from work, the lights went on and off, stereos on and on, and the whole house was throbbing. Again and again I tried to sleep, each time drifting off only to be awakened once more. At some indeterminate hour, I heard whispering all around me. Then the whole bunk began to shake. What was going on? Cameron was giving it to one of the Japanese ladies in the bed above me....

The next morning I awoke with a throbbing, ICBM headache. The smell of kerosene suffused the room. Gaspings and snorts came from behind curtains. Everywhere were empties, wrappers, peels, condoms, and other sheddings and moltings. I got up, dressed, carefully cleared away some of the junk, and sat by the heater. And read. I remembered that when I had first come to San Francisco I had studied the *Tao*, and it had helped me, brought peace and purpose to my mind. For some reason Basho wasn't working—it read flat. Suddenly the door opened and the guy who had been there the day before came in—the guy with the magic foot. He sat down by the heater and asked me how my first day had gone. His name was James, he said. From New Zealand. I told him about my disorienting walk through the neighborhood.

"You were supposed to get lost—that's the way they planned it."

"Oh," I said. That sounded interesting but also a little crazy. "Who are they?"

"Tokyo's a castle town," he said, swinging his almond-cookie toe. "Designed so invading armies couldn't find their way to Edojo, the castle."

"To know it you have to know it," I said.

"Yeah."

He went on to tell me about some of the major centers and subcenters. Shinjuku, Shibuya, Ikebukuro. Just names that I would have to fill in. I mentioned that it had been noisy last night and that I hadn't gotten much sleep.

"You can block it out," he said.

I wondered how.

For the next few days I worked hard at adjusting my schedule to that of Edo House. I went to bed later, got up later. It was still hard, if not impossible to sleep and there was virtually no privacy. The showers were filthy and the toilets frequently clogged. The sign over one of them said NO USE. Precisely. Could there have been a better colloquial translation of Dante's "Abandon Hope"? I spent as much time away from Edo House as possible. The afternoons I allocated to walking. I wanted to know as much about Tokyo as I could before I started looking for work. Consequently, I listened to people talk about the main destinations and areas, asked directions, and then visited the places they mentioned. I ate one meal per day and for the rest munched on snacks. In the evenings I went to the neighborhood *sento*, or public bath. I would stay there as long as possible, soaking and re-soaking in the hot water until I was rubicund. All the while I was up to my neck in the tub, I would observe the *sento*-regulars: the friendly father and his two boys; the "Bushi of the Bath"—the gruff, older guy who sat directly on the tiles, dispensing with the little stools; the bathers who lathered up until their faces looked like Noh masks and their whole bodies were white with soapy paste. But I couldn't stay there all night and sooner or later I had to return to Edo House. Slowly I would wend my way back, sometimes encountering the sweet-potato seller with his push-cart and haunting chant, *"Yaki imo, ishi yaki imo,"* which sounded to me like a sutra.

Edo House, to my dismay, increased in disorder and unruliness over the next weeks and the police came by frequently to quiet the place down. The guy with the magic foot lived in one of the back rooms—a single—and occasionally we chatted. He had been all over Asia. He talked about the beaches of Goa. The Taiwan trots. How he had come out of the jungle in Thailand. The taste of ice-cream in Chiang Mai. And so on. He was a funny guy. He had lots of practical knowledge, useful stuff, and seemed to want to help me. I guessed that he wanted to be my guru, or spiritual guide. I would listen to him, absorb what he had to say, but I wasn't sure I wanted his guidance. I think I believed that each person is ultimately his or her own guru.

After a reasonable period of time, I started looking around for work. Unlike most of the people at Edo House, I actually was a teacher, and as it turned out there was an open market for *eikaiwa* classes. I got tips from people, leads, and so on, and consequently was called in for quite a few interviews and received offers. This was all to the good, but it exacerbated the situation at Edo House. For many of these interviews I had to get up early in the morning. I took the interviews having had very little sleep. Edo House was like a nocturnal madhouse. People drifted in at all hours, sat down and carried on loud conversations. Cameron was rocking the bunk nightly. His old Daddy seemed to have taught him everything but the rudiments of civilized behavior. The open bunk was the designated venue for random sex. One night I awoke to see a young Japanese lady waving the curtain back and forth in front of the platinum headed English bloke. This must have been around three in the morning. He was sweating and trembling and swearing obscenities. The lullaby of Edo House. One night somebody came running through with a knife.

I redoubled my efforts at staying away from all this. Whenever I had an interview, I remained in that part of Tokyo for the day and explored the area. One of the drawbacks of this was that most areas in Tokyo were maximum-frenetic. This was during the bubble-economy, and the volume and intensity of spending was like a freakish free-for-all. Waves of people were always coming at you. Somebody told me that if you said *sumimasen* (excuse me) once, you'd have to say it a million times, so you didn't say it at all. One afternoon I found myself just riding the escalator in a Shibuya department store—up and up, down and down, almost delirious. I was overwhelmed by the constant bombardment, the exchange of money, wall-to wall humanity. I had had no sleep. No privacy. Had no place of refuge. I developed a spontaneous flu and was sick for several days. What I really had was a case of culture shock, a good dose of it. You couldn't have made a movie of what I was going through. I hadn't been thrown into a Latin American jail, been tortured by sadists, this wasn't the heart of darkness, but I was badly rattled. At forty-one what was I doing here? I had actually heard someone refer to me as "the old guy." I wondered if I shouldn't just go back to the States, grind out twenty years at some type of work, then retire, and call it a day. And yet I knew I would hate myself if I did.

Towards the end of winter that year there was a big snow in Tokyo, an onslaught that stranded cars and closed down several of the train lines. I happened to have brought some overshoes with me, so that evening I left the pandemonium of Edo House and walked through the snow-stilled neighborhood. I focused on every whitened twig and leaf, laboring branch, loaded bush and hedge. On and on I slogged through the snow, until I came by chance to a little street of small shops. Not many people were out and about, but one of the shops, a *sakaiya*, was open and glowing. The naked bulbs strung over the boxes and bins imbued the vegetables and fruits with a numinous quality. Sitting on a wooden platform was a short, wiry, simian-looking guy. The proprietor. As I passed him that snowy night, he suddenly flipped me three tangerines in quick succession. There was absolutely no expression on his face—it was closed tight. He was stone, except perhaps for the slightest unverifiable smile. But the tangerines were in my hand, like magic. I nodded, flashed the thumbs-up sign, and continued on, eating the wonderful fruit as the snow came down on me in huge flakes.

What had it been about, that incident? A small impish act of kindness during a big snow in the heart of Tokyo. I thought of the little man as The Tangerine Buddha. Somehow I drew strength from the incident, and I recalled the man often in the weeks that followed. As a consequence of the experience I began, or so I like to believe, my return to equilibrium. Something loosened in me and I became more receptive to what was good around me. Edo House, I found, had its rhythms—its calm periods and raucous ones. The frequent turnover of guests meant that the noisy intervals lasted only so long, and even though by the same calculus the serene intervals were just as transitory, I was grateful for them. I can't say I ever adjusted completely, but I got along, learning to deal with the small contained spaces, the cultural eclecticism, the jarring contiguities. With the arrival of spring the weather grew clement. The plums bloomed and then the cherries. I had turned down a number of job offers but at last one came along that was suitable, my working papers were approved, I found an apartment of my own, and left Edo House.

I have now been in Japan for over a decade. I have seen many Buddhas in the course of that time. Buddhas of all sizes, materials, and postures. The little man, The Tangerine Buddha, is among them. In my mind the three tangerines seem always in the air, a perpetual juggle. Orbs of light in a cold season.

Michael Fessler is a teacher and writer whose work has appeared in Kyoto Journal, Hawaii Review, Modern Haiku, Wind Magazine, *and other publications as well as writing a chapbook of haiku,* The Sweet Potato Sutra. *Although he was born in Kansas and grew up in Kentucky, he now makes Japan his home.*

✳

At about four o'clock I came to a part of the river that had been turned into a lake by the construction of a dam. In a dark, tiny sweet shop near the dam an old woman advised me to spend the night at the *saikuringu taminary* ("Cycling Terminal"), a hot-spring lodging house which I presume was so called because it catered to the hundreds of students who came through these hills in the summer on bikes. I recognized the turnoff to the lodging house, which I reached about an hour later, by a brightly lit electric sign glowing an effusive welcome. The place itself was about a kilometer and a half along a track that ran up into the hills, and when I arrived a large barking dog greeted me equally effusively. The doors of the lodging house were curtained and locked and it took five minutes of rattling them to rouse the white-shirted custodian, who bustled out finally to tell me that they were closed.

"But you've got a sign all lit up down on the highway."

"Yes. We always keep it lit."

"What for, for goodness' sake?"

"To make people feel welcome."

"But you're closed!"

"That's right."

Which was, perhaps, the most quintessentially Oriental conversation of the entire trip.

—Alan Booth, *The Roads to Sata: A 2000-Mile Walk Through Japan*

CATHY N. DAVIDSON

✷ ✷ ✷

Grief

An unexpected tragedy fosters unexpected behavior.

WHEN THE CALL COMES ON CHRISTMAS EVE, TED IS GRADING A few last papers up in his office at Kansai Women's University. Since I've finished my grading, I'm down in the English Department office, where I sip green tea with some of our colleagues and the English Department staff. We're talking about how the term is going, plans for the holidays, typical departmental chitchat.

The mood is festive. It is the last day of class. For the foreign teachers, it is Christmas Eve. For the Japanese it is the end-of-year celebrations that precede *Oshogatsu*, New Year, the most important holiday in Japan and one that brings the whole culture to a three-day halt. Miss Sumida, the head departmental secretary, explains that, although *Oshogatsu* itself only lasts three days, the celebrations really fill a whole month. First there are *bonen-kai* (weeks of parties to speed the passing of the old year), then *Oshogatsu* (New Year, in which, for three days virtually all shops and buildings are closed), and finally *shinnen-kai* (another few weeks of parties to welcome in the New Year before normal activities begin again). The Year of the Monkey is about to yield to the Year of the Rooster, a lucky year.

When she's on the telephone, Miss Sumida uncharacteristically

218

turns away from us as she speaks, first in Japanese, then in English, huddling her body over the phone, muffling her voice. Instead of calling me over, she puts the receiver down on the desk and comes to me. I cannot remember her exact words, but she conveys to me and to everyone else in the room that this will not be happy news from home. She takes my arm and solicitously leads me to the phone, as one might guide an invalid. It is an extraordinary gesture in a culture where people are respectful of one another's physical space, rarely touching one another as so often happens in casual Western conversation. Miss Sumida stands near, almost touching me, for most of the conversation. My colleagues—another American and two or three Japanese—sit alert in their chairs, ready to help in any way they can, as I keep asking my brother-in-law to repeat himself, not wanting to believe.

The connection is terrible. My brain won't cancel out the static, attend to the blurred voice on the other end of the line. I can't seem to make meaning. Instead, my hand records what my mind resists. Somewhere, in the mass of clippings and flyers I brought back with me from Japan, I still have the small white piece of paper from Miss Sumida's desk on which I took dreadful dictation: *Christmas Eve. Driving home. Park and Sheena—dead. Bruce—multiple injuries. Ross and Karina—???*

We learn the details later. Ted's brother, Park, and his wife, Sheena, were driving home through the Canadian Rockies to spend Christmas Eve with Ted's parents and his sister. They were in a Volkswagen camper van, the three kids (Karina, a first-year-college student; Bruce and Ross in high school and junior high) in the back of the van. A blizzard came up unexpectedly, ice first and then snow. The Mounties closed the mountain highway, but not soon enough to stop a pickup truck coming from the east and Park's van from the west. On a treacherous curve, both vehicles went out of control and met in a head-on collision. Park and Sheena were killed instantly. The kids were trapped in the car for several hours until the Mounties arrived.

I have said enough for my colleagues to know what has happened before I hang up the phone. Their eyes are large with concern and empathy, and everywhere there are enfolding arms. Later I realize that one of the American teachers at Kansai Women's University, an avuncular eccentric known as PK, must have come on the phone and taken my brother-in-law's phone number, because when Ted goes to call Ken, we find the number there, at the bottom of the sheet, in a handwriting we do not recognize. I remember saying over and over that I must find Ted and tell him. But my colleagues insist I sit for a few seconds and drink the rest of my tea. Someone—I do not remember who—says that it is unimportant now, of course, but at some point we will start worrying about our responsibilities at the University and he wants us to remember, then, that our colleagues will take over whatever needs to be done. We must not worry in any way about our responsibilities here. He says this in a commanding voice, more bracing than the tea. His practical comments bring me back an inch closer to the world of the ordinary.

A colleague walks me to the wing where Ted's office is and watches as I enter the room. How will Ted take this awful news? He and Park were born fourteen months apart, adorable together in baby pictures, blond-haired blue-eyed Ted in feet-pajamas holding his little brother, an urchin with masses of black curly hair and bright dark eyes. Ted's mother was a teacher in a small, four-room schoolhouse in Mountain View, Alberta, a ranching community in the foothills of the Canadian Rockies. She taught Park everything that Ted was learning so that Park could skip a grade and the boys could go through school together, eleven years in the same class.

"My brother Park and I only had one fight the whole time we were growing up," Ted sometimes would say. "It was over a pair of socks."

As adults, the two men were as different in personality as in appearance, yet they retained an eerie compatibility, almost like twins. And both had gone on from the four-room school in Mountain View to earn Ph.D.'s, Ted in English literature, Park in psychology. We had been on the phone with Park only a few weeks before the accident, arranging for him to visit Japan to lecture at a nearby university where one of our Japanese friends taught psychology. Park was planning to come early in the New Year.

I still remember the details of that day. How Ted sits at his desk turned slightly away from me with his elbows resting on the traditional Japanese handmade paper in the desk blotter. The paper is of an intense, emeraldlike hue that we would call green but that the Japanese call *aoi*, blue, like the blue of traffic lights or grass. As I tell him what happened, he reaches over and takes the piece of notepaper on which I recorded disaster. He holds it in both hands and just looks at it, not reading, just looking. Ted's boyish face turns, for an instant, into something stony and mask-like. Color drains from his cheeks. His face is white; in any language, deathly white.

"We have to go home," he says quietly.

I am not sure if he means home to our apartment in Nigawa, Japan, a mile from the university, or home to Mountain View, Canada.

We walk down the hill to the train together, holding hands, ignoring the taboo against a man and woman holding hands in public. At first, we are glad that we recognize no one. But soon I begin to realize that we are not just going unnoticed. We are being avoided. Normally, Japanese do not look at one another in public, do not make eye contact. But curiosity at seeing a foreigner up close often overrides the Japanese insistence on privacy and on maintaining a respectful distance from others in public spaces. As a *gaijin* in Japan, one grows used to stares. But today we must be communicating

———)———

Shiko [baseball] players were forbidden to use the word *ouch!*—no matter how much a ball stung their hands on a frozen winter's day or how badly they bruised their bodies during sliding practice. Those who could not suppress the pain were allowed to use the word *kayui* (it itches). It was their way of demonstrating spirit, the sine qua non of any good Japanese athlete.

◆

—Robert Whiting,
You Gotta Have Wa

something different, tragic. Neither of us cries but we are obviously repressing deep emotions, and people, sensing this, avert their gaze.

I feel more alien, isolated, and alone than I have ever felt in my life. I am surprised by a sudden surge of something that feels like rage, as if our being here, away, has caused this terrible thing to happen. The emotion reformulates itself: terrible things happen when you go away.

Somewhere deep inside me is a strange, displaced emotion, guilt masked as anger, my hostility directed, inexplicably, at everyone who dares to ride that train with us and not feel what we are feeling. We violate public decorum again by sitting pressed against one another, holding both of each other's hands in both hands, the fingers as intertwined as we can make them. I am a *gaijin*—outsider, foreigner, nonperson—and I don't care what they think, these people who see green and call it blue....

We want to fly home at once, but Ted's family asks us not to. There will be no funeral. Neither Park nor Sheena wanted one. They say it would work much better for everyone if we finish up our school year as soon as possible and then fly to Vancouver to stay for a while, to help. The Japanese academic year ends in early March. If we could work things so that we could come home five or six weeks early—in late January, say—we could fly directly to Vancouver and be there when the kids get out of the hospital. We could then help to settle financial matters (there seems to be no will) and to set up new living arrangements. Ted's dad, a retired rancher in Alberta and recently divorced from his second wife, will live with the boys in Vancouver so that they won't have to leave their house, their school, and all their friends. He would like us to come to Vancouver to help him out for the first few months and before we have to be back at our regular teaching positions in the United States.

We agree. We know this makes the most sense for everyone. But we also feel severed, cut off from family, from rituals, left alone with our own sense of loss....

The Japanese apartment that we once found charming is suddenly a torture chamber. The walls have grown too close together. Soon we won't be able to breathe. My head is throbbing with pain; Ted feels dizzy. Yet we feel a need to go somewhere busy, distracting, loud, a place that can preoccupy.

We decide to spend the day in Osaka, a 30-minute train ride from our apartment. It is Christmas Day.

Despite weeks and weeks of pre-Christmas hoopla, Christmas in Japan is a day like any other. The Japanese have taken up with gusto Christmas music, Santa Claus, and gaudy red-and-green decorations, but the month-long blaring of "Rudolph the Red-Nosed Reindeer" and "Silent Night" turns out to be an elaborate preparation for absolutely nothing. When December 25 finally rolls around, the Christmas trees and bows and bangles come down to be replaced by the ritual decorations for *Oshogatsu.*

> ──── ☽ ────
>
> *I*n the first graveyard a mother and her daughter had set up a small bamboo table in front of a grave. On the table they had placed handfuls of cooked rice wrapped in lotus leaves, slices of watermelon, a tomato, some beans, crackers still in their cellophane wrappings, and a little cup of the cold green tea they were sitting drinking.
> The rain ran down their umbrellas and pattered onto the plastic sheets they sat on, but they laughed as they talked and drank their tea.
>
> ◆
>
> —Alan Booth,
> *The Roads to Sata: A 2000-Mile Walk Through Japan*

We spend the day wandering through department stores where shoppers busily prepare for *Oshogatsu* amid the iconography of cute Baby Jesuses and adorable elves. The aisles are packed, and Bing Crosby croons "White Christmas" at ear-splitting decibels. We visit the gigantic food basement where salespeople in traditional cotton *happi* coats use electronic megaphones to announce specials on various seasonal items. They shout in highly stylized voices—like the piercing declamations in kabuki opera. The smells are strange too: seaweed, fermented soybeans, pink and yellow pickles, sweetly acrid like mildew and old fish. It's more than we can handle today.

We flee to the clothing floor, where there is, at least, less aural and olfactory chaos. Ted buys himself a tie. I purchase a tiny, collapsible umbrella. Both cost far more than we would normally spend, but it's Christmas, we say.

After a few hours, we realize how useless it all is and we return to our austere apartment, make a few more calls to Canada and to my family in the United States. Although some American expatriate friends had earlier invited us for Christmas dinner, we are in no mood for socializing. We remember still other invitations for Japanese end-of-year celebrations that must be canceled.

That is how we feel: canceled.

But our friends will not leave us alone. Normally no Japanese ever, ever comes to a home without being very specifically invited. It's unusual to entertain at home in Japan and frequently colleagues will work together ten or twenty years without ever seeing where one another lives or without ever meeting a coworker's spouse and children. Outside/inside, public/private. These are borders not easily crossed.

Yet Japanese friends keep showing up on our doorstep unannounced and uninvited. While we were away in Osaka someone managed to get into our apartment to fill the refrigerator with food. We are not alarmed at this because our apartment is owned by the university and people on the maintenance staff have a key. But we are astonished by this flagrant breach of one of the cardinal rules of Japanese sociability, something we learned soon after arriving in Japan.

"What does it mean," I asked Professor Sano, our department head, early on, "when someone says, 'Please come to my house?' We keep getting invited, even by strangers we happen to meet in the supermarket. I don't get it."

"Please come to my house," Professor Sano said, smiling, "means

(Please don't come to my house.) No one ever goes to a person's house without an invitation that includes a definite, prearranged time—and a map."

The map is crucial. Since most streets are unnamed in Japan and houses are typically numbered in the order in which they are built, having just an address usually gets you nowhere. Business cards often have a small schematic map on the back, as do store ads in newspapers or other commercial announcements. Privacy—the home—is institutionalized by the very anonymity of the streets. The seeming public disorder is itself almost a system; it's a *choice* the Japanese have made. Tokyo has been destroyed twice in the 20th century, once by earthquake, once by war. Each time the Japanese have chosen to rebuild the city as disordered as before. Maps to particular places allow one to penetrate the maze, by appointment as it were. Privacy is not just a privilege; it is a fundamental value and an escape valve for Japan's collective life. It is the still center amid the whirlwind.

Yet, mysteriously, our Japanese friends violate this rule. This isn't collusion, since people we know who do not know one another all show up at the apartment, uninvited. A colleague we barely know comes with a beautiful plant, an enormous yellow mum with russet edging on each petal. We've been told that chrysanthemums are commemorative flowers, used at funerals, but she explains that she has chosen these because yellow and orange are colors of life. The plant is for us because a lucky new year is coming, she says. She bows deeply before leaving, then, choking back tears, reaches out and grasps first my hands, then Ted's, as if intuiting that just now we crave touch.

Another colleague arrives with the papers we might need to

O bon—festival of the dead—occurs in August when all families return to their ancestral homes to welcome the return of their dead relatives.

♦

—DWG & AGC

leave the country for the funeral and then to reenter again. Mr.
Higuchi is afraid we will be caught in the *Oshogatsu* bureaucratic
shutdown and will not be able to get the proper exit papers and
entry visas. Somehow, without our aid or signatures, he has managed to secure every document we might require to make the
trip home immediately and then return to Japan for the rest of
the academic year. When we tell him that there will only be a
very small ceremony at the graveside in Mountain View and that
Ted's family has asked that we not come now but, instead, finish
up our year as early as possible and then come to help with the
kids in Vancouver, Mr. Higuchi doesn't bat an eye. This practical
solution must seem incomprehensible to him: how unnatural to
miss one's brother's funeral. But he shows no sign of surprise.
Instead, he pulls a legal pad and a calendar from his briefcase and
heads for the phone. After a few calls in which he makes arrangements in rapid Japanese, he returns to show us neatly and clearly
how we can wrap everything up in less than a month and be
gone. He gives us a choice of dates, then proceeds to call the airlines for us and changes our supposedly nonchangeable tickets.
We can return home early without paying a penalty, he reports.
He next calls the tax bureau so that we will have the necessary
papers before we leave. We don't understand why he tells us that
he has informed the tax office that Ted is the oldest son and that
there has been a death in the immediate family. But when the tax
assessment comes, we realize that Ted has received an official tax
break because of each of those circumstances. Mr. Higuchi hasn't
missed a thing.

Ted and I sit dazed. I heat and then reheat water for tea, a welcome distraction, as various visitors enter, tend to our lives, leave.
At one point Ted and I discuss how strange this must be for the
Japanese, our staying here in Japan instead of flying home for the
funeral. Ted's family is not religious. A funeral is not what is important; it is putting together a life for our nephews and niece,
helping to make things as comfortable as possible for Ted's father.
Rationally, we know all this, but we still feel amputated.

We have heard that in Japan death stops the culture. A new set of rules and procedures comes into play when a loved one dies, but we don't know what the rules are. This is totally outside our experience—it's not in the guidebooks—and we have no way of knowing if the treatment we receive is typical or special because we are foreigners. We suspect that our friends are trying to compensate for our alone-ness. The closed quality of Japanese society, the collective nature of the culture, must make our situation—alone in our grief—seem unendurable. Our friends help us to endure. They intuit what it must be like feeling sorrow so far from home. Individually and collectively, they refuse to allow us to be foreigners through our worst pain.

Several people anticipate that, in the grief of the moment, we might forget to stock up on the food and supplies necessary for the three days of New Year, when the stores all close. People bring everything from milk to canned goods to toilet paper. Neighbors and students, some of whom we barely recognize, come only to the *genkan*, drop something off, and then leave. The *genkan* is where you remove your outdoor shoes and replace them with slippers. But like all features of Japanese domestic architecture, the *genkan* is also symbolic and serves an important cultural function. Physically inside the apartment or house, the *genkan* is symbolically outside, a mediation between inside and outside is so great in Japanese culture that you actually need this place to pause and prepare for the transition, from one kind of space (and self) to another. It is not just a space but a *concept*. We understand this function better when some acquaintances whom we barely know enter the *genkan* with gifts but refuse to remove their shoes and step up into the apartment itself. This, they insist, would be an invasion of our privacy.

Our Japanese friends do not leave us alone. We are moved by their attentions, including many reiterated invitations for the various events of *Oshogatsu*. But we realize here, too, our Japanese acquaintances are violating a social taboo. Someone who has experienced a death in the family in the previous year does not normally join in *Oshogatsu* celebrations beyond the immediate family. This is institutionalized in Japan through the ritual of the *ningajo*, the New Year's cards. The post office somehow collects and holds everybody's *ningajo* until New Year's morning, when they are all delivered to your home in a tidy bundle. It is exhilarating to run to the mailbox to find the cards and know that people all across the country are also reading dozens, even hundreds, of greetings from friends and loved ones. But if a relative has died in the previous year, you send a card edged in black, a wordless announcement and a way of excusing yourself from the festivities. *Oshogatsu* is all about establishing good omens for the coming year. The bereaved stay home with their families and their sorrow, regrouping in privacy for the New Year. They skip the second and third days of *Oshogatsu*, days reserved for visiting with business associates and friends. Privacy, again; but also a keen sense that one must be respectful of others' happiness. One does not inflict one's personal sadness on others at this happy time of the year. We know about this custom, and make a point of excusing ourselves from the traditional Oshogatsu activities to which we have been invited by friends and colleagues.

As New Year's Eve approaches, our close friends, Maryvonne and Ichiro Okamoto, insist that we spend *Oshogatsu* with them.

"I'm French," Maryvonne argues on one of her food visits, this time bringing a wonderful bouillabaisse. "I don't give a shit"—she pronounces it "sheet"—"about Japanese customs or superstitions. It's New Year's Eve. You are spending the night with us."

"Maryvonne, we're just not up to it."

"Never mind!" she insists. "Ichiro and I and our friend Takashi will come to get you if you're not at our house by ten o'clock tonight. I mean it."

Maryvonne is five feet tall—but no one messes with Maryvonne. At ten o'clock, dreading having to spend the next three hours in celebration, we drag ourselves the block and a half to the Okamotos' house.

On television is the annual New Year's competition called the "Red and White." It's a rather inane exercise in nostalgia, where both past and current pop stars assemble to sing songs, the men against the women, the white team against the red, each song more lugubrious than the last. It's ostensibly a contest but no one cares who wins. What matters is how the songs evoke a torrent of *natsukashisa*, the bittersweet remembrance of things past, one of the most fundamental, powerful, and prized of all emotions for the Japanese.

When the last note of the "Red and White" dies out, when the points are tallied and the applause is over, it is midnight in Japan. The scene on the TV switches dramatically. A monk in yellow robes pulls a coarse hemp rope that is attached to a thick log that he swings back and forth with more and more force until it thunders against the striking seat of the huge cast-bronze temple bell. The sound is deep, melodious, impressive. At every temple in Japan, a bell booms forth the New Year 108 times, spelling, by one interpretation, the twelve months, twenty-four atmospheres, and seventy-two climates of the earth and, by another, casting out the 108 world worries of the year gone by.

Cameras are set up throughout the country so that, with each boom, the picture changes to show another temple, in another place. Urbanites in Tokyo or Osaka watch to see the bell of the local temple of their hometown, the place they left behind.

The Okamotos summon us outside to hear the ringing of the bell at Kabuto-yama Daishi. Often we have hiked up "Helmet Mountain" to visit the serenely beautiful temple there. Tonight the winter air is resonant with the somber sound of the bell at Kabuto-yama Daishi, 108 rings, repeated and distant like yearning.

It is a clear night with stars but too cold for gazing. We hurry back inside and huddle together under the *kotatsu*, the traditional heating device, the center of the Japanese home. Some people have argued that the divorce rate is rising in Japan because more efficient space heaters have replaced the *kotatsu*, a low square table containing a coiled heating element underneath and a long quilted skirt to keep in the warmth. Friends and families sit close together around the *kotatsu*, their legs extended beneath the thick quilt. The heat is so mellow and constant and close it seems to emanate from deep inside your body. Radiantly warm together under the Okamotos' *kotatsu*, we now eat *toshi-koshi soba*, the delicious ritual

New Year's "long life noodles," slurped from lacquer bowls passed down for generations in Ichiro's family

At one point, Ichiro excuses himself to bring *toshi-koshi soba* to his mother. A *shamisen* player and beloved teacher, she is ill in her bed on the first floor of the house. Upstairs, we toast her with the special New Year's sake, rice wine, and, on her behalf, slurp the *soba* loud and long. Ichiro's father is impressed by how well Ted and I have mastered this special slurping technique: it is something we have practiced in the privacy of our own home.

It has been a pleasant evening. We have done our duty. We have celebrated. But we are exhausted by this reentry into sociability. We want to go home.

"No!" Ichiro and Takashi say together. "It's time for the Red and White, American-style!"

Classical musicians by profession, Takashi was once Ichiro's lute student. But both confess that they originally learned to play guitar and did so from an adolescent adoration of Western pop music. They realized earlier in the night that their favorite American songs are probably our favorites, too. Ted and Ichiro are the same age. Takashi and I are each thirteen years younger ("And our music is much better," Takashi jokes).

"Please sit for a few minutes," Ichiro leads us back to the *kotatsu*. They tune up and I notice, not for the first time, the beauty of Ichiro's delicate, seemingly boneless tapered fingers, and remember reading once that most hand models in the United States are Asian.

Like the New Year's Eve television show, Ichiro and Takashi alternate songs. But these songs are all in English. Ichiro's English is excellent. Takashi, who barely understands a word, *sings* English perfectly. They both know not only every chorus, but every single word to every verse of seemingly every American pop song of the fifties and sixties....

By two a.m., Ichiro and Takashi still haven't exhausted the pop repertoire of our respective youths. Ichiro croons some silly song about a yellow-haired girl whose feet go "paddy whack," whatever that means. "One-eyed, One-horned, Flying Purple People Eater" is Takashi's rejoinder.

We all claim "Weemaway," both generations, even Maryvonne, whose birth year falls in between Ted's and mine, and who has only sung background vocals tonight. Maryvonne has the deep melancholy voice of a French cabaret singer. She has not sung a solo tonight, I know, because her Piaf style can coax tears from a stone—and this is not a time for tears. We've Tennessee Waltzed, Mashed Potatoed, and Twisted the night away. We are in a house in Nigawa, Japan, singing, dancing, and, miraculously, Ted and I are laughing.

In the morning, there is a knock on our front door. It is Mrs. Yanase, who refuses to enter past the *genkan* but who insists that we will come to her traditional New Year's dinner at one o'clock or her husband will send his whole football team to pull us out of our apartment and carry us to the Yanase house.

"But we know this is against Japanese tradition," we insist.

"It is also against tradition for me to be here now. Please be at my house by one."...

At the Yanases, we enjoy the array of traditional foods of *Oshogatsu* and one of the fellow guests kindly assumes the task of explaining to us the symbolism of everything we eat and drink. All the food is prepared in advance, we learn, so that even the cook has a three-day holiday from the usual domestic chores. Since Mrs. Yanase must run back and forth serving things during the whole of the meal, it hardly seems like a holiday for her, but she insists, laughing, that *symbolically* she's having a vacation.

The meal begins with water that was drawn at daybreak in order that we will have good health throughout the year, and then *ozoni*, a clear soup broth containing an assortment of unfamiliar vegetables, as well as *omochi*, a rice cake made from rice that has been pulverized with large wooden mallets to form a sticky paste. *Omochi* symbolizes long life. *Koi*, carp, is served both raw and pickled on *Oshogatsu* because no fish is more able to surmount obstacles than the carp. The Japanese written character for chestnut is a pun on the word for *prowess* or *mastery*, so chestnuts, too, are part of the New Year's meal as are black peas (a pun on *robust*), and dried seaweed (*happiness*). The root of the sacred lotus plant assures spirituality. No one explains what the *daikon* means, but the symbolism of this hard, white, foot-long radish is easy to guess.

All of these symbolic dishes are washed down with *otoso*, a form of sake flavored with Japanese pepper, yet another symbol of life, vitality, and energy: *genki*, as the Japanese say, the best thing a person can have.

Throughout the meal, food appears, plates are cleared, our tea and sake cups have been kept full. We haven't had to ask for or decide a thing today, as if our hosts realize that at a time like this mundane decisions become impossible. We can see the soft expression in their eyes, caring and solicitous, watchful. They are quick to change any conversation that might remind us of our sorrow and even quicker to respond to requests we don't even realize we're making. Once, my eyes start to fill with tears and I excuse myself and go to find the bathroom. Before I can get there, Mrs. Yanase is beside me, offering a tissue. Briefly, she holds my hand. Another time, when Ted looks sad and distracted, Mr. Yanase starts planning ahead to our next trip to Japan when, he suggests, he and Ted might think about team-teaching a course together. For a few minutes, Ted is removed from present pain and feels enthusiasm for the future. Silently, tacitly, they cushion us against loss and loneliness by showing us life again and friendship. They make us feel loved.

We are aware that our Japanese friends are handling this situation differently than would our American friends. Back home, our friends would have wanted to talk about it all; they would have coaxed us to express our feelings, urged us to cry. Such talk is not the usual way here when a friendship is as new as ours. Out of decorum or cultural differences or simply not-knowing-what-to-do, our Japanese friends have not really mentioned the deaths, although in some other unspoken sense the accident has been the point of every interaction. An overt reference to Ted's brother might cause us to weep and, in a formal situation, where some of the guests are strangers, this might embarrass us. These Japanese friends do not want to add to our pain in even the slightest way.

We can feel this in their gestures, in the way they hover over us. They are taking care of us today, and we feel grateful for their attention. For days, Ted and I have done nothing but think, talk, weep. Now, it is a relief to be able to put the pain aside for a few hours. In this situation, at this moment, we feel comforted by this generous form of Japanese empathy which does not require our self-revelation.

At the conclusion of the meal, Mr. Yanase has all of the guests toast Ted and me. Once again, there is no overt mention of the accident but that is what this has all been about. Mr. Yanase says he knows that this is simply the first of many *Oshogatsu* celebrations that we will spend together. We all applaud and drink to reunion. And then all of the guests, new friends, wish us *genki* in this, the new year, the propitious Year of the Rooster. We thank them, and, in turn, toast them, too. All the omens look good.

As we walk home, we talk about how both groups of friends have adapted the

———) ———

Several nights ago I asked my teacher again about his own beginnings.

"How did you decide to come to Miyama?" I asked. "Didn't you worry whether it was the right decision?"

"Water always finds its way around the rocks," he answered with a laugh. "You think too much and your smile goes away." Although he often made fun of Zen, and the idea of Westerners sitting zazen in remote Japanese temples put him in hysterics, at times he could be as cryptic as an old monk. Once again I turn my hands slowly in the light, Nagayoshi-san watches me. Neither of us speaks in the kiln's steady roar. Suddenly he looks down at the temperature gauge and grins.

"What was the name of that king in Shakespeare," he says suddenly, "that king who couldn't decide—Hamurreto?" He grins. Cocking his head to one side, he looks so like a song-bird that I laugh.

◆

—Leila Philip,
The Road Through Miyama

Japanese New Year's rituals to our situation. It is a cliché, of course, that the Japanese are brilliant at adaptation, but this is amazing. They have taken traditional symbols and reassigned them to us, an American and a Canadian reeling from death and loss and separation. Adrift after the news of the accident, we have been buoyed by their kindness. In the midst of this terrible time, they have given us something precious.

We are beginning to understand that there's another level here, too, something beyond simple kindness. The Buddhist causality. *Because* of this terrible accident, we have been offered something precious. Nothing we do, nothing anyone else does, will ever change the fact of the accident. What can be changed is how we view its relationship to our life. Everyone experiences pain; everyone has a story to tell. How one understands the story is what's important. This is a matter of choice. We can see the accident as an indication that the universe is fundamentally unfair and we can wrap ourselves in this unfairness, armor ourselves against the world. Or we can see the way a community of people, all strangers less than a year ago, has come together in our time of pain. Community is essential; it is the one bulwark against inevitable grief and loss.

Jiko. Accident. The grief doesn't go away. But the reverse side has a reverse side, too. We will always be *gaijin*, foreigners, in Japan but we are aware that, because of a tragedy, we have been given entrance to a different aspect of Japanese life.

Cathy N. Davidson also contributed the story "Bilingual Laughter" in Part Two.

*

Dawn, the earth smiles, the small-blossomed peach trees shine in an old farm. Leaning against my train window I see the bony, tortured body of Japan. Mountains made of lava, extinguished volcanoes—some still smoking, ravines opened by earthquakes, hot springs, all the tragic history of Japan is written with stones, boiling water and flames. And if the atmosphere is so clear, Japan pays dearly for this purity. It is created by violent atmospheric currents which sometimes break into terrible typhoons, uprooting cities and villages.

But when the earth and the air calm down, the Japanese rise, rebuild their houses and temples; the air has been cleared, the earth puts on again its fresh mask full of flowers, and the Japanese soul rejoices as if awakened from a bad dream. And, as if the soul is in a hurry to enjoy itself before the nightmare engulfs it again, it carves on wood and on stone the joyful gods, picks up the plume and writes small migratory songs of seventeen syllables, the haiku, and of thirty-one syllables, the *tanka*; it takes the brush and paints the beauty of the world becomingly, as light as frost.

> The color of the flower withered away
> At the moment I admired, in vain,
> The passing of myself through the world!

So the great Japanese poetess Okono-Kumassi sang a thousand years ago. But this concept of the ephemeral is transubstantiated in the brave soul of the Japanese; and instead of becoming fatalism and despair, it becomes craving for joy, for work, for creation before the earthquake, the hurricane and death.

For that reason the Japanese selected as their supreme symbols the rising sun, a flower (the chrysanthemum) and a fish (the carp). The sun symbolizes the three great virtues: knowledge, kindness and bravery. The chrysanthemum endures and blooms in the snow. And the carp rushes up against the current of the river and defeats the force that pushes it down...

—Nikos Kazantzakis, *Japan China,* translated by George Pappageotes

DAVID MURA

Dance Through the Wall
of the Body

A visit into the strange world of Butoh dance.

I AM GOING TO MY FIRST BUTOH *KEIKO* (TRAINING). ON THE
train I read V.S. Naipaul's *The Crocodiles of Yamoussoukro*, about his
travels through the Ivory Coast, a trip to the President's palace,
where the crocodiles, in an afternoon ritual, are fed a live chicken.
Stations pass, their names unknown to me, sounding almost
African—Shinokubo, Toteneki, Nakano. Since none of them is my
destination, each creates a further uncertainty: I've boarded the
wrong train, will be stranded at some station with no one to call,
no way home. Reiko was unable to accompany me on this first
trip, and I am, despite my worries, grateful for this. I feel I already
owe her so much, without her taking the two-hour trip to Ono's
studio. Still, en route to Ono's house in Yokohama, beyond the familiar confines of Tokyo, I find my newfound confidence ebbing.
Again, I feel beset by the fears of a foreigner, an illiterate, a peasant
in the city, a primitive man.

As the train rumbles on, Naipaul is talking to a professor of
African drummologie. "The world of the white men is real," says
the professor. "But, but. We black Africans, we have all they have,
we have all of that in the world of the night, the world of darkness." And so, says Naipaul, the talk turns away from the modern

236

African city of hotels and golf courses, the Mercedes and its chauffeur, the overextended French restaurants with their shoddy service. It turns away and moves into the night, the other world. It is the world of *djinns* and doubles, of travel where the body stays, sitting placidly while the spirit travels to another continent, to the world of the dead, seeking a father, a mother, a son.

We arrive at my stop. I get off under the eye of the video camera, which shows me on a screen with the crowd erupting from the train, moving down the platform. As I enter the station, I don't know where I am. All around are the ever-present crowds, the faces of strangers, the faces of my ancestors. My next train is leaving. But I don't know where the platform is. And I enter, as I have so many times these first few weeks in Japan, a state of panic. I'm lost. I'm late. I'll never arrive. As I scramble through the giant Yokohama station, frantically asking directions, the image of Ono's dance pops into my head and I think, What in the world am I doing? Why do I want to study with this man? An hour later, I enter a room, a long gray hall with dark wooden floors. On one wall, there's an abstract etching, like the Nazca lines, and then a color drawing of Ono; beneath, lined against the wall, are women's shoes, including a silver pair of high heels. A snare drum and cymbal behind the old battered couch. Last month's calendar next to a cabinet with vases and artificial flowers on top, a book of pictures of Mishima, porcelain horses, a horn, a Japanese doll. Surrounded by the couch and a couple of old chairs, there's a coffee table cluttered with papers, bottles of Creap creamer, a bottle of Brim. Twisted roots of ginger from Korea, bottled in honey. Kleenex, tea bags, sugar, fruit in a basket, sweet *sembei* (rice crackers).

Ono goes to his house next door. I introduce myself to a man in gray sweat pants with the body of a gymnast or a soldier, his torso naked, muscular, lean, his biceps pronounced. His head is closely cropped, a crew cut; his face is shaved, but the stubble is dark; his eyebrows are thick, close, his eyes deep-set. His face reminds me of the great Japanese author Yukio Mishima; so does his body. It implies strength, a taut wire, the hint of cruelty. I stumble through my Japanese, letting him know where I'm from. (Later I learn that Hideshima has been studying with Ono-san for twelve years. The other students call him "the first student.")

He sits down in a chair as I go to the back to change to my sweats. I pass a table with a makeup mirror, flowers, capes. I suddenly begin sweating and feel incredibly awkward.

The other students, all fairly young, in their late twenties or early thirties, arrive. In comparison to Hideshima, they are smaller, slighter, their bodies less obviously those of dancers. I hand out my newly printed *meishi* (business cards), as I've been instructed, a Japanese ritual. Yet I feel like an impostor, afraid of being discovered, my lack of Japanese exposed. I try to nod appropriately, to smile when the others smile. The others don't seem to notice I'm faking. They are talking to each other. I feel self-conscious writing down notes in English. The man next to me notices.

Ono hands a book of poems to Hideshima, then gives a slighter, smaller man a different book. Another dancer, her face hidden by bangs, her body lost in gray baggy sweats, looks at a magazine with pictures of Ono in a black dress cavorting on an English lawn, while his son, in white makeup and shaved head, stands behind him attentively, like a butler. Long moments of silence as the other six students, now in dark, unmatching sweats, t-shirts, or long underwear, lounge about and look at the books.

Ono is wearing a gray, prison-striped, Mexican-style shirt with a long pointed collar, and blue cotton pants. Barefoot, he squats in the chair, knees settling his lower legs in a V. Not the posture of a European but of a man used to sitting on floors.

Without any formal signal for the class to commence, he begins to talk. I notice that his hands seem enormously large, expressive, the thumb and little finger often moving in opposition to the middle fingers. Frequently, they hang limp from a forearm held parallel to the ground; at times, in this position, especially when he strains his chest forward, showing the motion of a dance movement, he looks like a baby chick emerging weakly from the egg, feebly pulling its head up into the light. And yet these movements are strong, timeless, and, through a slight twisting or raising of the arms, a twist of the torso, a thrust of the neck, the dropping of the jaw, a guttural sound in the throat (his flexibility makes it hard to believe he is eighty), his body appears capable of an infinite expressiveness. I have no idea really what he is talking about, but the gestures command my attention.

A dog barks in the yard, snapping through the sound of crickets, the wind. Ono's hands seem to move of their own accord, his voice breaking from time to time into repetition. He translates a few words from the last of the New Testament, and I try to connect the gestures, the cadences of the speech, the frail thinness and absolute strength of the body with the skinny Christ of the crucifix, his grace and agony. As the arms are swinging through the air, all I pick up through the Japanese is *"Kangaenai...kangaenai..."*—Don't think, don't think. I feel I might be wasting my time, it might have been a mistake to come. I keep hoping the *sensei* will not look at me, not see I don't understand. I edge back a bit; I bend my head closer, still attempting to listen. I don't understand. I think of Susie, visiting a friend and a Japanese family in a cabin near Mt. Fuji. I wish I were there.

A few minutes later, another student walks in. I am saved: Sekai, Ono says, will translate for me. Sekai is in his late twenties, with short cropped hair and thick, wire-rim glasses, with a puffiness about his features that makes him look slower than he is. I later learn that he's a photographer and is studying with Ono to learn more about the soul. Although Sekai's English is not really fluent, his translations help, and slowly I feel myself falling under Ono's spell.

As he talks, I watch the gentleness in Ono's hands, their strength, the repetition of certain words emphasized with repeated shakes—not the emphatic insistence of didacticism, but the repetition of dance, the retrieval of motion from randomness into expression, the cadence of music and body coming together. At times, he opens his hands as if presenting an offering. When he speaks about the cosmos, he spreads his arms up and then outward in a circle; when he speaks of hugging a dead man, he wraps his arms around himself and rolls gently back and forth. I feel less that I am listening to a harsh Japanese *sensei*, or even to the calm, pure wisdom and emptiness of a Buddhist master, and more that I'm in the presence of some shaman, some Native American wise man, a guide between this world and the next.

"Even if a person does not cry physical tears, that person may be sad inside. In dance, sadness does not just show itself on the outside, tears must be inside too. The body reacts because it's alive. I can't separate the two. And what is present is both the physical and non-physical. When you are sad, it is not just your single self who is sad, but all the dead people, the great number of souls who are living inside you...

"The dead people say they won't or can't cry. So I will cry for them. And the cosmos is crying too. In Butoh, then, I have to enter the world of the dead, and even though I can't talk to the dead, because the dead do not talk, I know through my body, my body is there, and I feel very happy hugging a dead person.

"There are people who say the dead don't cry, and it's true, sometimes it's hard to tell if someone is crying or happy.

"When you dance, you must dance through the wall of the body. During my dance of Mozart, on the video, I am not doing a lot outside, but I am moving inside. If I move too much outside, I lose the within, the source or energy, the feeling that propels the dance. In order to break through the wall, I must hold on to and not forget what's inside. It's the relationship between what is living inside me and the living realm of the dead that is dance..."

And then the talking is done. It is time to dance. Ono motions for me to join the others. Not knowing whether I was coming here as an observer or a student, I hesitate. Will I make a fool of myself? Am I imposing? What right do I have to claim to be here as a student?

$\mathcal{N}$oh—a 14th century dramatic play form relying heavily on symbolism and nuance.

Butoh—a form of Japanese interpretive, modern dance.

◆

—DWG & AGC

And then easily, quickly, my hesitations fall away. I join the others.

The Japanese are extremely polite and will go to immense lengths to avoid criticizing or confronting others. Foreign artists frequently remark that because of this lack of open criticism, Japanese artists don't develop and are unable to talk about their art with any vehemence or sense of the struggle to improve. These foreign artists often miss how much is imparted in Japanese society without words or direct expression. They also fail to see how, at least in the Japanese traditional arts, much of the learning that takes place is in the process of imitating the master. After years of study, most pupils don't need to be told how they fall short. Still, this charge that the Japanese lack the stomach for direct criticism has some truth.

> ———)———
>
> *In* the end my own views reluctantly began to change. I had only to look around to see that much of the world of Japanese traditional arts was concerned with name, status and lineage. "Form first, content after" is a well-known Japanese saying.
>
> ◆
>
> —Leila Philip,
> *The Road Through Miyama*

Yet this attitude toward direct criticism provides a wonderful atmosphere for beginners; it allows one to develop an interest, to gain a foothold of understanding and technique, while overcoming self-doubts or self-consciousness. As Zeami, the great theorist of Noh, wrote: "At first [the apprentice actor] should be allowed to act as he pleases in what he happens to take up naturally and follow his own inclinations. He should not be instructed in minute detail, or told that this or that is good or bad. If he is taught too strictly he will lose heart and also become uninterested in the Noh and forthwith cease to make any progress in performance."

I'm sure I sensed such an attitude from Ono. Otherwise I would never have made such a fool of myself.

The dancers spread out across the wooden floor, doing knee bends and stretches, rolling their necks back and forth, in a ritual of loosening I try to imitate. Ono snaps a tape into the machine: a Japanese flute begins to play, the notes quavering, low, a series of drones and moans. The others around me start moving, very slowly, drifting, shifting into a trance.

I start with a squatting position, what seems the least affected to me. I put my hands on the floor in front of me and begin to lower myself into a crawling and then a prone position, all the while trying to keep thoughts about appearing ridiculous out of my mind, trying not to see the whole situation as an American, or someone unfamiliar with Butoh, might.

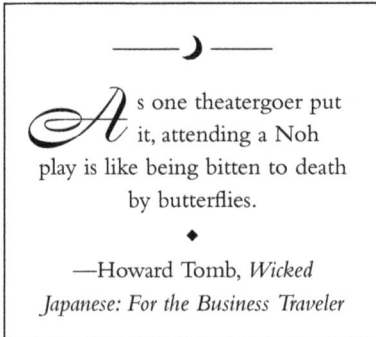

——— ☽ ———

*A*s one theatergoer put it, attending a Noh play is like being bitten to death by butterflies.

◆

—Howard Tomb, *Wicked Japanese: For the Business Traveler*

I look at the others around me, one woman lowering herself also into a crouch, and then slowly lowering herself to the ground; another man, staring forward, arms held as if in some karate pose called the praying mantis or the twisted crane; another moving with arms strapped across his chest, hugging his body as if trapped in a straitjacket. I am crawling on the floor, and as I close my eyes, Ono, who has been muttering, "Free, free" and "*Kangaenai, kangaenai*," stops everyone and says that in Butoh you keep your eyes open, slightly raised above eye-level vision. If you close your eyes, you lose the spirit, the process of giving and receiving, of creating a flow between what you see outside you and what is inside you; your eyes should take in the whole field of vision, but should not be focused on any particular object. Only the dead do not see, and when you are dancing you should be neither asleep nor dead, though you should be communicating, exchanging with the world of the dead.

A bit later, he stops someone and tells him to slow down. By slowing down you make your movements larger, says Ono; everything in the dance changes. After a few more minutes, he gives me an artificial oversized lily and tells me to look at it without focusing my eyes. It is an offering, he says. Somehow I sense he wants me to stop conceptualizing, to stop thinking how ridiculously or awkwardly or poorly I might be dancing, to forget what I am trying to represent with the dance, what I am trying to symbolize or imitate.

And, at certain moments, I do stop thinking. A brief, unnameable sadness seems to well up within me, and yet is offset by a rising joy. I start walking toward the screen door, where I see my grandfather and grandmother. I present them with the flower, a greeting bearing some part of me that has wandered through the world, unwhole, lost, bewildered, alien, fading in and out of the sense of playacting, of pleasing the *sensei*. I get a glimpse of what my self-consciousness misses.

David Mura, a Sansei, *third-generation Japanese-American, is an essayist and poet whose work has appeared in* The Nation, The Partisan Review *and other magazines. He has also been a recipient of an NEA Fellowship and the winner of* The Nation's *Discovery Prize.*

✳

Boon watched spellbound. The *shamisen* jarred on the last of the five notes of its theme, repeating it querulously until Corn Flower raised her head and revealed the lower half of her face, her bright red lips and white cheeks. The last note shuddered into silence, the dancer was obediently still. The *shamisen* attacked at a high pitch; her body jerked with a spasm, as if she had been stung, and with sharp, stiff movements of her hands and arms, warding off the jangle of chromatic sounds, the dancer began to retreat. She moved backwards to the left side of the stage, her face blind in the shadow of the wide-tilted hat, her body in profile to the audience displaying a classic kimono figure, one straight line from the head to the small of the back, bent knees pulling the material taut under the curve of her buttocks, both suppliant and erotic. Her white *tabi* never left the ground. She raised each heel slowly, the instep arched, sliding the sole of her foot noiselessly over the polished floor, lowered the heel. The rhythm of the *shamisen* became faster and more aggressive, breaking the dancer's controlled sequence of movements and forcing her into confusion; the straight neck suddenly buckled and slumped, no more than a few degrees, Boon saw, but exaggerated by the corresponding tilt of her hat. She stopped, flounced, pitching her head back and her buttocks out, straightened, shuffled forward a few paces and stopped again, turned from side to side as if searching for an escape and fluttered submissively to her knees. The strident, masterful music of the *shamisen* beat her still further down, she drew her arms into her sleeves and gently sank, nothing but white and gold, back into exhausted repose.

—John David Morley, *Pictures from the Water Trade: Adventures of a Westerner in Japan*

ALEX KERR

* * *

In Search of Beauty

How impossible is possible?

DAVID TAUGHT ME AN IMPORTANT LESSON WHICH I WOULD NEVER have heard from art historians and curators: beauty comes first. "It should be old, it should be valuable," he said. "But first ask yourself, 'Is it beautiful?'"

"How can I know if a new thing I have bought is beautiful, or if I have simply become carried away?" I asked.

He answered, "There are two ways. One is to have a beautiful house. The other is to surround the new thing with beautiful things. If it's not right, they will reject it."

After that, whenever I bought an antique, I would put it in David's living room to see how it looked. Most of the time my purchase would be revealed as an eyesore. But one time I bought an old Chinese table in Kyoto, brought it back to David's and set it in a *tokonoma* without telling anyone. We got through the whole evening without David noticing it, and so I knew that the table was good.

Fascinated as I was by David's collection, I was in no position to start collecting jades and Chinese ceramics. Instead, I continued with old books and calligraphy. By 1977 I had moved to Kameoka, so I had ample time to explore the antique shops of Kyoto. One

245

day, the master of an old bookstore showed me a set of ten *shikishi* (square plaques) and *tanzaku* (rectangular plaques)—small pieces of paper with calligraphy in an archaic and refined style. They were decorated very delicately with gold, silver and mica, on papers dyed red and blue. He was offering them to me for 5000 yen each, roughly $20 at the time. I turned them over and was shocked to read "Prince Konoe, Regent Nijo, Minister of the Left Karasumaru," and so on. These were genuine pieces of calligraphy by court nobles of the 17th century! I could not believe that they could be bought so cheaply, but at the time there was simply no interest in Japan in such things. So I began collecting *shikishi* and *tanzaku*. After I had acquired several dozen of them and the general style became clear, my curiosity was aroused. The hair-thin lines of elegant calligraphy on these plaques were different from anything I had ever seen in Japan. I began to inquire into the history of these princes and ministers, and was thus introduced to the world of the *kuge*, the court nobles.

The *kuge* were descended from the Fujiwara family, who ruled every aspect of court life during the Heian period. They controlled almost all the important court posts, reducing the Emperor to puppet status. It was the Fujiwara nobles and related families who built fantasy pavilions like Byodoin near Nara, and penned the poems and novels for which the Heian period is famous. After several hundred years of Fujiwara dominance, the extended family grew so large that it became necessary to distinguish between the various branches. So people started calling the branch lineages by their street addresses in Kyoto: the Imadegawa family, etc. Over time, there grew to be about one hundred families, called the *kuge*. They were seen as having semi-Imperial status, and were carefully distinguished from the *buke*, or *samurai* families.

When the *samurai* class overthrew the system of noble rule at the end of the 12th century, the *kuge* lost all their lands and revenue. They had no choice but to find work, but after four hundred years of writing poetry by moonlight, the only work they were able to do was in the field of the arts. So they became teachers of poetry, calligraphy, court dance and ritual. Over time, they developed a system of hereditary franchises, in which each family purported to be the holder of "secrets" passed down to the head of the house. Outsiders could only acquire these secrets by paying for them.

The next step, naturally, was the proliferation of secrets. The *kuge* organized their secrets into hierarchies, with lesser secrets for beginners and more profound secrets for advanced students, on an ascending pay scale. This was to become the prototype for the "schools" of tea ceremony, flower arrangement and martial arts predominant today. Typically, these schools have a hereditary Grand Master, a system of expensive titles and licenses granted to students, and ranks (such as the different colored belts in karate and judo).

With the coming of peace and prosperity at the beginning of the Edo era in the

> Every artist is a ghostly worker. Not by years of groping and sacrifice does he find his highest expression; the sacrificial past is within him; his art is an inheritance; his fingers are guided by the dead in the delineation of a flying bird, of the vapors of mountains, of the colors of the morning and evening, of the shape of branches and the spring burst of flowers: generations of skilled workmen have given him their cunning, and revive in the wonder of his drawing.
>
> —Lafcadio Hearn,
> *Writings from Japan*

early 1600s, a renaissance of *kuge* culture occurred in Kyoto. Each family taught its specialty, the Reizei concentrating on poetry, the Jimyoin on Imperial calligraphy, the Washio family on Shinto music, and so on. The one art they all had in common was their delicate calligraphy, which they wrote on *shikishi* and *tanzaku* at tea parties and poem festivals.

The *kuge* lived in cramped quarters in a village surrounding the Imperial palace. They never had money. The story goes that right up until World War II, they would pay a visit to their neighbors just before the New Year, when all debts must be settled. "I am very sorry," the *kuge* would say in polite accents, "but our family will not have enough money to pay our debts by the end of the year, so we will have to set fire to the house and flee in the night. I hope that will be no trouble to you." This was a disguised threat, since setting fire to one house in the crowded inner city of Kyoto might destroy an entire district. So the neighbors would take up a collection and bring the money over to the *kuge* on the last day of the year.

All the impoverished *kuge* possessed was their memory of the Heian era's refinement, so they developed ways of living elegantly in poverty. Examples of this can be seen in every *kuge* art, and it exercised an incalculable influence on the city of Kyoto. For example, the construction of teahouses such as the famous Katsura Detached Palace, the utensils of tea ceremony, even the dainty displays one sees today in store windows can be traced back to the *kuge*.

People who come to Kyoto hear much about Zen and tea ceremony. But Kyoto is not just Zen and tea; it was also the center of the culture which grew from the fine-grained sensibility of the *kuge*. When the capital was moved to Tokyo in 1868, many of the *kuge* moved north with the Emperor. Their village around the Imperial palace was razed, leaving the large open spaces you see today surrounding the palace. As a result, almost nothing tangible remains of *kuge* history, and their culture never became a tourist attraction; there is very little written about their world, so most people are hardly aware that it ever existed. Nevertheless, their romantically delicate sensibility survives in *waka* poetry, incense ceremony, *geisha* dance and Shinto ritual. But if I had not purchased a few 5000-yen *shikishi* on a whim, I would never have discovered it.

As the years I spent in Kyoto went by, the scope of my collection grew. The next step from *shikishi* and *tanzaku* was hanging scrolls, and then folding screens, ceramics, furniture, Buddhist sculpture, and more. My collection expanded to include not only Japanese art but pieces from China, Tibet and Southeast Asia as well. However, no matter how underpriced the folding screens or

Buddhist statues were, they never cost just hundreds or thousands of yen, so collecting began to involve real money. In order to pay for it, I began to sell or trade pieces to friends, and before I knew it, I had become an art dealer.

As the business grew, I eventually found my way into Kyoto's art auction; in Kyoto, these auctions are called *kai*, or "gatherings." These gatherings are a closed world known only to dealers. They are completely unlike Christie's or Sotheby's, where the auction houses research the pieces and publish a catalogue in advance, and buyers can examine objects at their leisure before bidding. In a Kyoto *kai*, no information is made available, and there is no time to even get a close look at the work. With a flourish, the auctioneer unrolls a handscroll across a long table, and with no mention of the work's author or date, the bidding commences. Buyers have only an instant in which to look over the seals and signature on the work and to examine the quality of the paper and ink before placing their bids. So participation in these auctions requires a highly trained eye, to say the least. At first I found myself utterly at a loss.

Rescue came in the form of my scroll mounter, Kusaka. At eighty, Kusaka had close to sixty years' experience of the Kyoto auctions, and over that time had seen tens of thousands of screens and hanging scrolls. I had sent him some of my screens for repair, and through this connection, he allowed me to accompany him to the *kai*. As a mounter, Kusaka could judge paper and ink with the eyes of an expert, and he had an encyclopedic memory of signatures and seals. Muttering, "No signature, but that's the seal of Kaiho Yusho—looks like the real thing..." or "The characters have vigor, but the paper is dubious. Maybe you ought to pass this one by...," Kusaka became my teacher at the *kai*. In this fashion, I was able to acquire knowledge that decades of university study could never bring.

There are two types of antiques. One consists of objects already circulating in the art world, in good condition and with artist, period and provenance well documented. The other type is made up of objects which in Kyoto are called *ubu* (literally infant). *Ubu* objects are those surfacing in the art world for the first time; very often they have sat for years in old storehouses. These storehouses, called *kura*, have defined the special character of the Japanese art market.

Traditionally, most houses in Japan of any size or wealth had a *kura* built alongside. These storehouses were necessary because of the "empty room" ethos. Furniture, paintings, screens, trays and tables appeared in a Japanese house only when needed, and varied by season and by occasion. I was once shown into a *kura* belonging to a prominent family in the mountains of Okayama. The mistress of the house explained that she kept three full sets of lacquer trays and bowls there—one for the household, one for guests, and one for VIPs. Well-to-do families needed a place, separated from the house itself, where they could store such things. You can spot *kura* by their unique architecture: tall, squarish structures with peaked roofs, a few tiny windows and walls of thick white plaster. The plaster walls protected the buildings against damage from the fires and earthquakes which were the scourge of Japan.

There was a strong taboo against entering the *kura* unless you were the head of the house. In Kyoto, a maid would boast about her status by saying. "I'm the number one maid. I'm allowed to enter the *kura*." Even in the prewar years, when Japan's culture was still more or less intact, *kura* were rarely entered, and obscure objects inside tended to get forgotten. And after the cultural shock of World War II, there was suddenly no need at all for the trays, plates and screens kept inside them, so their huge wooden doors were shut for good. Their present-day owners, caught up in the rush for modernization, deem the *kura* and their contents almost completely worthless: when it comes time to tear down an old compound, the owner calls in an antique handler, or "runner," who buys the entire contents of the *kura* in one lot, more or less as scrap. The runner carts it all away in a truck and delivers it to the auctions, where dealers such as myself see it for the first time. These things are *ubu*. When an artwork which has been sleeping for years in a *kura* arrives at auction, it is as if it has popped out of history. Sometimes I open a screen—stiff from mildew, damp and insect

damage—and realize that I am likely to be the first person to see
it in a century. At such times, memories come welling up of a child
unwrapping straw rope from Imari plates in Motomachi long ago.

Ubu objects are the ultimate risky venture for an art collector.
There are no guarantees, and huge problems of repair and restora-
tion. But this is where the excitement lies. David Kidd once said
to me, "Having a lot of money and using it to buy great pieces of
art on the world market—anyone can do that. Not having money,
but still being able to buy great pieces—that's fun."

Which brings me to the secret of how "impossible was possible" for David and me. Neither of us had much money at first, but
we were able to build art collections wildly out of proportion to
our means. And we didn't achieve this in some poverty-stricken
Third World country, but in an advanced economic superpower. It
was possible because of the lack of interest of the Japanese in their
own cultural heritage. Chinese art maintains its value on the world
market because as the Chinese get rich, the first thing they do is
invest in traditional cultural objects; there is a large community of
Chinese art collectors. In prewar Japan there existed such a community, in which Japanese collectors vied with each other for fine
paintings, calligraphies and ceramics. They were the ones who
stocked the *kura*.

After the war, this community evaporated, so today there are almost no significant private collectors of Japanese art. The only exception is tea masters. The tea-ceremony world is still very active
so utensils such as tea bowls, scoops and scrolls for the tearoom are
highly valued; in fact, they are very often overvalued, and command ridiculous prices. But step outside the world of tea, and
Japanese artworks sell for a song. For example, I made quite a collection of handscrolls, some of them with calligraphy by artists
greatly prized by tea masters. Handscrolls roll sideways and can be
ten or even twenty meters long. Unlike hanging scrolls, they are
difficult to use in the tearoom. So they sell for a fraction of the cost
of hanging scrolls, although they have equivalent, or even greater,
artistic and historical value.

I once acquired a handscroll of the Kabuki play *Chushingura*

(*The Forty-Seven Samurai*), an enormous piece just over one meter high and ten meters long. It was originally a banner illustrating each of the eleven acts of the play, and was probably used by a traveling Kabuki troupe in the mid-19th century. On doing some research, I found there was nothing comparable in any of Japan's museums, and that possibly I had chanced into ownership of the finest *Chushingura* scroll in all Japan. But being young and very poor I had no choice but to sell the work.

I first approached my friends in the Kabuki world. But these actors spend their daily life immersed in Kabuki trappings, and they told me that the scroll was hardly what they would want to relax with at home. I could see their point, so I then tried selling the piece to Shochiku Inc., the entertainment giant that produces movies and manages Kabuki. They weren't interested. Foreign companies in Japan often display gold screens or folk art in their lobbies, so I thought Japanese firms might do the same. I took every opportunity to look around the premises when I happened to be visiting an office building. But everywhere I turned, Western Impressionists hung from the walls, and I could only conclude that Japanese companies had zero interest in the traditional art of their country.

Next, I decided to try my luck with Japan's art museums. However, on hearing of this, my veteran art-dealer friends in Kyoto were quick to dissuade me. Without proper introductions, there was virtually no chance that these museums would give a young foreigner like me a hearing. I tried other avenues, such as approaching the Sengaku-ji Temple in Tokyo, which is dedicated to the memory of the 47 *samurai*, but received only a brusque rebuff on the telephone. In the end, an American friend bought the scroll for the absurdly low price of $4000, and it went to Fargo, North Dakota.

Alex Kerr also contributed "Osaka: Bumpers and Runners" to Part Two. This story was excerpted from his book, Lost Japan.

✳

"There!" he said suddenly. "That's what I like best."

The boat had rounded the spit. There, on the other side, was a tiny island, high, a rockery, the kind of rocks one sees in Chinese Sung paintings. At the very top, surrounded by wind-bent pines, was a small shrine.

The entire prospect was superbly beautiful, even if one remembered gossip about its presiding goddess. The scene was made of so little—the horizon of the sea, some rocks piled high, a pine or two, the little shrine, the sky. Views are rarely this simple. This one was so right, so appropriate, that it seemed ideal. And like all ideal things it did not seem real, but more like a mirage floating on the surface of the sea.

If I had seen a picture of it, I would have said it was pretty—a postcard view, typical Japan. But coming upon it in a boat under a summer morning sky, I was startled into beholding its simplicity. It was accidental, this beauty. And it is difficult for us to believe or remember or admit that the greatest beauty is always accidental.

And this accidental quality is to be captured only if the full context is shown. Japanese scenery is like Japanese poetry. Both its beauty and meaning depend upon a context of things perhaps incongruous. One observes a relationship that had always hitherto escaped notice but which, once seen, becomes inevitable.

Such an island as this exists, but its beauty exists in the morning sky, in the endless expanse of sea, in the light that hovers and bathes. Japanese scenic beauty is a whole beauty because it requires this context before it can be recognized. Since it is whole, it creates in the viewer a sense of wholeness, however fugitive. Travelers from our fragmented West are ravished by the vision of such wholeness, such natural inclusion of everything in the world. I gaze. The beauty lies not in the single lovely object standing alone. It is in this combination that slides into and out of its background. The shrine is not beautiful, nor are these pines. It is their being so much a part of the sea and the sky that makes them beautiful.

—Donald Richie, *The Inland Sea*

STEVEN WARDELL

* * *

Capsule Cure

Coffin anyone?

THE HEART OF TOKYO'S BUSINESS DISTRICT, SHINJUKU, IS A congested, confusing realm where winding streets converge. One will lead to the Green Plaza Capsule Hotel, my destination for the night.

A *bijinesuman* and two colleagues emerge from a cramped basement bar. The leader pauses half-way up the white-tiled stairway to throw up on his shoes, and then sinks to his knees. Shaking off help, he continues his wobbly ascent. His followers succeed in reaching the top, whereupon they wipe off their ankles with delicate silk handkerchiefs. Arm in arm, the tipsy three jostle each other into a nearby office building and then into an elevator with me. One of them presses the fourth-floor button: KAPUSERU HOTERU. It is 11:30 p.m.

The doors snap open onto a bright, clean, quiet lobby, where the elevator's beery smell quickly dissipates. Half a dozen subdued men in charcoal or blue business suits and stocking feet are lined up at the registration desk. I deposit my shoes at the shoe-check window and join them. As they wait, the men watch two television screens suspended above the registration desk. The sets display strategically blurred American pornographic videos.

I am noticed immediately. The clerk calls to the back room, and the manager emerges to open up a new check-in line, just for me. The manager wants to make sure I'm in the right place. Twice he points to his desk and says, "*Kapuseru hoteru.*" I nod in turn. He asks hopefully, "*Kapuseru ja nai?*" ("Not capsule?") A toothy grin: You're not, after all, interested in checking in, are you?

"*Hai, kapuseru,*" I correct him.

The manager sucks his teeth for a few seconds, while the clerk glances at him sideways. In desperation he tosses out a few English words. "Understand...*hmmmm*...unusual hotel."

"*Hai,*" I say. "I understand."

I am here to experience the uniquely Japanese capsule hotel, totally foreign to my notion of an overnight stay. Beyond the lobby, I know, are hundreds of tiny prefabricated units, roughly three feet by three feet by six feet six inches, stacked two-high like Pullman berths. Or as I can also picture them, like a double row of coffins, pointed feet-first toward the aisle.

I pre-pay for the night. Escorting me to the locker room, the manager straps a locker key on my wrist with a velcro band. These babying precautions are not only for foreigners but for all guests, because they're likely to be drunk and unconcerned about their own safety.

Over the public-address system a soft, sexy woman's voice repeats the instructions every few minutes: change into the underpants and *happi* coat provided by the hotel and lock up everything else. Men change at their lockers in awkward slow motion, requiring the support of the walls and the guidance of the sweet-sounding voice as they take ten minutes, on average, to do the job. Some keep up a slow, friendly banter—not the common talk of friends but more like that of off-duty soldiers, bonded by their escape to this capsule retreat. They are here with their comrades. They are safe now, among allies.

Uninhibitedly nude, they pause for long blank stretches before putting on fresh blue boxer shorts and a skimpy white *happi* coat that resembles a hospital gown. (No provision is made for women guests at the Green Plaza; none are expected.) They are reassessing themselves, changing modes, transforming themselves from businessmen into recuperating capsuleers. One jovial elderly guest tries to carry his wrist bag—with his money, keys, business cards, status-brand gum, and train pass—beyond the locker room. He has not fully changed, but he has already locked his locker. An employee solicitously reminds him that he will surely lose his wrist bag. Pleased by the special attention, the old man donates his wrist bag to the startled employee, pats him on the hand, and coos words of gratitude.

The employee is far younger than the client but uses the voice of an elder brother to stop the old man and instruct him to finish changing. After the white-haired guest has donned his uniform, the staffer velcroes the key back onto his wrist, wipes his nose for him, and leads him to the next stop.

The manager, who has supervised my metamorphosis, points me toward the rest of the hotel. As I enter the common room, *Dallas* is playing on the television. Bivouacking businessmen watch from lounge chairs, encircled by vending machines that sell sodas, pep drinks, isotonic drinks, hot drinks, dried squid, seaweed, Cheez Doodles, and chocolate bars. After I have taken a seat, one of the TV-watchers, Takeshi Matsuoka, leans over to speak to me in English. A clean-cut, pleasant-looking man, he surprises me, not just because he's speaking English but because everyone except the manager has studiously ignored the foreigner, and I have just gotten used to that.

Matsuoka is not one of the drunks. Tomorrow he will attend a seminar here in Shinjuku at 6:00 a.m. Because he lives in Chiba, a far suburb, there is, he says, no train early enough. He is not pleased about the hour set for the meeting or about having to pay for a hotel. He asks why I'm here.

I explain that I want to experience something uniquely Japanese. To me this hotel seems a symbol of modern Japan—its crowding, but also its group spirit, sacrifice, and practicality. "Don't you have the same thing in America?" Matsuoka asks. I tell him that we probably never will, because in America staying in a capsule hotel would be an admission of failure, suggesting an inability to afford something grander, plus a drinking problem.

"In Japan a capsule hotel is a sign of victory," Matsuoka counters. "It's a major convenience and a triumph of efficiency. Some *bijinesuman* stay in capsules half the week to avoid a long commute. They like watching TV instead of standing for two hours on a crowded train. Peak use is Wednesday and Thursday nights, when some workers may stay at their desks past eleven and then find themselves too tired to go home. But this is Friday, so many are here tonight because of too much drink."

After *Dallas* these common-room convalescents watch two more American shows dubbed in Japanese—one about a horse farm in the Midwest, the other about a private eye in California. During a commercial break I hear the rousing music of the Regain march, advertising a pep tonic. The ad portrays a businessman sallying forth, larger than life, to conquer the world, lightning flashing from his eye, attaché case and a yellow-and-black bottle of Regain in his hands.

Matsuoka translates the first stanza and the refrain for me:

"Yellow and black is the sign of courage. Can you fight for twenty-four hours? Regain, Regain, our Regain. In the attaché case put the sign of courage. Can you fight all over the world?

"Businessman, businessman, Japanese businessman."

Barefoot like everyone else, I visit the lavatory-washroom and find two flip-flop slippers outside the entrance. (In Japan a lavatory's ceramic floors are "not clean" by convention, and require their own slippers.) The man before me must have put on two left slippers; I slip into the remaining pair of right ones. The bare, peach-tiled washroom dispenses free disposable toothbrushes. Paste has already been applied, presumably in case an unsteady guest can't get it together.

Two floors above, a dozen men float on their backs, arms propped on the edges of three white-tiled hot pools, each a yard or so deep and a little larger than a king-size bed. Two young women in white slacks provide massages in open stalls, where men lie on gurneys, partly covered by towels. A weight machine and an exercise bicycle occupy a room to the side, along with do-it-yourself hair-care stations stocked with combs in an ultrasound sterilizer and a variety of mousses, gels, and hair tonics. The blue glow from a tanning booth chills the white walls of the room. If anyone still has work to do—and is fit to do it—the hotel is prepared. Private studies the size of a couple of phone booths are each furnished with a desk, a chair, and a banker's lamp.

Continuing my tour of the hotel, I descend a flight to the restaurant. At 1:30 a.m. businessmen are relaxing after a light meal by taking off their *happi* coats and tipping back in their chairs. The restaurant is very simple, serving mostly noodles. Its decor includes a fake fireplace and small tables spread over a large carpeted area. On each table free cigarettes are stuffed into a beer glass, and there are dispensers for disposable chopsticks and toothpicks. The tables form a semicircle around a TV broadcasting a golf match from Scotland. The men laugh, josh each other, smoke, slurp noodles—enjoying themselves as if among pals. Some of the older troops play *go*.

I can't read the menu, so I order *ramen*, a noodle dish for 550 yen (more than $5). The waiter writes my wristband number on the bill. I will pay in the morning, in exchange for my shoes. The fellow next to me falls asleep, his forehead slowly descending into his bowl. The waiter deftly cradles the head, removing it from the bowl, and rests it sidelong on the table without waking the man up. I try to start a conversation in English—my Japanese isn't good enough—with several apparently inert men sitting near me. The third time I succeed. My question is "Why are you here tonight?" This one smiles and slowly explains in English: "To...*not* the wife."

Glass walls separate the restaurant from a room on the same floor where 50 patrons rest on fully reclined chaises. Closely packed, the chaises resemble deck chairs around a pool. The lights are on, and noise travels through the glass from the restaurant's television and noodle-slurpers, yet most of the patrons seem able to sleep. They are restless, though, tossing their arms and legs across their comrades. The bodies slump, twist, and contort, as if writhing from some form of shell shock—casualties, one might think, of Japan's international trade wars.

At 3:00 a.m. the restaurant area is as full as ever. Why aren't they asleep? Most of them could be at home in bed by now. These men are putting something off, deliberately not surrendering to sleep. They prefer to lie paralyzed in front of the TV. Most of them are still up at 3:30, when I withdraw to my capsule.

The hotel's stacks of beige plastic capsules are located within an angular labyrinth, eerily reminiscent of a columbarium or a morgue. To enter an upper capsule, you climb two steps on a small ladder attached at one side of the lower capsule's square opening and then twist sideways to sit on the edge of the upper opening. Then you

> ——)——
>
> *A*nd so it has come to be that the beauty of a Japanese room depends on a variation of shadows, heavy shadows against light shadows— it has nothing else.
>
> ◆
>
> —Jun'ichiro Tanizaki, *In Praise of Shadows*

lean back and launch yourself in headfirst, horizontally. Presumably the less athletically inclined guests (not to mention the drunk ones) are assigned to bottom-level capsules, for reasons of triage.

The smell inside the capsule is a mixture of chlorine vapors descending from the bath area, the soaps and deodorants of the capsuleers, and the new-car smell of the fresh, shiny capsules themselves. A one-inch-thick futon slightly cushions the length of the capsule. After scooting backward inside, you lean forward and pull down a translucent plastic shade to cover the opening. But the shade doesn't shut out the presence of the bodies surrounding you. Like a high-tech pup tent, the capsule shuts out nothing except the view.

At the entrance, where the foot of the bed is located, a white bedsheet and a beige blanket lie folded together like computer paper. I am more than six feet tall, and although the capsule is barely long enough, the covers aren't. If I pull the sheet and blanket up to cover the top of my chest, they slide off my toes, which then catch a breeze from the aisle just outside. Inside the capsule there is room for only a few activities, most of which require you to prop yourself up on one elbow. The capsule contains a television, a radio, a mirror, a shelf for toiletries, a reading light, an alarm clock, and a fire alarm (with a no-smoking sign). The speaker for the television is positioned right next to your ear, so that the sound won't annoy others (except that it does). Among the offerings are the same pornographic videos being shown above the registration desk.

All around me is snoring. The vibrations feel as though my comrade on the left were shoveling the phlegm in his nasal cavity back and forth. He almost swallows it on the intake. When he exhales, it flaps out at the edge of his nostrils before he catches it and breathes it back in. The noise is loud.

Somewhere very close, two men are snoring alternately at the same speed. One snores "*zzzz*" in and breathes out silently, by which time the other is snoring inward. Together they generate a constant dull growl that sounds as though I were sitting near the jet engines on an airplane.

From the capsules come the sounds of:

- a cellophane wrapper being torn and wadded
- squid being chewed for a very long time by someone who doesn't shut his mouth
- a televised sports game of some sort
- teeth being brushed (someone has returned from the washroom with the toothbrush still in his mouth)
- heavy breathing.

I feel the press of bodies; five human beings within three radial feet of me. Each has a force that extends three feet all around and presses against my force, my personal space. I feel uncomfortable. I also think I'm the only one feeling this way.

The person below me shifts violently against the side of his capsule, shaking mine. Something that can only be his face smacks the plastic wall like a slab of ham. I feel him drag his arm along the capsule's squeaky-clean wall. Someone struggles to close the shade at the foot of his capsule. Hooking the latch at the bottom is the only complicated operation in the whole hotel. Each attempt sends the spring-loaded shade chattering up like a machine gun. He is successful on his eighth try. *"Ehche ehche ehcheche"* the sound of dry retching issues from another capsule. Someone shifts from side to side all night. A distant TV broadcasts until morning; that guy must have fallen asleep watching the palm-sized screen suspended less than two feet from his face.

In the morning everyone leaves quickly, quietly, separately, without even a nod to last night's comrades. Girding themselves anew in their business suits, some of the men depart to face the family for a weekend. Others will return to the front lines. They try hard to organize themselves and their clothing, clearly not quite ready for Tokyo and the renewal of their struggle. As the occupants leave, ancient, sexless *obasans* ("grandmothers") in face masks and rubber gloves whip out the washable futons and sheets and swab the insides of the capsules. These tiny ladies rouse the heaviest sleepers, including me, by twisting our feet like a steering wheel.

The late risers slip into the locker room, where the public-address system emits the bright sound of chirping birds. A woman's voice, quivering with emotion, interjects *"Ohaiyo gozaimasu?* ("Good morning") at intervals. On the way out rumpled or dirtied guests can buy new shirts at reasonable prices, and also socks and boxer shorts, or a Hanes undershirt that calls itself a "great American original." A dry-cleaning service has opened out of nowhere in a corner of the registration area. You do not have to take your sweaty, vomit-encrusted clothes home or to the office. They will be ready when you next check in.

The elevator whisks my comrades from their capsule stronghold. Out of the little black handbags that they clutch to their chests come sunglasses, useful defenses against the sun's bright attack. Some stop to buy a "wellness" drink from a vending machine on the street.

Beyond the sanitized capsule refuge the city, too, has been refreshed. This busy consumer area of Tokyo is once again litterless and sparkling. The men of Mister Donut are scrubbing their sidewalk. Japan is neat and cute again. Last night's dank confusion has been transformed into a shopping mecca for Saturday-morning homemakers—the industrial warriors' wives. The throbbing hum of Tokyo continues, at a different pitch.

Steven Wardell is a writer whose work appears in The Atlantic Monthly *and other publications.*

★

After the banquet began, I found myself in for another surprise. People were going around eagerly pouring drinks for one another, scarcely glancing at their food. Clearly, the main purpose of the banquet was not to enjoy one's food but to drink. This explained why the quality of the food was a nonissue.

I patiently explained that I was not a drinker, but such quibbles were swept aside as I was urged, "Drink up, drink up!" Evidently noticing my troubled expression, someone gave me some advice as he poured me a drink.

"It's not like this in the provinces. There, they have a hole in the sake-cup that you have to keep your finger over, or else the sake runs out the bottom. It's served good and hot, too, so you'll scald your finger unless you gulp it down fast. Anyway, it's a good idea to train yourself to be able to drink."

What a difference in the method of pouring drinks, I couldn't help thinking. In the West, a *sommelier* pours wine; to abstain, all you need do is lay your fingers lightly across your wineglass. As a result, it is possible to remain in control of your own drinking. Accustomed to that approach, I was truly amazed by the kind of boozing that went on during this office trip.

The main purpose of the banquet, I soon learned, was to get drunk together. Moreover, I observed that even people whom everyone knew to have a low tolerance of alcohol were forced to drink whether they liked it or not.

"Government officials have to be able to hold their liquor. This is for your own good," such hapless individuals are assured. In fact, however, the sight of one's victim suffering the ill effects of alcohol is a source of endless amusement. Nobody interferes; everyone enjoys the spectacle. In the Japanese world of seniority systems and lifelong employment, when a superior offers to pour you a drink, it's hard to say no.

—Masao Miyamoto, M.D., *Straitjacket Society: An Insider's Irreverent View of Bureaucratic Japan*

LOUISE RAFKIN

✴ ✴ ✴

A Yen for Cleaning

Zen and the art of water closet maintenance.

A FRIEND HAD TOLD ME ABOUT SHO ISHIKAWA, WHO HAD GROWN up in Ittoen, a commune near Kyoto where toilet cleaning was considered a path to self-knowledge. Sho's parents had spent most of their lives in the commune. Indeed, his father was in some ways one of the present spiritual leaders.

Sho himself now lived in Manhattan and worked in public accounting. "It is difficult to imagine cleaning for your whole life," he warned me during the first of our phone conversations.

But perhaps I could. To augment my earnings as a writer, I had been cleaning professionally for six years.

Ittoen, "One Light" or "One-Lamp Garden," is a community inspired by the spiritual awakening, teachings, and life example of a man named Tenko Nishida (1872-1968). Not a religion in the sense of a creed with a specific object of worship or set of scriptures, Ittoen honored Tenko-san's "Oneness of Light" philosophy while embracing all spiritualities grounded in the ideal of humble service. Both Buddha and Christ lived the life of the homeless, I would be reminded later, and both washed the feet of others.

Tenko-san had first become disenchanted with capitalism in the late 1880s. Unwilling to struggle against others for his own survival, he challenged the assumption that one worked in order to live. Tenko-san's awakening came after three days of meditation: Life was given freely to all by "the Light," or by God, and was not something that had to be worked for. Work was therefore a way of offering thanksgiving for the gift of life.

Renouncing his family, his status, and all possessions. Tenko-san began to serve others. He scrubbed, chopped wood, and cleaned privies. Declining all but the bare necessities, he connected with others through service. For him, this was enlightenment. Over the years, Tenko-san attracted followers, and in 1928, some land was donated for the establishment of a community. In the 50's and 60s, the commune had hundreds of members. Now, nearly thirty years after his death, only about one hundred and fifty remained.

I don't think Sho quite knew *why* I wanted to travel ten thousand miles to scrub toilets with a bunch of people I couldn't even talk to, and I wasn't sure myself. Nevertheless, after a succession of phone calls to Japan, a week-long visit was arranged that would culminate on the national Day of Labor, a day the entire community went cleaning. Sho's English teacher, a woman close to seventy who had lived over forty years in the commune, would be my official host.

The Ittoen compound is tucked into the hills east of Kyoto. Gorgeously kept grounds—maples and mossy, rolling hills—hug an odd array of buildings. Several older women were sweeping leaves with traditional bamboo brooms.

Outside the office, I met Sho's teacher, Ayako Isayama, a slight, short-haired woman in a black, karate-*gi* like smock. She politely invited me to follow her to my room, then took off at such a clip that in order to keep up I was forced into a gallop.

I had imagined a small group of dedicated cleaners, living in spartan quarters, buckets and sponges always at hand. Instead, I found a highly organized group who run what is essentially a small town with its own complicated economy. I would soon learn that although members own little personal property—all possessions are given up upon joining—the commune supports itself by operating various businesses, including schools, a press, a theater group, and a "theme park," dedicated to the ideal of peace, located in a southern province.

The group also facilitates training sessions for young factory workers and businesspeople, and as we approached the building in which I was to stay, we encountered a line of gi-clad men and women who looked, as they jogged past, to be in their early twenties. Though it was late afternoon and the fall air was crisp, they wore their flip-flops barefoot, without *tabi*, the split-toed Japanese socks.

"Mr. Donut workers," Ayako explained. "Four days' training. Humble toilet cleaning, door-to-door service."

Four thousand Mr. Donut workers spend time at Ittoen each year; the training is meant to promote humility and facilitate group dynamics. They are assigned specific houses in nearby towns for toilet cleaning. And they seek out a variety of other tasks—washing clothes, babysitting, weeding—wherever they are needed, undertaking such service in the tradition of *takuhatsu*, the "begging-bowl rounds" practiced by Zen monks, who still visit households reciting sutras. The last day is set aside for the workers to reflect on their training.

It's a stretch for me to imagine a group of American workers, say from Dunkin' Donuts or Burger King, jogging door-to-door, heads bowed, begging to clean toilets.

That night, Ayako made dinner in the quiet, dark kitchen of our dormitory. We chatted in simple English. I asked if I might be able to clean with the Mr. Donut trainees. Ayako, considering my request, looked away from me. "Difficult, with no Japanese," she short-handed. "May not be possible." She rose and began to wash the dishes. "Saturday," she said. "You clean then, with the group." It was Monday. "Morning service at 5:30," she announced.

At dawn's light I followed Ayako down the dusky corridor of our ancient building, where she sped off towards the Spirit Hall. Inside the bare wood hall, both Buddhist and Christian images flanked the altar. At center position was a round window opening onto a view of the forest. Ittoen elders and Mr. Donut people were seated on both sides of the room, kneeling on tatami platforms,

men on one side and women on the other. I took a seat behind
Ayako. We began with a song recounting Ittoen history, and then
chanted a Buddhist sutra, the gist of which was non-attachment to
worldly goods.

After the service, I raced behind Ayako back to our place for the
daily morning cleaning. She offered me a choice of toilet brush or
broom. I went with the brush and was handed a bucket and rag.
Ayako set off to mop the entire building, and was, of course, finished before me. Experience and a lifetime of cleaning, I told myself consolingly.

In the week that followed, I asked Ayako several times about
going door-to-door, but each time she seemed evasive. Aside
from our morning service, and helping her with some translating,
my time was my own. Couldn't I take the initiative myself, even
go into town on my own? The thought of knocking on a door
without a translator was daunting. Would they invite me into
their bathrooms?

One evening, I flipped through the pages of one of Ayako's
many scrapbooks while she talked about her life. She spoke of her
own spiritual awakening, which literally happened after cleaning
a toilet.

"I swept the cobwebs and began to scrub. After about thirty
minutes the grain of the floor came to be seen and the stool became white. Wiping my sweat, I looked behind me and saw the
lady of the house chanting Buddha's name, her hands in prayer. It
was a meeting of two persons, in prayer and in peace. I went outside and saw a tiny blue flower blooming by the roadside. I talked
with the blue flower, just like I am talking to you."

I nodded, but never in my toilet-cleaning life had I ever come
close to this kind of feeling, or spoken to a flower.

"In my heart I saw a big tree, with everything in its branches.
You, me, air, birds, flowers. I knew everything was related. That was
my realization after cleaning that toilet."

I flipped pages; the photos dated back decades. Many pictures
documented *roto*, the "life of the homeless," and showed lines of
uniformed disciples marching across the countryside or through

small Japanese villages. In these, Ayako was often at the head of the group beside Tenko-san.

"Were you ever scared?" I asked. "Not knowing where you'd end up each night?" "Once," she said. "In America."

She pulled an album from the bottom of the stack. Inside, there were pictures of Ayako with American families, on a farm, one next to a Washington, D.C., apartment building. And there were newspaper clippings, circa mid-70's, about a young Japanese "nun" who had volunteered to massage feet at several retirement homes. "For over one month I did humble service. I spent six dollars," she said. "Two dollars I gave to a church."

I drew out the whole story, beginning with Ayako's middle-of-the-night arrival at JFK Airport and the taxi driver who carted her to Manhattan for free at the end of his shift. At Penn Station, while waiting for a bus to rural New Jersey, she cleaned toilets and massaged the feet of a homeless woman.

It was in New Jersey, during a four-hour trek down a country road, that Ayako had felt afraid. She didn't know where she was going and felt so lonely she was almost crying. When she finally stumbled onto a family home, she explained her mission simply to the woman of the house. "I live in Japan. My work is to help people. May I work for you?" she asked, with her hands in prayer.

She stayed at this house almost a week, cleaning, cooking Japanese food, and working in the garden. "They asked me always to pray over their food," she said, translating the Ittoen grace: "True faithfulness consists of doing service for others and ignoring your own interests."

At 6:30 on Saturday morning, about seventy people gathered on the school grounds, each dressed in full Ittoen gear. Our destination was in Osaka, where, as a group, we were to clean a large Buddhist temple. After an official toilet-cleaning poem was recited, we marched out of the compound in a single line, while those staying behind bowed us on our way. With Ittoen flags flying and buckets looped over left arms, we snaked our way down to the nearby town where our buses waited.

Arriving in Osaka around eight, I was escorted with my team

to a graveled area about the size of a football field. I was given a bamboo broom. At first look, the ground seemed clean, but closer inspection revealed tiny leaves, cigarette butts, and scraps of litter.

Sweep too hard and the gravel comes up, producing a mound of leaves, dirt, and trash, while leaving bald patches of ground. Sweep lightly and nothing moves. I watched as members of my team flicked their brooms expertly with the precise amount of oomph. In hopes of getting the "trick," I experimented with left-handed, right-handed, and back-handed techniques. After an hour, I had barely swept a quarter of the space completed by the others.

As we approached a particularly dirty and trash-laden area, I noticed a group of men sprawled on some stairs outside an abandoned building. Even at this early hour, most had been drinking. Red-faced and weary, they were watching us work. It made me nervous.

As we neared, several men got up and began throwing trash in the bins and stacking empty bottles. Then I remembered something Ayako had told me about Tenko-san. In his day, when down-and-outs came to Ittoen, as many did following the war's devastation, each was welcomed and given food and shelter. But after two days, they were required to join work groups or do *roto*. Tenko-san believed handouts would brew resentment and keep people disempowered. Work would reveal a heart of thanksgiving.

Over the course of the day, I had felt like my sweeping was improving, but at quitting time, I realized that someone from my group had always been working some distance behind me. I looked at the path that I'd cleared and then at the ground they had passed over. Shards of leaves and a tiny confetti of trash spotted my work. Where they had swept, the ground was pristine, a carpet of smooth, gray rock.

Suddenly, I was really tired.

On the bus ride back to Ittoen, the skyscrapers of Osaka disappearing behind me, I questioned if I were capable of selfless cleaning. The week's experience had set me face-to-face with my shortcomings and fears. In my cleaning world I got things—money, free time, acknowledgment, Here, cleaning was about giving everything up.

And yet, the complications of *my* life—what to do or be, where to live—fell away against the backdrop of this selfless community. Dust to dust? Who really believes it?

My last teatime with Ayako was brief. She offered tangerines, tart and juicy.

"How can others—how can I—live Ittoen principles out there? In America?"

Ayako's eyes were downcast. She carefully separated the sections of her fruit and didn't say anything for what seemed a long time, though this wasn't unusual during our talks.

"Live a simple life with an affluent spirit."

I sipped my tea and flipped again through my favorite photo album, the one with pictures of early Ittoen life. There were several photos of Ayako and Tenko-san cleaning together, which now, after my own cleaning experience, seemed truly beautiful. And another: Ayako with her headscarf tied behind her ears, barely visible over the right shoulder of an aged Tenko-san, he steadying himself with a staff, the misty Ittoen hillside in the background.

"Take whatever you wish," Ayako said.

"But these are originals. You must want them?" I asked. "Others must want them?"

"I'll die soon," Ayako said. "A few will be saved. The others will go with my body and with the ashes of others, with the ashes of Tenko-san."

I peeled several photos from the book.

"Take care of everything you have," she added. "Everything given to us is in trust from the Light."

I thought of the place I owned in the Bay Area. Eight years ago, when I had first quit my job and set off for a writer's colony, an adventure I thought might last a year, I had sublet the house. Since then, I had lived in at least seven cities, on several continents, snagged at least a dozen sublets myself, and begun my cleaning life.

I knew the basement of my house was now crammed full of other people's castoffs, and what had been a neatly tended garden was overgrown. The once-bountiful fruit trees were in desperate need of husbandry and no longer producing. A tenant had recently sent me pictures of my bedroom, post-1989 earthquake: cracks and hairline fractures crisscrossed the walls.

It was time to clean house.

Louise Rafkin is the author of Other People's Dirt. *She has written for* The New York Times Magazine, Tricycle: The Buddhist Review, Cosmopolitan, OUT, *and other publications as well as commentary for National Public Radio.*

✳

The Japan Toilet Association was officially founded in May of 1985 and thereafter has been nothing short of a keenly focused organization. A promotional pamphlet entitled *The Restroom Revolution of Japan* described the group as "entirely committed to the toilet, the only association of its kind in the world." Its membership was comprised of a voluntary network of planners, designers, and researchers. With far-reaching vision, they had set out to transform the unsafe and unsanitary image of public restrooms, a largely expected condition worldwide, referred to in Japanese as the "Four K's"—*katanai, kural, kowai,* and *kusai* (dirty, dark, scary, and smelly).

The Four K's are seen as representative of a variety of urban and environmental issues, including the discrimination faced by senior citizens, children, and the disabled. In the less economically advantaged parts of the world, add to that list women and the poor. The Japan Toilet Association, through a series of national and international symposiums, study teams that travel abroad, even such things as restroom design contests and toilet essay competitions, soon captured the attention of their government and the Japanese public. A progressive toilet culture has since grown up around the construction or remodeling, the beautification, and the successful maintenance of urban public restrooms.

—Kathleen Meyer, "Toiletopia: Plunging into 'Things Japanese'"

CLEO PASKAL

✳ ✳ ✳

Love Boat, Japanese–Style

The author goes to great lengths to get a date.

HE WAS GORGEOUS, OK? IT'S MY ONLY EXCUSE BUT IT'S A DAMN good one. I had been in Japan for over a month. Lonely place, Japan. Not that easy to get a date. Unless you are a Western male. A lot of Japanese women go for Western men on the daring assumption that they are not as mindbogglingly sexist as Japanese men. But I'm a Western female. All my countrymen were already dating Ms. Yukiko Perfect and most Japanese men willing to go out with a Western woman were, let's just say, a bit odd. One too many *Anne of Green Gables* movies, or something. I had tried everything. In desperation, I had even bound and gagged my pride and had a go at the traditional Japanese way of getting a date.

My friend Metz took me to visit his steamed-apple-face grandma. She is an *o-miai* co-ordinator, a match-maker. Rumour is, about a third of all Japanese marriages are arranged through an *o-miai* co-ordinator but stats are hard to come by as most Japanese would prefer to say they met their partners through AA than through *o-miai*. Metz's grandmother had been the mysterious, but beaming, guest of honour at over 250 weddings. Not that I was looking to get married, more like a subtle urge for some honeymoon-type action.

I was appraised over a dinner. My chopstick technique was good. I even passed the picking up soft tofu test. I ate *sushi* with a smile. I went "mmmm" as I choked down the slimy seaweed salad. I slurped my noodles. I managed over an hour of sitting on my knees on the *tatami* floor. I was an all-around, full-on candidate for *Karate Kid III*. Wax On Wax Off this, grandma.

During dinner, grandma was all smiles and nods. Afterwards, she gave me a kimono and showed me how to put it on. Slightly more complicated than bandaging yourself up after an arm amputation. Things (though not necessarily me) were looking good.

Grandma grinned proudly as she put the finishing tweaks on the big bow that held the kimono together, effectively gift wrapping me. Through Metz, I asked her what the criteria were for a good match. With the certainty of an expert in the field, she replied that there were only two things important in a marriage: that the man be taller than the woman, and that he also be better educated. Given how short and dumb I was, she beamed, she thought she could make me a good match. More than 250 weddings based on that? Had Cosmo lied to me?

I could understand being wanted for my 34DDs, but because my feet dangled on public transport and I had failed Moral Philosophy? I think not. It's the little differences that make travel so exciting. I told grandma the matchmaking equivalent of "just browsing, thanks," gathered up my kimono and went home. Alone.

Another Saturday night and I ain't got nobody…

After moping around for a couple of days, the husband of the family I was staying with, either through pity or a strong desire to get me out of his house, arranged for his brother to take me out. Sad, I know. But a body is a terrible thing to waste. So, the next Friday, I arranged to meet Hiroshi in the cafe of a fancy downtown hotel (typical Japanese first date). I spotted him right away, sitting at a corner table, cigarette dangling from the corner of his mouth, looking intently at the lounge's automated piano as it plonked out "Piano Man." He was gorgeous. The cool suit and shades of Chow Yung Fat with the lithe, panther pose of Jackie Chan. Mmmmm. And this time, I meant it.

The rest of the date progressed pretty much as one would hope. After overpriced lousy tea in lovely, paper-thin china, we drove down to the docks in his black throbbing, limited edition, only-for-the-Japanese-market Mitsubishi. He showed me where he used to drag race as a youth. As I took over his stick shift, our hands touched.

Which is where it gets complicated. The Japanese are not overly bound up by Judeo-Christian constraints on sex. Even good girls do it. And who am I to go against local traditions? But everyone in Japan seems to live in tiny apartments with loads of relatives. Hiroshi lived with his mom. I was sharing a two bedroom flat with a family of four. And the Mitsubishi wasn't designed for everything. To get to the climax, so to speak, of a long story stretched out over several dates, I ended up at a Japanese love hotel. Solely out of anthropological interest, of course.

Look, he was gorgeous, OK?

—————)—————

*Y*ou might call it erotica or pornography, dirty or sexy, perversion or human nature, but the museum at the Taga Shrine is three floors of floor-to-ceiling (and across the ceiling) displays of private parts and sexual acts. It is cases and cases of phalli and vulvas, wallpaper of pinups and pornography. It is everything you ever wanted to know about sex and a few things you never imagined without blushing.

And it is the lifework of a priest.

Aimaur Kubo is a small man with a finely-shaped head, white and purple vestments, and a nervous laugh. He has spent 40 years bringing together a collection that would make granny wash your eyes out with soap if she knew you'd seen it.

Mr. Kubo says he collects these things because sex is the origin of human nature, the origin of religion. He says this as he shows visitors around, pointing at various renderings of genitalia or couples in the carnal clinch, to illustrate his points.

♦

—Sophia Dembling, "Sex and a Single Priest," *Dallas Morning News*

You see love hotels everywhere in Japan, especially near the off-ramps of large highways. Unlike the rest of Japanese architecture, which is either achingly beautiful or heartlessly functional, love hotels are flights of Disney-esque fancy. There are ones shaped like UFOs and castles and boots. And even the relatively normal-looking ones offer themed bedrooms. A night in the Dungeon Room, anyone?

Friday. Hiroshi picked me up and we drove over an hour out of Tokyo, into the mountains. He turned off the highway and we headed down a small side road to an alpine lake surrounded by fir trees. Floating on the far side of the lake was the QE II. Cool, who thought it could navigate the treacherous inter-coastal waters of Japan? Turns out, it can't. The QE II was actually a love hotel, solidly built on the opposite shore. We parked "below deck" in the underground garage.

I think the idea of love hotels is that, in an overpopulated country, it is the one place you can go and never see anyone else. Check-in consisted of an empty lobby with a lit panel displaying photos of all available rooms: the Cowboy Room, where the bed is in the back of a pick-up; Arabian Nights Room, with lots of billowing sheets; Jungle Room, overgrown and very green. We opted for the '70's Disco Room. The photo was a bit blurry, but it looked like it had a mini-dance floor, complete with a mirrored ball suspended from the ceiling. I pushed the button corresponding to the room and a key card slid out of the slot next to the panel. We went up the elevator to the third deck, then down the hall to starboard. The light was flashing above the door. Thoughtful touch. I slid in the key and we entered our "cabin."

How *not* to start a romantic evening: on sight of the bedroom, try to refrain from collapsing on the floor in a fit of hysterical laughter. Red. The whole room was very red. The heart-shaped bed was covered in red velour. The red satin duvet was covered in red sequins in the shape of, you guessed it, hearts. The ceiling, where not mirrored, was quilted in red plushy stuff. Next to the bed, there was indeed a mini-dance floor. With a rotating mirrored ball suspended from the ceiling. And multi-coloured floor panels.

And a juke box. And a mini-piano. On the other side of the bed, there was a TV and VCR, with kindly provided videos (undoubtedly of *Saturday Night Fever*, though my anthropological interest didn't extend far enough to find out). Next to that, there was a video trivia game in Japanese.

In a superb example of the Japanese habit of mishmashing American culture, the wall that partitioned off the bathroom had a stained glass representation of an American '50s waitress with a poodle skirt and a tray full of Cokes. The bathroom itself was normal but the sink-side freebies included a condom and, for some reason, a green hair elastic. It all just puts you in the Mood Fer Luv. Especially since my date couldn't understand why I was wiping away tears of laughter. I pretended they were tears of joy. He was appeased. Boys.

We were on the all-night pricing plan (you can also get the rooms in four-hour chunks—for the businessman and office lady on the go), and I am pleased to say the next few hours shall remain forever a mystery. Largely because I myself have only a vague idea of what happened. Calisthenics? Judo? Tantric shiatsu? All I know is that stereotypes and several blood vessels were soundly shattered.

Finally it was time to gather up our belongings. Thankfully, none of our stuff was red, otherwise it might have been lost forever in that vermilion vortex. Checking out consisted of paying a vending machine that controlled the door lock. No pay, no leave. Which made me wonder if there were other couples, slowly starving in the back seats of clown cars behind the door of the Big Top theme room for want of exact change. We paid (cheaper than "normal" Japanese hotels) and we left. Never saw another soul.

Over the next couple of months, Hiroshi was kind enough to assist with my research at several other love hotels. Normally, people stick to just one place because you can get member's cards that earn you points every time you visit. A frequent flyer sort of thing. Tragically though, the prizes are designed to appeal to Japanese girls and tend towards the pink and fluffy. So, I didn't leave Japan with a souvenir koala, but I do have the world's most extensive collection of green hair elastics. And every time I plait my hair I find myself singing "Mmmm Mmm Mmm Mmm staying alive, staying alive." God, he was gorgeous.

*Foreign correspondent and travel writer Cleo Paskal (*The Economist,
The Independent, *BBC and* CBC *radio) has done all sorts of odd things
to ensure absolute accuracy in her stories. But she does have her limits and
will not be writing follow-up pieces about eating horse sushi or hunting the
noddy birds of Nauru with a butterfly net.*

✳

"Oh no," Sato wailed. "You can't do it...You won't fit!"

"What are you saying?" I protested.

"Japanese girls are too small," Ishikawa declared, "especially in that *important* place. For Japanese men it's okay, but for foreigners..."

Was I, in biological fact, being denied access to this secret sanctum of Japan, or was this just another artificial trade barrier? After all, if I could use chopsticks, then surely I could handle this challenge.

But Sato and Ishikawa were deadly serious. Sato reached across the counter and grabbed a bottle of Tabasco sauce.

"You see this?" he said, waving the bottle in front of my face. "This is your average Japanese man—about ten to thirteen centimeters long. You are longer, right?"

"Uh, well..."

"It's true," he burst in. "But although yours may be longer, mine is harder. Japanese men are short but strong. American men are soft."

While I pondered this new cross-cultural theory, Sato disappeared briefly into the kitchen and emerged brandishing an empty teakettle that he proceeded to fill with water. With great flourish and bravado, he held the Tabasco bottle to his crotch and suspended the teakettle from the neck of the bottle. *Ta-dum.*

"There," he shouted, as if he had just pulled a rabbit from a hat, "I can do that...Can you?"

"I'm afraid I don't know," I replied humbly, hoping he would resist the temptation to test my virility right there in the middle of the Potato. "I never tried. But does this really mean I can't go to a love hotel?"

"Let's just say," Ishikawa remarked, "that it would be difficult."

—Bruce S. Feiler, *Learning to Bow: Inside the Heart of Japan*

MARIANNE DRESSER

* * *

A Queer Night in Tokyo

A foray into an unusual bar scene.

"I'LL SEE YOU IN ROPPONGI AT 11:00," ULRIKE SAID AND HUNG UP the phone. I hurriedly wrote down the specific instructions— which corner of the train station, which exit: north or south, the nearest architectural landmark, and what commercial logo to look for on which neon billboard—all necessary reference points for successfully arranging a rendezvous in the vast urban chaos that is Tokyo. After two and a half months in Japan, I was at last going to sample some of its hidden *rezubian* subculture.

Well, perhaps "subculture" is too grand a term, implying a more obvious presence, a recognizable community. There *are* lesbians in Japan, but unlike the flaming gay boys who throng the streets of Shinjuku, Tokyo's oddly antiseptic "sleazy" quarter, they are well hidden to the point of invisibility. Hardly surprising, given the patriarchal cast of Japanese society with its feudal cultural and gender codes still firmly in place underneath an outward appearance of cutting-edge modernism.

So I was delighted that my intrepid friend, a Dutch lesbian photographer on a year-long student exchange program, had managed not only to find a real Japanese *rezubian* bar, but had also acquired the personal contact there that would allow us access. Without a

277

preliminary introduction, a *gaijin*, or foreigner, would never get past the elaborate politeness that masks the iron-clad impenetrability of Japanese society.

After another typically confusing day at my job serving as the token *gaijin* in a small, hip architectural firm, I negotiated the clockwork commute from midtown Tokyo to the tiny, pristine apartment in a northern suburb that I shared with my girlfriend. Janet had been here for over a year, engaging in a well-paid but ultimately futile attempt to teach English to Japanese teenagers at a private school. Following my fervent but terribly misguided heart, I had relocated to Tokyo to be with her. Although neither of us was willing to admit it, we were enacting an expat queer version of a "Can this marriage be saved?" scenario.

Worried that she might lose her job, Janet was emphatically *not* out; we played our public role as two Western women "friends" living abroad. But no foreigner in Japan has any real privacy, and every shopkeeper within a mile knew exactly where the two strange American women lived. Although I was too obedient to ever say so, I thought our precautions were ridiculous. We were incontrovertibly *gaijin*, and secretly I was beginning to enjoy my newfound capacity to elicit squeals of delighted fright from small children or whiplash-inducing headspins from blue-suited *sararimen*. We were already seen as particularly interesting specimens of alien creatures, freaks of nature, so I didn't see how any other queerness on our part could possibly matter. In the end, Janet's paranoia and her mastery of passive-aggressive control tactics won the day, and so we carried on with the transparent pretense, fooling no one but ourselves.

But after-hours and away from the incessant curiosity of her students, Janet was as eager as I to check out the *rezubian* bar. So, after our evening rice and *miso*, we began the important work of planning our respective costumes for the night's outing. After some deliberation, we both ended up in the little-boy drag that was the current unisex fashion rage for trendy Tokyoites. Maintaining the conventions of heterosexual femininity to which she would eventually revert, Janet tipped the scales of her gender-bent image with eye shadow and lipstick. Bravely we ventured out in our baggy black Comme des Garçons suits, downscaled men's shoes, and short slicked-back hair. The subway ride was no more nor less alienating and hilarious than usual. We received the requisite ambiguous stares and were correctly identified by two kids shouting *"Gaijin-san!"* (roughly translatable as "Mister Foreigner"). Thankfully, no one attempted to practice their English on us.

Our Dutch friend met us at the designated place, her solid northern European body stretching the contours of a dark-blue Japanese schoolboy uniform. With Ulrike in our midst, looking like a Eurodyke version of an obsessed Mishima character, any notions of blending in with the crowd were discarded. We three unlikely pilgrims set off on the convoluted back-alley route to a non-descript bar tucked between a *yakitori-ya* and a karaoke place emitting a thin stream of heartfelt (if off-key) wailing.

Ulrike knocked on the door, and conducted the elaborate display of baroque pleasantries, roundabout introductions, and name-dropping that allowed us entry. We were ushered into a narrow room veiled in cigarette smoke. A long, dark wood bar paralleled the left side of the room. Leaning against it were five or six gray-and blue-suited businessmen carrying on with one another in the characteristically gruff, casual speech reserved for Japanese males. A few women clad in frilly pastel dresses were seated demurely at the tables in the no-man's land between the bar and the entryway. The exaggerated

> *I* met an American man who'd recently been to a Tokyo gay bar. In this gay bar, the bartender asks you the type of person you are looking for, young slender, young big, mature Caucasian, etc., and gives you a coaster with your drink. The patterns and colors on your coaster form a code by which others can tell your preferences. With this system embarrassment is minimized.
>
> ♦
>
> —George Vincent Wright, "A World of Bathhouses"

birdlike tones of *onnakotoba*, "women's speech," floated toward us
from their conspiratorial conversations.

I was seriously confused, certain that there had been a mistake.
This was just another typical Tokyo dive filled with *sararimen* and
bar "hostesses" whose job was to make sure their male customers'
glasses were never empty and provide inane, ego-stroking conversation at their whim. Our arrival had caused a noticeable ripple
among the inhabitants; we were being thoroughly scrutinized with
dozens of brief, oblique glances from every set of eyes in the room.
But no one approached us, and we made our way to a deserted
corner table. Ulrike went off to the bar for drinks, for once amazingly preempting the instantaneous service that is standard in
Japanese public places. Janet and I gazed at the scene and each
other and laughed incredulously.

When Ulrike returned with our drinks, I accosted her immediately: "I thought you said this was a lesbian bar. What are all these
guys doing here?"

"It took a long time to find this place. Let's just stay for a while.
Kampai!" she toasted, and drank.

We drank, looked at each other and at the other patrons, while
they appraised us with intense sidelong glances. I sensed an immi-
nent approach; the knot of excited voices at the bar signaled that
someone was screwing up the courage to cross the great cultural
divide to actually *talk* with the strange trio holed up in the corner.
After about fifteen minutes of mutual inspection, two self-
appointed emissaries swaggered over nervously. They wore the
uniform of the thousands of corporate drudges and petty bureaucrats who elbowed me in the subway every morning: blue suits,
stiff white shirts, perfect replicas of British club-striped ties. It was
only when they began to speak to us in their heavily-accented
English that I realized these garden-variety businessmen were in
fact women. Despite the flawlessly executed, typically male manner in speech, stance, and gesture, their voices heard up close,
pitched higher by nervousness and coerced bravado, revealed an
elaborate gender ruse in progress.

Our new friends exchanged a few rapid-fire salvos with their compatriots at the bar and we were soon faced by a phalanx of extremely curious, extremely "male-identified" Japanese *rezubians*. When summoned by their dates, a few of the flashy femmes joined us, plying us with bottomless glasses of sake and *shochu* while their masculinist counterparts proceeded to grill us about Western lesbian habits. Our bizarre conversation, conducted in a mixture of broken English and equally maimed Japanese, ran the gamut from what kind of underwear we wore to whether our wives were pretty.

Our *wives?* In her serviceable Japanese augmented by a few crude gestures, Janet explained that she and I were "together." This was met with utter incredulity. None of our eager interrogators would be caught dead going out with their "wives." The other women in the bar were either their "mistresses" or a queer variant of the bar hostesses I had imagined them to be. Like typical Japanese married ladies, the wives waited patiently at home, kept dinner warm, and would, on their return at 2:00 or 3:00 a.m., get up immediately to prepare a meal or a hot bath for their "husbands." Didn't we have wives too? How could we two "boys" be together?

By now an alcoholic haze was descending, and the verbal exchange was reduced to monosyllabic grunts and headshaking incomprehension at our mutual strangeness. Janet, Ulrike, and I managed to extricate ourselves from our hosts' inexhaustible hospitality and stumbled out. We walked back to the train station sharing our bemusement, smug in our notions of cultural superiority. In a twisted parallel to the youth culture obsessions currently sweeping Tokyo—James Dean, rockabilly rebel posturing, and completely unattainable *Route 66* road trip fantasies—Japanese lesbians seemed to be living in a slightly twisted version of a '50s butch/femme universe. We Western dykes were *far* beyond that. We weren't internalizing our homophobia, participating in our own oppression, or reenacting the patriarchal heterosexist model. We didn't have "wives," we had partners, colleagues, sisters in the struggle, fellow radical lesbian feminist separatists. Right on!

And yet, all the way back to our tiny closet in Takinogawa, I

kept thinking about the *rezubian* bar and the women we had met
there. Those passing Japanese androgynes, their "wives" and "mistresses," were negotiating a particularly virulent form of *samurai*
patriarchy. In a society that considered its women lost if they
weren't married by age 23, a few lesbians had found a way to be
together. The "businessmen" in the bar spent every day of their
lives conforming to the corporate monolith in order to support
themselves and the women who depended on them, and who
loved them.

Some part of me recoiled from the oppressive gender-coded
social mimicry in which they lived. But even though it made me
uneasy to admit it, I found these women oddly beautiful and brave.
And the more I thought about the fallacious equality of my relationship with Janet, the more I envied the clarity and brutal simplicity of their tyrannical coupling. While we American dykes hashed
about in mushy realms of "compromise" and "process," those *rezubians* knew who wore the pants and who steamed the rice.

I never made it back to the *rezubian* bar, and after a couple of
months I left Tokyo, and Janet, to pick up the shreds of my
abandoned life in San Francisco. And I learned how to steam my
own rice.

*San Francisco Bay Area-based writer/editor Marianne Dresser has published
essays and stories in several anthologies, including* Travelers' Tales Food
and The Road Within, *and is the editor of* Buddhist Women on the
Edge: Contemporary Perspectives from the Western Frontier. *This
story is part of an ongoing series based on various adventures living, studying, and wandering in Asia.*

★

Nor should a courtesan, when she is entertaining a customer at sake,
lard her conversation with over-clever repartee and display her parts
with much ingenious talk. Such tactics may avail if her companion is
a real gallant and well versed in the ways of the world; but, if he is an
inexperienced man who had only dabbled in these paths, he will be
abashed by such a show and will acquit himself ill with the woman.

—Iharu Saikaku, *Fille de Joie*

BRUCE S. FEILER

Red Lights and Green Tea

The author discovers the primary lesson
for a new teacher in Japan.

THE TOHOKU SUPER EXPRESSWAY STRETCHES EIGHT LANES WIDE
and reaches over eight hundred kilometers north from Tokyo into
the hinterlands of central Japan. From its start near the heart of the
city, the road winds its way through the bustling urban sprawl of
the capital, spans two colorless rivers hurrying toward their
dénouement in the depths of Tokyo Bay, then heads inland toward
the vast provincial region that the Japanese call *inaka*, or what people from my home in Georgia would refer to as "up the country."
Soon the clamor of neon fades from view and steel girders cease
piercing the sky. The endless queues of cramped apartment blocks
and towering concrete factory walls slowly back away from the ad-
vancing road as if to make room for the tile-roof buildings and
moistened rice fields that will soon take their place. Several hours
down the road, a small city rises from the grassy lowlands where
the Tohoku bends toward the north. In the parking lot just off the
highway, a towering sign salutes the new arrival: "WELCOME TO
SANO. PATIENCE AND HUMILITY PREVENT ACCIDENTS."

Sano is a city—a *shi*. In Japanese, places are separated into cate-
gories by size and then labeled with identifying tags, not unlike
socks in a well-ordered drawer. The classification is based on

population—up to ten thousand is a village, ten to twenty thousand is a town, and above that is a city. Thus the city of Sano becomes Sano-*shi*, and the town of Kuzu, Kuzu-*machi*.

For the newcomer such names are helpful. That is especially true in this community, where one might never guess from its surface that Sano—whose two Japanese characters translate somewhat forebodingly into English as "left field"—could actually qualify as a city. Although it has a population of close to fifty thousand people, one train station, two department stores, and more than its share of stoplights, Sano has no curbs. Downtown, buildings seem to melt into streets, and residents step out of their homes in the morning into lines of oncoming traffic. In summer, when people in cars roll their windows down and people at home leave their doors ajar, a driver can sit in his car at a red light and watch a baseball game on a TV set in a house by the side of the road.

Leaving my two-room second-floor apartment each morning, I would stop to admire the delicate Japanese garden that my landlady had tended for over sixty years. Short-leaf pines and persimmon trees hunched over the tiny courtyard, a pale green moss shrouded the ground, and three aging carp mingled quietly in the still, black waters of a homemade pond. Retrieving my bike from astride her stone fence, I would pedal down the narrow lane, past the barbershop and the lean stone pillars of our neighborhood Shinto shrine, and head toward the shadow of the Hotel Sunroute, an eight-story beige concrete box that was the tallest and ugliest building in Sano. As I crossed the railroad tracks every day heading away from town, the same women would be gathered outside the same stores, having, it seemed, the same conversations—"Sure is hot today." "How is your daughter doing?" "Did you hear the mayor is having an affair?" These women would bring out their burnable garbage for collection on Tuesdays, their bottles on Wednesdays, and their used batteries in small plastic bags every other Saturday morning. Most of them had probably never been to the Kentucky Fried Chicken on the other side of town or the Mos Burger Store just around the block.

Before coming to Japan, I had often heard that Japan is the

wealthiest country in the world. I had read stories about toilets that talk and robots that answer the telephone. I had seen pictures of fancy buildings all over the world which the Japanese recently bought. With this introduction I half expected to find an island paradise overflowing with expensive cars, spiral escalators, and extravagant buildings that the Japanese already owned. But in Sano I found a world quite different from the polish and poshness of Tokyo and far closer to the disheveled tin-roof towns I remembered from my childhood in the American South. Although Japan has the highest per capita gross national product in the world, the lives and homes of most Japanese people do not reflect this statistic. My apartment, for example, had no heating, no insulation, no hot running water in the sink, and no overhead lighting. My toilet had no seat. Still, my Japanese friends told me I had the nicest apartment they had seen in town. My American friends, meanwhile, had a different name for this lifestyle: they called it creative camping.

After a ten-minute ride through the traffic, I would arrive on the outskirts of town. Here, away from the crowded down-town alleys and narrow single-lane streets, away from the faded plastic hydrangeas that drape the main street in summer, away from the gray tin aura of old-town Sano, a shining new building appears along the road. The five-story hall is wrapped in white-washed stucco and gray metallic windows. Along with the other trophy towers in town, the Hotel Sunroute, the Jusco Department Store, and the "Happy Home" Wedding Palace, it has one of the few elevators in Sano. On the top floor of this government building, the elevator doors open directly across from the Ansoku Regional Branch of the Tochigi Prefectural Board of the Japanese Ministry of Education.

It was here, on a Monday morning in August, fresh from my inaugural bath, that I first reported for work.

According to legend, when the American army moved into Japan at the end of World War II, they brought their own desks—large, solid, U.S. government-issue, gray metal desks. Perhaps because of their durability, perhaps because of the Japanese custom of adopting things foreign, perhaps because of mere fashion, these desks have remained ever since. To this day, these indestructible desks are the staple of government, and many non-government, offices across Japan. On my first day as a government employee in Japan, I too was given my very own gray metal desk, with a hard-back gray metal chair to match.

"This is Mr. Bruce's desk," Mr. Cherry Blossom said as I arrived, using his junior high school English in front of his colleagues and plopping down a sign that said, indeed, "MR. BRUCE'S DESK."

The crowded room had three groupings of desks spaced evenly across the white tile floor. My desk was in the middle section of nine, along with Mr. C's. Our group was arranged in tight formation, with four desks lined up end to end like football players in a line of scrimmage, facing four oth-

> Japan is like an oyster. An oyster dislikes foreign objects: when even the smallest grain of sand or broken shell finds its way inside the oyster shell, the oyster finds the invasion intolerable, so it secretes layer after layer of nacre upon the surface of the offending particle, eventually creating a beautiful pearl. However, while pearls may vary slightly in size or luster, they all look very much alike. In the process of coating, not a trace remains of the shape or color of the grain of sand inside. In like manner, Japan coats all culture from abroad, transforming it into a Japanese-style pearl.
>
> —Alex Kerr, *Lost Japan*

ers directly across. The section chief, like a referee, was perpendicular at the top. Since all the desks in this double-file line were touching, they formed what amounted to a giant tabletop that stretched from the door to the plate-glass windows overlooking downtown Sano. In this huddle, every conversation and every minor memo became the business of the whole group. Every four desks, moreover, shared one telephone.

As soon as Mr. C had introduced me to my seat, two women came rushing over with hot rags to wipe off the top of the desk.

"This is Arai-*san*," he said, pointing to the older of the two secretaries, whom the Japanese call "O.L.s," office ladies. She was a middle-aged woman with a tapered neck, an elongated face, and black hair pulled back from her face.

"How do you do," she whispered shyly, drawing her hand to her mouth and grabbing her assistant for protection. The younger woman, in her mid-twenties, was taller, with straight hair that hung down her back and a timid gaze across her face like that of an animal frightened from sleep.

"This is Eh-*chan*," Mr. C said, resisting what seemed like the temptation to pat her on the rear. "She is not yet married."

Slowly, allowing for bows and handshakes, Mr. C led me around the phalanx of desks and formally introduced me to each person.

"This is Mimura-*sensei*. He teaches science."

"Mogi-*shido*. He is a student adviser."

"Nanmoku-*kacho*. He is the section head."

At first glance all the desks in this formation appeared equal, like beds in a hospital ward, but a closer look revealed a subtle order. Younger people sat at the bottom of each line, seniors higher along, and the section chief alone at the end. As a worker advanced along this route, he was allowed to keep more paper on his desk, more cushions on his chair, and perhaps even a pair of slippers underneath. In this office, one desk stood out. It was placed in the center of the room, separate and unequal from the rest, and its chair was draped in a sheepskin rug. Above the desk a lone sign dangled from a fluorescent light. It read, simply, *shocho*: Director.

"Welcome to our office," said Kato-*sensei*, now tucked into a blue polyester suit and looking less fat than he had in the bath. "Please have a seat." He gestured toward a brown vinyl sofa and two easy chairs that were grouped together in front of his desk. Arai-*san* went dashing across the hall to a small kitchen and returned with two cups of tea and a basket of crackers, which she set on the knee-high coffee table between the sofa and the chairs.

"Can you eat Japanese crackers?" she asked. "They are made of Japanese rice."

I assured her that I could.

"Ahhh," she said, nodding her head up and down and resting her finger on her chin. "That's amazing."

Kato-sensei and I chatted for a while. He asked about my new apartment and offered to buy me a rice cooker. Then he started to explain my duties. This would be my home office, he said, but after the start of the fall term the following week, I would come here only on Wednesdays and visit schools on all other days. Most of the time I would be teaching at Sano Junior High, although I would have to make short visits to many of the other schools in the area. Unlike Japanese teachers, I would have Saturdays off. "If you have a problem," he said, "you can talk with Mr. Manager, Mr. Personnel Director, or Mr. Section Chief. They will be glad to help you."

In addition to reading desks in Japan, one must also be deft at hearing titles. All the men in the office were former teachers and were thus entitled to have the word *sensei*, teacher, attached to their names. But in this office, *sensei* was just the minimum. Mr. C was also a *shido*, adviser; Nanmoku was a *kacho*, chief. When they addressed one another, the teachers dropped their names and used titles instead: "Mr. Section Chief, telephone for you."

Even the titles for the two secretaries showed rank. The older woman, Arai, earned the term *san*, and the younger only *chan*, a diminutive term used mostly for children and unmarried girls. Like the difference between a *shi* and a *machi*, the difference between a *san* and a *chan* is part of a cultural code that maintains order and assures that hierarchy is preserved.

For most of my first days in Sano, I participated in introductions of this kind, known formally as *aisatsu*. In less than five days I was introduced to all the other government workers in my building, the mayor, the head librarian, the director of the Public Health Department, the manager of the train station, and—to cover all bets—the chief of police. At the end of my first week, Mr. C decided I was ready to meet my most important protector, the principal of my school.

Sano Junior High School occupies a small plot of land on the west side of the city, at the foot of a large span of rice fields leading into the mountains of central Tochigi. Although the school was founded just after the Second World War, the building itself is new, standing three stories tall, with the same white-washed stucco as the government office building across town. The front of the school faces an open parking lot and a covered courtyard where students leave their bicycles, and the back of the school overlooks an enclosed dirt field, bordered by two soccer goals, a swimming pool, and a gymnasium. With its thick walls, lack of landscaping, concrete, and sterile air, the building looked to me more like a prison than a schoolhouse.

Once we were inside, Mr. C led me into a big, open room where several dozen people were working. Reading the desks, he quickly discerned the most prominent person in the room and asked him if the principal was in his office. Within seconds a large, broad-shouldered man dressed in a light gray suit, white shirt, and dark blue tie shuffled out to meet us. His face was square, with a flat, tense smile and thick black-rimmed glasses. His glistening gray hair had been stretched taut with a comb and matted to his head with a brand of hair tonic that smelled like distilled vinegar. Mr. C apologized for the inconvenience, bowed, and asked for permission to perform an introduction. Without objection, the principal excused himself before his colleagues and announced that a formal greeting was in order. All those at their desks dutifully rose and pulled on their coats from the backs of their chairs.

With everyone in place, the principal addressed the office and introduced the go-between, Mr. C. We bowed. The go-between then introduced the guest of honor. Again a bow. I then introduced myself. Another bow, this time deeper. Finally the principal thanked all of us for our consideration, and life returned to normal. We bowed a final time.

At this point we were shuffled into the host's receiving room and invited to partake in a customary snack. The principal's room was spacious and carpeted but had the same gray metal desk and brown vinyl furniture as every other office I had visited.

"Please sit anywhere," he said to me.

When I first began my round of visits I accepted offers like this at face value and sat in any seat. After a while, however, Mr. C pulled me aside and told me that I should not sit just anywhere but should confine myself to the couch. The easy chairs are for the host, he said, and the couch is for the guests.

"*Hajimemashite*," the principal said. "We are meeting for the first time. My name is Sakamoto." He held his business card with two hands above his head and bowed until both his head and the card dipped below his waist. I rose to accept his offering and bowed deeply in return.

"I am the principal of this school," he said. "Do you see those pictures on the wall?" He pointed to a series of tinted black and white photographs that hung against one of the paneled walls. "There have been twelve principals before me in the forty-year history of this school. You are the first foreign teacher ever to come here. We are honored to have you with us."

Soon an office lady appeared with three cups of green tea, three lacquer saucers, and a plate of sponge cakes, which were stuffed with purple bean paste, wrapped in plastic, taped, and placed in a box with a ribbon. For several minutes no one acknowledged the tea; then the principal gestured and said, "Please," and we partook with a short apology and an expression of thanks.

As the guest, I remained quiet through most of these meetings while the go-between spoke on my behalf. But this host was eager to speak with me.

"I hear you come from Georgia," he said to me. "I like *Gone with the Wind* very much."

Mr. C nodded and looked at me in surprise. He hadn't known that this movie took place in my home state, he said.

"Do you know what this is?" the principal asked, pointing to a small flowerpot on the floor. A bare trunk stuck out of the dirt and several naked branches protruded from the side.

I told him I didn't know.

"It's a cotton bush!" he cried. "Just like you have in Georgia."

"I didn't know cotton grows in Japan," I said.

"It doesn't," he said. "We don't have the right soil. Plus we don't have any slaves…" He paused as if to consider his next line. Then slowly a smile crept across his face. "All we have is our wives." The two men laughed uproariously at this comment: Mr. C, a wiry little pug with a chipper laugh; and Sakamoto-*sensei*, a Great Dane with a sturdy bass guffaw.

I assured them we didn't have slaves anymore either, but they didn't seem to listen. After a moment Mr. C jumped up from the sofa and pulled me up beside him.

"You see, Mr. Bruce, I'm sure Mr. Principal will take good care of you. He already knows your heart."

Aisatsu greeting ceremonies like this occurred in school and in my office no fewer than eight times in the course of a normal day—and more during busy seasons. That meant eight times a day everyone must rise and bow to the guest. Eight trays of tea that must be made, served, drunk, retrieved, and cleaned. Eight plates of sponge cakes stuffed with bean paste, fancy rice crackers, cookies, or plastic containers of jelly that must be eaten. It didn't seem to matter what was said in these meetings. Their purpose was to establish the unofficial paths along which

———)———

*O*ver dessert I asked about something I'd read in a travel book—that one should not blow one's nose while in Japan. Yasuko's fierce grimacing told me that the Japanese positively revile the act of blowing your nose; it is perhaps tantamount in Western culture to a raspy clearing of the throat and firing a viscous glob onto a fine linen tablecloth. Tissues and hankies are though disgusting and unsanitary. Stuff a soiled one back in your pocket? Never! Swab the end of your nose? Uncouth! Yasuko offered a demonstration in how to use a dinner napkin. A woman might delicately blot her mouth, once. More for affect, it seemed, than anything utilitarian. There would be no wiping, no sneaking of the corner past a dripping nose.

♦

—Kathleen Meyer, "Toiletopia: Plunging into 'Things Japanese'"

tacit deals and arrangements are made. As I was making my way around Sano, drinking tea and bowing to strangers, I was creating lines along which I could later walk, if need be. In Australia, the Aborigines called such paths "songlines." In Japan, they are called *ningen-kankei*, the web of human relations.

"Japanese culture runs on *ningen-kankei*," Mr. C explained to me after our visits were done. "We Japanese like to work with people we know. Japan has one race, so we never had strong laws. The laws of human relations are our laws."

My initiation into Japanese laws was swift. Early in my stay, I developed the habit of speeding through town on my bicycle with some abandon. Darting in and out of streets, at times I startled local children, and at other times a storekeeper flagged me down in order to ask one of those questions—"What are doghouses like in America?" If during one of these journeys I happened to come to a red light, and if the hour was late and the roads were empty, I would ride through that red light and continue on my way. That was my own law, but the law of human relations worked differently.

Sure enough, some citizen in town eventually witnessed my showing such wanton disrespect for the law, and she telephoned my office to express her disapproval. Like an insect flying unaware through the woods, I had been trapped in a web. As a distinguished foreign teacher at the Board of Education, I had gained special access to many people in town; thus I could hardly expect to excuse myself from various rules because they didn't suit my needs.

"You are a teacher," Mr. C. explained as he pulled me aside one day to explain that red means stop in Japan and green means go. "During school or after school you are always a teacher. You must obey the rules."

This was the primary lesson for a new teacher in Japan: the closer you get to the songlines, the stronger the pull of the web.

Bruce Feiler also contributed "P's and Q's and Envelope Blues" to Part One.

⋆

As time went on, the banquet became increasingly rowdy. Some people were chugging sake down as if it were a test of manhood. Others were shouting out loud, or drinking stripped to the waist, or dancing in the nude, or drinking themselves into oblivion. I could only sit and wonder about the nature of human dignity.

In a Western-style formal banquet, alcohol increases the humor, esprit, and wit of the conversation. While I do realize that not every issue can be reduced to a simple comparison between Japan and the West, from what I've seen of ministry-sponsored banquets, I would have to say that in this case, the West gets my nod—even though, as one who takes pride in the overall sophistication of Japanese culture, it pains me to admit it.

A bunch of drunken, pot-bellied, middle-aged men whooping it up, with *yukata* in disarray, makes an unimaginably ignominious sight. The only reason they can get away with such escapades is, I think, that women rarely participate.

Close observation reveals that such male-only banquets have two characteristics. For one thing, participants' speech and actions become extremely juvenile. For another, men begin to hang on one another in a way that appears to carry homosexual nuances. Then and only then do they let their *honne*—their gut opinions—out. Everyone's pet dissatisfactions, including criticism of the boss, come flying out in no uncertain terms. Meanwhile the director pretends to be intoxicated, while listening tolerantly with a wry smile.

My habit of speaking my mind when I'm sober has invited criticism and even a measure of ostracism. But in the atmosphere of such a banquet, nothing you say is held against you. Normally, outward harmony is maintained; yet in fact, there is considerable underlying stress. People do have their complaints and dissatisfactions. The annual banquet serves as a safety valve to release the stress that builds up in the shadow of the supposed harmony. Peace is preserved by letting off steam periodically in this way.

—Masao Miyamoto, M.D., *Straightjacket Society: An Insider's Irreverent View of Bureaucratic Japan*

LEILA PHILIP

Rice Harvest

Knee-deep in muck, snakes swirling,
the seedlings get planted.

NAGATA-SAN CAME TO MIYAMA AS A YOUNG BRIDE FROM THE
coastal town of Kaminokawa over the hill. But her husband died
early, leaving her with two children to raise alone. She has never
remarried. A back injury in youth left her with a crooked rolling
gait, one hip and leg dragging slightly behind. Now she is in her
late sixties, and her gaunt face, carved by daily exposure to wind
and sun, is ridged in a steady scowl. Even when saying good
morning, she reminds me of an angry skunk. In order to supple-
ment an income from rice growing, she began working as grounds
and kitchen help at the Chin Jukan workshop, a job she has kept
for the past twenty-five years. Most of the older men and women
in Miyama gather daily on the village exercise field to socialize
and play gateball, a game similar to croquet, but Nagata-san shuns
these events.

After several chance meetings last spring, we have become
friends of a sort. My morning walks often take me past her *tambo*
(rice paddies), and one day she walked slowly back toward the village with me, telling me of her main trouble. Her unmarried son,
who is almost thirty, won't accept any *omiai*, or matchmaking offers. He lives with her, commuting daily to his job in a small

company outside of Kagoshima. I met him once. In accordance
with rural chic his hair was permed and greased back Elvis Presley
style. He wore tight-fitting white jeans, a red shirt and dark sunglasses with Playboy bunnies on the sides.

"He can't find a wife," she complained. "It's terrible. He won't
listen to me, I don't know what to do."

"There's still time. Lots of young people don't marry early," I offered. "Maybe he just wants to find someone he likes."

"Life starts at marriage," Reiko often said. By the time she was
my age she had already had her first child. According to Nagata-
san, at twenty-two I myself was almost past the "suitable age."

"You'd better marry soon yourself," she retorted sharply, shaking her head. "No one wants a bride who's too old, you know!"

One Sunday in the May tea harvest, I stopped to help Nagata-
san pick tea leaves from the bushes surrounding her house. She had
offered to let me come to the rice planting in June. But weeks
later, when I asked about the planting, she had frowned. "A foreigner in a rice field? Impossible!" she answered. "You don't even
have the right shoes." She stalked away, one hand steadying her
rolling hip.

I gambled that this was more her manner than a direct refusal.
Villagers knew Nagata-san as the *obasan* with the "bad mouth" and
kept out of her way. Her eyes had a habit of slipping to one side as
she talked, as if looking for something she'd left behind.
Nagayoshi-san said that with her wide brow and high cheekbones,
she had one of the few "Korean" faces left in the village. Even after
ten years she will not address Reiko or Nagayoshi-san—they are
yoso no hito, from Tokyo, and she will have nothing to do with
them. I sometimes wonder why she even speaks to me. Perhaps a
gaijin is outside village disputes and etiquette. Perhaps she finds my
enthusiasm for field work amusing. I don't mind her dark moods
or her complaints, half of which I can't understand anyway.

Nagata-san had seeded her nursery beds in April. When the
slim blades were six to eight inches tall, a sea of waving green
shoots, she had transplanted them into the *tambo.* In May fast-
growing clover spread out over the fields in a thick carpet of

purple and white. I would pass her rice paddies on my *tuns* to the coast and think for a moment that I was back in Vermont, staring at a rise of clover-rich pasture. After tilling the clover into the ground with a large-bladed hoe, Nagata-san opened the channel for irrigation.

Each day during the last week in May another field was irrigated, until the entire area was brimming with water, the individual paddies a series of muddy reflecting pools. Across the way, villagers gathered at the Aiko store daily to exchange news and information about the planting.

"Just about time for *otaue*, isn't it?"

"When is your *otaue*?"

"Finished *otaue* yet?"

Miyama farmers, who, like farmers across Japan, are mostly women, called children home to help and prepared large picnics, making it a festive occasion. Even the Emperor donned his rubber boots and appeared on TV planting a few symbolic seedlings. When Nagata-san's earliest-maturing paddy by the cedar was brimming with brown water, the *obasan* of the Aiko store said that she would plant soon. It would probably be on a Sunday, when she had the day off. I simply had to show up at her house on time.

I had looked forward to walking through the wet paddies under a blazing sun like a peasant in a grade B samurai movie. I always enjoyed being with Miyama *obasan*. With their weathered hands and faces, and floral-print shirts, their slow way of pouring tea as if time didn't matter, their comforting

> "Scientists go to the moon and say, 'This is what is real,' but we Japanese think that is a superficial view. Even if our culture is changing fast, our hearts stay the same. We want to live where we were born; we want to die on *tatami*. The sun shines and the rice grows, and that is the power of the *kamisama!*"
>
> ◆
>
> —Gretel Ehrlich, *Islands, The Universe, Home*

blend of severity and warmth, they reminded me of my own grandmother, and of a time before the sleek modern life that now dominates Japan. After the concentration the workshop demanded, it felt good to stretch and bend under the open sky. In the fields no one noticed if you spilled your rice or slopped the tea. The *obasan* were easy company, and, if only briefly, our lives overlapped in the shared activity of the work at hand. I slowly slid one foot into the rice paddy, and then the other. Suddenly I was knee-deep in mud that reeked worse than any cattle wallow. The thick bog swirled with threadlike red and black worms, long leeches and multitudes of floating insects. Frogs croaked everywhere at once, like summer crickets. Through my thin rubber-soled boots I felt each twig and stone on the paddy bottom. Hot, rank slime pressed through my thin cotton *mompei,* covering my calves and knees. In the far corner of the field Nagata-san was busy running a guide string across a deep spot. I watched in horror as the hot mud encased her legs, reaching almost to her hips as she waded across the paddy, and felt grateful for my slight advantage in height.

Ignoring my grimace, Nagata-san showed me how to tuck the spiky green seedlings into the mud, just deep enough to hold them steady.

"Whatever you do, don't run," she said gruffly. "It ruins the mud." I had no intention of running anywhere. The motion of planting wasn't hard, but walking on the slippery bottom was a lesson in balance. The very thought of falling and what I might land on made me freeze in place, storklike, one foot poised in the air.

"Hurry up. The seedlings won't live if you just stand there," barked Nagata-san.

"*Hai.* I'm going," I said quickly, and pushed the seedling down into the paddy, feeling the warm mud slip like a glove up over my wrist. Staring down at my half-submerged arm, I wondered what was living, dying, breeding, spawning, birthing under this teeming slough of mud and water and why I had insisted on coming along.

Just ahead of me Nagai-san and Takara-san plodded slowly through the mud. Talking and laughing as they worked, they were a sharp contrast to my English students in Kagoshima City, who'd been horrified when I'd told them about my weekend plans.

"You, planting rice in the mud," Junko exclaimed. "But, why?"

"I'm curious. We don't grow rice where I live," I said, trying to explain. "And besides, I like working outside." The two sisters shook their heads, delicately covering their mouths with napkins while they giggled.

"Your skin will get brown," said Junko.

"You'll smell," her sister added.

Suddenly I felt depressed, and I finished the lesson in a sour mood.

When I told Reiko that I hoped to help plant the rice that Sunday, she too had wrinkled up her nose in digust.

"Did you ever work in a rice field?" I had asked.

"Certainly not," she responded stiffly. "My family came from Kobe. We were not farmers." Like most urban Japanese, Reiko would no more consider stepping into a rice paddy than she would wear *mompei*. Working in the fields was considered lower-class and feudalistic. But before I was to go she reluctantly dug up a sunshade and a pair of gloves for me to wear. Nagayoshi-san, who came from a poor family of rice farmers, thought it amusing that I wanted to help plant and gave me the entire day off.

Although born in Kagoshima, the two sisters whom I taught English conversation weekly knew little about growing rice, and had no desire to learn more. Both of them worked in offices in Kagoshima City. They took English classes, they said, because they wanted to visit the United States someday, and they liked Americans because we were *akarui*—bright, lively. But neither of them ever studied, and our "free conversation" classes always drifted to the topic of American men: at twenty-seven and thirty, their main concern was marriage.

With their perfectly ironed dresses and knee-length skirts, my students looked as if they'd stepped out of *Leave It to Beaver*. Like young Japanese women everywhere, they preferred pastel colors, polka dots and things that were *kawaii*—"cute." They spent their weekends shopping, and a row of pink and white teddy bears lined the rear window of their new white Nissan.

Although intelligent and educated, they affected a cultivated silliness and, around men, assumed the shyness of eleven-year-old girls and soft childlike voices. I was accustomed to hearing this formal women's speech, which to me sounded like baby talk, from the young women who worked in department stores, but it seemed odd to me that it was considered not only polite but seductive. While boy-crazy American girls labor at sophistication, Japanese women of marriageable age tend to act like girls, and are popularly called *burikko*—"pretending kids."

At times *burikko, okusan* and *obasan* acted so differently from one another, it was hard to believe they all belonged to the same culture. With marriage, however, the girlish veneer I saw in my students drops like a wet blanket; as wives and mothers, Japanese women may baby their husbands and spoil their sons, but they rule the icebox, the house, the children and even the family finances with an iron fist. A typical "salary man" may work like a drone, yet see no more of his paycheck than the monthly "allowance" his wife doles out.

At fifty, it is as if another veil drops, revealing the solid steel of the *obasan*. In Miyama, census records show that village *obasan* have historically outlived their men, and *obasan* far outnumber the men in the rice paddies and construction sites along the road. Having reached an age of respect in Japanese society, rural women drop the pro forma female subservience. They are outspoken and frank, and seem to shun the company of older men, preferring their own circles. They till the gardens, mind the stores, sweep the shrine, take care of the grandchildren and know every villager's business. I remembered passing a roof-patching party where two grizzled old men sat in the shade quietly drinking *shochu* while three stocky *obasan* took turns kneading straw into red-clay mud with their bare feet amid much bantering and laughter.

My students would never gain the bawdy freedom of rural *obasan*, who did what they pleased, regardless of protocol, but in

Japan, old women everywhere commanded respect. "How could you come here alone?" Junko and her sister had asked incredulously when we first met. "Didn't your father oppose your traveling so far? Weren't you afraid?" No matter how many times I explained that where I came from, college was seen as a transition time away from family, or that I liked traveling alone precisely because of the solitude, they continued to look upon me with a disquieting degree of awe.

But Junko, the elder of the two, had told me of her "secret" plan to move to Tokyo and get a new job of some kind for a year or two, away from her parents. She was attractive, with a soft, reaching smile, but she had been through ten or eleven rounds of *omiai* without any luck. She liked someone, but he was from Tanegashima, just south of Kagoshima, and her parents had vehemently opposed her marrying one of the southern "islanders" looked down upon by mainland Japanese. She was bored with her office job at a small company, but didn't know what else she wanted to do. I had encouraged her to make a change, to get out of Kagoshima and try something new, until I realized that if she quit her job she would forfeit her chances of finding comparable work on return. Companies preferred young, single women whom they could hire cheaply as "temporary workers" on the expectation that they would quit work when they married. In the end, Junko had given up the idea, saying that once word got around of her *kawatta*—"abnormal"—behavior, her younger sister would have trouble in her own attempts at *omiai*.

Yet Junko herself seemed ambivalent about marriage, and she spoke with unconcealed admiration of the single "career women" on the rise in Tokyo. Even in Kagoshima, more opportunities for women were opening up and a growing number of young women were delaying marriage for jobs and careers outside the home. Like most young Japanese women I knew, Junko kept such a busy schedule of "secret" rendezvous and schemes that I never could keep it all straight. Another young working woman I knew, who also lived at home with her parents, had carefully engineered a strategy for maintaining a private social life. She didn't even dare visit her boyfriend's apartment because she was afraid that the neighbors might see her there and tell her parents, but she and two female friends who also lived at home had rented an apartment that they used for parties and trysts.

Other couples, their faces covered, slipped in through the underground entrances of one of the "love hotels" scattered throughout Kagoshima City, especially behind the train station, to rent rooms by the hour. The hotels provided an accepted, if not openly discussed, place for married men to carry on affairs, prostitutes to conduct business, college students to take their dates and young unmarried couples to meet. In a burst of sisterly solicitude, my friend had once told me how to "read" the neon signs outside the hotels. If some of the bulbs were dark, then there were vacancies; if all were lit, the hotel was full.

Once, after teaching my classes and dining in Kagoshima City, I had driven back to the village with Okada-san, an apprentice at the Sataro workshop. When we stopped at a gas station on the way back, the attendant addressed me as Okusan, giving Okada-san a knowing wink. Then I began to notice neon signs bearing such names as Pink Chalet, Castle Romance, and Love Inn appearing with regularity along the road. Apparently we'd found our way onto a love-hotel strip. The whole thing seemed amusing and I was about to say so when I glanced over at Okada-san. Usually calm and collected, he was hunched over the wheel, driving as fast as he could, his face scarlet. Even my sense of humor was closer to that of an *obasan* than to my Japanese peers'.

Midmorning, the hot June sun glanced off the rice field in a brown headache glare. I was used to the sewer odors, the constant motion of planting, and ready for tea break. Wedging clay in the cool workshop suddenly seemed inviting. I wouldn't even mind practicing teacups. Already sharp pains ran up and down my back from the constant stooping. I thought of Nagayoshi-san's stories of places where the rice paddies are so deep that farmers push the seedlings about on wooden rafts, half-swimming through the fertile mud.

Suddenly a shriek from the bank made us all start. "Snake!"

shouted Nagata-san. Crouching on the bank, she showered rocks and curses upon a large black serpent on the shoreline. No one could see the snake, but Nagata-san, stalking the unseen foe with a large stick in one hand and a flat rock in the other, looked possessed. I froze in place. Glancing at my pale face, Takara-san laughed. "*Ooi, Hebi-san, Hebi-san*—Hey, Mr. Snake, Mr. Snake," she teased, and threw a clump of rice shoots at my feet. Under the deep mud, my toes curled up instinctively.

Soon the thick black snakes became a common sight. They basked in irrigation ditches and along the banks, tongues flicking as they watched us stomp around in their boggy home. The rest of the day was a steady haze of heat, rank slosh and fragile green shoots. When the sun at last sank and cool pink light came over the cedar tops, we headed back to town. Takara-san carried a small glass jar containing three small fishlike salamanders that she had scooped out of the paddy mud and said she would eat for dinner that night. I walked down the road more bent and exhausted than my sixty-year-old friends. Back at the workshop Nagayoshi-san, his hands still coated with clay, was standing by the hedge when I arrived. "Phew, that smells!" Laughing, he called for Reiko, who handed me a towel and a bucket through the back door. "Here, wash off and leave your clothes in the yard. The ofuro is ready, but hurry up, guests are coming for dinner."

Too tired to be modest, I stole a quick glance toward the hedge, peeled off my mud-soaked clothes and darted for the tub. Satisfied that I had carried back no leeches, I sank into the scalding bathwater and stared at the tips of my pink toes; just visible above the steamy bath, they looked vulnerable-bite-sized.

Leila Philip grew up in Manhattan but spent lots of time in upstate New York surrounded by apples. She did a two-year pottery apprenticeship in the Japanese village of Miyama, then went on to get a master's degree in creative writing from Columbia University and wrote The Road Through Miyama, *from which this story was excerpted.*

In Japan, stages in life seemed as rigorously demarcated as the hours of the day: just as people changed kimono or bracelets with the seasons, just as restaurants served different kinds of rice, or tea, according to the time of year—customs that we, not imprisoned by them, could afford to find enchanting—so Japanese people had to change roles and identity on cue, with the seasons of their lives.

Age, therefore, was always stressed in Japan as much as it was downplayed in the U.S. (where, in California at least, a sixteen-year-old girl often looked so much older than her age, and her forty-year-old mother so much younger, that mother and daughter truly did end up looking like sisters, as the soap ads promised). One reason Japanese generally asked one another, as soon as they were introduced, "How old are you?" was station—a thirty-year-old was expected to defer to someone thirty-five and to have priority over someone twenty-five. But it was also, and relatedly, to give, and enforce, a sense of identity. Just as Sachiko's life was set up so that she gave her mornings to herself, her afternoons to her children, her evenings to her parents, and her nights to her husband, so the stages of a woman's life seemed all but scheduled in advance: 0-5 for shiny bowl cuts and indulgence; 6-18 for ponytails and the blue-and-white sailor-suits of school; 19-24 for bangs, high fashion, and a stint in an office; 25-45 for child raising in jeans and pretty sweaters; and the years that followed for sober matronhood in perms, a return to the workplace, perhaps, and, at last, a rounding of the cycle in the licensed second childhood of old age. The *Kurisumasu keki* phenomenon was only the most flagrant example of a system that propelled its people into stages as forcibly as commuters into train compartments.

—Pico Iyer, *The Lady and the Monk: Four Seasons in Kyoto*

MICHAEL WARD

✦ ✦ ✦

Last Train to Takatsuki

From a simple English teacher to hardened criminal
in the course of an evening.

ONE NIGHT IN JANUARY, AT KAWARAMACHI STATION IN KYOTO, I
missed a train. Even considering Japan's superb rail system—
frequent departures adhering to a schedule that runs like clockwork—the particular train which I failed to board, a local train
stopping at all stations on its way to Osaka, was a particularly bad
one to miss. It was the last of the night.

After a long day teaching in Osaka, I was in Kyoto to attend a
reading of *A Midsummer Night's Dream* that some friends planned
to stage in the grounds of a local temple. I had only given the platform timetable at Kawaramachi a cursory glance; the departure
times of Osaka-bound trains later that night ran until around
eleven thirty, and the 11:19 looked a good bet, the last of the night,
if things went that late. I'd be home in Takatsuki—a small city
roughly half way between Osaka and Kyoto—just before midnight, in bed by five past. Or so I thought.

The rehearsal began late. We were meeting at Lanai's place, an
old-style Japanese house that was cluttered with the ephemera of
her five-year stay in Japan: English grammar books, family photographs from California tacked to a cork message board, two

guitars, a shelf of dog-eared paperbacks, a pile of cassettes, masks, subscription magazines from the States, a bonsai tree, a second hand kimono. Lanai said she was going home in September, but I knew that Japan was a great seductress; one year stays became three, three became six, and Lanai's room filled up....

The reading proceeded smoothly. We read through our scenes a number of times and talked about "character" and "group dynamics." Lanai handed out photocopied essays on the comic role of the artisan in Shakespeare's plays and we talked about group dynamics some more. Before I knew it, it was after eleven. One of the cast members, Curtis, offered me a lift downtown on his motorbike. We'd have to hurry.

On a Tuesday night, Kyoto isn't particularly crowded. I gripped Curt as his motorcycle wove effortlessly through the light traffic, speeding down backstreets past dark temples and glowing neighbourhood noodle bars, eventually turning onto Kawaramachi dori, where our progress was slowed by a coagulum of taxis inching about intersections in search of fares. Brilliant blue and green neon signs atop the low buildings advertised Fuji. Nikon, Lotte, Asahi, and TDK. The last of the diehard gamblers, their dark blue suits crumpled and spotted with cigarette ash, were emerging from the smoky pachinko parlours that lined the street. The bars were emptying. Diligent workers just out of the office shuffled along the footpath. Everyone was making for Kawaramachi station.

Curt dropped me off near the steps leading underground and buzzed off through a red light. I checked the time. It was 11:17. Two minutes! I bolted down the steps three at a time, pulling out my wallet as I ran. At the station concourse I turned the corner and sprinted over to the ticket machines, fumbling for some change.

There was a line. Three people in front of me. I had about ninety seconds before the train left. I switched to another line, which of course you always do and it is almost always a mistake: now the line I had just left sped up, leaving me stuck behind an old grandmother who appeared to be depositing her life savings into the ticket machine. I ducked back into the original line just as it ceased to exist and thrust my coins into the slot. I tore the ticket away, turned and ran, force feeding my ticket through the automatic barriers and hurtling down the stairs to the platforms below.

The conductor's whistle blew, a shrill, painful sound, and suddenly time slowed down, fragmented. Like some manic triple jumper I launched myself through the air from the bottom of the stairs—and seemed to float for an eternity, free of gravity. I stuttered momentarily as I hit the platform—again time stretched, like warm toffee—then sprang with a final desperate bound between the train's closing doors. Almost in slow motion, but with an emphatic clunk that seemed to echo in my head, the doors slammed together—and I found myself on the inside of the carriage. I'd made the last train of the night..

I slumped against the doors, breathing heavily, as the train accelerated out of the station and into the darkness of the tunnel. Almost everyone at my end of the carriage was gawking at me, some open mouthed, as if I'd just performed a death-defying stunt. That's nothing—you should see me board a bus, I felt like telling them.

I could see plenty of green velour throughout the carriage; there were a surprising amount of seats vacant for what was ordinarily a crowded train—the last of the night to return to Osaka. Crossing the aisle, I sat down between a dozing salaryman and a schoolboy reading a comic book. A young man sitting opposite me was cracking his knuckles loudly. I removed the *Japan Times* from my backpack and began reading a report on the fifth day of the Tokyo *sumo basho*.

We pulled into Katsura, the fourth station from Kawaramachi. The train eased smoothly to a halt and the doors slid open. I looked up from the paper. The schoolboy who'd been sitting next to me was gone and the sleepy salaryman was wobbling to his feet; I could see the knucklecracker through the window, striding off along the platform amongst a crowd of people.

Alarm bells registered inside me. Everybody was getting off! In a few moments, rows of empty green seats lined the train and I was alone. Discarded *manga* comics sat on the overhead racks, an evening newspaper lay scattered on the seat opposite; at the far end of the carriage I could make out a pool of vomit splashed across the floor. Three cars back, I could see the conductor, making his way steadily through the deserted carriages, looking for dozing drunks or mislaid bags.

"Last stop, Katsura," he said when he reached me.

"Is there another train going to Osaka tonight?" I asked hopefully.

"No more trains tonight." The conductor stood waiting for me to leave.

"Are you sure?"

"Yes. There are no other trains to Osaka. You must get off here." He made no motion to leave.

"OK, thank you." I automatically adopted the kind of air that suggested what he had just told me confirmed information I had been well aware of. Nodding my head sagely, I stood and walked out onto the empty platform. Yes, I think everything seems to be in order. Of course I'm not some poor, idiot *gaijin* who has quite possibly just missed his last train home.

I stood on the deserted platform as the train pulled out, watching the flipping *kanji* characters on the destination board above the platform eventually disappear altogether. I found it impossible to believe there were no other trains tonight. It wasn't yet quarter to twelve! I walked the length of the platform, climbed the steps into the station and went straight to the timetable. I ran my finger along the columns of information. Weekdays. PM. Kyoto-Osaka. I swore. There were no other trains returning to Osaka tonight. The facts were there in front of me, on a brand new timetable. Unbelievable. I really had missed the last train of the night that could take me home.

I stood there, momentarily at a loss for a course of action. Below me through a window I could see empty carparks and shuttered shops, the last of the train's passengers disappearing down unlit lanes. A few taxis idled under streetlights. To my right I could see a salaryman making a call from a public telephone, probably asking his wife to come and collect him. A young couple close by were leaving the front of a Lawson's convenience store on their bicycles. There were no buses in sight.

No trains and no buses. A taxi? I took out my wallet and tallied its contents. I knew it was pointless even as I counted—the wallet contained only coins, no notes. I had 700 yen, barely enough to let me sit in a taxi. I was seven stations from Takatsuki, over thirty kilometres by road. I'd need at least ten times the amount I had. I considered the only realistic option open to me: borrowing the taxi fare at the end of the ride from Judy, my girlfriend with whom I shared a tiny apartment. This would be no problem, but did she have the money?

I stepped into a telephone booth that was covered with dozens of glossy stickers displaying pictures of scantily clad girls, a price and a telephone number. On top of the telephone was a crushed can of Pocari Sweat, a popular sports drink. There was an empty packet of Lark cigarettes on the ground and a dozen or so butts surrounding it, most only half smoked.

I punched our telephone number and heard the phone ring three times before the answering machine clicked on: "Hi, Judy or Michael can't come to the phone right now, but if you leave—

Judy's voice cut in. "Hello?"

"Hi Jude, it's Michael."

"Where are you?"

"I'm in Katsura. Listen Jude, do you have any money on you?"

"Why?"

"I need money for a taxi. Could you check for me please?"

"Wait a minute." I heard a clunk as Judy put the phone down. In the background I could hear the dull drone of the TV.

Her voice came back on line. "I've only got a thousand. Why do you need to catch a taxi?"

"I got on a train that I thought was going to Takatsuki but it only went as far as Katsura. I missed the last train and I've only got 700 yen on me. Are you sure you don't have any more money? What should I do?"

"How did you miss the last train?"

"I don't know, I just did! The last train left at quarter past eleven or some ridiculous time. Can you believe it? Jeez!" I swiped the can of Pocari Sweat from the top of the telephone.

"Maybe Jun could lend you the money," Judy suggested. Jun was the Japanese owner of The Sunnyside Up, a small bar close to where we lived.

"Jude, today's Tuesday. Sunnyside Up is closed."

"Well I don't know Michael. What are you going to do?"

"I–I'll think of something...see you soon...OK?"

"OK."

I hung up the phone.

A great sense of calm, of inevitability, descends when all logical options are positively ruled out. For a moment life takes on a comforting simplicity. As I stood there in the phone booth, amongst the girlie stickers and the cigarette butts, I knew I had only one option open to me if I wanted to get home tonight. I'd have to walk. Walk over thirty kilometres without a map, in the dark.

The thought instantly excited me. Ahead I imagined a treacherous journey through an unknown land, a nocturnal odyssey fraught with peril. Like some Homeric hero I would wander, until I eventually triumphed and arrived home, proud and unbeaten, to the sleepy embrace of Judy.

I seized upon the idea of this epic undertaking. Somewhere far back inside my mind, the flickering idea of returning to Lanai's house to stay the night was quietly extinguished—too spiritless a choice! No, I was resolute. I would follow the railway line as closely as possible and it would eventually lead me all the way to Takatsuki.

So with the dark silhouette of the mountains to my right, I stepped out of the telephone booth and began walking. The night had grown cool, but pleasantly so, and a light breeze blew in my face as I walked. Far away across the mass of dark, gently swaying rice fields, trucks rumbled along the Meishin Expressway.

I fell into a brisk, rhythmic stride as I followed the main road leading from Katsura and thought: I could be anywhere in the world.

There was nothing around me identifiably "Japan"—no crowds of Japanese, no signs in *kanji*, no temples or pachinko parlours or coffee shops with plastic food models in the window. Just a road

310 *Travelers' Tales ★ Japan*

running along a railway line. The scene could have belonged to a million places.

But it was Japan. In the first few months after arriving in Osaka, a thought had once or twice struck me like a thunderbolt, jolting me from my blase day to day acceptance of life in a foreign country: I was living in Japan! The mysterious land from my childhood of Godzilla, geisha, sumo wrestlers, kamikaze pilots, Astroboy, The Samurai, "Made In Japan"—and now I was here!

And loving it. The food and the beer were wonderful. I loved Osaka's entertainment district, Shinsaibashi, a neon wonderland of narrow streets straight out of *Bladerunner* lined with bars, noodle stands, cinemas, restaurants and clubs. I loved the distinct seasons of Japan: the reds and yellows of autumn in Kyoto; spring and the cherry blossoms in bloom around Osaka castle; the humid summers that ushered in the rainy season; even the freezing winters were bearable. I was a big fan of sumo wrestling, adored the simple aesthetics of old Japanese houses with their *tatami* floors and sliding *shoji* doors, and the place was a music lover's paradise with a vast array of CDs available everywhere. And Japan was so safe— I had never, ever, felt threatened—at any time or in any place.

I had been walking parallel to the tracks for perhaps thirty minutes when I came to my first impasse. The road I was on turned abruptly left at the padlocked gates of a lumberyard and led a considerable distance away from the tracks across some barren fields. A large wire fence prevented access to the railway line on the right, and it would be dangerous, and probably illegal, to try and climb over. I had no alternative but to turn left, follow the road and try to cut right as soon as I could.

I turned my back on the tracks and began my detour, hoping it would be short lived, peering ahead in the dim light for any sign of traffic lights or crossroads. After about a kilometre, the road narrowed, gradually rising until it stood a metre or so above the brown grassy expanse it bisected. Stagnant water lay in shallow ditches on either side of the bitumen. There was no traffic.

Any hope of getting from Katsura to Takatsuki as the crow flew were already starting to look decidedly unrealistic. If I were to zigzag this aimlessly all night, I'd still be wandering the countryside when school started in nine hours' time. I imagined a trio of students sitting patiently, waiting for a teacher who, at that moment, was looking for a left hand turn out of a rice field in Arashiyama.

On impulse I decided to abandon the road and cut across the field on the right, hoping to stumble onto a path that would lead me back to the railway line. I leapt the ditch and instantly regretted my haste—a vision of landing in six inches of mud flashed through my mind—however I met only solid ground when I tumbled amongst the knee-high grass. Although the sky was almost starless, the light of the moon was enough to guide me across the sparse field and soon I came upon a narrow track, hidden amongst the grass, that ran back towards the railway line. On course again!

Once more I was walking parallel to the train tracks. Ahead I could just make out the dark forms of trains in a shunting yard, clustered silently together, empty of their commuter cargo and seeing the deserted carriages, with the faintest glint of moonlight reflecting from their windows, I suddenly felt a pang of loneliness. This wasn't right, wandering after one in the morning here in the middle of nowhere. What was I doing? It felt like the whole world was asleep, secure at home where they belonged, while here I was, invading a landscape that, in the darkness after midnight at least, had no place for the human soul. The silent trains, the dark mountains, the rice fields rippling in the breeze, the sleeping neighbourhoods behind me all seemed to whisper, "What exactly are you doing here?"

I walked on. The world was silent, except for the quiet clicking of my footsteps on the road and the murmur of the breeze when it sprang up. I was now passing through a small residential enclave nestled next to the railway line and the road had narrowed to a serpentine lane. There was no sign of life from any of the houses, not even a lamp glowing dully behind a curtain. For all the world, the squat wood, brick and tile buildings on either side of me may have been home to ghosts. Behind the lifeless facade, however, I knew there slept the same kinds of people I saw every day on the crowded trains and bustling streets of Osaka or Kyoto: pretty secretaries with the cultivated little girl look that was so popular with many Japanese women; middle aged salarymen who lived for their company, and occasionally, died for it (*karoshi*—death by overwork); university students, as free as they'd ever be before joining the corporate treadmill for the next thirty years of their lives; cute little children—sometimes on their way to classes before dawn; often home from *juku*, or cram school, well after dark; the elderly—tiny, hunched witnesses to the post-war miracle that had propelled Japan to its economic powerhouse status; bored housewives, weekend punks, sailor-suited schoolgirls, happy families...they all slept and dreamed behind those dark walls.

And I was a *gaijin*, or outside person. I could stay in Japan for the rest of my life, become fluent in the language, marry a Japanese woman, settle down—but I would always be a *gaijin*. I could never really get inside.

My watch said it was almost two. Time had warped; it felt like five or six hours since I'd called Judy, while the meeting in Kyoto seemed like yesterday.

The lane I was ambling along had widened again, and ahead there loomed a dark, rectangular shape between the tracks. As I drew closer I realised that I had arrived at Omiya, the next station down the line from Katsura. A wave of despair swept over me. All this effort, this time, and I had advanced merely a single station towards Takatsuki. Enthusiasm drained from my body as if I'd been punctured; my backpack suddenly felt heavier, my feet wearier, the night colder. I realised now I could never make it home before the trains recommenced at five. I would spend the next three hours zigzagging across the countryside, all in the name of some crazy adventure that only began because I was fool enough to misread a train timetable.

I eyed the empty station. Perhaps I could just slump down inside, admit defeat and see out an uncomfortable three hours on a cold, concrete floor. Peering around me to see if there was anyone about, I cautiously crossed the tracks at a railway crossing. The boom gates pointed straight up into the sky, the red warning signals as dead as glass eyes. In front of the station, amber lights flashed rhythmically over a pedestrian crossing like indefatigable sentinels. I strode across the deserted street and walked into a dark building.

Although the light was dim, I could see that everything inside the station was spotlessly clean. The red tiled floor had probably been mopped only a few hours earlier. Metal shutters had been pulled down over the ticket windows and the ticket barriers were closed. Cartoon posters advertising upcoming community events were taped neatly to the wall opposite the newspaper stand. Clean, cold and uninviting.

I walked outside and around to an adjoining compound full of bicycles. The compound was surrounded by an eight foot wire fence and was protected from the rain by a blue corrugated steel roof. I could see the bicycles closest to me, just behind the wire fence, all secured with the typical Japanese bicycle lock—a short piece of metal locked in place between the wheel spokes, preventing forward movement.

Suddenly I decided to steal a bicycle. Just like that. Take somebody's bicycle and ride it home. In two hours I could be snug in bed, all of this foolishness behind me, nothing but a dream. My criminal impulse brought with it no immediate twinge of guilt; there appeared no friend at my shoulder giving cause to a second thought, nor stranger to cast a suspicious glance my way and bring me to my senses. No, the moment the idea of thievery entered my head, any alternative course of action became impossible. Before me stood rows of

This morning in a supermarket down in the Tojin district, I passed a bulletin board on the wall nearest the cash registers, the kind of board used in the States for handwritten notices of cars for sale, apartments wanted. Among the various local notices on this board, there were two credit cards some shoppers had dropped or misplaced. They were just hanging there, attached with scotch tape, waiting for the owners to return.

◆

—James D. Houston, *In the Ring of Fire: A Pacific Basin Journey*

314 *Travelers' Tales * Japan*

bicycles…so many of them in their cage in the dark…and all I had
to do was find one that was unlocked. And what was a single missing bicycle going to matter? Bicycles went missing in Osaka every
day. Everybody stole bicycles and anyway, I rationalised, I had all
the more reason: this was an emergency!

bicycles…so many of them in their cage in the dark…and all I had to do was find one that was unlocked. And what was a single missing bicycle going to matter? Bicycles went missing in Osaka every day. Everybody stole bicycles and anyway, I rationalised, I had all the more reason: this was an emergency!

I blocked from my mind any thoughts of reversing my decision. Think too long and moral guilt will always lead you astray. I sprang at the fence, shaking it noisily, and clambered for the top. Within seconds I was balanced precariously on my stomach at the height of the fence, wavering, trying clumsily to throw a leg over, and then half-falling, half-leaping to the concrete floor of the compound below. Crouching low in what I imagined was the stealthy stance of the trained commando, I squinted through the wire fence nervously, expecting discovery at any instant, but the area around Omiya station remained dark and deserted. Quickly and quietly I began gliding between bicycles, searching for one that had been left unlocked, but unfortunately (for would-be thieves like myself) most of the bicycle owners had secured their spoke locks; indeed, some prudent owners even had a padlocked chain looped around their bike's back wheel for extra protection.

Then I spied an unlocked bicycle. I darted over to it and, still crouching, gently wheeled it forward. Yes, it was free of chain and lock and what's more it wasn't one of those ubiquitous shopping bicycles with a basket between the handles, but a sleek, black, smaller model with thicker tyres and a well-padded seat. The perfect getaway bicycle.

Once again I surveyed the scene. The streets were empty, the houses dark. The pedestrian crossing lights flashed. There were no taxis about. No witnesses to the crime I was about to commit.

Picking up the bike by the frame—it was amazingly light—I hoisted it to the top of the fence and tried to keep it balanced while shakily climbing after it. My plan was to silently lower the bicycle from the top of the fence onto the footpath below, but I had barely taken both feet off the ground when the bicycle went crashing down from the top of the fence with a clatter I was sure would wake half the neighbourhood. I hastily scaled the wire, leapt from the top almost as ungracefully as the bicycle had fallen (on the right side of the compound, thank goodness) and quickly picked up the tangled wreck, which was, happily, still in one piece.

Everything was accelerating now. My mind was racing with fear and excitement, my heart pounding behind my ribs, my eyes darting in every direction. With a final, paranoid glance at the rows of dark houses—was that a light flicking on? A face at a window?—I jumped in the bike saddle and began peddling wildly. Immediately a feeling of exhilaration swept over me, as tangible as the wind sweeping through my hair. I was free! I'd done it! The scene of the crime was fast disappearing behind me as I careered off down the road. Adrenaline pumped in my veins and a soundtrack thumped in my head: Steppenwolf's "Born to be Wild…"

I rode furiously, snaking between houses, bowling down narrow lanes and deserted streets, speeding along quiet backroads that skirted wide fields of rice. I tried as much as possible to run parallel to the train line, but this often proved difficult, especially when the tracks led across terrain that was inaccessible and I soon found myself taking ever-widening detours, the bicycle zigzagging to the left and right of the tracks via low bridges and dim underpasses.

After forty-five minutes of hard cycling I still hadn't arrived at the next station along the line and I began to feel that I had somehow lost my way. The rail lines had multiplied like hydra heads, branching out in all directions from a jumble to my left, and ahead I could make out a network of murky, sludge-filled canals that looked to offer few, if any, opportune crossing points. I wondered how I could stay on course. And now, with tracks running to all compass points, which direction was the right direction?

I rode the bike slowly up a gravel path onto the raised bank of the nearest canal and dismounted to stretch my tired legs. Once again, I felt ridiculously out of place. In the last week—or month, or year—who had stood where I was standing now? Had anybody ever stood here, on this particular patch of ground? From this precise angle, at this particular time, in this exact place, no human gaze had ever fallen across the industrial panorama that lay before me. It was decaying, a timeless process that was private, never meant to be seen. And here I was, invading like some idiot voyeur.

I decided that the only course of action open to me now was to get onto the Meishin Expressway. My meandering had deposited me closer to its access ramps than at any time since leaving Katsura, and the route—once I was barrelling down its wide lanes—would be speedier and more direct than negotiating the maze of byways, fields and canals that otherwise lay ahead. I now realised I should have made for the expressway back at Omiya, even Katsura, but at the time (it seemed so long ago!) a cross country jaunt had had infinitely more appeal. Well, I didn't care for adventure now. Resolute, I again set off on the stolen bicycle, speeding along the canal bank towards the expressway, the wind whipping my tie over my shoulder.

Soon I found myself travelling along a wide road that was flanked on either side by plastic orange witches' hats. The bitumen was smooth and black, recently laid, and the lines marked down the centre of the road appeared freshly painted. After a time the road steepened and crossed the canal which I had been following earlier, and then suddenly, as if a heavy veil had been lifted, the discernible rumble of heavy trucks disturbed the air.

The road continued to rise gradually, the noise continued to build, and minutes later my hopes were confirmed when I pulled exhausted onto the Meishin Expressway. This was Japan in the early hours of a Wednesday morning on an expressway between two major cities: semi-trailers barrelling along through the night, blinding headlights approaching, red tail lights fading, tiny blue warning lights blurring with speed. The trucks carried anything and everything—produce, lumber, electrical goods, newspapers, rice. They wheezed into the driveways of all night petrol stations, brakes hissing. Their drivers sated their appetites at Lawson's convenience stores and brightly lit roadside noodle stands, talking of sumo and politics and money through mouths full of food. The drivers and their trucks owned the Meishin Expressway at this hour of the morning; very few cars drove amongst their number, and pedestrians and bicycles simply did not exist.

The noise of the trucks on the expressway rose and crashed like waves.

For a time, there would lie a moment of calm, an eerie silence on the empty road. To my ears, every sound during this fleeting respite seemed amplified a hundredfold: the hum of the bike's tyres along the bitumen; my shallow breathing; the whirr of the greased chain in constant motion. Then the greater silence would break. In the distance, a faint rumble, building slowly in intensity. Was the sound coming from behind, or in front of me? I was unable to tell. As it grew louder, however, I was able to ascertain its origin, but by then the source of the cacophony was upon me: a speeding truck bearing down from behind, its thunderous howl crashing around my ears. Hurtling past, the truck's roar threatened to knock me from my bike and send me sprawling headlong, tumbling over and over in its wake...

According to the Japanese

*R*eal bike shops are often reluctant to work on bikes sold by other stores, so when the bike needs attention, the owner just abandons it and buys another new bike at discount, starting the cycle of bicycle pollution over again.

The question you might be asking at this point is how to distinguish, for moral as well as legal purposes, between bike recycling and bike theft.

The answer is time. Very simply, if a good bike has remained locked and obviously unmoved in the same location for more than a few weeks, chances are it has been abandoned. Once the police notice it, the bike is likely to be tagged with an appeal to the owner to move it or lose it. At this point I usually act. Try recycling a bike sometime and see if it doesn't make you feel good inside.

◆

—Byran Harrell, *Cycling Japan: A Personal Guide to Exploring Japan by Bicycle* and English lettering on the large green sign above me, Takatsuki was now only seven kilometres away.

Seven kilometres. After the ups and downs and crisscrossings of my journey to date, the distance was trifling. I rubbed one eye and looked at my watch. Just after 3 a.m. I'd be home before the first train of the morning, with time to snatch a little sleep before heading off to school.

I pedalled my way along steadily, on the fringes of the city now, scanning the road ahead for the next indication of the distance that remained until Takatsuki's centre. Trucks seemed fewer now; those that did occasionally pass by were travelling perceptively slower through the built up area in which I now found myself.

I wondered about Judy. Would she be worried about me? Up, bleary eyed, pacing the floor of our apartment, waiting anxiously for another phone call? More likely I thought, she'd be asleep. And when I told her later today of my thievery, what would she think of me?

Moral questions hadn't bothered me since my rush of adrenaline at Omiya. Even now, as I considered Judy's reaction to my crime, I remained free of any overwhelming sense of guilt. I had known the moment I had started pedaling that returning the bicycle the next day, or any day after that, was impossible. Unless I was prepared to ride all the way back to the station—very doubtful after tonight's debacle (and bicycles were not allowed on trains)—the bicycle would be mine, regardless of Judy's thoughts on my perfect crime.

The sudden flash of blue lights to my right broke into my thoughts. A police car had cruised up beside me, silently, like a shark, and the two policemen inside were motioning for me to pull over to the curb. Instantly my heart contracted into a tight ball of muscle. Waves of heat were spreading across my chest and questions were flashing through my head. What was this? Where had the police come from? Surely their presence was unrelated to my theft over an hour ago? Or had it taken them this long to track me down? I'd seen no one at Omiya—but had someone seen me? I had to believe their presence was sheer coincidence, but I felt guilt pouring out of me like a broken dam. The police!

I stopped cycling and pulled over to the side of the road while the police car slowed and parked a short distance behind me. I stared straight ahead and heard the motor turn off; I could sense the blue lights still flashing rhythmically, their beams playing across my back. Waiting there, heart thumping, face red with guilt, I heard two doors open and quietly shut, then the squeak of approaching leather shoes.

Seconds later two policemen stood either side of me. They were dressed in black uniforms with white trim, carried truncheons slung close to their hips and had small walkie-talkies tucked into their breast pockets. The younger of the two policemen flicked on a small torch and shone it at the front wheel of the bicycle.

"You should have that light on."

I looked down and remembered I hadn't clicked the wheel-powered light into place.

"Sorry," I mumbled, and reached down to correct my error.

The other policeman spoke. "Is this your bicycle?" He too was young, but bigger than his colleague; his uniform seemed a size too small for him, tight around the shoulders. His hair was shiny and straight, but cut in a terrible bowl style that made his head appear oddly small upon his large body. Beneath his low fringe was a rounded face with a flat nose and thick lips curved into a slight smile, which gave him the appearance of a contented pug.

"Um, no...it's a friend's bicycle," I stuttered.

The pug nodded and removed a spiral bound notebook and pen from inside his jacket, then squatted next to the bicycle's front wheel. His colleague took the torch and directed the beam at the front mudguard, illuminating half a dozen large, blue *kanji* characters that clearly spelt out the name of the bicycle's true owner. I felt sick. Suddenly hundreds of identifiable marks seemed to leap from the bicycle, eagerly proclaiming my guilt: a sticker here, a scratch there, the address beneath the owner's name...

The policeman with the notebook asked me politely to

dismount. I kicked the stand up, got off the bicycle and stood watching on the footpath, hands thrust into my pockets, as he shifted his attention to the bike's serial number, stamped in the frame just below the seat.

"What are you doing riding at this time of the morning?" the younger policeman asked me. His confident, slightly sarcastic tone seemed at odds with his boyish face; he couldn't have been any older than mid-twenties I guessed. He had traces of acne on his forehead and cheeks.

"I missed my train," I said, fumbling for the tattered train schedule I carried in my wallet. I held it out to him, hopelessly attempting to lend credence to a lie rapidly inventing itself on the spot. The policeman nodded and looked at me, waiting.

"I borrowed the bike from a friend," I continued, glancing down at the kanji-inscribed mudguard.

"What is your friend's name?"

I had no idea what the *kanji* read.

"I don't know," I answered like a complete moron. "Actually it's my friend's friend's bicycle."

"Name?"

"Judy Lemke. L-E-M-K-E."

I am a terrible liar. At the slightest confrontation with authority, my brain shuts down and my tongue goes into scrupulously-honest mode. Of a million names I could have invented there and then, I produced a real one—and my girlfriend's at that.

"Where does your friend live?" the puggish policeman asked, putting away his notebook as he rose.

"Address?" I said, stalling. "Er, she lives at the same address as me." I gave them our address.

"And where does her friend live?" the pug continued patiently.

I squinted and looked at the sky, hoping to give the impression that I was cooperatively racking my brains.

"I'm not exactly sure...Near, umm, Omiya, I think."

The younger policeman asked to see my alien registration card. This was an ID card that every foreigner living in Japan was obliged to carry about with them at all times. A stay in the country longer than three months required the "alien" to register their name, address, occupation and other details at the municipal offices closest to where they were currently residing. Fingerprinting—despite the indignity—was standard procedure.

I produced my card and handed it to the policeman. He took it and glanced from the card to my face and back again, comparing the photograph with the red-faced foreigner in front of him. Convinced my picture and I were one and the same, he turned and sidled away towards the police car. The pug said nothing. I waited.

Of course my story held no more water than a sieve. "Yes officer, rather than let me spend the night at their house or pay for a taxi, my friend's friend (whose name I cannot recall) was good enough to lend me his bicycle at 2 a.m. in the morning to find my way home over a distance of twenty kilometres." Oh yes, highly plausible. How tangled my pathetic web of deception was!

As the younger policeman returned with my card and began questioning me again, I resigned myself to the fact that I was past the point of a quick release. This pick up may have begun routinely enough—I was desperately unlucky to have been pulled over for the unlit light—but it was now clearly evident that my interrogators had me for theft of the bicycle and all that stood between them and a conviction was my sad self-

---)---

I went to a gay bathhouse in Tokyo, a small place with tiny rooms and futons on the floor. I wandered the halls, the doors to some of the rooms were open...and on the futons, two or three or four young, slightly effeminate men, gaggled together like puppies, bursting out with mirthful, high-pitched giggles, which were then rapidly muffled by a hand covering the mouth in embarrassment: the typical Japanese gesture which, so it seems, allows one to break out beyond decorum by making constant gestures to acknowledge its violation.

◆

—George Vincent Wright, "A World of Bathhouses"

delusion that I could talk my way out of this. My options were nil. There was no recourse but to admit the truth, play the dumb *gaijin* and hope for lenience.

"Wait a minute," I began...

My sudden admission of guilt signalled little surprise on the Japanese faces. They simply nodded understandingly. Admitting one's mistakes and seeking forgiveness is a very big deal in Japan. I was politely ushered towards the police car and the stolen bicycle was placed in the boot. The pug did a U-turn and we drove off, the flashing lights mercifully extinguished.

Ten minutes later I found myself sitting in a cramped, two room neighbourhood police box, or *koban*. Across a small desk, I faced— I assumed—the officer in charge. He was middle-aged, with bright, alert eyes and a shock of thick black hair, and wore the same immaculately pressed black and white uniform as his subordinates. He was examining my alien registration card.

After a moment, apparently satisfied, he put the card down. He had said nothing since my arrival and had only spoken briefly with his colleagues when they had first brought me in. I wondered whether he'd ever had a foreigner sitting opposite him at his desk before.

He glanced towards his fellow policemen standing in the doorway that led to the other room. For an instant I thought I saw smiles flicker across the lips of the three Japanese, a silent joke shared, but when the officer turned to face me again, his face bore no trace of humour.

"My name is Masutani," he said. A smile blossomed on his face, revealing perfect teeth.

I concentrated on the essence of humility; head bowed, eyes lowered and a slightly pronounced bottom lip. My voice was very low.

"Where do you come from?" he continued conversationally.

"Australia."

"Ahh, Australia! Very beautiful country!"

"Thank you very much."

"How long do you stay in Japan?"

I sensed he was referring to the time I had already spent in the country.

"I've been in Japan about seven months," I answered.

The policeman seemed to pick up on my subtle correction.

"I'm sorry. English is very difficult for Japanese people." He looked sheepishly towards his colleagues, who could hardly contain their amusement.

"No, no, you speak it very well!" I said.

"Thank you. Would you like some tea?"

The pug disappeared into the adjoining room and emerged moments later with a tray bearing a mug of hot tea. He placed it on the desk in front of me.

"Thank you," I said, picking up the mug.

Then the pug surprised me. Screwing up his face, almost as if he were in pain, he asked in faltering English, "What is...your hobby?"

This was a serious question in Japan, a common icebreaker. I answered mechanically as I had dozens of times before; the policeman smiled, obviously pleased with his question and my response.

What was going on? I couldn't believe I was sitting here, in a *koban*, after being caught riding a stolen bicycle and the Japanese police seemed to have little better to do than practise their English on me, their captive native speaker! I realised the novelty of the situation, certainly, but surely it was only a matter of minutes before the pleasantries ceased and I was fined or imprisoned for the remainder of the night—or worse...

Then, the first sign of getting down to the matter at hand. Masutani placed before me a form, in triplicate, and handed me a pen. As I couldn't read Japanese, the police officer pointed to the spaces I had to fill in and translated: name, address, alien registration number, place of employment, date of arrival in Japan and so on. When the form was complete he produced a small ink pad from a desk drawer. Fingerprinting! Now my worst fears were confirmed! All that remained, I thought, before the full extent of Japanese justice was unleashed upon me, were the mug shots in front of the wall: turn to the left, FLASH! Turn to the right, FLASH!

Masutani spoke as he pressed my finger to the ink pad. "Don't worry. Stealing a bicycle is not a serious crime in Japan. First time, no problem. It's OK. But second time...very serious." He passed me a tissue to wipe the ink from my finger and handed the completed forms to the younger policeman.

The words hung tantalisingly in the air. No problem. OK. Don't worry. I felt a spark of hope ignite inside me, but I was careful not to let this hope pierce my humble exterior; Masutani's reassurances did not necessarily preclude some form of punishment. He might be saying, don't worry, it's OK, you're not going to jail, but here's a fifty thousand yen fine for you. However, with proceedings so far rather genial, I decided to risk broaching the question of the penalty facing me over my little transgression. I was primarily concerned with my working holiday visa status; if my misdemeanour showed up on any kind of record, I could have trouble obtaining an extension on my stay in Japan.

"No problem," Masutani assured me when I asked him what my fate might be. The answer was still rather ambiguous, but for some reason, I believed him. His face seemed to invite reassurance: There was nothing to worry about, his eyes seemed to say. A first time mistake. You've seen the error of your ways.

A combination of relief and something akin to true humility washed over me. I wanted to thank this policeman profusely, I wanted to shake his hand, to be his friend.

"Please tell the owner of the bicycle that I'm very sorry, that I missed the last train and..." My voice trailed off.

Masutani's eyes lowered, a smile tightened on his face. Was he for some reason embarrassed? Then he nodded, rose and said that it was time to take me home.

An hour later, after a lengthy interlude at the main police station in Takatsuki, where the paperwork was lodged, I directed Masutani and the happy pug policeman through the streets of Tonda, a suburb of Takatsuki, to the double story apartment block where I lived. It was a quarter to five in the morning. Throughout the drive home Masutani and I chatted amiably about Japan, Australia and policework; we were getting on so well that tentative plans were made to go out drinking one night in the near future.

As we walked up the steps to my apartment in the cool morning air, Masutani informed me that Judy would be required to complete a form similar to mine and would also have to be fingerprinted. I couldn't believe it! My hopes of quietly slipping into bed and breaking my wild story to her a few hours later were ruined; humiliatingly I'd have to rouse her from her sleep and involve her in the whole ridiculous affair.

I invited the policemen into my darkened apartment. They entered first, slipping off their black leather shoes just inside the doorway, and stood waiting inside my tiny kitchen in their socks, looking awkward and embarrassed. Thin bars of moonlight streamed diagonally across the carpet from the apartment's only window. I crossed the floor in a few steps and padded silently up the ladder to the loft where Judy lay sleeping, facing me. Her eyes opened slowly. I told her what had happened, and that the police needed her fingerprints.

"Police here?" she said.

"Please Jude. It'll only take five minutes. Nothing's going to happen."

Judy's eyes closed, then reopened. She sighed. "OK."

Judy dangled her arm from the loft and the police fingerprinted her, then filled in the required paperwork. Masutani politely informed me that the matter was now closed. I thanked him and showed him into the kitchen, where the other policeman was already slipping on his shoes. I opened the door and with a slight bow the policemen turned and were gone.

Five minutes later I lay in bed, trying my best to tell Judy of my night in more detail, but my narrative was constantly interrupted by my jaw-wrenching yawns. My head felt as if it were sinking into my pillow, subsiding slowly into a bottomless pit full of feathers—in moments its weight would drag my leaden body after it and I would disappear forever. I felt something soft pass over my eyelids—Judy's palm?—helping them fall...down...down... knockknockknock—

"Michael? Michael?" Judy's voice, a harsh whisper. "Someone's at the door!"

Shaking my head I sat up. A knock came again. I clambered down the ladder to the living room and opened the front door to the only possible callers: the two policemen were back.

Masutani said: "We're very sorry, but your friend's fingerprint has been taken from the wrong hand. It is our mistake. We must make another print."

Once again the police entered our apartment and removed their shoes; once again the younger policeman remained in the kitchen while Masutani followed me into the living room. Judy's finger was inked—this time from her opposite hand—and she filled in a fresh form. Then with a smile and a bow, Masutani left the apartment with his colleague. I watched them walk down the darkened apartment block corridor towards a small, faint square of light. The rising sun.

That night, home in our apartment after a hazy teaching day of stifled yawns and heavy eyelids, the telephone rang around eleven o'clock. Halfway through the recorded message on the answering machine, I heard a familiar voice. It was Masutani.

"Michael-san? We are very sorry, but there has been a mistake. The wrong forms were completed yesterday. I am very sorry. We have some new forms. Is tonight convenient for us to visit?"

We never did have that drink together, Masutani and I.

Michael Ward is a writer based in Melbourne, Australia. Since returning from Japan, he has proven himself to be a model citizen, and now tends not to go anywhere without some "emergency money" wrapped in the corner of his handkerchief.

★

A group of us had ordered turkeys from the foreign buyer's club (cheaper) and I had picked up mine and one belonging to a friend. So, needing to deliver it, and always trying to efficiently do at least two things at once, I wrapped it with a frozen pack in some newspaper, stuck the whole thing in an old carry-on bag, and put it in the side basket of my bike, as my front basket was full of some other groceries I was delivering along with books for my class.

I left home and went southwest a few miles to a hospital to visit Peggy, our church pianist, to admire her newborn baby. No problems. I left there for a leisurely ride of about 4 miles going east to teach my Bible class (turkey delivery was going to be one block from class). After about 6 blocks, I happened to glance at my side basket. Guess what? It is old and the bottom had dropped through—and I had no turkey. What to do?

I retraced my tracks—back over the highway; back to the hospital—no sign of a turkey. But WHERE could I have lost a turkey? WHAT was I going to say to this poor woman waiting for her Thanksgiving dinner (it's not like one can run down to the corner store and get another). And, I HAVE to get to class. At the point of giving up, having searched the route twice, four young men stop me. Am I looking for something? Yes, Well, they had found a bag and taken it to the police box. Off I go, following these helpful guys to the police box, where I must fill out a form describing what I have lost, giving my fingerprint as proof that I am the one claiming it, etc. (How many other people are liable to come in and claim a frozen turkey?)

—Mary Kay Sapp, "You Lost a What?"

PART FOUR

IN THE SHADOWS

(Shadow)

ROBERT WHITING

✳ ✳ ✳

The *Wa* of Baseball

Foreigners must obey or else....

IF YOU ASKED A JAPANESE MANAGER WHAT HE CONSIDERS THE most important ingredient of a winning team, he would likely answer *wa*. If you asked him how to knock a team's *wa* awry, he would probably say, "Hire an American."

Foreign ballplayers, most of them refugees from the American major leagues, have been an active part of Japanese baseball since the postwar era. And for most of that time, there has been a limit of two per team. The somewhat lower level of play in Japan has given these *gaijin* a temporary reprieve from the athletic scrap heap. And although the Japanese have paid the *gaijin* high salaries, it hasn't always been a mutually rewarding experience.

Money is a particular sore point. Foreigners always make two to three times as much as Japanese players of comparable ability. This fact, combined with the free Western-style house and other perks that the

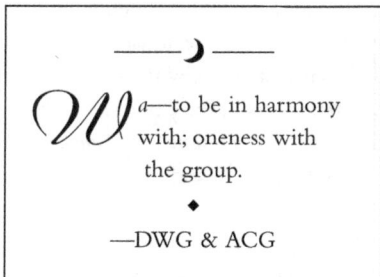

> *Wa*—to be in harmony with; oneness with the group.
>
> ◆
>
> —DWG & ACG

gaijin seem to view as inalienable rights, sets them too far above their teammates.

Despite the special treatment, the foreigner is often unable to adjust to the different style of play in Japan. Roughly half of all new *gaijin* recruits each year are not invited back for a second. Said one American of his initial season, "I was in a daze for six months."

In 1981, the Yomiuri Giants signed former major leaguer Gary Thomasson to what was then the highest-paying contract in the history of Japanese baseball: three years at a total of $1.2 million. This compared to the $270,000 a year earned by the highest paid Japanese player, Koji Yamamoto of the Hiroshima Carp. While Yamamoto was winning his third straight home run crown with 44 homers, Thomasson compiled a batting average of .261, hit 20 homers, and struck out 132 times. The Giants benched him during the last week of the season, perhaps to spare Thomasson the embarrassment of breaking the Central League strikeout record of 136, held by another American named Lee Stanton. Thomasson was dubbed "The Giant Human Fan" by Japan's merciless sports press, which also frequently spelled his name using the Chinese character *son*, meaning "loss" or "damage." He was released the following year.

But finance is only part of it. Deportment is the rest. Although few Americans hold Japanese batting or

---

> ——— ☽ ———
>
> *T*he government asked them whether they were glad they had had firsthand exposure to Japan. Most of them said no.
>
> The same poll asked the foreigners what had most irritated them about their time in Japan. Anyone who has lived in the country could guess the answer without looking at the results: Non-Japanese, in Japan, felt ground down by the constant reminders of the perceived racial gap between *ware-ware Nihonjin* (we Japanese) and everyone else.
>
> ◆
>
> —James Fallows,
> *Looking at the Sun: The Rise of the New East Asian Economic and Political System*

pitching records, many have established new lows in the area of bad conduct. Records for most smashed batting helmets, ejections from games, and broken clubhouse windows, for example, are all held by individual *gaijin*. Indeed, the clash of free-spirited individualism with Japanese group-think has perhaps caused more grief than all the American strikeouts and errors put together.

There was ex-San Francisco Giant Daryl Spencer, for example. Like most former major leaguers, Spencer insisted on following his own training routine, and it was considerably easier than his teammate's. One night, as he was lackadaisically going through his pregame workout, his manager on the Hankyu Braves, Yukio Nishimoto, decided something had to be done.

"You don't look sharp, Spencer-san," he said. "You need a rest."

"What do you mean, I need a rest?" Spencer growled. "Who's leading this team in home runs, anyway?"

"I don't think you can hit this pitcher," Nishimoto said.

"I can't hit him? I'm batting .340 against that guy."

"Not tonight. That's my feeling. You're out."

That was too much for Spencer to take. He was in the dressing room changing into street clothes when he heard his name announced in the starting lineup. Nishimoto had put Spencer down as the third batter, but only because he was planning to "fool" the opposition by inserting a pinch hitter in the first inning.

Now Spencer was smoldering. When the game began and he heard the name of the second batter over the loudspeaker, he decided to get even. Clad in his shorts and shower clogs, he headed for the dugout. Grabbing a bat and smirking in the direction of Nishimoto, he strode out to the on-deck circle to take a few practice swings.

Spencer's entrance delighted the fans, and his picture was in all the papers the next day. Nishimoto, however, was not amused. He ordered Spencer off the field and slapped him with a suspension and a two-hundred-dollar fine. Spencer paid up, later reporting with a wide grin, "It was worth every penny."

Other Americans have followed in Spencer's shower-clogged footsteps.

Willie Kirkland, who had played for the Giants, Indians, Orioles, and Senators, was a happy-go-lucky sort who liked to tease his teammates. One day Kirkland was bemusedly watching an aging infielder (who had recently been elevated to player-coach) straining through a batting drill. "Hey, man, you're a coach now," Kirkland yelled playfully. "You don't have to practice anymore."

The player-coach took Kirkland's jest as a comment on his declining usefulness and he launched a roundhouse right that barely missed the American. It took half a dozen men to restrain the coach. "I was just joking," Kirkland protested.

"He was making fun of me," the unappeased coach retorted.

The Japanese didn't find Richie Scheinblum a barrel of laughs, either. A noted clubhouse wit in the U.S., Scheinblum spent his two years (1975-76) as a Hiroshima Carp baiting the umpires. Shane, as he was known on the club's official roster, was frequently agitated by the plate umpire's idea of Scheinblum's strike zone; that is, it was considerably larger than the one Shane had in mind.

Scheinblum searched for a Japanese phrase to convey his sentiments to the men in blue, something that would really get under their collective skins. A Japanese friend came to the rescue, and soon Scheinblum was muttering, "You lousy Korean" to arbiters who crossed him.

There is, historically, not much love lost between Koreans and Japanese, and to the umpires, Scheinblum's taunts were intolerable. To stop him, they imposed a stiff fine each time he uttered the dreaded epithet. When Scheinblum finally departed Japan, no cries of "Come back, Shane!" were heard—at least, not from the umpires.

It was not until Clyde Wright came along that the rules of behavior for foreigners were to be finally codified. Wright, a pitcher of some note with the California Angels, Milwaukee Brewers, and Texas Rangers, made his first Japanese appearance in Japan with the Yomiuri Giants in 1976. A self-described "farm boy" from eastern Tennessee, Wright was regarded by those who knew him in America as a "tough-as-nails" competitor who didn't believe in hiding his feelings.

The Giants, of course, were by a million miles the most popular team in Japan, and their manager, Shigeo Nagashima, was in-
disputably the most beloved sports figure in the land. As a player
he had been personally responsible for the most exciting moment
in Japanese baseball history: a game-winning (or *sayonara*) home
run in the first professional game Emperor Hirohito ever attended.
He had charisma that no one, not even famed teammate Sadaharu
Oh, could match.

The Giants were also the self-appointed custodians of national
virtue. Popular belief had it that their players were neater, better
mannered, more disciplined, and more respectful than those of
other clubs. Their *wa* was in better tune.

In early 1977, when one writer, a former Giants player turned
magazine reporter, suggested otherwise in print, he was banned
from the Giants' home stadium, Tokyo's Korankuen, for a whole
year. Among his horrifying revelations were: (1) Some Giants players did not like other players on the team; (2) A few players
thought Nagashima could be a better manager; (3) Some younger
Giants living in the team dormitory did not especially care for the
Saturday night 10:00 p.m. curfew; (4) Some Giants' wives objected
to the season-long "energy-conserving" rule forbidding them to
request sexual relations with their husbands. It was tame material
as far as exposés go, but to the shoguns of Yomiuri, the Giants'
name had been desecrated, and someone had to pay.

Wright also faced the difficulty of being a foreigner on a team
that traditionally liked to consider itself pure-blooded—Oh's
Chinese ancestry and the few closet Koreans on the Giants not
withstanding. Wright was only the second non-Oriental *gaijin* to
play for the team, and the sight of a fair-skinned American in a
Giants uniform was a bit unsettling to the Japanese multitudes.

Wright, like many other *gaijin*, seemed to the Japanese to be of
a breed apart. He was a muscular and hairy six footer who seemed
selfish and crude to Giants fans, many of whom considered themselves the height of refinement.

Wright soon gave them reason to be more unnerved. In the
sixth inning of an early-season game, with the score tied 1-1,

Wright allowed the first two batters to get on base. Nagashima walked out on the field to take him out of the game. Few American managers would have removed him so abruptly. It was Nagashima's feeling, however, that Wright was getting weak and that was that.

When Wright realized what was happening, he blew a gasket. To the horror of fifty thousand fans and a Saturday night TV audience of millions, he brushed aside Nagashima's request for the ball and stormed off the mound, an angry scowl on his face. Halfway to the bench, he threw the ball against the dugout wall, cursed, and disappeared inside.

Once inside, he kicked over a trash can, ripped off his uniform, shredded it and flung it into the team bath. Amidst a rapid-fire discharge of obscenities, he finally said something that the official team interpreter was able to understand, "Stupidest damn baseball I've ever seen. If this is the way the Giants treat their foreign ballplayers, I'm going, I've had it."

Nothing like this had ever happened on the Giants. Other teams had problems, but not the proud Kyojin, as the Giants were called in Japanese. No one had ever shown this much disrespect for Nagashima. "Crazy" Wright, as he was instantly renamed by the press, became headline news in the sports dailies the next day. Letters, telegrams, and phone calls poured into the Yomiuri offices. Outrageous! Inexcusable! Wright should be released. Deported. Shot. Drawn and quartered. And not necessarily in that order.

Only Nagashima kept his cool. First he patiently explained to his American pitcher that what he had done was not "stupid" baseball but simply the Japanese way of playing the game. It's a group effort. Then the manager faced the angry masses. There would be no disciplinary action. He was glad that Wright cared so much about winning. And he wished that some of his Japanese players would show as much fight.

Such benevolent words from the prince of Japanese baseball dissipated much of the public's antagonism toward Crazy Wright. It did not, however, pacify the front office. Management was not as eager as Nagashima-*san* to let Western ways penetrate the organization. They issued a set of ten rules of etiquette that Wright and every other American player the Giants might henceforth deem worthy of their uniform would be obliged to obey.

The Japanese press quickly gave it a name: The Gaijin Ten Commandments. This is how they went:

1. Obey all orders issued by the manager.

2. Do not criticize the strategy of the manager.

3. Take good care of your uniform.

4. Do not scream and yell in the dugout or destroy objects in the clubhouse.

5. Do not reveal team secrets to other foreign players.

6. Do not severely tease your teammates.

7. In the event of injury, follow the treatment prescribed by the team.

8. Be on time.

9. Do not return home during the season.

10. Do not disturb the harmony of the team.

Robert Whiting graduated from Sophia University in Tokyo, where he began his career as an author and columnist. His work has appeared in Winds, Smithsonian, Sports Illustrated, *and many other publications, and he is the author of many books, both in English and Japanese. This story was excerpted from his book* You Gotta Have Wa.

❈

Always be ready! That is the great commandment of the samurai. When you go out of your house, you should go as if you were never to return. Thus, the commandments of the samurai were gradually codified, and the *Bushido,* the guide of knighthood, was created. Strict commandments, a Japanese hierarchy of values:

1. Honor and duty above all.

2. Blind obedience to the emperor.

3. Boldness, disdain of death; be ready to die at any moment.

4. Relentless discipline of soul and body.

5. Polite and kind behavior to friends.

6. Ruthless vengeance for the enemy.

7. Generosity (frugality is one of the forms of cowardice).

With these fiery commandments, pure, hot-headed Don Quixotes, the *samurai*, flooded Japanese history. With the same commandments, they fought, elevating Bushido to a new religion. The contemporary Japanese tried to mold the new generation of entirely modernized knights who would flood the world history.

—Nikos Kazantzakis, *Japan China*, translated by George Pappageotes

AMY GREIMANN CARLSON

Whose Hand is This?

A trip downtown transforms a polite young lady
into a red-faced, gun-wielding Rambo.

I HAD ALWAYS THOUGHT OF THE JAPANESE AS THE EPITOME OF
polite and demure behavior, reserved and proper. Most stereotypes, however, die when faced with experience. There I was, 23
years old, ten thousand miles away from home, by myself in a
strange country where it was obligatory to slurp your noodles and
you were NOT to blow your nose in public; sniffling was preferred. You read vertically from right to left, and Mother Goose
didn't exist. No assumptions could be made about even the simplest of things.

7:00 a.m.—I bolted out of bed to the blaring ritualistic tunes of
the exercise music across the street in the Mitsubishi yard.
Everyone was out doing their morning calisthenics perfectly syn-
chronized to the beat and to each other. As I watched from my 5th
floor apartment, their fluorescent orange work overalls reflected
the morning sun on the wall above my tea cup. I averted my eyes
from the brightness. Groaning, I slowly rose and trudged into the
bathroom to get ready to meet the day.

I had to go to the heart of Nagoya to teach English to a bunch
of housewives who liked to study. It was their hobby. I enjoyed their
giggles and their delight in things foreign. Each time we would

gather, they wished to teach me about what it meant to be Japanese, so I was never quite sure who was teacher and who was student. That day I was to meet them in a foul mood and we WOULD discuss what it meant to be Japanese, especially the male kind!

As the doors of the subway car slid shut, I drew in my breath and slunk through the morning rush hour throng to a free air space hovering over an elderly gentleman. He was sitting unmoved, unmoveable, placid; even his wrinkles lay at rest. I began to sweat as my knuckles turned white from grasping the overhead rings as the black-haired hoard pressed upon my back, making me lean dangerously closer to the gentleman's lap. I strained to keep my balance, dropping my bag to reach up with my second hand. The bag did not make it to the floor. It jammed between bodies, stuck to my thigh. I ignored it as my attention focused on the tension in my arms. They ached badly. I needed to move, but I couldn't. I needed oxygen, but there was none. The closed windows dripped with condensation.

"Get me out of here!" I screamed silently.

The next stop approached as I plotted to procure more space, not to mention air. The doors opened and the sea of black-haired passengers began to flow like the changing of the tide—out...in. The man below me continued to sit, unmoved, unmoveable. I continued to hang precariously over his lap, not able to accomplish my plan due to the strong current of bodies. Suddenly this small elderly gentleman, who up to this moment could have been mistaken for a Buddha statue in his stillness, became a blur in his swiftness. Jumping into action, he ripped my arms from the rings above as he shoved me aside. As I toppled into the now empty seat, he grabbed a handful

> *T*o create an awkward moment is a sin in Japan; to cause disruption puts one beyond the pale.
>
> ◆
>
> —J.D. Brown, *The Sudden Disappearance of Japan: Journeys Through a Hidden Land*

of my youthful bottom and gave it a generous squeeze. I just froze there, mouth agape like a fish out of water as the slimey fellow exercised precision timing and propelled himself out of the closing doors. As the train slowly began to move away from the platform, I exploded with a string of profanities that flew around the tight confines of the car like machine gun fire, hitting many innocent bystanders. I felt like a terrorist. Red-faced and hopping, I was politely given a circle of space to be an American female Rambo.

Who had had time for "DARE NO TE? I didn't! Those infamous first words of Japanese were taught to us in Tokyo for our protection on crowded trains: "If you are being fondled, quickly grab the offender's hand, jerk it up into the air and scream, "Whose hand is this?!"

At the time I had thought it ludicrous, never imagining myself having to use such a tactic and wondering why they had even felt it necessary to teach us this phrase, even before "hello". Japanese men were polite and would never behave in such a perverse manner! Even after the unfortunate incident on the subway, I clung to my ideal, despite male street hecklers, blatant chauvinistic displays by Japanese colleagues, and other unpleasant, far-from-polite happenings.

My stereotype finally crashed for good on the eve of my departure from Japan. I was headed home after almost three years in a foreign place. I stood in Shinjuku, one of the busiest train stations in the world, with a group of other Americans on the same program as me. Some of us were on our way out, others were just arriving. Linda, my perky replacement, looked fresh, enthusiastic, and ready for adventure. Without warning, out of the masses strode a man who headed straight for this spring of youthful exuberance, grabbed her breasts and groped her for what seemed like minutes while we all just stood there, again, with mouths agape. He calmly walked away while we all stared at each other like dull-eyed cows ready for slaughter. So much for "DARE NO TE" and so much for the ideal polite and proper Japanese male! It was too bad that I had to leave Japan with this memory so fresh in my mind. I kind of liked the stereotype better.

Amy Greimann Carlson is a teacher, editor, and gardener who lives in Leavenworth, Washington with her husband Reed, juggling many projects including building a house.

★

By Western standards, the Japanese are subdued in public; I hardly ever heard anybody laughing out loud. I did see a lot of comic books, which are a huge industry in Japan, but most of them are not meant to be humorous. They're more like novels or action-adventure series with pictures, and they tend to contain a lot of violence and sex. Several times, riding in the Tokyo subway, I'd be standing next to a middle-aged businessman in his business suit, and he'd have a fat comic book, which he'd be frowning at studiously, as though it were the Third Quarter Sales Trends, and I'd glance at the page he was looking at, and there would be a naked woman with hooters so large that I half expected to see a little cartoon Woody Allen running away from them.

—Dave Barry, *Dave Barry Does Japan*

CLAYTON NAFF

* * *

Every Yen's Worth

The Japanese work ethic threatens to destroy.

THE *JAPAN TIMES*, ALTHOUGH NOT PARTICULARLY AUTHORITARIAN, consciously tried to be a traditional Japanese company. It made a clear distinction between the "lifetime" employees and the contract-based help. It had a company union. Big decisions were subject to *ringi*, the passing around of a proposal to all permanent employees for them to approve by affixing their personal seals.

Hardly anybody took their full allotment of personal vacation. In lieu of this, the *Japan Times*, along with all the other national newspapers, observed seven or eight "newspaper holidays" a year, most of which fell on a Sunday. (We *gaijin* were permitted to take up to three weeks leave a year—without pay.)

However, you could sense the reach of authority from beyond the company boundaries. One night, as we were closing the late edition, one of the deskmen looked at some dry, statistic-laden piece we were publishing and snapped. "Why are we putting this out? It doesn't mean anything."

"Beats me," I replied.

"I want to get out and report, talk to real people about real issues," he continued.

"So why don't you?" I asked.

343

"I don't know. We just get pinned down," he said, and concluded with conviction: "It's the system."

> *B*efore leaving for Japan
> to teach English under
> the auspices of the Lutheran
> Church, my pastor gave me a
> copy of Shisaku Endo's novel,
> *Silence*, to read on the plane. I
> read it before I left. A mistake?
> His characters, missionary priests
> of the 1600s, spoke to me and
> my direction, causing me serious
> doubts about my imminent
> journey: "This country is a
> swamp. In time you will come
> to see that for yourself. This
> country is a more terrible
> swamp than you can imagine.
> Whenever you plant a sapling in
> this swamp the roots begin to
> rot; the leaves grow yellow and
> wither. And we have planted
> the sapling of Christianity in
> this swamp."
>
> ◆
>
> —AGC

The *Japan Times* did report on real issues and real people. However, for nearly all of its government and business news, it had little choice but to be spoon-fed meaningless statistics by nameless government sources or corporate flaks. Japan has evolved an ingenious press club system that throws a muffling blanket over nearly all controversy. (The exception is politics, which provides an entertaining sideshow.) Every government agency, right down to the local police station, and every major company or business group has a "*kisha* club." Members are coddled with closed briefings (to the fury of foreign reporters, who have long been excluded), but the implicit bargain is that all reports will be limited to agreed-upon facts.

The upshot is that many Japanese reporters know a great deal more than they are able to tell in print. Being ignorant of this in my early days at the JT, I was surprised to learn from Doi-san, a bright star on the desk, that the ruling Liberal Democrats frequently paid their bitter opponents, the Socialists, to act as go-betweens with the North Koreans. I found this hard to believe. I certainly hadn't read it in the *Japan Times*. But in 1991

Doi-san was proved absolutely correct. Shin Kanemaru, the LDP "godfather" who kept millions in gold stashed under his floorboards, went hand in hand with Socialist leader Makoto Tanabe on a diplomatic foray into North Korea. There they dined with the Great Leader himself, Kim Il Sung, Korea's answer to Stalin. Kanemaru bungled the trip, promising more than Japan's bureaucrats were prepared to give. A year later, he fell from grace when a shady businessman confessed that he had wheeled a shopping cart stuffed with $4 million in Japanese banknotes into an underground garage to pay off Kanemaru for political favors. The businessman was backed by right-wing gangsters. But money politics holds ideology cheap. Some of that $4 million undoubtedly snaked its way through the political swamp into the clutches of North Korean commissars. After all, arranging a trip to Pyongyang costs money.

Eventually, things came full circle. Kanemaru's fall toppled the ruling party itself, and the Socialists, blinking with astonishment, found themselves partners in a ruling coalition led by defectors from the LDP. Less than a year later, the Socialists walked out of that coalition and into a deal with the very Liberal Democrats who were ostensibly their bitter opponents. Together, they formed one of the strangest governments democracy has ever seen: a conservative cabinet with a Socialist face. And the Japanese press had, in some sense, been a silent witness to the corruption that made it all happen.

So are Japanese reporters lazy? Hardly. Many are ambitious and most are hardworking. Important politicians like Kanemaru were followed around the clock by squads of reporters. The only thing comparable in America is the press corps that dogs a front-running presidential candidate. But unlike their American brethren, Japanese reporters tend to keep a lid on the juicy stuff until a press club—say, at the prosecutor's office—validates it.

Japanese reporters are reluctant to let go of the *kisha* club system because of the security it affords them. Nevertheless, the foreign press in Japan is battering away at it. The *kisha* club members were especially galled, for example, when T.R. Reid of *The Washington Post* broke the news of Crown Prince Naruhito's engagement to Masako Owada. All the Japanese media had known about it for weeks, but had obeyed a government request to withhold the news until the Imperial Household Agency gave them the green light.

David Butts, my boss at UPI, who went on to become Tokyo bureau chief of *Bloomberg Business News*, dealt the system another blow in the summer of 1993. After years of quietly seeking membership in the stock exchange press club, which like most press clubs had no provision to admit foreign members, David finally began a highly public series of protests inside the club. I accompanied him the day CNN came to film the scene. It was highly amusing to watch him shout, "We're all journalists! We're not supposed to restrict information!" at a club member who hid out of camera range behind a bookcase.

However, the press club later showed that it was not amused: Its members voted to relax the rules, but in a demonstration that in Japan the nail that sticks up still gets hammered down, they admitted Bloomberg's chief rival, Reuters, but rejected Bloomberg itself.

Of course, the press was not the only industry whose actions were influenced by the government. About the time I started working for the *Japan Times*, [my wife] Rumiko was being courted by Nippon Steel, one of Japan's biggest companies. Nippon Steel, once the centerpiece of Japan's industrial policy, was getting a little long in the tooth. What's more, it was under pressure from the bureaucracy to make some helpful gesture toward reducing trade friction with the United States. Demand for its steel was slipping, so it had to close down several sprawling old factories in Kitakyushu, on the northern tip of Japan's southermost main isle. But Nippon Steel still had one of the country's largest private workforces—more than 60,000 people. The era of personnel "restructuring" had not quite arrived, so it needed to find new jobs for the thousands of workers who had been employed in the shuttered plants. The managers settled on a plan that, for a staid old company like Nippon Steel, was positively radical. They would convert an outdated foundry into a theme park called Space World. Going from manufacturing to service was a big leap, but theme parks were a growth industry at the time, thanks largely to government encouragement.

Since leisure was what Americans knew best, Nippon Steel would go a step further: It would incorporate the best of American amusement park know-how and technology. This would not only solve the problem of what to do with the old factory, it would earn the company brownie points with the government for reducing international trade friction.

That's where Rumiko came in. As a Japanese architect with a U.S. graduate degree, she could help them deal with the Americans and furnish designs appropriate to a Japanese project. Normally a company like Nippon Steel would be loath to hire a woman in her thirties for a professional job. The firm prided itself on having in-house expertise of all sorts, even architects. The vast majority of its employees were hired right after graduation and, if male, would stay with them until retirement. If female, they would normally be nudged into marriage with a suitable man, possibly from within the company, and retired after five years of service.

But the times they were a-changing, and Nippon Steel was determined to keep up with them. When the need arose for someone to deal with the Americans, they turned to one of those newfangled headhunters. They did not flinch when the man the headhunter produced turned out to be a woman.

Engrossed in my own work, I had only the vaguest idea of all this. One night, I returned from a shift at the *Japan Times* to find Rumiko standing in the middle of our living room/dining room/kitchen, looking disoriented and pale. A flush of anger coursed through me. Some high school boys, realizing that I was away in the evenings, had lately been harassing her, tapping on the windows of our ground-floor "mansion" and making unspeakable suggestions. Just a week ago I had switched worknights and staked out the corner. Sure enough, about 9:30 a couple of guys in black, Prussian-style school uniforms, no doubt on their way home from cram school, came sneaking up to our bedroom window and tapped on it. I caught them red-handed. Well, I almost caught

them. Cursing them out in fractured Japanese must have slowed
me down. But at least I thought I had scared them off for good.
Now I was not so sure.

"What's happened?" I asked.

"They made me an offer," Rumiko replied. "I think I might
accept."

Rumiko often says things that surprise me. Even after years of
living with her, I'm amazed to find how rarely our thoughts move
in parallel channels. At this juncture, however, I was shrewd
enough to suspect that we were talking at cross-purposes. I re-
quested details.

Rumiko sighed. As a Japanese, it really irritates her to have to
spell out everything for me. She can't understand why I can't grasp
the meaning from her…her whatever it is I'm supposed to grasp.
The Japanese call it *haragei*, "belly-talk." How you are supposed to
read someone's belly, even on the remote chance that it is exposed,
remains a mystery to me. I poured a couple of beers in hopes of
loosening her tongue.

Eventually, Rumiko enlightened me. Nippon Steel was now offering her a one-year contract at the salary equivalent to that of a
man with ten years' service to the company. There probably wasn't
another woman in the company who could command its equal.

This was clear but confounding. Rumiko had just launched a
private practice, in partnership with some old friends. Their firm,
Square Inc., was out of the shoals and spinning off a modest income for each partner. Becoming a partner in one's own firm rep-
resents an enormous step in the career of an architect. What's
more, although Square required hard work and plenty of it,
Rumiko could adapt her hours to our schedule. I was disturbed
by the idea of her working a nine-to-five job at Nippon Steel
while I worked from early evening till late at night. But, large-
souled creature that I am, I naturally said, "Go for it." After all,
Nippon Steel's offer amounted to Big Money, something in the
neighborhood of $60,000. It never occurred to me that they
would get every yen's worth. Nine-to-five, indeed. Hah!

Soon after the Space World project got started, Rumiko hit the road. In characteristic Japanese style, Nippon Steel dispatched its employees to learn everything they could about amusement parks. Rumiko and several colleagues roamed the world in search of perfect leisure knowledge. One day they were examining the giant roller coaster at a mall in Edmonton, Canada, the next they were somewhere in Alabama. Rumiko quickly racked up enough miles to become a premier member of United Airlines' frequent flyer club.

Even when she was back in Tokyo, Rumiko rarely got home before ten or eleven. But at least she did get home. The men in her office were frequently obliged either by the actual volume of work or by peer pressure to stay overnight at a nearby hotel.

As the pace picked up, her weekends vanished into a black hole of work. When I saw her at all, Rumiko looked drained. Her eyes were dull and her voice flat. She ground her teeth in her sleep.

I grew more and more frustrated with the situation. Finally, one Sunday afternoon, to Rumiko's great embarrassment, I called her at the office and insisted she come home. "Tell them you have an emergency at home!" I said. She didn't have to; they could guess. For a spouse to call the office on a matter less urgent than death was unusual, and the anger in my voice must have tipped off whoever had answered the phone. They let her leave.

Back home, I paced furiously until she arrived. What was going on? I demanded to know. "Meetings," she replied wearily. Long, endlessly long meetings in which everyone tried to figure out what everyone else was feeling without tipping their own hand. Politics—tense, back-stabbing, power-play politics in which various managers who had come to the project from different backgrounds tried to line up factions against one another. All this had to be done without creating so much as a ripple on the surface of the pool (harmony must be preserved!), so naturally it took far more time than open warfare would. And of course, work itself: The original task had quickly doubled in scope and budget as ambitions grew, but the schedule had not. Only the hours grew longer.

Despite my anger, it seemed there was nothing to be done

about the situation. Rumiko felt she was already getting off light compared with the others in the office. It was the Japanese version of the prisoner's dilemma: If one left, the others suffered more.

> To expand Japan Inc., the bureaucracy introduced the philosophy of *messhi hoko*, or self-sacrifice for the sake of the group. This philosophy requires the subordination of individual lives to the good of the whole....
>
> The Japanese are educated so that even if they are frustrated or unhappy, they will resign themselves to the situation. This education is very important since, if people do not complain, it is easier to propagate the philosophy of *messhi hoko*.
>
> ◆
>
> —Maseo Miyamoto, *Straightjacket Society: An Insider's Irreverent View of Bureaucratic Japan*

There was no overt command to stay. But because responsibility lay undivided with the group, everyone felt obliged to hang around for the sake of the others. No one ever felt sure that his day's work was done.

The next morning, Rumiko was out the door again before eight o'clock. I barely saw her again for a week, and when I did she was little more than a sleepwalker.

I started to worry about her health, not to mention the health of our marriage. One night, I decided to voice my concerns. "Rumiko," I said in a voice intended to convey both reason and compassion, "you are young and strong, but you're not invulnerable, for Chrissakes. If things go on the way they are, who knows what…"

She exploded. I don't recall exactly what she said, through the tears and rage, but the gist of it was that I was only making things worse. She was under tremendous pressure and what she needed from me was support and practical help, not advice. My feelings were hurt, but it later struck me as bitter comedy that I was being asked to play the role of the "good wife" to her salaryman shtick. Not that I was ironing her chemises or anything. But she was telling me that I should be indulgent and supportive rather than critical and challenging.

I shrugged and got on with my own work. But the situation grew intolerable. Finally, we hit on a mutually agreeable solution: Have a baby!

We went to work with a will. If anything, life was even more exhausting now, but at least it had its fun moments. Finally, one of the little pregnancy testing strips turned blue: We were going to be parents. As it happened, this was too late to trim any time off Rumiko's contract, but it gave her a reason to lighten up her schedule somewhat in the later stages.

Rumiko was lucky. As a mother, she had no choice but to be present for the birth of her child. One of her colleagues at Nippon Steel was not so fortunate: When his wife gave birth to their first child, he was on assignment hundreds of miles away. Many weeks passed before he got to see his child. Another colleague of hers was a man eager to start a family. But to the rich amusement of everyone around him, he simply lacked sufficient opportunity for intimacy with his wife. It seemed that he always got home too late or too exhausted.

But the excesses of work proved tragically unfunny in the end. Shortly before the project was completed, one of Rumiko's supervisors—a lean, hard-driven man in his forties—flew down to Kyushu to inspect the site yet once more. Shortly after arriving, he dropped dead in his tracks. It was plain to all that overwork had felled him. Nippon Steel might have a new vision of its business, but its corporate culture had hardly changed a whit.

Clayton Naff, an American journalist, went to Japan on assignment, married into a Japanese family, and became known as an expert on Japanese affairs. He has reported for National Public Radio and other media.

*

"Don't be late," I continued, "means that you must be at work—that is, at your desk—before anyone else; you don't actually have to be working. You could be reading the paper, or looking at a comic book, or having a cup of coffee. The important thing is to let people around you know that you arrived before starting time.

"The second principle, Don't take time off, means, as far as possible, you avoid taking paid vacations. Even if you get sick, you don't take time off until you've let your co-workers see you suffering with a fever. And when you do take off because of sickness, then and only then do you use your paid leave. Officially guaranteed sick leave goes unused. It's also important not only to work overtime but to perform a kind of unpaid 'voluntary' overtime. This overtime exists in a multitude of forms: sympathy overtime, which means staying late with co-workers when they have extra work to do, even if you don't; study groups and research teams; take-home work; going out for a few drinks with your superiors; Sunday golf, section trips, baseball tournaments, sports days; helping someone move; attending weddings and funerals...the list goes on and on. The idea is to demonstrate your willingness to sacrifice your own time in order to contribute to the organization."

—Maseo Miyamoto, *Straightjacket Society: An Insider's Irreverent View of Bureaucratic Japan*

ALAN BOOTH

* * *

A Thousand Cranes,
A Thousand Suns

Uncomfortable moments steeped
in darkness end in prayer.

At the point where the atomic bomb was dropped on Hiroshima there is a Peace Park, and in the Peace Park there is a museum. I visited the museum with no illusions that I would be able to write about what I saw and little real hope that I would comprehend it. The three hours that I spent there, forcing myself to look at every item, reading each caption in English and again in Japanese, brought me no closer to an understanding but they knocked a gaping hole in my spirit.

It is not the vastness of the destruction that moves you so much as the relics of individual suffering. These speak with the most eloquence, a melted desktop Buddha, a burned watch, the scorched blazer of a thirteen-year-old schoolboy, one of more than six thousand who had been led out to participate in an air-raid defense program and so were on the unprotected streets when the bomb fell. There are photographs of a little girl, her will snapped, refusing the cup of water that might have made her death easier; of a young soldier bleeding obscenely from the pores, who died two hours after his picture was taken; of keloid formation on the face and body of a teenage boy, bald as an egg; of a young housewife who had put on, in these last breathless days of the war, a bright cheerfully patterned summer kimono and the dye of the cloth had burned lines and squares into her back and arms and neck so that she looked, in her death agony, like a plaid doll.

There is a display in which two or three department store mannequins have been dressed in rags and smeared with rubber latex to represent the peeling off of their skin. They slouch through a yellow cardboard inferno, so gross, so like a comic strip that I could not bear to look at it. For the three hours I was in the museum my eyes kept drifting to the windows and, through them, into an impossibly remote world where fountains played in the sunlight of the park.

I was staggered to see so many schoolchildren being shepherded round the exhibits by their teachers. They were very young and very quiet, shuffling along wide-eyed in their little yellow hats, some holding each other's hands, some pointing and asking their teachers questions that were answered in an almost inaudible drone. I did not see a single child smile, and the seriousness of their faces made them appear very much older and wiser than they were. Many stared as they passed me, and I could feel the bewilderment and tension in their little bodies. One boy turned round from an exhibit to find me standing close behind

———)———

"*E*very Japanese junior high school student knows about Hiroshima and Nagasaki," Denver lamented, "but they don't know about Nanking."

♦

—Bruce S. Feiler, *Learning to Bow: Inside the Heart of Japan*

♦ ♦ ♦

*I*n 1937, the Japanese systematically massacred over 300,000 Chinese in what was then the capital of China, Nanking. This atrocity has become known as "The Rape of Nanking," and is left out of Japanese history books.

♦

—DWG & AGC

him and threw up an arm as though to protect his face from a slap. None of the children laughed at me or shouted greetings, but several whispered to each other, quietly and seriously, "Look, it's a foreigner. Look, it's a foreigner." Slowly I shuffled past the exhibits toward the exit with my sunglasses on my foreigner's face, breathing easier because I was almost out of the museum, and quite unprepared for what happened next.

I was looking at one of the last displays—a shelf of melted rooftiles and bottles that had fused together in the twelve-thousand-degree heat of the bomb—a heat sufficient to melt human bones. I felt a nudge at my elbow and looked round to find a man in his early thirties—too young, I think, to have remembered much about the bombing—standing beside me wearing workman's clothes and smelling (or perhaps I imagined this) of sake.

He said: "Your country did this."

My eyes must have altered behind my sunglasses. I slid away from him and stopped in front of a large photograph of a junior high school girl with half her face missing. I felt the same nudge and now the man was grinning.

"Do you like this picture?" he asked. "Do you find it interesting at all? Does it amuse you? Do you find it amusing?"

And suddenly the part of the museum where we were standing was very still because, suddenly, it contained no other people, only a young man with a camera—a student, I think—who came up and slipped quietly between us and said to the workman: "Stop it, please. Please, stop it. Please, leave him alone. He's not an American. Please, stop it."

But the workman would not be stopped now, and his voice had begun to rise.

"He was rude to me," he said. "He turned his back when I spoke to him. He mustn't do that to me. I'm Japanese!"

I drifted on toward the exit, past another group of staring children whose teachers had stopped answering their questions and were looking vacantly at the windows or at the walls. I could hear the workman and the student still arguing and I managed to pause at the souvenir stand long enough to buy some books I wanted—one that contained poems by survivors of the bombing, one with the photograph of the schoolgirl who had no face. When these were wrapped and paid for, I turned round to find the workman waiting for me in the doorway.

At first I pretended I hadn't seen him and tried to walk past him, through the pool of space that other visitors had left around him, out into the impossible world where the fountains played. But it was a narrow doorway, and as I stepped through it, he prodded me and I took a deep breath and swung round and looked him in the face.

"I'm very sorry," he said.

"It's all right," I said. "I'm sorry I was rude."

"I'm sorry I was rude," he said.

"No," I said, babbling like an idiot, "I'm sorry, I'm sorry. This is the Peace Park."

"I'm sorry," he said.

"No, I'm sorry too," I said.

I left him in the doorway and went and sat on a bench with my books still wrapped in their paper bag and watched the autumn sun light the leaves of Hiroshima trees.

It was from a cloudless sky like this that the bomb dropped—"brighter," say the people who saw it, "than a thousand suns." Later, in the north and east of the city, the sky turned dark and a "black rain" fell. As painful as the deaths and the lingering disease was surely the bewilderment of the stunned survivors: no such suns, no such rain had ever before intruded into mankind's history.

From my seat under the trees in the Peace Park I watched an old man sweep colored garbage into a heap that he arranged very carefully beside one of the park's stone monuments. When I passed it on my way to the gate I saw that it was not a heap of garbage but thousands upon thousands of tiny folded paper cranes.

There is a story told about a little girl who fell desperately ill some two or three months after the bombing. For a long time the exact nature of "A-bomb sickness" was only dimly understood, and treatment was haphazard and ineffectual. This fact, combined with the soaring black-market prices of foreign medicines in postwar Japan, condemned most of those who contracted radiation-induced diseases to an agonizing death. But the girl's mother was stubborn and resourceful and hung onto her wits far longer than most mothers would have. Patiently she persuaded her little daughter that if she could fold one thousand paper cranes and string them together like a rosary she would recover. Millions of these tiny cranes—the work of well-wishers and pilgrims—hang today in colored festoons from the stone monuments in the park, and it was these that the old man was arranging in heaps. The little girl began to make her cranes, but daily her fingers lost their strength, and eventually the sheer effort of folding them was a torture both to her and to her mother. Still her mother—by now, and of necessity, a believer in the myth she had concocted—stubbornly urged her daughter to fold another crane and then another, and painfully the little girl folded another crane and then another, and painfully the little girl folded her cranes and one by one the number grew. She died after making nine hundred and sixty-four.

I have found it extremely difficult and depressing to write even this much about Hiroshima, but others have taken greater pains. Among the pieces of writing that move me is a short childlike poem by Toje Sankichi—a man of twenty-eight when the bomb fell, who died of radiation disease eight years later. The poem is reproduced in stone on a Peace Park monument.

> Give back my father, give back my mother.
> Give back the old.
> Give back the children.
> Give me back myself, give back
> all people who are part of me.
> For as long as this world is a human world,
> Give me peace.
> Give me peace that will last.

The sun was still bright when I walked out of the Peace Park, and the fountains and the monuments and the paper cranes. It was hard this cloudless autumn day—95 days since the start of my journey, 11,890 days since the dropping of the Hiroshima bomb—to realize how quickly time had passed and, in passing, how completely it had stolen away memory. Some 200,000 people are thought to have died as a result of the world's first atomic holocaust, and their names are contained in a stone chest that is one of the park's simplest and most eloquent memorials. But looking at the words carved on the chest, I couldn't help wondering whether the passing of time had not transformed their ringing promise into a strangled, wholly incredible prayer:

> $\smile$
>
> We are painfully conscious of your sentiments today, you, Our subjects. Therefore, We have decided, in accordance with the dictates of fate and of the present time, to pave the road toward a great peace for generations to come by enduring the unendurable and supporting the insupportable.
>
> ◆
>
> —Imperial decree, broadcast August 15, 1945

Sleep in peace.
The mistake will not be repeated.

Alan Booth also contributed "Taiko Drumming" to Part One.

✳

Waiting for a Nagasaki streetcar the next morning, we watch two men at work, both smoking as they flap their black and white checkered flags. They toot on whistles like gym coaches and cavort in whatever way it takes to hail passing cars and induce them to enter their parking garages for the day. From across the street I can hear the steel rain of steel balls in a pachinko parlor. It is Monday morning all over Japan, and everything is untangled from the shadows.

At Nagasaki's downtown Mazda dealership the sales force is lined up two rows deep in the showroom, men in front, for the 9 a.m. pep rally.

The gas stations are outfitted with washing machines to keep the towels and chamois clean. Everyone gets their windshield wiped; car mats, too; the works—no boom in self-service here. As a customer pulls away with a full tank, uniformed gas jockeys bow.

The last sign we see leaving Nagasaki is on an office;

INSTITUTE FOR RESEARCH IN HUMAN HAPPINESS

Its venetian blinds are drawn shut, but I see a brilliant flash of light as if from an explosion inside an empty glass vault. Perhaps this is an underground entrance to a parallel cyclotron; but whether fashioned of aging wood or polished plutonium, I can't tell.

At the Atomic Bomb Museum the most haunting relic is a lump of glass in which the ashes of a human hand are embedded, "a grudging hand that remains forever," says the museum brochure—a hand print on the century.

—Nicolas Bouvier, *The Japanese Chronicles,*
translated by Anne Dickerson

CLEO PASKAL

Why I Burned the Flag

How a mild-mannered supermarket owner
became a world-famous radical.

THE OKINAWAN ISLANDS, DOTTED ALONG THE SOUTHERN TIP OF
the Japanese archipelago, should be known for their coral beaches
and hyacinth groves. They're not. They're known for having been
the only bit of Japan actually captured during the Second World
War. The Americans are still there. It was directly occupied until
1972 and Okinawa's main island still has the highest concentration
of U.S. bases outside the continental United States.

It was well after midnight at Birdy's bar, an off-base club for
American Green Berets from nearby Kadena base. It was the
Friday after payday but there were no soldiers in the bar. They
were all in Somalia. Rumours were that some of them were
among the 18 who had died in the botched attack on Aideed.
The Okinawan barmaid casually wondered who had been among
the dead.

The Green Berets might not have been there in person, but
their spirit was pervasive. On one side of the cash register was a
photo of Nixon and Elvis shaking hands. On the other side was
the "Welcome Military Personnel" sign given to favoured business
during occupation. Tacked above the bar was currency from all the
places the Americans had visited or perhaps invaded including a
Canadian two dollar bill. Faded, lacquered, movies posters papered

the walls. Grant, Garbo, and Bogart smiled down at the patrons. In a corner was a transcript of Martin Luther King's "I had a dream" speech. In another corner was a karaoke machine. Fish tanks rainbowed with tropical fish and plastic American Indians were on the counter and behind the bar. A Russian officer's hat hung from the wall like a trophy. It had the feeling of a cozy, well-worn officer's club, which, of course, is basically what it was.

I was there to meet one of Japan's most notorious radicals. But I didn't know what he looked like. I sat down at the bar. As I sat, the man next to me turned and smiled. "Hello," he said, "my name is Chibana Shoichi. I own a supermarket, a small supermarket."

It wasn't exactly an understatement but it definitely wasn't the whole story. Everyone in Japan knows Chibana Shoichi, though they might not recognize his name. People usually refer to him as "You know, that Okinawan guy who burned the Japanese flag." Sometimes they'll add some reference to heroism or treason, depending on their politics. But everyone knows him.

In 1987, at a baseball game on a U.S. Army base in Okinawa, he took off his shoes, scaled a concrete wall, and set fire to the Hinomaru, the Japanese flag, with his pocket lighter. He climbed back down and waited to be arrested. The police were so shocked they didn't know what to do. So Chibana went to the local McDonald's and had lunch while the prosecutors tried to put together a warrant. Then he turned himself in.

Since then, he has been vilified by right wingers and beatified by left-wingers. Now he was buying me a drink.

The bartender, looking rather effete in oiled down curls and Lennon glasses, served us our beers and quietly left. I asked Chibana the obvious: "Why?"

"Do you know much about the history of Okinawa?" He asked.

I said I knew the islands had been independent until the Japanese had unilaterally annexed them in the late 19th century. The Japanese had done their best to eradicate local languages and culture and replace them with Japanese and Emperor worship. Then came the decimation of the war and American occupation.

"That's all true," he said, "but empty. It doesn't explain the damage Japanese education did to Okinawa, to Okinawans. During the war, we were taught that the Japanese were divine. That there was no worse shame than to be captured by the barbaric Americans. Because of that, thousands of Okinawans committed suicide rather than surrender. When the Americans landed, mothers slit their daughter's throats then set themselves on fire. They killed the ones they loved best to save them from what they were taught to believe was a fate worse than death. Okinawans who did try to surrender were killed by Japanese soldiers who thought they would betray them. All this was done in the name of the Hinomaru, the flag of the Japanese military during the war. Now that flag is the unofficial flag of Japan. Germany changed their flag. So did Italy. But Japan didn't. The war isn't over here. We still have Japanese education and U.S. bases. When they decided to fly the Hinomaru in my village, a village where hundreds died in its name, a village that is built around a U.S. base, many old people came to me and asked me to stop it from happening. I was the logical choice because I am self-employed and can't be fired.

"I didn't think it was such a big deal. The response was shocking. East Timorese, Puerto Ricans, American Indians all come to me. I say 'Please don't consider me a representative of Okinawan dissent,' but they still come.

"I didn't expect the response from right-wingers either. They tried to burn my store. I couldn't imagine that. But there was also unexpected support. sixty-five lawyers from as far away as Tokyo have volunteered to defend me. I don't even know most of their names.

"Honestly, the thing that surprised me most was that no one had burned the Hinomaru before. People think I am a crazy radical. In the context of Japan, the act looks crazy, but in the context of the community, it was not so strange. A supermarket without customers is impossible. If they thought I was crazy, my customers would go elsewhere. They didn't stop coming.

"Speaking of which, I have to go. If I don't get home soon, I won't be able to get any sleep before the farmer's market opens in the morning. You have to get there by 5 or else all the good fruit is gone. It's not easy running a supermarket."

Chibana Shoichi got up and, smiling, waved goodbye to the barmaid and bartender. They warmly smiled back as he went out into the night.

Cleo Paskal also contributed "Love Boat Revisted" in Part Three.

*

I was quick to dismiss Japanese laments over the fragile nature of existence until my first earthquake, when the house felt as if it were being picked up and dropped, for sport. I shielded by head and looked up, not knowing what I was looking for except what might be coming down. I was helpless and afraid. The next day I went out and bought bottled water, six cans of tuna, a flashlight, and extra batteries, and stuffed them all into a backpack that sat by the door. Having had my hint of catastrophe, I was taking no chances.

Buildings could be built to sway. Seismologists might even be able to forecast the big quake long overdue. But in the end, when the earth began moving and the sea churned, you were stuck, on your own, like everyone else, trying to stay on your feet, losing control. In Japan handwringing talk of natural disaster was too often the excuse for social rigidity—rigidity that could tyrannize the spirit and sap the life from what I still saw as the pleasure in spontaneity. Though I wearied of the tiresome talk of people bonded in their understanding of the way things were done, that belief was nonetheless rooted in a historical fear of death from above or below. It was not environment alone that had made Japan resistant to change. The environment only accentuated and gave credence to what I had come to see as they very natural human inclination to wake up every morning knowing where the world began and ended. My nation's myths may have told of endless possibilities built upon the promise of change. But those were myths; and in the everyday business of living I recognized that the Japanese were not alone in seeking sameness. They had simply used the valid concern over their shaky homeland as the basis for attaching virtue to predictability.

—Michael Shapiro, *Japan: In the Land of the Brokenhearted*

ALAN BOOTH

* * *

Raw Horsemeat

It's not easy being an alien.

THAT EVENING I LEARNED THAT RAW HORSEMEAT WAS A specialty of the area, so instead of eating dinner at my *ryokan*, I went to a little restaurant near Kumamoto station with my mind made up to try some. It was disappointingly stringy and, having come straight out of the refrigerator, was hard with bits of ice. I sat for a long time sipping beer, waiting for the horsemeat to thaw, while the only other customer in the restaurant had a private conversation with the owner.

"Foreigners are a weird lot, aren't they? I had my fill of them when I was in the States. So impolite and opinionated. Always on the look out for a confrontation. I kept telling myself how lucky I was to have been born a Japanese."

It is true that the Dutch, like all foreigners, were reputed, probably for good reason, to smell like rotting meat; one popular joke even claimed that when the *komos* (redheads) went on a trip to Kyoto, all of Kyushu's flies followed them there.

♦

—Nicholas Bouvier,
The Japanese Chronicles,
translated by Anne Dickerson

I asked for another beer, and the owner brought it over and put it down on my table without a word.

"I tried to buy a raincoat in New York, but I couldn't find one to fit. It wasn't just that they were all too big. Foreigners are a funny shape. Japanese bodies are so much better proportioned."

My second beer bottle was still full and I'd hardly touched the horsemeat, but I got up and went over to the cash register to pay my bill. The conversation had been going on for twenty minutes and I no longer found it amusing.

"I don't speak English," the owner said to me and winked at his customer.

"Wah yah frum?" the customer grinned.

I paid the bill and left the shop. The night in Kumamoto city was cool, and I was still hungry and wanted a drink, so I strolled twenty yards up the road by the station and sauntered into another, similar shop. But no sooner had I slid the door closed behind me than I knew how impossible the night would be. One of the three customers sitting at the counter turned to his friends and announced in a voice loud enough to fill the place:

"Look! A *hen na gaijin* (funny foreigner) has arrived!"

I sat down and took the warm towel the master offered me and dabbed my hands and face with it.

"I'm not a funny foreigner," I said. "I'm an ordinary foreigner."

There was a short silence, and the master coughed.

"Er...what...er...would you like to drink?"

"He heard me!" laughed the customer.

"Yes," I said, "you have quite a loud voice."

The traditional pantomine followed, in which the customer went through the motions of an elaborate and completely insincere apology, and ending with an offer to buy me some beer.

"No thanks," I said. "I've ordered some of my own."

Alan Booth also contributed "Taiko Drumming" to Part One and "A Thousand Cranes, A Thousands Suns" to Part Four.

If I were as remote as I imagined myself, why could moments that irritated me no end also please me? Why was I reacting viscerally, and in contradictory ways, to the same stimuli? Little boys would approach and ask for my autograph for no reason other than my foreignness. I smiled and complied, seeing in the encounter an innocence I never saw at home. Yet when those boys of the same age and intent called out to me, "Harro, harro," I wanted to grab them by the backs of their collars, lead them home, and explain to their parents that foreigners were not mere objects of curiosity.

—Michael Shapiro, *Japan: In the Land of the Brokenhearted*

PART FIVE

THE LAST WORD

智

(Wisdom)

LAFCADIO HEARN

* * *

Reflections

The ancient place has changed and shall
change again until there is no place.

I HAVE ALREADY BECOME A LITTLE TOO FOND OF MY DWELLING-place. Each day, after returning from my college duties, and ex-changing my teacher's uniform for the infinitely more comfortable Japanese robe, I find more than compensation for the weariness of five class-hours in the simple pleasure of squatting on the shaded veranda overlooking the gardens. Those antique garden walls, high-mossed below their ruined coping of tiles, seem to shut out even the murmur of the city's life. There are no sounds but the voices of birds, the shrilling of *semi*, or, at long, lazy intervals, the solitary splash of a diving frog. Nay, those walls seclude me from much more than city streets. Outside them hums the changed Japan of telegraphs and newspapers and steamships; within dwell the all-reposing peace of nature and the dreams of the sixteenth century. There is a charm of quaintness in the very air, a faint sense of something viewless and sweet all about one; perhaps the gentle haunting of dead ladies who looked like the ladies of the old pic-ture-books, and who lived here when all this was new. Even in the summer light—touching the gray strange shapes of stone, thrilling through the foliage of the long-loved trees—there is the tender-ness of a phantom caress. These are the gardens of the past. The

369

future will know them only as dreams, creations of a forgotten art, whose charm no genius may reproduce.

Of the human tenants here no creature seems to be afraid. The little frogs resting upon the lotus-leaves scarcely shrink from my touch; the lizards sun themselves within easy reach of my hand; the water-snakes glide across my shadow without fear; bands of *semi* establish their deafening orchestra on a plum branch just above my head, and a praying mantis insolently poses on my knee. Swallows and sparrows not only build their nests on my roof, but even enter my rooms without concern—one swallow has actually built its nest in the ceiling of the bathroom—and the weasel purloins fish under my very eyes without any scruples of conscience. A wild uguisu perches on a cedar by the window, and in a burst of savage sweetness challenges my caged pet to a contest in song; and always through the golden air, from the green twilight of the mountain pines, there purls to me the plaintive, caressing, delicious call of the *yamabato:*

Tété
poppo,
Kaka
poppo,
Tété
poppo,
Kaka
poppo,
Tété...

No European dove has such a cry. He who can hear, for the first time, the voice of the *yamabato* without feeling a new sensation at his heart little deserves to dwell in this happy world.

Yet all this—the old *katchiu-yashiki* and its gardens—will doubtless have vanished forever before many years. Already a multitude of gardens, more spacious and more beautiful than mine, have been converted into rice-fields or bamboo groves; and the quaint Izumo city, touched at last by some long-projected railway line—perhaps even within the present decade—will swell, and change, and grow common-place, and demand these grounds for the building of factories and mills. Not from here alone, but from all the land the ancient peace and the ancient charm seem doomed to pass away. For impermanency is the nature of things, more particularly in Japan; and the changes shall also be changed until there is found no place for them—and regret is vanity. The dead art that made the beauty of this place was the art, also, of that faith to which belongs the all-consoling text, "*Verily, even plants and trees, rocks and stones, all shall enter into Nirvana.*"

Lafcadio Hearn, a roving English-Greek journalist and devotee of the exotic in the late 1800s, was commissioned by Harper's Weekly *to visit Japan and write about the culture. He went—and never returned, adopting the culture as his own and living the last fourteen years of his life there. His eloquent and prolific writings introduced Japan to the West—and to this day are considered classics.*

WHAT YOU NEED TO KNOW

WHEN TO GO/WEATHER

Enjoying Japan depends on many factors, two of which are weather and people flow. The size of California, Japan varies greatly in its climate zones, equivalent to traveling from Maine to Florida. If you like hot and humid, go in the summer to the islands of Honshu, Kyushu, or Shikoku. If you like skiing and cold, go to Hokkaido in the winter. Spring and fall, however, are the most temperate and dynamic seasons for the Japanese landscape. Springtime ushers in the famous cherry blossom explosion. Waves of blooming petals move from Kyushu in early March, to Tokyo by mid-April. Even the television news shows, along with the weather forecasts, give you a cherry blossom update. Fleeting blossoms occupy the national consciousness and everyone's travel plans. The masses descend during the last week of April and the beginning of May for a national holiday called Golden Week. The whole country is on the go—a bad time to travel unless you book way ahead of time! Other mass exodus periods include New Year's Week and in August for Obon, a time when people travel to their ancestral prefecture to honor their dead. And then there's fall, a time when crowds dissipate, the weather cools, and the color of the fall foliage rivals that of New England. Whatever season you decide to spend in this magical land, prepare to layer. Carry a small backpack on your outings for that extra clothing you remove when hot, or put on when chilled. Be prepared.

VISAS/PERMITS

If you are a tourist or business visitor and intend on staying less than 90 days, your passport is the only necessary documentation you will need. If you plan on working, going to school, or staying longer than 90 days, you must apply for a visa. Check with the Japanese embassy closest to you.

CUSTOMS AND ARRIVAL

When entering Japan, non-residents are allowed three 760ml bottles of alcohol; 500 grams of tobacco (or 400 cigarettes or 100 cigars); 57 grams of perfume; and other goods/gifts worth 200,000 yen or less. There are no limits on the amount of foreign currency you can have with you as you enter, but you are allowed no more than 5 million yen as you exit; for anything over 5 million yen, you need authorization. If you would like to get yourself detained or deported, never to return, try entering with firearms, narcotics, or pornography. The Japanese are funny about pubic hair in pictures, including in art books. Beware. Also, certain animals, fruits/vegetables, and plants are also illegal and will be confiscated.

𝒢ETTING INTO THE CITY

To get into Tokyo from Narita International Airport, the easiest way is by train on either the JR Narita line or the private Keisei line, which will bring you into the heart of the city. Unless you rob a bank, taxis are out of the question since the airport is more than 60km away. There is an airport bus, but you take a chance on traffic and may end up sitting for two hours or more. If you rent a car, you will face the same fate. Trains really are the way to travel in this country.

You can access Osaka, Kobe, or Kyoto with ease from Kansai International Airport. Kansai is a new facility and it provides excellent, fast rail service and/or ferry service. Check upon arrival for schedules.

All other destinations can be reached by flying into either Tokyo or Osaka and taking the bullet train, *shinkansen,* which gets you there fast, in style, and you can see the countryside on your way. Enjoy!

𝓗EALTH

Start your trip healthy. In the event you become ill while in Japan, do not worry, there are many medical facilities available to you. Contact JNTO's Tourist Information Centers for a list of English-speaking doctors and hospitals. If your own health insurance does not cover you outside of the U.S., it is advisable to buy supplemental coverage for your trip. There are no immunizations needed to travel in Japan and there are no restrictions as to the foods you eat (although parasites do live in raw fish) or the water you drink (but use your common sense—drinking out of streams in the mountains can give you giardia anywhere in the world). You will want to bring with you those personal items that you depend on, such as an extra pair of glasses, your medication, and contraceptives. If by chance you have large feet and your shoes fall apart while you are there, you will be out of luck, so bring an extra pair for such an emergency. All in all, you don't have to worry about much except getting crushed by rush hour crowds.

Emergency Assistance

For emergency help in English, try contacting a TIC Office (see 'Important Contacts') for a list of hospitals that have English-speaking physicians nearest you.

Travel Insurance & Assistance

Several companies in the U.S. and Europe provide emergency medical assistance for travelers worldwide, including 24-hour help lines and English-speaking doctors. Travel agents and tour companies can recommend policies that can work for you.

Global Emergency Medical Services Network (GEMSN)
PMB339, 1500A Lafayette Rd., Portsmouth, NH 03801
contact: gemsn@gemsn.bigstep.com; www.gemsn.com

International Association for Medical Assistance to Travelers (IAMAT)
1623 Military Rd., #279, Niagara Falls, NY 14304
(716) 754-4883
email: info@iamat.org; www.iamat.org

IME

Time is truly relative when today is tomorrow. Nine hours ahead of Greenwich Mean Time, the Japanese are eating lunch at noon on the 13th, while Americans in Seattle are eating a 7:00 p.m. supper the night before on the 12th; New Yorkers are having a night on the town at

THE NEXT STEP

10:00 p.m. on the 12th; in London everyone is in bed and dreaming at 3:00 a.m., the morning of the 13th; and so on and so forth.

All clocks in Japan work on 24-hour time:
1:00 am = 1:00
2:00 am = 2:00
3:00 am = 3:00
and so on, until
12:00 p.m. = 12:00
1:00 p.m. = 13:00
2:00 p.m. = 14:00
and so on, until
12:00 a.m. = 24:00

BUSINESS HOURS

Government offices and most businesses are open from 9 a.m. to 5 p.m. weekdays, but are closed on Saturdays, Sundays, and public holidays. Banks are open from 9 a.m. to 3 p.m. weekdays, but are closed on Saturdays, Sundays, and public holidays. Local post offices have their doors open weekdays from 9 a.m. to 5 p.m., but again, are closed on Saturdays, Sundays, and public holidays. District post offices have hours of 9 a.m. to 7 p.m. weekdays, and are closed on Saturdays, Sundays, and public holidays. *But,* they keep open a reception counter that handles only express and air mail around the clock. Department stores are usually open from 10 a.m. to 7 p.m., seven days a week, closing only occasionally, which varies according to store. Mom & pop shops are an exception. They have hours of 10 a.m. to 8 p.m., seven days-a-week, and are usually open even on holidays. Also, the ubiquitous convenience store remains open anytime, anywhere.

MONEY

The unit of currency in Japan is the yen. There are 1 yen, 5 yen, 10 yen, 50 yen, 100 yen, and 500 yen coins, and bills of 1000 yen, 5000 yen, 10,000 yen or *man*. To give you an idea, a *man* is anywhere between $30 and $50 depending upon the rate, but the exchange rate varies from day to day, so to get an idea of the worth of your currency, check with your travel agent or bank right before leaving.

Japan remains a cash-based society. Credit is a foreign word unless you are in Tokyo or other metropolitan areas. Visa, Mastercard, American Express, and Diner's Club are the preferred cards, but don't count on using any of these out in the country or even in smaller shops in the city. So what do you do? Carry cash. Carrying sizable amounts of currency is relatively safe since the crime rate is low, but still exercise your common sense. ATMs are now available, again, in the urban areas, but you had best check with your home bank about reprogramming of your PIN number to the Japanese system and even then, don't count on them. Traveler's cheques are acceptable in most places, except again, cash in the country is a good rule of thumb.

To exchange money, do so at the airport, an "Authorized Foreign Bank," or large hotels. Even some of the larger stores will exchange for yen, though the rate may be exorbitant.

$\mathscr{E}$ LECTRICITY

If you are concerned about plugging things in, certainly bring an adapter and a converter. The U.S. runs on 110 volts, 60 cycles AC, while the Japanese have a unique electric current of 100 volts with 60 cycles AC in western Japan and 100 volts with 50 cycles in eastern Japan. The two-prong outlet reigns, so remember to bring a plug adapter for your grounded three-prong appliances.

$\mathscr{M}$ EDIA: NEWSPAPERS, RADIO, TELEVISION

Found primarily in urban centers, there are several English-edition news-papers which can be purchased at train stations, newsstands, hotels, and bookstores: The *Japan Times*, which is Japan's leading rag and has a worth-while international section; *The Mainichi Daily News; The Daily Yomiuri* which, on Saturday, includes stories from Los Angeles; *The Asahi Evening News*, good for an entertainment listing for Tokyo.

✎HE NEXT STEP

English magazines are few, but do include *Time* and *Newsweek*. There are also area-specific journals which are aimed at the expatriate community, such as *Tokyo Journal* for those meandering around Tokyo and *Kansai Time Out* for those in Osaka.

Both radio and TV present problems if you don't speak Japanese, and even if you do, chances are you wouldn't want to listen to them anyway. Both are filled with empty jabbering talk shows and inane variety hype. You can get the ever-present U.S. Armed Forces network on your radio, but.... There is one television network, NHK, that does attempt to give the foreign community an evening news broadcast which includes international stories of import.

✎OUCHING BASE: PHONE CALLS, FAXES, POSTAGE, E-MAIL

Japan is the home of the phone-card. Purchased from vending machines, telephone company establishments, and many stores, these prepaid cards offer access to a highly developed communication system. If you don't have a card, local calls cost approximately 10 yen for 1 minute, and a **pocketful** of change is necessary for long-distance or international calls. Public pay phones are found almost everywhere, but you must know which color phone to use. Pink and red phones are being phased out so don't bother with them. Green phones accept phone-cards, 10 and 100 yen coins, and can be used for all local and domestic long distance calls...and then there are the grey phones. If you want to dial a direct international call, this is the public phone for you, although not all grey phones will accommodate this act. Look for an International sign on the phone. It is advisable, however, to simply plan on making any overseas calls from your hotel room, as this is the easiest and most understandable approach. Also try dialing direct whenever possible, for operator-assisted calls are very pricey! There are three telephone companies in Japan that provide international service: IDC (0061), Japan Telecom (0041), and the largest, KDD (001). To dial direct, enter the company code, followed by the country code, followed by the number of the party you wish to reach. If you want to use your AT&T Calling Card, do so by dialing 0039-111, the phone number in the U.S., followed by your card number. If you need to use an international operator, all of whom speak English, dial 0051.

The Japanese postal system is fast and efficient, but fairly expensive. To mail a postcard to anywhere in the world, it will cost, as of this writing, 70 yen; an aerogram, 90 yen. To mail a letter weighing 25 grams or less, it will cost you 90 yen to Asia, Guam and Midway; 110 yen to North America, Central America, Down Under, The Middle East, and Europe; 130 yen to Africa and South America. Be sure to watch for the works of art on Japanese stamps, some are breathtaking and worth saving.

You tell yourself you are in a progressive technological country, faxing should be easy. On the contrary, sending a fax can be an exercise in frustration for most of the post offices do not offer the service, nor do hotels, unless you are a guest. In other words, forget it. Use another mode.

E-mailing can be done if you are either with America Online or Compuserve. You can pick up mail using local Japanese access numbers which you need to get from your servers before traveling to Japan.

Find internet cafés and other access points in most major cities. Rates vary, usually ranging between 200 yen to 700 yen per hour.

CULTURAL CONSIDERATIONS

🖉 OCAL CUSTOMS: DOS AND DONT'S ─────────

Many books have been written on this subject in depth. To capture the essence of these do's and don't's there is one mandate that you need to follow: BE POLITE. Japan is *the* most polite country in the world and has myriad rules of behavior grounded in this principle. Here are a few:

- Do not eat food while walking down the street.
- Do not blow your nose in public. Sniffling is recommended.
- Do slurp your noodles (actually, they are inhaled).
- Do give a slight bow upon meeting someone; a lower bow if they are your elder or boss.

⑦HE NEXT STEP

- Don't wear shoes or slippers on *tatami* mats or you will cause heart failure.
- Don't give anyone 4 of anything, because the word for 4 sounds like the word for death: *shi.*
- Say *sumimasen* after everything you say. This word is an all-purpose polite word meaning everything from excuse me to thank you to hello.
- Don't smile in formal pictures.
- Do give your business card, with a slight bow, immediately upon meeting a business colleague.
- Always give your seat up for children on trains.
- Don't stick your chopsticks upright in a bowl of rice. This is only done at funerals as an invitation to the dead to come eat.
- Don't wear shorts to temples or shrines, wear skirts or long pants. Be respectful.
- When sitting on the floor, do not point your feet at anyone. It is considered insulting; base; filthy.
- When visiting in a Japanese home, bring a small gift such as flowers, chocolate, or a present from home.
- Never be direct. Listen to what is *not* said.
- Wash *before* you get into the tub.
- Don't laugh with your mouth wide open. Like the feet, the mouth is considered a place to cover; dirty.
- …and the list goes on. For further reading try *Culture Shock! Japan* by Rex Shelley, 1997 or *Japan Made Easy* by Boye Lafayette De Mente, 1995.

ℰ VENTS & HOLIDAYS ──────────────────

National holidays⋆ are times *not* to travel in Japan unless you have reservations, and even then…. But festivals, especially local neighborhood ceremonies, are an integral part of the Japanese psyche; a must-see. For a schedule of such events, please contact the JNTO.

January

1–3   ★New Year's (Oshogatsu) This holiday includes feasting and visiting family, shrines, temples and colleagues.

15   ★Adults' Day (Seijin-No-Hi): A time to celebrate the coming-of-age of those turning 20.

February

3   Halloween's equivalent (Setsubun): Chase away the evil spirits.

11   ★Foundation Day (Kenkoku Kinen-No-Hi)

March

3   The Doll Festival (Ohina Matsuri): Doll collections, fashioned after the emperor of old and his entourage, come out of the closet and are set up in the home of female children and added to.

21   ★Spring Equinox (Shumbun-No-Hi): A time to appreciate the dawning of spring.

     Blossom-viewing Time (Ohanami) occurs from late February through April. This is one of the times when reservations are absolutely necessary to book way ahead of time. Plum and cherry blossoms send everyone traveling; a national movement.

April

29   ★Green Day (Midori-No-Hi): This day celebrates nature.

29   Golden Week starts on April 29 and goes through May 5. This holiday week includes Green Day, Constitution Day, and Children's Day. This also includes the now-deceased Emperor Hirohito's birthday on the 29th of April. Again, if you travel in this week, please know that you will be accompanied by millions of others. Act accordingly.

☞HE NEXT STEP

May

3   ★Constitution Day (Kempo Kinen-Bi]: A day set aside to honor
         the constitution.

5   ★Children's Day (Kodomo-No-Hi): This day celebrates the youth
         of the nation, especially boys (the counterpart to the doll festival
         for girls). Many homes with male children bring out the samurai
         paraphernalia and fly flags shaped like carp. The carp is an old
         symbol of toughness and endurance. As the fish swim against river
         currents, building strength, so do the boys in the family.

June

         Check with JNTO for local festivals nearest you.

July

7   Star Festival (Tanabata Matsuri): Based upon a legend about the
         Milky Way, this day celebrates star-crossed lovers.

20   Marine Day (Umi-No-Hi): A time to celebrate the ocean.

August

13-16   Festival of the Dead (Obon): This is a time when it is believed
         that ancestors return from the dead and visit their place of origin.
         All of Japan travels home to honor the dead and speed the spirits
         back to the underworld through the symbolic lighting of paper
         lanterns which then float away down rivers, streams, lakes. Out of
         any time of the year, this is *the* most difficult time to find room
         on the bullet train or in that favorite Japanese inn, though a most
         interesting occasion.

September

15   ★Respect for the Elderly Day (Keiro-No-Hi): This is a day to cel-
         ebrate the wisdom of age.

23   Autumn Equinox (Shubun-No-Hi): A time to revel in the arrival
         of fall.

October

10   *Sports & Health Day (Taiku-No-Hi]: A day when many people, especially school children, participate in sports rallies.

November

3   *Culture Day (Bunka-No-Hi): A day to appreciate the arts and the Japanese culture.

23   *Labor Thanksgiving Day (Kinro Kansha-No-Hi): A day of rest for the weary and thanks for blessings.

December

23   *Emperor's Birthday (Tenno Tanjobi)

Note: There is currently thought of changing certain official holidays to Mondays so that everyone can have a three-day holiday. Stay-tuned.

IMPORTANT CONTACTS

$\mathscr{F}$OREIGN EMBASSIES IN TOKYO: ————————————

- Australia   03-5232-4111
- Canada   03-5412-6200
- China   03-3403-3388
- France   03-5420-8800
- Germany   03-5791-7700
- India   03-3262-2391
- Italy   03-3453-5291
- Sweden   03-5562-5050
- Thailand   03-3441-1386
- UK   03-3265-5511
- USA   03-3224-5000

THE NEXT STEP

TOURIST OFFICES AND THEIR PHONE NUMBERS ——————

The Japan National Tourist Organization or JNTO is the clearinghouse of travel information in Japan. They generally do not handle reservations, but disseminate anything and everything you would ever want to know about the country. Operating Tourist Information Centers or TIC around the nation, their main offices include:

In Tokyo -   TIC
                10th floor, Tokyo Kōtsu Kaikan Building
                2-10-1 Yurakuchō
                Chiyoda-Ku, Tokyo 100-006
                03-3201-3331
                Open weekdays 9 a.m. to 5 p.m. and Saturdays, 9-noon

                Narita International Airport
                Terminal Building 2
                Chiba Prefecture 282-0004
                0476-34-6251
                Open everyday from 9 a.m. to 8 p.m.

In Kyoto -   Kyoto Tower Building, First Floor
                Higashi-Shiokojicho
                Shimogyo-ku, Kyoto 600-8216
                075-371-5649
                Open weekdays 9 a.m. to 5 p.m.

In Osaka -   Kansai International Airport
                Passenger Terminal Building
                Izumi-Sano, Osaka 549-0011
                0724-56-6025
                Open everyday 9 a.m. to 9p.m.

If you wish to contact the JNTO before you leave, offices can be found in:

New York -   1 Rockefeller Center, Suite 1250
                New York, NY 10020
                212-757-5640

San Francisco -   1 Daniel Burnham Court, Suite 250C
                    San Francisco, CA 94109
                    415-292-5686

ACTIVITIES

$\mathscr{F}$IFTEEN FUN THINGS TO DO

- Find out from The Nippon Kodo in Tokyo the local ceremony schedule for *kodo*, the incense burning ritual, and treat yourself to a bit of ancient aromatherapy.

- For a good chuckle, go on a t-shirt hunt in the covered mall or the underground shopping street and gather a collection of shirts with interesting English slogans (an understatement) to give as gifts to your friends.

- If you are lucky enough to be in Tokyo or Nagoya during sumo tournament season, find out from the local temple priest where they are practicing and go watch. Each "team" is called a "stable" and usually is affiliated with a temple in town where they then practice. It costs nothing to watch and you can get much closer than in the fighting arena.

- Try *odori zushi,* otherwise known as dancing *sushi.* Can you guess what it is? Your friends will never believe you if you partake…just close your eyes and bite fast!

- Be the first in line at the daily opening of a big department store like Matsuzakaya or Mitsukoshi and feel like royalty as you enter, then go (usually down) into their deli section for some taste-testing, then back upstairs to view the latest exhibit. Most up-scale departo have elaborate exhibits of many Japanese art forms such as *ikebana* and *shuji.* Enjoy!

- Take a trip to the fertility shrine, Tagata Jinja, outside of Nagoya for a little titter, but be respectful.

THE NEXT STEP

- Late at night, take a seat at a four-stool *oden* cart and sample the savory specialties, from boiled eggs and baked potato chunks in broth to less familiar but equally tasty delights.
- Wherever you travel in Japan, there will be a public bath. Go. This is an experience that should not be missed. If you are staying in one place for a while, go to the same local bath every evening around 7:00 p.m. and become a regular. It is the best way to get to know Japan intimately, and don't try the electric bath if you have heart problems!
- Skip Mt. Fuji and the masses. Climb Hakusan near Kanazawa and get a true Japanese wilderness experience, or go into the *chuo* Alps, the middle Alps, and take a ropeway up Komagatake to get to some good ridge-top hiking. It's an easy day over the peak. Contact the Japanese Alpine Club through the JNTO for further information.
- Find out where in your neighborhood there might be a *tofuyasan*, a maker of tofu, and go visit the operation. In the neighborhood of Ozone in Nagoya there was one such gentleman that did his business out of a shack, a cool, dark place where vats of refrigerated water kept slabs of fresh tofu in all forms from creamy to hard. He would let you sample...mmmmm, on a hot summer day!
- Listen at night for the *yaki-imo* street vendor who calls plaintively to his customers as he rolls his cart 'round the neighborhood seeking business. At around 10:00 p.m. you might hear a song of the sweet potato man. Keep your ears open and your mouths ready. It's a treat, if you can find him.
- Rent a bicycle in Tokyo and get off the beaten track. Explore the neighborhood, but take a map and the address where you are staying written in Japanese. Tokyo is a maze of small roads leading nowhere. After the war, the city was rebuilt on the foot paths created around the rubble. You can tell by the haphazard web of streets, but that is what makes it fun. Know your landmarks and be prepared to get lost!
- Take part in or organize a moon-viewing party, an age-old tradition of gathering beneath the full moon in a park with friends to write poetry, drink rice wine, and sing, especially during cherry blossom season.

- Try playing the national pastime of *pachinko*, a vertical pin-ball machine game, popular especially in the Kansai District (Osaka). Noisy, smoky, frenetic, watch the intensity with which the Japanese play.
- Get your hair cut at a local beauty salon and get treated like royalty as they marvel at your hair, especially if you are a blonde.

☞ATIONAL PARKS

Japan is not only a land filled with man-made gardens, it is 60% forested and covered with mountains, ranging from sub-tropical to sub-arctic conditions. From the island of Kyushu to the island of Hokkaido, the government, in the 1930s, established 28 national parks, *kokuritsu koen*, and 55 quasi-parks to preserve the wilderness. Fashioned after the U.S. model, the parks have an extensive trail network which can be easily accessed. Many of the trails that are near population centers will be crowded. To get away from it all, you must travel far and deep into the mountains. For further information, contact the JNTO for listings of different hiking clubs.

ADDITIONAL RESOURCES

☞APAN ONLINE ————————————————————

- Asahi Shimburi: www.asahi.com/english/english.html
- AOL: travel/Asia/Japan
- Daily Yomiuri: www.yomiuri.co.jp/index-e.htm
- HBC: www.hbc.co.jp/
- Info Hub: www.infohub.com/TRAVEL/TRAVELLER/ASIA/ japan.html
- JNTO Internet Homepage, an online information service: www.jnto.go.jp
- Japan Garden Database: pobox.upenn.edu/~cheetham/jgarden
- Japan Information Network: jin.jcic.or.jp/
- Japan National Tourist Organization: www.jnto.go.jp
- Japan Travel Guide: www.japan-guide.com

THE NEXT STEP

- The Japan Times: www.japantimes.co.jp/
- Japan Youth Hostel Assoc: web.kyoto-inet.or/jp/org
- Lonely Planet: www.lonelyplanet.com
- Outdoor Japan: www.outdoorjapan.com
- Radio Japan: www.nhk.or.jp
- Travel Library—Japan travel and tourism information: www.travel-library.com/asia/japan/
- World Travel Guide-Japan: http://www.travel-guide.com/country.asp

GIVING BACK

There is a lot to be gained by traveling in Japan, and many people are moved to support good causes once they've returned home. A few organizations that do good work and could use contributions follow. For more non-profit organizations go to the Japan Information Network and do a search for "NGOs," "non-profit," "aid," "environment," "foundation," or other related topics. www.jinjapan.org or web-jpn.org

AMDA—Asian Medical Doctors Association is a multinational medical NGO founded in 1984 to promote the health and well-being of the needy and underprivileged in Asia and other continents. Some of their focuses include: implementing community-based sustainable development programs, and initiating and participating in emergency relief programs worldwide. *Contact: 1-310 Narazu Okayama, 701-1202, Japan; Email: nakanot@amda.or.jp; Website: www.amda.or.jp/index_e.html*

Aozara Foundation Center for the Redevelopment of Pollution-Damaged Areas in Japan was established to carry out projects including surveys, research, interchanges, and environmental studies, which will make Japan's pollution experience useful in community development. They hope to be of service arresting pollution around the world by providing information on Japan's pollution experience, and by building an international citizens' network meant for redeveloping pollution-debilitated areas. *Contact: Sanyo Bldg. 4F, 1-1-1 Chibune, Nishiyodogawa-ku, Osaka 555; Tel: 06-475-8885; Fax: 06-478-5885; Email: webmaster@aozara.or.jp; Website: www.aozara.or.jp/English/esyoukai.htm.*

THE NEXT STEP

International Rivers Network is a non-profit organization in the United States that works with Japanese NGOs to build their capacity to preserve and restore Japan's rivers and watersheds. They also have an extensive program for Japanese interns. *Contact: 1847 Berkeley Way, Berkeley, CA 94703 USA; Tel: 510-848-1155; Fax: 510-848-1008; Email:irn@irn.org; Web site: www.irn.org.*

WWF Japan—World Wide Fund for Nature is the largest and most influential non-governmental international conservation organization. Besides participating in the activities via WWF's international network, WWF Japan has been conducting it's own projects to conserve the unique nature of Nasei Shoto islands, wetlands, marine areas, and to promote environmental education. *www.wwf.or.jp*

RECOMMENDED READING

Ainsley, Robert. *Bluff Your Way in Japan.* Lincoln: Centennial Press, 1989.

Barry, Dave. *Dave Barry Does Japan.* New York: Fawcett Columbine, 1993.

Booth, Alan. *The Roads to Sata: A 2000-Mile Walk through Japan.* New York: Penguin Books, 1985.

Bouvier, Nicolas. *The Japanese Chronicles.* San Francisco: Mercury House, 1992.

Brown, J.D. *The Sudden Disappearance of Japan: Journeys Through a Hidden Land.* Santa Barbara: Capra Press, 1994.

Butler, Linda. *Rural Japan: Radiance of the Ordinary.* Washington, D.C.: Smithsonian Institution Press, 1992.

Carey, Peter. *Wrong About Japan.* New York: Alfred A. Knopf, 2005.

Chang, Iris. *The Rape of Nanking.* New York: Basic Books, 1997.

Davidson, Cathy N. *36 Views of Mount Fuji: On Finding Myself in Japan.* New York: Penguin Books, 1993.

Ehrlich, Gretel. *Islands, The Universe, Home.* New York: Viking Penguin, 1991.

THE NEXT STEP

Endo, Shusaku, William Johnston, trans. *Silence*. New York: Taplinger
   Publishing Co, 1976.
Fallows, James. *Looking at the Sun: The Rise of the New East Asian
   Economic and Political System*. New York: Pantheon. 1994.
Feiler, Bruce S. *Learning to Bow: Inside the Heart of Japan*. New York:
   Ticknor & Fields, 1991.
Harrell, Bryan. *Cycling Japan: A Personal Guide to Exploring Japan by
   Bicycle*. New York: Kodansha, 1993.
Hearn, Lafcadio (Francis King, ed.). *Writings from Japan: An Anthology*.
   New York: Penguin Books, 1984.
Houston, James D. *In the Ring of Fire: A Pacific Basin Journey*. San
   Francisco: Mercury House, 1997.
Iyer, Pico. *The Lady and the Monk: Four Seasons in Kyoto*. New York:
   Random House, 1991.
Jones, Patricia. *21st-Century Gardening Series #166: Japanese-Inspired
   Gardens: Adapting Japan's Design Traditions for Your Garden*. New
   York: Brooklyn Botanic Garden, 2001.
Kazantzakis, Nikos. *Japan China*. Berkeley: Creative Arts Book
   Company, 1982.
Kerr, Alex. *Lost Japan*. Australia: Lonely Planet Publications, 1996.
LaFarge, John. *An Artist's Letters from Japan*. London: Kegan Paul
   International Ltd, 2001.
Miyamoto, Masao, M.D. *Straitjacket Society: An Insider's Irreverent View
   of Bureaucratic Japan*. New York: Kodansha, 1994.
Morley, John. *Pictures from the Water Trade: Adventures of a Westerner in
   Japan*. Boston: The Atlantic Monthly Press, 1985.
Mura, David. *Turning Japanese: Memoirs of a Sansei*. New York: The
   Atlantic Monthly Press, 1991.
Naff, Clayton. *About Face: How I Stumbled onto Japan's Social
   Revolution*. New York: Kodansha, 1994.
Newsham, Brad. *All the Right Places*. New York: Vintage Departures,
   1990.
Philip, Leila. *The Road Through Miyama*. New York: Vintage Books,
   1989.

Rappaport, Roger and Marguerita Castanera, eds. *I Should Have Stayed Home: The Worst Trips of Great Writers*. California: Book Passage Press, 1994.

Richie, Donald. *The Inland Sea*. New York: Weatherhill, Inc., 1971.

Saikaku, Iharu. *Fille de Joie: The Book of Courtesans, Sporting Girls, Ladies of the Evening, Madams, A Few Occasionals & Some Royal Favorites*. New York: Barnes & Nobles Books, 1967.

Sen, Soshitsu. *Tea Life, Tea Mind*. New York: Weatherhill, Inc., 1979.

Shapiro, Michael. *Japan: In the Land of the Brokenhearted*. New York: Henry Holt & Company, 1989.

Statler, Oliver. *Japanese Inn*. New York: Pyramid Books, 1961.

Tanizaki, Jun'ichiro. *In Praise of Shadows*. Stony Creek, Connecticut: Leete's Island Books, 1977.

Tomb, Howard. *Wicked Japanese: For the Business Traveler*. New York: Workman Publishing Co. Inc., 1991.

Whiting, Robert. *You Gotta Have Wa*. New York: Random House, 1989.

Yee, Chiang. *The Silent Traveller in Japan*. New York: W.W. Norton & Co., 1972.

"THE NEXT STEP" WAS PREPARED BY AMY GREIMANN CARLSON AND THE STAFF AT TRAVELERS' TALES, INC.

Glossary

aisatsu	formal introductions
akarui	bright; lively
aoi	the color blue
"Ara"	an exclamatory outburst
arigato gozaimasu	thank you
arigato	thanks
atariya	"bumpers," people who make a living crashing into others
bijin	beautiful women
bijinesuman/bizunesuman	businessman
buke	the samurai families
burikko	pretending to be kids
chan	like "san" only reserved for children and unmarried women
Chushingura	famous, popular traditional tale of loyalty and revenge
daikon	radish
Dare no te	"Whose hand?"
denki furo	electric bath
Doitashimashite	"You're welcome," "Don't mention it"
domo arigato gozaimashita	thank you very much
fude	brushes for calligraphy
fugu	blow fish

fujitarosugi	tall red tree; literally "boy cedar tree to Fuji"
fukusa	special cloth used in a tea ceremony to wipe the tea scoop
fusuma	paper sliding doors
futon	Japanese bed
gaijin	foreigner; literally "outside person"
gaman	persistence
geisha	a highly-skilled woman who entertains guests at parties with music, dance, conversation, etc.
genkan	a foyer in a Japanese home
genki	full of vitality; life
go-con	get-together of people from special interest clubs
gomi	garbage
gyoji	referee
gyudon	beef atop rice served in a bowl
haiku	poetry consisting of 17 syllables
Hajimemashite	"How do you do"; literally "We are meeting for the first time"
hana	flower
happi	belted blue tunic
hebi-san	Mr. Snake
hen na gaijin	weird foreigner
hiragana	the Japanese word for alphabet
honne	what one truly thinks; gut opinons
ichi go, ichi e	"one meeting, one chance"
ichiko	baseball
ikebana	flower arranging
inaka	countryside
jiko	accident
jo, ha, kyu, zanshin	literally "slow, fast, faster, stop," a basic rhythm of nature

juku	after-school cram-school
jushi	secondary branches
kacho	section head; chief
kai	gatherings; meetings
kaiseki ryori	multi-dish meal using seasonal ingredients, served artfully in small portions
kamakboko	fish sausage
kamisama	god
kana	the Japanese syllabary including *hiragana* and *katakana*
kangaenai	"don't think"
kanji	Chinese characters
kanpai	toast; cheers
kapseru hoteru	capsule hotel
karate	a Japanese martial art
karesansuidry	landscape
karoshi	death by overwork
katakana	the foreign loan word for alphabet
kata	prescribed "forms" of movement
katchiu-yashiki	traditional samurai dwelling
kawaii	cute
kawatta	abnormal
kejime	finishing one stage before going to the next
kendo	a Japanese martial art using bamboo rods
kenzan	flower arranging frog
kisama	"honorable you," considered derogatory
koban	neighborhood police box
kofude	a small brush for calligraphy
koi	carp
konnichiwa	good afternoon

kotatsu	a low table under which is attached an infrared bulb to provide heat to the legs of those sitting
kuge	the court nobles descended from the Fujiwara family
kura	old storehouses
kurisumasu keki	literally "Christmas cake"; an unmarried woman over 25 is referred to as an "old Christmas cake"
kuruwa	an enclosure within an ancient city
machiya	traditional wooden house
manzai	comic free association
meishi	business cards
messhi hoko	self-sacrifice for the sake of the group
miso	soybean paste soup
mompei	field clothes
mura	small town
nakama	the insiders group
nakodo	the formal go-between in an arranged marriage situation
natsukashi-sa	bittersweet memories
ningajo	New Year's cards
ningen-kankei	the human relations web
obasan	grandmother
obento	lunch box
oden	a type of noodle
ofude	a large brush for calligraphy
ofuro	Japanese bath
Ohaiyo gozaimasu	"Good morning"
ohanami	flower-viewing party
oishi	delicious

ojichan	grandfather
okachan	mother
okaeri nasai	"welcome home"
okonomiyaki	do-it-yourself Japanese-style pizza
okyaku-sama	customers
omatcha	tea ceremony
omiai	arranged marriage meeting
omochi	specially prepared New Year's rice cakes
onnarashii	very feminine
Oshogatsu	New Year's
otochan	father
otoso	a form of sake
Oyasuminasai	"Goodnight"
pachinko	vertical pinball game
pica-pica	the sound of starlight
poku poku	a rhythm
rakkon	red stamp used by artists to "sign" their work
ramen	a thin noodle
rezubian	lesbian
ri	3.927 kilometers, an old-fashioned measure
romaji	the Japanese language written phonetically with English letters
ryokan	Japanese inn
sake	rice wine
sakura	cherry tree
sama	a more formal version of *san*
samurai	warrior
san	the Japanese equivalent of Mr. and Mrs.
sararimen	salarymen
sashimi	raw fish or meat

sazae	clam
sembei	rice crackers
sensei	teacher
sento	public bath
shakkei	borrowed scenery
shamisen	traditional stringed instrument
shiatsu	special Japanese massage technique
shi	city
shido	advisor
shikishi	square plaques on which artists create calligraphy or paintings
shin, soe, hikae	terms in flower arranging coinciding with three levels: "heaven, earth, man"
shinnenkai	New Year's parties
shito-shito & goro-goro	the sound of thunder
shocho	director
shochu	cheap, popular rice wine
shodo	the Way of Writing
shogi	Japanese chess
shogun	a Japanese ruler
shoji	wooden sliding doors with panes
shuji	the Practice of Letters
soba	noodle
sumi o suru	literally "doing _sumi_," rubbing the ink block in water to become ink
sumi-e	Japanese painting with black ink
sumi	black ink
sumimasen	excuse me; sorry; thank you
sushi	vingared rice; often topped by slices of raw fish, boiled shrimp, etc.
tabi	socks with a separate big toe sleeve

Tadaima	"I'm home"
taiko	large bass drum
takoyaki	octopus dumplings
takuhatsu	the Zen practice of begging with bowls
tambo	rice field
tanka	poetry of 31 syllables
tansu	hope chest
tanzaku	rectangular plaques on which artists calligraphy or paint
taray	three-wheeled motorized wagon
tatami	grass mat
teisai buru	doing something for the sake of appearences
tempura	lightly-battered and fried vegetables/ shrimp, etc.
tokai	city
tokonoma	special alcoves for displays
torii	Shinto shrine gates
toshi-koshi soba	"long-life" noodles
tsubo	architectural measurement of two *tatami* mats (3.3m squared)
tsukemono	pickles
tsunokakushi	an elaborate bridal headgear
ubu	antiques surfacing for the first time
uni	sea urchin
wa	harmony
waka	romantic poetry
waraji	ceremonial straw sandals
Ware-ware Nihonjin	"We Japanese"
wu	essence
yaki-imo	mountain potatoes roasted in charcoal

yakiin	a brand burned into a hiking stick to mark your progress
yakisoba	fried noodles
yakitori-ya	a chicken restaurant
yakuza	Japanese Mafia
yamabato	dove
yokan	sticky bean paste cake
yoso no hito	outside person
yozakura	viewing of the cherry blossoms at night
yukata	cotton kimono used primarily in summer or after bath
_za-za_	the sound of heavy rain
zabuton	pillow
zori	flip-flop-like sandals, rubber thongs

Index

Index of Contributors

Acknowledgments

First of all, I want to thank Larry Habegger and James O'Reilly, longtime friends and colleagues, who had the vision to want to do this book originally and the loyalty and persistence to make it happen.

In addition to Larry and James, the primary credit for this collection must go to its endlessly energetic, perspicaceous and disciplined co-editor, Amy Carlson, who spent years assembling, extracting, and editing hundreds of stories and book excerpts about Japan as possible entries.

The collection would also not exist without the kindness and home office of Travelers' Tales staffer Susan Brady, who turned her home over to Amy and me for a long, long weekend surrounded by those hundreds of stories and excerpts—until we emerged with a manuscript.

I want to thank my parents, who first inspired me to see the wonders of the road and later gave me the essential encouragement to explore those wonders on my own.

I want to thank my parents-in-law, for graciously allowing me to transport their precious daughter to this far away second homeland—and for welcoming us so warmly whenever we return to visit that first home.

And especially I want to thank my wife Kuniko, and my children, Jenny and Jeremy, for supporting and guiding and delighting me through all our years together, and for making my life deeper and richer than I ever could have imagined.

—Donald W. George

I hate watching the Academy Awards..."And a thank you to everyone and their uncle who has ever worked with me, for me, by me, or on me." Here I am, doing the same.

Thanks first, of course, to my parents Millie and Stan Greimann, who have fostered in me the yearning to learn. What a gift. To my husband, Reed Carlson, for all of his insights, hugs, cooking, and sake. He is my #1 consultant and partner. To Don, my co-editor, for his delightful humor and gentleness. "*Kanpai*, Donaldsan!"

Thanks to the O'Reilly family for having more faith in me than I have in myself and dragging me into this project. To Susan Brady, the production whiz, whose energy we could not do without and for her grasp of the bigger picture, to the Grunewald Guild for the space and the time to spread out and think, to Miki Aoki for his ever-patient, ever-helpful assistance in gathering and checking information…and last, but not least, "thank you to everyone and their uncle who has ever worked with me, for me, by me, or on me."

—Amy Greimann Carlson

"Taiko Drumming," "A Thousand Cranes, A Thousand Suns," and "Raw Horsemeat" by Alan Booth excerpted from *The Roads to Sata: A 2000-Mile Walk through Japan* by Alan Booth. Copyright © 1985 by Alan Booth. Reprinted by permission of Penguin Putnam Books.

"The Magic of Miyajima" by Donald Richie excerpted from *The Inland Sea* by Donald Richie. Copyright © 1971 by Donald Richie. Reprinted by permission of the author.

"I Feel Coke" by Pico Iyer excerpted from *The Lady and the Monk: Four Seasons in Kyoto* by Pico Iyer. Copyright © 1991 by Pico Iyer. Reprinted by permission of Random House, Inc.

"When the Heart Becomes Quiet" by John David Morley excerpted from *Pictures from the Water Trade: Adventures of a Westerner in Japan* by John David Morley. Reprinted with permission from the author. Copyright © 1985 by John David Morley.

"Smo" and "Rain Droppings" by Brad Newsham excerpted from *All the Right Places* by Brad Newsham. Copyright © 1989 by Brad Newsham. Reprinted by permission of the author.

"Somebody Stab Him Again" by Dave Barry excerpted from *Dave Barry Does Japan* by Dave Barry. Copyright © 1992 by Dave Barry. Reprinted by permission of Random House, Inc.

"The Essence of Japan" by Donald Richie reprinted from the October 1984 issue of *Travel & Leisure*. Copyright © 1984. Reprinted by permission of the author.

"When the Cherries Bloom" by Donald W. George reprinted from the February 28, 1993 issue of the *San Francisco Examiner*. Copyright © 1993 by the *San Francisco Examiner*. Reprinted by permission of the *San Francisco Examiner*.

"Into the *Denki Furo*" by Jeff Greenwald excerpted from *I Should Have Stayed Home: The Worst Trips of Great Writers* edited by Roger Rapoport & Maguerita Castanera. Reprinted by permission of RDR Books. Copyright © 1994 by RDR Books.

"P's and Q's and Envelope Blues" and "Red Lights and Green Tea" by Bruce S. Feiler excerpted from *Learning to Bow: Inside the Heart of Japan* by Bruce S. Feiler. Copyright © 1991 by Bruce S. Feiler. Reprinted by permission of

Selection from *Cycling Japan: A Personal Guide to Exploring Japan by Bicycle* by Bryan Harrell copyright © 1993 by Bryan Harrell. Reprinted by permission of Kodansha America, Inc.

Selections from *Dave Barry Does Japan* by Dave Barry copyright © 1992 by Dave Barry. Reprinted by permission of Random House, Inc.

Selection from *Fille de Joie: The Book of Courtesans, Sporting Girls, Ladies of the Evening, Madams, A Few Occasionals & Some Royal Favorites* by Iharu Saikaku copyright © 1967 by Balance House, Ltd. Reprinted by permission of Balance House, Ltd.

Selection from *In Praise of Shadows* by Jun'ichiro Tanizaki copyright © 1977 by Jun'ichiro Tanizaki. Reprinted by Leete's Island Books.

Selections from *In the Ring of Fire: A Pacific Basin Journey* by James D. Houston, published by Mercury House. Reprinted by permission of the author. Copyright © 1997 by James D. Houston.

Selections from *The Inland Sea* by Donald Richie copyright © 1971 by Donald Richie. Reprinted by permission of the author.

Selection from "Is Japan Too Civilized for the '90s?" by Nicholas D. Kristof reprinted from *The New York Times*. Copyright © *The New York Times*. Reprinted by permission of *The New York Times*.

Selection from *Islands, The Universe, Home* by Gretel Ehrlich copyright © 1991 by Gretel Ehrlich. Reprinted by permission of Viking Penguin, a division of Penguin Putnam Inc.

Selections from *Japan China* by Nikos Kazantzakis copyright © 1982 by Nikos Kazantzakis. Reprinted by permission of the author's estate.

Selections from *Japan: In the Land of the Brokenhearted* by Michael Shapiro. Copyright © 1989 by Michael Shapiro. Reprinted by permission of Henry Holt and Company.

Selection from "Japanese Bath" by Naomi W. Caldwell published with permission from the author. Copyright © 1998 by Naomi W. Caldwell.

Selections from *The Japanese Chronicles* by Nicolas Bouvier, translated by Anne Dickerson copyright © 1989. Published by Mercury House, San Francisco, California, and reprinted by permission.

Selections from *The Lady and the Monk: Four Seasons in Kyoto* by Pico Iyer copyright © 1991 by Pico Iyer. Reprinted by permission of Random House, Inc.

Selection from *Learning to Bow: Inside the Heart of Japan* by Bruce S. Feiler copyright © 1991 by Bruce S. Feiler. Reprinted by permission of Ticknor & Fields/Houghton Mifflin Company and Jane Dystel Literary Management. All rights reserved.

Selection from *Looking at the Sun: The Rise of the New East Asian Economic and Political System* by James Fallows copyright © 1994 by James Fallows. Reprinted by permission of Pantheon Books, a division of Random House, Inc. and the Wendy Weil Agency.

Selections from *Lost Japan* by Alex Kerr copyright © 1996 by Alex Kerr. Reprinted by permission of Lonely Planet Publications.

Selection from "Nippon No Tabi" by Marge Wyngaarden published with permission from the author. Copyright © 1998 by Marge Wyngaarden.

Selections from "A World of Bathhouses" by George Vincent Wright published by permission of the author. Copyright © 1998 by George Vincent Wright.

Selections from *Writings from Japan: An Anthology* by Lafcadio Hearn, edited by Francis King. Selection copyright © 1984 by Francis King. Reprinted by permission of Penguin Books Ltd.

Selection from *You Gotta Have Wa* by Robert Whiting reprinted by permission of Macmillan USA, a division of Simon & Schuster Macmillan Company. Copyright © 1989 by Robert Whiting.

Selection from "You Lost a What?" by Mary Kay Sapp published with permission from the author. Copyright © 1998 by Mary Kay Sapp.

About the Editors

Donald W. George first traveled to Japan on a Princeton-in-Asia Fellowship in 1977. On the two-year fellowship, he taught English writing and literature at International Christian University in Tokyo; he also hosted an English-language talk show for the educational division of NHK-TV, Japan's national broadcasting network. Living in Japan changed his life, teaching him that many of the cultural concepts he'd assimilated growing up weren't necessarily true—and even more importantly, introducing him to the wise and lovely woman who would become his wife, Kuniko Ninomiya.

Don returned to the U.S. in 1980, settling in the San Francisco Bay Area, where he was joined by Kuniko in 1982—and where they continue to live, now with two wonderful children, Jennifer Ayako and Jeremy Naoki, immeasurably enriching their lives.

From 1980-86, Don was a travel writer and then a magazine editor for the *San Francisco Examiner*. He became the Examiner's Travel Editor in 1987 and remained in that position, roaming the globe and writing a weekly column, until 1995, when he leapt into cyberspace to work for GNN, once the Internet division of America Online. In February 1997 Don joined many of his former Examiner colleagues at the Internet magazine *Salon,* where he founded and edited the acclaimed travel site, Wanderlust.

Today Don is the Global Travel Editor for Lonely Planet Publications. He frequently appears on TV and radio and in print as Lonely Planet's spokesperson. He also writes the weekly "What Would Don George Do?" travel advice column for lonely-planet.com; oversees Lonely Planet's nationally syndicated newspaper column, "Travels with Lonely Planet"; and commissions books for the publisher's literary travel series. Don is the author of *Travel Writing* and the editor of five anthologies, including *By the Seat of My Pants, The Kindness of Strangers* and *A House Somewhere: Tales of Life Abroad*. Don has published more than 600 articles in magazines and newspapers around the globe and has received dozens of awards for his writing and editing, including, most recently, the Pacific Area Travel Association's Gold Award for Best Travel Article and the Society of American Travel Writers Lowell Thomas Award.

Don is co-founder and chairman of the annual Book Passage Travel Writers Conference, which is held every summer in Northern California, and has been a Visiting Lecturer at the University of California, Berkeley, Graduate School of Journalism; he frequently speaks about travel writing and travel industry issues around the world.

Amy Carlson was born a Bushido Barbie, destined to edit a book on Japan, her many identities include:

English Teacher Barbie,
Snow Plower Barbie,
House Builder Barbie,
World Traveler Barbie,
Gardener Barbie,
Flute Player Barbie,
Seminary Student Barbie,
Church Lady Barbie,
Mountain Climber Barbie,
Poet Barbie,

…in other words, she's a Jane-of-All-Trades; a female George Plimpton; a restless soul living with her husband Reed in Washington State; a sojourner who seeks enlightenment and truth.

www.ingramcontent.com/pod-product-compliance
Lightning Source LLC
Chambersburg PA
CBHW030252100426
42812CB00002B/400